Democracy, Intermediation, and Voting on Four Continents

Edited by

Richard Gunther, José Ramón Montero,
and Hans-Jürgen Puhle

OXFORD
UNIVERSITY PRESS

OXFORD
UNIVERSITY PRESS

Great Clarendon Street, Oxford ox2 6DP

Oxford University Press is a department of the University of Oxford.
It furthers the University's objective of excellence in research, scholarship,
and education by publishing worldwide in

Oxford New York

Auckland Cape Town Dar es Salaam Hong Kong Karachi
Kuala Lumpur Madrid Melbourne Mexico City Nairobi
New Delhi Shanghai Taipei Toronto

With offices in

Argentina Austria Brazil Chile Czech Republic France Greece
Guatemala Hungary Italy Japan Poland Portugal Singapore
South Korea Switzerland Thailand Turkey Ukraine Vietnam

Oxford is a registered trade mark of Oxford University Press
in the UK and in certain other countries

Published in the United States
by Oxford University Press Inc., New York

© The Several Contributors 2007

British Library Cataloguing in Publication Data
Data available

Library of Congress Cataloging in Publication Data
Data available

Typeset by SPi Publisher Services, Pondicherry, India
Printed in Great Britain
on acid-free paper by
Biddles Ltd., King's Lynn, Norfolk

ISBN 978-0-19-920283-6
ISBN 978-0-19-920284-3 (pbk)

Foreword
The Elmira Project—fifty years later

The reference is to an important election study, a four-wave panel survey of voters in Elmira, New York during the 1948 presidential election, the contest of Harry S. Truman, Thomas E. Dewey, and several others. The result was a volume by Bernard Berelson, Paul F. Lazarsfeld, and William N. McPhee entitled *Voting: A Study of Opinion Formation in a Presidential Election* (1954). It was a collective effort, the work of Columbia University sociologists, but the main ideas I think were those of Lazarsfeld. I joined the effort, over fifty years ago, as a research assistant to Bill McPhee.

By way of background, I offer a note on personal intellectual history, on some generational effects. I was 15 when the Second World War ended, a catastrophe that, in three ways, had an impact on my rather sheltered life. Over five years, those wartime events had figured prominently in my consciousness. What we forever after would call 'the war', provided an agenda for thought, an invitation to address a very big problem.

A few years later, many of us entered universities where 'the veterans' were among our classmates. Those men were serious, hard-working, and dedicated in purpose and, as a result, they provided a quiet but important influence on campus life. They were, in the then-current phrase, 'making up for lost time'. We had to follow their example. Even if we had thought about it, in those years there was no place for Joe College antics on the nations' campuses.

The third influence was that of the exile scholars. Among them, at the University of Chicago, was Gerhart E. O. Meyer, a man with an encyclopedic mind and extraordinary analytical abilities. Later, at Columbia University, there was Paul Lazarsfeld and, in another department, Franz Neumann. It was an experience never likely to be repeated—that a nation with a leading intellectual tradition would expel hundreds of its outstanding minds.

The Columbia Sociology Department when I entered it in 1950 was the best in the nation. Its two leading figures were Robert K. Merton and Paul Lazarsfeld. The two were advocates and practitioners working for the unity of theory and research. Robert S. Lynd, co-author of two famous community studies, *Middletown* and *Middletown in Transition*, was also there. He had been instrumental in bringing Lazarsfeld to Columbia. A young student of Lynd's, Seymour Martin Lipset, was a recent addition to the department. He had just brought out his first book, *Agrarian Socialism*. Also at Columbia, although not in the department, was another young man, C. Wright Mills, who with Hans Gerth had published essays from Max Weber and was about to bring out his first major publication, *White Collar*. Another of the exiles joined the department for several years, Herbert Marcuse. And, by a circuitous route, another younger exile arrived, first as a fellow-graduate student then as faculty member, Juan José Linz Storch de Gracia.

Paul Lazarsfeld was frequently defined as a researcher, as an empiricist, the suggestion being that he offered no serious theoretical contribution. But within that book, *Voting*, there is an eminently useful theoretical position, one that has been called the social- or personal-influence model. It might be summarized as follows:

1. Values (political, religious, cultural, etc.) are learned from one's parents, this called primary socialization. Parental influence was the no. 1 predictor of party preferences and issue orientations.

2. Those values might be reinforced or modified by subsequent social influences, called secondary socialization. The stress, however, was on reinforcement, most people choose a like environment, like friends, like news sources, and so on. Most people, for example, marry within the same religion. The most frequent changes of religion follow out-marriage, taking a partner of a different faith.

3. The centrality of socialization means that 'other factors' are of limited importance. The mass media, for example, had rather limited impacts, an empirically based finding. The authors were arguing a reversal of the usual causal statement: instead of mass media influence changing people's opinions, people chose media that supported or reinforced their previous views.

Personal influences are the key causal factors in this view. It is sometimes referred to as the social-bases position.

Some intellectuals found this position unattractive. For them it was of little interest; for some it deserved only disdain. Many social commentators prefer to deal with 'big' world-historical events—industrialization, urbanization, uprooted masses, alienation, classes, and class struggle. For them, 'powerful forces' were declared to be operating—the consciousness of 'the masses' was formed by 'the media' that were controlled by 'big business'. But the *Voting* framework rejected those claims, focusing instead on family and the acceptance of parental direction. It was an account of intergenerational continuity, of conformity. Many subsequent commentators found a revived Marxism more 'interesting', more 'exciting'. Many found the mass society theory more useful, more appropriate for their purposes.

One principal finding reported in *Voting* has relevance for both of those theoretical perspectives. One table shows the vote by class and religion. The high-status Protestants showed a remarkable consensus—98 per cent support for the Republicans. High-status Catholics, in contrast, divided evenly between the major parties. Parallel findings appeared in all of the classes, all showing comparable sizeable divisions between Protestants and Catholics. That finding signalled both the persistence and weight of a communal factor. It presented a serious challenge to both Marxism and the mass society theories. But the importance of the finding went largely unnoticed.

I made use of the Berelson–Lazarsfeld framework in my first book, *Affluence and the French Worker* (1967), finding it useful for explaining both the variations and the persistence of Communist voting in France. I made much greater use of it in my second book, *Class and Politics in the United States* (1972), essentially following through on many themes from *Voting*. At a later point, I was studying the rise of the Nazis in Weimar Germany where, in the course of four years the Nazi vote went from 3 to 37 per cent. Here too, much to my surprise, I found the framework very useful (see *Who Voted for Hitler* [1982]).

Commentators, then and later, declared that the Nazi support came from 'the lower-middle class'—but they supplied no evidence to support that claim. A communal factor was present and of towering importance in those elections. Protestant towns and villages ultimately voted overwhelmingly for the Nazis, 80 per cent plus; Catholic towns and villages voted overwhelmingly for Catholic parties, also 80 per cent plus. The importance of 'the religious factor' was easily seen in newspaper reports on the days following those elections. The persistence of that factor had obvious relevance for the mass society theory, a striking rejection of its claims, but the fact and implication went largely unrecognized. In the towns and villages that finding also meant that 'class' had to be of trivial importance. But the finding and the implication went unrecognized.

An 'interpersonal influence' factor proved useful for explanation of the sudden change in party preferences. The liberal parties of Germany, the so-called middle-class parties, were badly damaged at this point. The local leaders had to defend government policies in the midst of a serious depression. And those leaders, the town and village notables, were ageing and largely without successors. Wartime mortality varied directly with rank up to captains. And military rank correlated with civilian rank which means the sons of the local notables were very disproportionately among the fallen of the Great War. And entering into the towns and villages to challenge the traditional notables were the Nazi activists, very capable war-trained veterans of the same war. They made their greatest gains when campaigning against those badly weakened leadership coteries.

The lay leaders in equivalent Catholic communities would also have suffered heavy losses in the successor generations. But there, the Nazi activists faced unified opposition from all local notables, clerical and lay, and from the local press. Similarly against the still intact leadership groups in working-class communities, the Nazis had limited success.

Lazarsfeld and Berelson discovered a limited, but important, media impact. Harry Truman emphasized domestic liberalism issues in his campaigning. And those themes, communicated through the mass media, brought a return of Democrats who had 'defected' earlier in the year. And that return led to Truman's re-election. In Germany too, there was a media impact. In those cities where the Nazis had outspoken newspaper support, in Essen, Braunschweig, Chemnitz, and Kiel, they received their highest voter support.

In my judgement, clearly, the Lazarsfeld position is very useful. Unfortunately, this contribution was largely neglected in later social science efforts. We have evidence attesting to that neglect. The four best-selling university-level introductory sociology textbooks command half of the market (and they in turn influence the other contenders). Two of the four textbooks make no reference at all to the Lazarsfeld–Berelson–McPhee work. The other two textbooks make brief mention of the man but refer only to minor peripheral works. A review of four leading American government textbooks yielded a similar result. Only one mentioned Lazarsfeld, even that referring to an early media study. The students in those classes would learn nothing about the importance of this contribution.

Many things have changed since 1948. The study antedates television, e-mail, websites, and all the rest. Organized political efforts, lobbying, pressure groups, etc. have a presence that one could hardly imagine in 1948. And many millions in later generations have experienced higher education with its many influences both personal and impersonal, all of which might challenge the primacy of family socialization. One should always keep in mind the most important lesson from the heritage of ancient Greece, those being the words of Heraclitus—'All is flux, nothing is stationary'.

The participants in the Comparative National Election study deserve commendation, for their revival of the *Voting* framework, for its development and extension.

Richard F. Hamilton

Preface
From Lazarsfeld to CNEP: the return and integration of a research tradition

The work of Paul F. Lazarsfeld and his Columbia University colleagues, as described earlier by Richard Hamilton, dominated the emerging field of American voting behaviour during the late 1950s and 1960s. As the first theoretically driven survey-based studies, this landmark work moved the study of voting beyond its traditional focus on geographically aggregated voting outcomes and their ecological correlates—and the inevitable demographic-variable explanations of the voting decision. The Columbia scholars' more refined emphasis on sociological factors and especially the voter's social context, though, was soon displaced by a focus on *personal* rather than *social* factors in voting.[1]

The turn to personal factors was led by scholars at the University of Michigan in their classic work, *The American Voter* (Campbell et al. 1960). As discussed more extensively in the introductory chapter of this volume, their so-called 'Michigan model' conceptualized the vote as a function of short-term attitudes towards the candidates and parties and long-term predispositions embedded in what they called 'party identification'. Sociological factors and, to a lesser degree, social context were not absent from these studies. Instead, they were relegated to a background or distal role as determinants of vote choice operating through the party identifications that reflected the prevailing political cleavages in the society. Party identifications, for those who had them, were viewed as psychological attachments to a particular party, which supplied frames through which the political world was viewed.

By the late 1960s, at first stealthily and then frontally, Anthony Downs' classic *An Economic Theory of Democracy* (1957) had emerged as a rival theoretical approach to the Michigan Model, especially as applied in Morris Fiorina's work (1981). This so-called 'rational actor' approach emphasized retrospective and prospective evaluations of governmental performance by the party in office and its opposition, often (though not necessarily) based on the voter's economic well-being. Fiorina also challenged the long-term stability and structuring influence of party identifications in showing how deviant vote decisions 'fed back' to weaken and even change them.

For all of the positioning of them as alternative socio-psychological and economic approaches to voting behaviour, the Michigan and the Downs–Fiorina approaches share an emphasis on the personal 'calculations' of an autonomously acting voter. They also share a methodological dependence for their data on sample surveys of *independent* individuals, which is the standard operating procedure in surveys to minimize the errors of sample estimates. This methodological procedure also removed voters from their social contexts, especially from the interactions among related individuals. One of the great insights of the Lazarsfeld studies had been that voters make their decisions within a social context rather than autonomously. With the turn to personal factors, attention was diverted from this insight for the next several decades. An incomplete view of the factors underlying voting behaviour was the unfortunate result. In treating the vote as a function of attitudes, identifications, and cost–benefit calculations, in other words, the personal approach neglected to consider that voting is as much a response to social situations and pressures as it is a private personal decision.

The idea that sparked the Cross-National Election Project (CNEP—now Comparative National Elections Project) was first developed in Tallahassee, Florida, when four Florida State University scholars—Russell Dalton, Scott Flanagan, Manfred Kuechler, and I—decided that a true cross-national analysis of voting behaviour was long overdue. Previous studies of voting in different countries had adopted one or more of the theoretical approaches described above, but none of them had applied their particular approach using the same research design and questionnaires in multiple countries.

At an organizational meeting in 1988 in a Florida panhandle resort where Tarzan movies had been filmed, my Florida State colleagues and I persuaded voting behaviour specialists involved in national studies in several other nations to join with us in an ambitious effort to conduct the first truly cross-national study of voting behaviour. We committed to employing a common theoretical approach, research design, and set of measures in the next national survey in their respective countries, so that they could become cases for cross-national comparison.[2] This agreement, operationalized in subsequent meetings, resulted in parallel surveys of voters in the first national elections of the 1990s in four countries—in Germany (1990), the United States (1992), the United Kingdom (1992), and Japan (1993)—and the subsequent addition of a survey in Spain (1993) to fill out the original CNEP (now referred to as CNEP I) group.[3]

In full appreciation of the rich research tradition in voting behaviour that had developed through the 1980s and of the different theoretical approaches previously pursued in the various country studies, we also decided on a comprehensive theoretical approach to our collaborative research. To this end, the five country studies integrated the sociological and social context approach of the early Lazarsfeld studies, the socio-psychological approach of the Michigan Model, and the Downs–Fiorina rational choice approach into a single study.

By then, variables reflecting the socio-psychological and rational choice approaches had become more or less standard fare in voting studies in the five countries. What was ignored in many of these studies, though, was the social context of the voting decision, as captured in the earlier work of Lazarsfeld and his colleagues. While there had been a reawakening to the importance of social context for voting decisions in some recent American and European studies, context was primarily measured by aggregating individuals' survey responses to create contextual variables for geographically defined units rather than by an attempt to build the voter's immediate social and political context through survey questions themselves.

The application of a comprehensive common theoretical approach to the cross-national studies required us to devote considerable attention to the measurement of social contexts. In thinking about how to best conceptualize and operationalize the voter's social context, we returned to the pioneering work of Lazarsfeld some fifty years before.

We conceptualized the social context as involving the three major *intermediaries* between the political world and the voter—the mass media, secondary organizations (including political party organizations), and personal discussion networks—and set about to measure messages from the particular intermediaries to which the voters in our surveys were exposed. By the late 1980s, each of these intermediaries already had established its own distinct research tradition, often outside the area of voting behaviour and out of touch with any of the other intermediaries.

Social networks research was developing into an exciting research frontier across the social sciences. We incorporated it into our cross-national studies by adding a battery of questions about the personal discussants, including the spouse, of the voters in our surveys. In several country cases, we even used snowball sampling techniques to identify and interview these discussants.

The mass media were widely credited with having transformed democratic politics, and their priming and framing functions were receiving increasing scrutiny. Rarely, however, were they employed as important variables in explaining voting choices. We developed batteries of questions on television, newspapers, and radio to assess the perceived partisan direction (what we called 'bias') of the messages emanating from each, as well as other important characteristics. In several CNEP countries, we even went so far as to content analyse the partisanship of the messages from the media in our analysis.

Secondary organizations too have been viewed as important intermediaries, but rarely have the campaign activities of organizations been factored into the voting behaviour of their members in election studies. We carefully assayed voters' membership organizations and their partisan message during the campaign. We also measured the contacts voters received in their respective countries from the various political parties.

While recognizing our intellectual debt to Paul F. Lazarsfeld and his Columbia colleagues in examining the social contexts defined by these intermediaries, I also want to acknowledge that our studies went well beyond his work in several important respects. Where the Columbia researchers studied contextual variation across individuals within a single community, the CNEP studies looked for variation across entire countries, and in the United States it radically clustered the sample so that we could compare communities with one another. Where the Lazarsfeld studies examined the major media of their time, newspapers and radio, we added the major medium of our time—television. Where they indirectly measured the flow of information from the intermediation sources, we relied directly on how they were received (and perceived) by the voter—and, in several countries, measured them at the source as well. Finally, where the Columbia studies operationalized a rather lean voting behaviour model, failing to treat the vote choice as the result of the personal attitudes and calculations that later were to become so central in studying voting behaviour, we employed comprehensive models.

And, as they say, 'the rest is history'. After the first round of so-called CNEP I studies in the early 1990s, surveys following the same design and instrumentation were carried out during the remainder of the decade in a new set of countries, including many new and reborn democracies. These countries plus the original five constitute the focus of this volume.

Paul Allen Beck

Notes

1. This distinction between personal and social approaches to voting behaviour— the former emphasizing personal attitudes and identifications, the latter emphasizing the influence of social contexts—is further developed in Beck et al. (2002).
2. The founding teams for the CNEP were Max Kaase, Hans-Dieter Klingemann, Manfred Kuechler, and Franz-Urban Pappi for Germany; Hiroshi Akuto, Scott Flanagan, Bradley Richardson, and Seizaburo Sato for Japan; Paul Beck, Russell Dalton, and Robert Huckfeldt for the United States; and John Curtice, Anthony Heath, and Roger Jowell for the United Kingdom.
3. The Spanish study was added to the initial four country studies after our original planning meetings. The principal members of its team were Richard Gunther and José Ramón Montero.

Acknowledgements

The debts, intellectual, economic and practical, to be acknowledged in an enterprise as large as this one are so many that it becomes almost impossible to do justice to all those who, in a variety of ways, have contributed to the conception, articulation, and realization of this project. From the very beginning, Paul Beck, John Curtice, Bradley Richardson, and other members of the original team of the Cross-National Election Project (subsequently referred to as CNEP I) were sources of inspiration and encouragement. Juan J. Linz and P. Nikiforos Diamandouros have given valuable advice at various stages of the project. The members of the various 'country teams' responsible for the coordination of the national surveys and the elaboration of the data, the participants of the working groups on specific research themes, the authors of the chapters, and our colleagues who have helped to organize the conferences and workshops, given papers and comments or served as discussants and resource persons (listed in Note 8 of the Introduction) have all been crucial for the successful conclusion of this study. They have demonstrated once more how important it is for an enterprise like ours to be able to count on the interest, support, and often enthusiasm of the members of an international network of social scientists from different backgrounds. Our heartfelt thanks go to all of them.

The second phase of what was re-christened as the Comparative National Elections Project (CNEP II) was launched at a conference on 'Democracy, Political Transition, Electoral Choice' held in Bologna on June 1998. It brought together key participants of the CNEP I group who had essentially analysed the older established democracies of Germany, Japan, the United Kingdom, the United States, and (as a late addition and a bridge to the third-wave democracies) Spain, and the members of the ACLS/SSRC Subcommittee on Southern Europe who had previously organized, with the generous financial support of the Volkswagen Foundation, a multi-year (and, in the end, five-book) project on 'The Nature and

Consequences of Democracy in the New Southern Europe'. The purpose of that meeting was to reflect on the principal conclusions of the Southern Europe project, to identify new research questions that were of particular relevance to newly established democratic systems, and to determine which of those themes were most amenable to analysis using the analytical tools created over the course of CNEP I. We are grateful to the Istituto Cattaneo for hosting that meeting, and to the Mershon Center of the Ohio State University, the SSRC, and the Volkswagen Foundation for providing the funding which made that crucial planning meeting possible.

In addition to continuing financial support from the Mershon Center, funds were made available for annual planning, research, and editorial meetings by the Volkswagen Foundation under a research project titled 'Political Intermediation and Democratic Legitimacy in New Democracies: Eastern Europe, Latin America, Southern Europe and Asia in Comparative Perspective'. The new research agenda of CNEP II led to seven conferences which were held in Budapest (1999), Yogyakarta (2000), Santiago de Chile (2001), Mannheim (2002), Columbus, Ohio (2003), Cape Town (2004), and the Casa de Mateus in Vila Real, Portugal (2005). In addition to providing an opportunity for the revision of research papers and their conversion into the chapters included in this volume, the last two conferences also made it possible for us to plan the further extension of this project, both geographically and thematically. The result was the launching of CNEP III in 2006, with the project now including new country teams from Africa, East Asia, and Latin America, as well as follow-up national election surveys in a number of CNEP I and II countries.

An ambitious cross-regional comparative study like ours could not have succeeded without the continuous support of two institutions which have become crucial to our endeavour: the Mershon Center of the Ohio State University and the Volkswagen Foundation. Both of them have not only provided essential financial support, but also friendly encouragement and professional advice. We wish to express our gratitude and sincere appreciation to those institutions, and in particular to Alfred Schmidt of the Volkswagen Foundation, and to Ned Lebow and Richard Herrmann of the Mershon Center. Invaluable staff support was also provided by Ann Powers, Linda Montaño, and Viki Jones of the Mershon Center over the course of several years of this project. Additional assistance was provided by the Center for Advanced Study in the Social Sciences of the Juan March Institute in Madrid, and the Institute for Political Science of the University of Frankfurt.

We are also most grateful to the local organizers and institutions that hosted our annual meetings. These include Paolo Segatti and the Istituto Carlo Cattaneo of Bologna, Tibor Gazso and the Századvég Policy Research Center in Budapest, Saiful Mujani and Gadjah Mada University in Yogyakarta, Eugenio Tironi and the Catholic University in Santiago de Chile, Rüdiger Schmitt-Beck and ZUMA in Mannheim, the Mershon Center of the Ohio State University in Columbus, Robert Mattes and the Centre for Social Science Research of the University of Cape Town, and Pedro Magalhães and the Mateus Foundation in Vila Real. Additional funding for these meetings was provided by the Mellon Foundation, the Gulbenkian Foundation, the Luso-American Foundation, the Orient Foundation, and the Social Sciences Institute of the University of Lisbon.

Our project would have been impossible without the various national surveys, as one can only compare data which have been previously collected and elaborated (and somehow made comparable). The surveys, in a way, are the core of the whole enterprise, even if they would remain silent without intelligent questions generated by creative teams of scholars. Here we are pleased to acknowledge the generous support of a number of institutions, including the Mershon Center (for the 1996 Bulgarian and 1999 Indonesian surveys), the Ohio State University (the 1992 and 2004 American studies), the North-South Center (Uruguay 1993 and Chile 2000), the Chilean Presidencia (Chile 1994), the Japanese Ministry of Education (Japan 1993), the Spanish Interministerial Commission for Science and Technology, the Catalan and Basque autonomous regional governments, and the Comité Conjunto Hispano-Norteamericano para la Cooperación Cultural y Educativa (Spain 1993), the Hong Kong research Grants Council (Hong Kong 1998), the Greek National Centre for Social Research (EKKE, for the 1996 and 2004 surveys), the Istituto Carlo Cattaneo (for the 1996 Italian study), and especially the National Science Foundation of the United States (for surveys conducted in 1992 and 2004 in the United States, 1982 and 1993 in Spain, 1998 in Hungary, 1999 in Indonesia [the opinions, findings, and conclusions expressed in this book, however, are those of the authors and do not necessarily reflect the views of the National Science Foundation]).

Finally, we are most grateful to Dominic Byatt, editor at Oxford University Press, for his encouragement and support for the publication of this book, and to Shuaib Ahmed for his excellent work in improving the style of our prose.

Contents

List of Figures   xxi
List of Tables   xxii
List of Appendices   xxv
Notes on Contributors   xxvi

1. Introduction: Intermediation, Information, and
   Electoral Politics   1
   Richard Gunther, José Ramón Montero, and Hans-Jürgen Puhle

2. Democracy and Intermediation: Some Attitudinal and
   Behavioural Dimensions   29
   Richard Gunther, José Ramón Montero, and Mariano Torcal

3. The Mass Media in Third-Wave Democracies: Gravediggers
   or Seedsmen of Democratic Consolidation?   75
   Rüdiger Schmitt-Beck and Katrin Voltmer

4. Intermediation Through Secondary Associations:
   The Organizational Context of Electoral Behaviour   135
   Paolo Bellucci, Marco Maraffi, and Paolo Segatti

5. The Flow of Political Information: Personal Discussants,
   the Media, and Partisans   183
   Bradley Richardson and Paul Allen Beck

6. Voting and Intermediation: Informational Biases and
   Electoral Choices in Comparative Perspective   208
   Pedro C. Magalhães

7. Value Cleavages and Partisan Conflict   255
   Richard Gunther and Kuan Hsin-chi

Contents

8. Conclusions: Processes of Intermediation, Electoral Politics, and
   Political Support in Old and New Democracies   321
   Hans-Jürgen Puhle, José Ramón Montero, and Richard Gunther

Notes   346
References   368
Index   395

List of Figures

3.1. Media effects on orientations towards aspects of political culture   82

3.2. The impact of mass media on components of political cultures   106

3.3. The impact of mass media on components of political cultures
     (less conservative estimates)   115

4.1. Overall associational membership   144

4.2. Association membership and association density   151

4.3. Association membership and political encapsulation of the electorate   175

List of Tables

2.1. Support for democracy in CNEP democracies, in comparative
perspective   35

2.2. The dimensionality of attitudes towards democracy: Spain,
Uruguay, Greece   38

2.3. The dimensionality of attitudes towards democracy: Portugal,
Bulgaria, Hungary   40

2.4. The dimensionality of attitudes towards democracy: Chile   43

2.5. Correlations among latent factors and RMSEA statistics from
confirmatory factor analysis   44

2.6. Correlations with organizational membership   47

2.7. Correlations between frequency of discussion of politics and
attitudes towards democracy   49

2.8. Behavioural correlates of attitudes towards democracy:
Spain, Uruguay, Greece   51

2.9. Behavioural correlates of attitudes towards democracy:
Portugal, Hungary   52

2.10. Behavioural correlates of attitudes towards democracy:
Bulgaria, Chile   53

2.11. Relationship between support for democracy and vote for
anti-system party   58

2.12. Correlations with involvement in politics   63

2.13. Regression analysis of involvement in politics   65

2.14. Correlations of disaffection scale with...   67

2.15. Behavioural correlates of disaffection   68

3.1. Political participation   91

3.2. Media penetration, political media exposure, and organization
membership   94

3.3. Correlates of media usage   101

4.1. Membership in voluntary associations 145

4.2. Membership by type of voluntary association and country 148

4.3. Logistic model of membership in voluntary associations 149

4.4. Density of membership in non-political voluntary associations 150

4.5. Intensity of participation in activities of voluntary non-political associations by country 153

4.6. Intensity of participation in activities of voluntary non-political associations by type of association and country 154

4.7. Non-political voluntary associations' electoral contacts by country and type of association 157

4.8. Non-political voluntary associations' electoral support by country and type of association 161

4.9. Zero-order probability and predicted probability of political cues and perception of partisan support 165

4.10. Average electoral turnout in CNEP countries 1961–99 168

4.11. Effects of association mobilization, individual resources, psychological involvement, and institutional context on turnout 170

4.12. Political encapsulation of the electorate 173

4.13. The political encapsulation of joiners by type of association 176

4.14. Logistic models of political encapsulation by associations 178

5.1. Levels of exposure to different sources of information 186

5.2. Perceived partisan bias in different information sources 189

5.3. Agreement between respondents' vote preferences and the perceived biases of information sources 193

5.4. Congruence in vote preference with primary discussant by type of relationship 196

5.5. Status equality–inequality and discussant–voter congruence in vote preference 196

5.6. Political knowledge levels and discussant–voter congruence in vote preference 199

5.7. Partisans and non-partisans 201

5.8. Perceptions of information source partisan bias among partisans and non-partisans 201

5.9. Partisanship strength and congruence in voter preference and source party bias 203

6.1. The association between partisanship and perceived intermediary bias 216

6.2. The role of intermediary biases   218

6.3. Intermediaries and short-term factors   220

6.4. The effects of perceived intermediary biases on voting behaviour, I   230

6.5. The effects of perceived intermediary biases on voting behaviour, II   231

6.6. Party identification and media biases   238

6.7. Intermediary influences on the vote in four countries   240

7.1. Mean scores on values items   267

7.2. Correlations between left–right self-placement and values items   272

7.3a. Factor analysis and correlations among values: Spain   277

7.3b. Factor analysis and correlations among values: Greece   278

7.3c. Factor analysis and correlations among values: United States   280

7.3d. Factor analysis and correlations among values: Uruguay   282

7.3e. Factor analysis and correlations among values: Chile   284

7.3f. Factor analysis and correlations among values: Hungary   285

7.3g. Factor analysis and correlations among values: Hong Kong   287

7.4. Confirmatory factor analyses of three-factor 'West European
     template' and two-factor model   288

7.5. Correlations between value scales and partisan preference   290

7.6a. Values quartiles by vote: Spain   292

7.6b. Values quartiles by vote: Greece   294

7.6c. Values quartiles by vote: Uruguay   294

7.6d. Values quartiles by vote: United States   295

7.7. Logit analyses of vote for parties of the left vs. right   298

7.8. Correlations between intermediation bias and vote for left vs. right   302

7.9. Correlations among value clusters, party identification, and
     left–right self-designation   316

7.10. Logit analyses of vote for parties of the left vs. right   318

List of Appendices

3.1. Classification of media   125

3.2. Overview of variables   127

3.3A1. Media exposure and political culture: Greece   129

3.3A2. Media exposure and political culture: Spain   130

3.3A3. Media exposure and political culture: Uruguay   131

3.3A4. Media exposure and political culture: Chile   132

3.3A5. Media exposure and political culture: Hungary   133

3.3A6. Media exposure and political culture: Bulgaria   134

6.1. Coding of variables   247

6.2. Coding of media exposure variables   254

Notes on Contributors

Paul Allen Beck, Dean of the College of Social and Behavioral Sciences, and Professor of Political Science at Ohio State University, specializes in the study of political parties and voting behaviour, primarily in the United States. His articles have appeared in the *American Political Science Review*, the *American Journal of Political Science*, and the *Journal of Politics*. He is author of *Party Politics in America* and co-editor of *Electoral Change in Advanced Industrial Democracies*. Beck has served as Book Review Editor of the *American Political Science Review*, and as Chair of the Strategic Planning Committee, of the Annual Meeting Program Committee, and of the section on Elections, Public Opinion, and Voting Behavior for the American Political Science Association, which awarded him the Goodnow Award for distinguished professional service. He has won the Distinguished Scholar and Distinguished University Service award from Ohio State University.

Paolo Bellucci is Professor of Political Science at the Università di Siena, where he teaches comparative political behaviour and political methodology. He is a member of the Italian National Election Study (ITANES) and principal investigator (with Paolo Segatti) of the 2006 Italian Election Study. Among his recent publications in English are *Italian Politics: The Return of Berlusconi* (ed. with Martin Bull 2002), and *Modelling Electoral Choice in the Twenty-First Century* (a Special Issue of *Electoral Studies*, ed. with Paul Whiteley 2006).

Richard Gunther is Professor of Political Science at the Ohio State University. He has served as Executive Director of International Studies at OSU and as co-chair (with P. Nikiforos Diamandouros) of the Subcommittee on Southern Europe of the American Council of Learned Societies and the Social Science Research Council. His recent publications include *Democracy and the State in the New Southern Europe* (with P. Nikiforos Diamandouros and Dimitri Sotiropoulos 2006), *Democracy in Modern Spain* (with José Ramón Montero and Joan Botella 2004),

Political Parties: Old Concepts and New Challenges (ed. with José Ramón Montero and Juan Linz 2002), *Political Parties and Democracy* (ed. with Larry Diamond 2001), *Parties, Politics and Democracy in the New Southern Europe* (ed. with P. Nikiforos Diamandouros 2001), *Democracy and the Media* (ed. with Anthony Mughan 2000), *The Politics of Democratic Consolidation* (ed. with P. Nikiforos Diamandouros and Hans-Jürgen Puhle 1995), and *Elites and Democratic Consolidation in Latin America and Southern Europe* (ed. with John Higley 1992). He is recipient of the Distinguished Scholar and the Distinguished University Service awards of the Ohio State University, and the Joan N. Huber Faculty Fellowship for Outstanding Scholarship.

Richard F. Hamilton is Emeritus Professor of Sociology and Political Science at the Ohio State University. Most of his work has focused on political sociology and historical sociology, as well as assessments of and commentary on relevant social theories. In addition to his seventy article-length publications, his books include *Affluence and the French Worker in the Fourth Republic* (1967), *Class and Politics in the United States* (1972), *Restraining Myths: Critical Studies of U.S. Social Structure and Politics* (1975), *Who Voted for Hitler* (1982), *The State of the Masses* (with James Wright 1986), *The Bourgeois Epoch: Marx and Engels on Britain, France and Germany* (1991), *The Origins of World War I* (ed. with Holger H. Herwig 2003), and *Decisions for War 1914–1917* (ed. with Holger H. Herwig 2004).

Kuan Hsin-chi is Professor of Government and Public Administration at The Chinese University of Hong Kong, and Academician of the Pontifical Academy of Social Sciences, Vatican. He is Chair of his department and Director of the Universities Service Centre, a leading research institution for post-1949 China studies. He is a member of several editorial boards, including *China Perspectives* and the *Journal of Contemporary China*. His current research focuses on elections in Hong Kong and the evolution of civil society in Greater China. He is co-author of *The Ethos of the Hong Kong Chinese* (1988), *The 1995 Legislative Council Elections in Hong Kong* (1996), and *Power Transfer and Electoral Politics: The First SAR Legislative Election in Hong Kong* (1999), in addition to many articles published in *Democratization*, *The China Journal*, the *Journal of Northeast Asian Studies*, and other scholarly journals.

Pedro C. Magalhães is a research scholar at the Social Sciences Institute of the University of Lisbon. He is one of the coordinators of the Portuguese Election Study. His research interests include comparative judicial politics, judicial behaviour, public opinion, and electoral behaviour. His book publications include *O parlamento português: uma reforma necessária* (with António de Aráujo, Cristina Leston-Bandeira, André Freire, and Marina Costa Lobo 2002), *A abstenção eleitoral em Portugal* (with André Freire 2002), *Portugal a votos: as eleições legislativas de 2002* (ed. with André Freire and Marina Costa Lobo 2004), and *Portugal: democracia y política* (ed. with António Barreto and Braulio Gómez Fortes 2003). He has also published articles in *Comparative Politics*, *West European Politics*, *International Journal of Public Opinion Research*, *South European Society and Politics*, and the *Journal of Southern Europe and the Balkans*. In 2004, he received the award of the Council of Graduate Schools for the best dissertation in the social sciences.

Marco Maraffi is Professor of Sociology at the University of Milan, where he is also head of the Department of Social and Political Studies and a member of the managing committee of the Graduate School in Social, Political and Economic Sciences. His research interests are in the field of interest representation, party organization, political culture, voting behaviour, voluntary associations, values and religion, decision-making processes, and choice mechanisms. Among his publications are *Social Capital and European Democracy* (ed. with Jan van Deth, Ken Newton, and Paul Whiteley 1999), *PCI, PDS, DS: La trasformazione dell'identità politica della sinistra di governo* (with Paolo Bellucci and Paolo Segatti 2000), and *Gli italiani e la politica* (ed., forthcoming).

José Ramón Montero is Professor of Political Science at the Universidad Autónoma de Madrid and at the Centro de Estudios Avanzados en Ciencias Sociales, Instituto Juan March, Madrid. He has taught at the universities of Granada, Santiago de Compostela, Zaragoza, Complutense de Madrid, and Cádiz (where he was Dean of the School of Law), and has been a visiting fellow at Harvard, the University of California at Berkeley, and Ohio State University. He has served as Deputy Director of the Centro de Investigaciones Sociológicas, head of the Economics and Social Science Program, Comisión Interministerial de Ciencia y Tecnología, and member of the Standing Committee for the Social Sciences, European Science Foundation, the Scientific Advisory Board of the European Social Survey, the Academic Europea, and the Editorial Committee of the *Revista Española de Ciencia Política*. He has published extensively on electoral behaviour, political parties, and political culture. His published books include *Political Dissatisfaction in Contemporary Democracies* (ed. with Mariano Torcal 2006), *Democracy in Modern Spain* (with Richard Gunther and Joan Botella 2004), *Political Parties: Old Concepts and New Challenges* (ed. with Richard Gunther and Juan J. Linz 2002), *El régimen electoral* (with Richard Gunther et al. 1996), *Elecciones autonómicas en Aragón* (ed. with Ricardo Chueca 1995), *Crisis y cambio: electores y partidos en la España de los años ochenta* (ed. with Juan J. Linz 1986), *El control parlamentario* (with Joaquín Morillo 1985), and *La CEDA: el catolicismo social y político en la II República* (1977).

Hans-Jürgen Puhle is Professor of Political Science at the Johann Wolfgang Goethe Universität Frankfurt am Main. He has held previous appointments at the universities of Münster and Bielefeld, and has been fellow or visiting professor at Harvard, Oxford, Cornell, and Stanford universities, the University of Tel Aviv, the Universidad de Chile in Santiago, FLACSO in Buenos Aires, and the Instituto Juan March in Madrid. He is a member of the editorial board of the journal *Geschichte und Gesellschaft*, and has published extensively in the fields of comparative social and political history of Europe and the Americas, problems of modernization, state functions and welfare capitalism, political parties, pressure groups and social movements, nationalism and regionalism, and regime transformation and problems of democratic consolidation. His recent books include *Kampf um den Wein: Modernisierung und Interessenpolitik im spanischen Weinbau* (with Ludger Mees and Klaus-Jürgen Nagel 2005), *Supermacht im Wandel: Die USA von Clinton zu Bush* (with Söhnke Schreyer and Jürgen Wilzewski 2004), *Defekte Demokratie: Vol. 1, Theorie* (with Wolfgang Merkel et al. 2003), *Parteienstaat in der Krise: Parteien und Politik zwischen Modernisierung und Fragmentierung* (2002), *Von der Diktatur zur Demokratie* (with Wolfgang Merkel 1999), *The Politics of Democratic Consolidation: Southern Europe in Comparative Perspective* (ed. with Richard Gunther and Nikiforos Diamandouros 1995), *Staaten, Nationen und Regionen in Europa* (1995), and *Von der Arbeiterbewegung zum modernen Sozialstaat* (ed. with Jürgen Kocka and Klaus Tenfelde 1994).

Bradley Richardson is Professor and Distinguished Scholar Emeritus in Political Science at Ohio State University. He is a specialist on Japanese society and politics, and is currently researching the changing microeconomic base of the Japanese economy. His publications include *Japanese Democracy* (1997), *The Japanese Voter* (1991), and numerous articles in the *American Political Science Review* and other prominent social science journals.

Rüdiger Schmitt-Beck is Professor of Political Science at the University of Duisburg-Essen, Germany. His research interests are in the areas of comparative political behaviour, especially public opinion, political communication, electoral behaviour, political culture, social movements, and political participation. His most recent books are *Politische Kommunikation und Wählerverhalten* (2000), *Do Political Campaigns Matter?* (ed. with David M. Farrell 2002), and *Sozialer und politischer Wandel in Deutschland* (ed. with Martina Wasmer and Achim Koch 2004). He has published in such journals as the *British Journal of Political Science*, the *European Journal of Political Research*, the *European Journal of Communication*, the *International Journal of Public Opinion Research*, and *Kölner Zeitschrift für Soziologie und Sozialpsychologie*.

Paolo Segatti is Professor of Political Science at the University of Milan, and is a member of the Italian National Election Study (ITANES) research team. He has conducted cross-national research on national identities, political disaffection, and the link between religiosity and voting behaviour. His most recent publications in English include *Italian Politics in 2003* (ed. with Jean Blondel), and 'Italy: Forty Years of Disaffection' in Montero and Torcal, eds., *Political Disaffection in Contemporary Democracies* (2006).

Mariano Torcal is Professor of Political Science at the Universitat Pompeu Fabra in Barcelona, and is National Coordinator of the European Social Survey in Spain, as well as a member of the steering committee of the INTUNE European Project. He has been a visiting professor at the University of Michigan, the Center for Advanced Studies in the Social Sciences of the Instituto Juan March, the Kellogg Institute at Notre Dame, and the Universidad Autónoma de Madrid. He has published studies of political culture and political behaviour in *Comparative Political Studies*, the *British Journal of Political Science*, the *International Journal of Public Opinion Research*, and other journals and edited volumes. The American Political Science Association awarded him 'Honorable Mention for the Gregory M. Luebbert Prize for best article in Comparative Politics of 1997', and the Spanish National Political Science Association (AECPA) gave him its award for the best article published in 2003. He is co-editor of *Disaffected Citizens: Social Capital, Institutions and Politics* (Routledge 2006).

Katrin Voltmer is Senior Lecturer of Political Communication, Director of Postgraduate Studies, and Head of the MA programme in Political Communication at the Institute of Communications Studies at the University of Leeds, UK. She has formerly held positions at the Science Center Berlin and the Free University of Berlin. Her research interests include the role of the media in democratic politics and in transitions to democracy, the quality of political news, and the media's impact on individual attitudes and participation. Her publications include *Mass Media and Political Communication in New Democracies* (2006).

1

Introduction: intermediation, information, and electoral politics

Richard Gunther, José Ramón Montero, and Hans-Jürgen Puhle

This book undertakes systematic, cross-national analyses of three themes that are central to the study of politics in democratic systems. The first two are broadly applicable to both new and long-established democracies. One involves the ways in which political attitudes and values are related to one another and to partisan preferences. The second deals with channels through which messages flow from parties and candidates to voters, and the ways in which such information flows affect voting decisions and levels of political participation. The third analytical focus of this book is particularly important for newly established or re-established democratic systems. It deals with the mass-level attitudinal underpinnings of democratic consolidation and the relationship between fundamental support for democracy, on the one hand, and other opinions and beliefs regarding satisfaction with democratic performance and the quality of citizen participation in democratic politics, on the other.

In one respect, this book represents a return to the very origins of the modern empirical study of electoral behaviour. Its centrepiece is a systematic examination of what we call *political intermediation*—that is, of the varying channels and processes through which voters receive information about partisan politics during the course of election campaigns and are mobilized to support one party or another. These include the flow of campaign messages and the exertion of influence through face-to-face contacts within personal networks, through membership and involvement in secondary associations, and through the mass communications media. These intermediation processes were the central focus of the very first modern survey-based studies of electoral behaviour undertaken by

Paul F. Lazarsfeld and his collaborators at the Bureau of Applied Social Research of the Columbia University in the late 1940s, but have largely been ignored by scholars since the mid-1950s.

In another respect, this book includes some substantial methodological and theoretical innovations. Foremost among these is the inclusion in several of these surveys of a substantial battery of questions tapping into several sets of attitudes towards democracy, as well as durable and deeply rooted socio-political values. These have not previously been systematically analysed in a comparative manner. As we see, some of these are important with regard to how citizens relate to their democratic political systems. Others have very substantial impact on voting decisions in most countries, particularly the United States, which has become severely polarized along the lines of 'values' cleavages. The systematic cross-national study of the electoral impact of values is a relatively new enterprise in comparative politics, and the approach that we adopt is a substantial departure even from the other studies included within this new school.

This book is a product of the Comparative National Elections Project (CNEP), which involves collaboration among teams of scholars in Western and Eastern Europe, North and South America, Asia, and Africa. A sizeable common core of items included in national election surveys makes possible cross-national and inter-regional analyses of several themes of both theoretical and empirical importance. This project was launched in 1990 and has grown subsequently over the following fifteen years, with the addition of new teams of researchers in Africa and Asia, and with second-wave surveys conducted in several of the original CNEP countries that will make possible analyses of change over the course of a decade. The current volume is based on surveys conducted in Germany (1990), Britain (1992), the United States (1992, 2004), Japan (1992), Spain (1993), Chile (1994), Uruguay (1994), Greece (1996), Italy (1996), Bulgaria (1996), Hong Kong (1998), and Hungary (1998). In addition, several other studies (conducted by scholars who were not yet members of the CNEP) included data that were directly comparable to ours, so from time to time we incorporate findings from those studies (of Spain in 1979, Italy in 1985, and Portugal in 2002) into our analysis.

Our sample of countries includes a number of political systems that were democratized in the course of the 'third wave' of political reforms in the late twentieth century. We are therefore able to test numerous hypotheses that have emerged from the literature on democratic transitions (which will be discussed more extensively below). Our post-communist East European cases include Bulgaria and Hungary, which contrast with each other in theoretically important ways: Bulgaria is the prototype of the post-totalitarian society (lacking an adequate degree of institutionalized pluralism), and has a powerful post-communist party whose commitment to democracy and economic liberalization have been questioned, while Hungary had undergone considerable economic and political liberalization well in advance of the collapse of the Soviet Bloc in 1989; Bulgaria's economy in the early to mid 1990s experienced a very deep depression, and maintenance of law and order collapsed, while Hungary was a reasonably prosperous and stable society. Our Latin American cases also provide useful contrasts which speak directly to key hypotheses in the literature on democratic transitions. The economy of Chile has boomed over the past decade, while that of Uruguay has continued to stagnate; but the persistent political intervention of General Augusto Pinochet (which meant that Chile could not be regarded as fully democratic until 1998) stands in contrast with the clean break from the authoritarian past in Uruguay. Our sample also includes the relatively new democracies of Greece and Spain, as well as the substantially restructured democracy of Italy. All three of these countries also experienced transitions to democracy (albeit at somewhat earlier periods) whose characteristics provide an invaluable baseline for the assessment of political and social change in the more recently established democratic regimes. And the incorporation of Hong Kong into this study constitutes a unique opportunity to monitor processes of political change whose ultimate outcome is very much in doubt. To what extent have these differing transition trajectories affected the vitality of and support for democracy in these countries? To what extent did the aforementioned intermediation processes contribute to these democratic transitions and the performance of democratic politics in these new regimes?

These questions are addressed in the six substantive chapters of this book. The first two deal with the nature and level of attitudes towards democracy and democratic politics. Richard Gunther, José Ramón Montero, and Mariano Torcal analyse the dimensional structure of various kinds of attitudes towards democracy, and then explore the behavioural correlates of three different kinds of such orientations. They also set forth a speculative explanation of cross-national variations in democratic support. In Chapter 3, Katrin Voltmer and Rüdiger Schmitt-Beck examine these same sets of political attitudes from a different perspective. In their analysis of the attitudinal and behavioural correlates of exposure to the mass communications media, they test the oft-stated media malaise hypothesis and its claim that media exposure exerts a negative influence on support for, and the level and quality of political participation within democratic systems.

The next three chapters are primarily concerned with partisanship and processes of electoral mobilization—that is, the role of intermediation channels in activating segments of the electorate during the course of election campaigns—in the aforementioned new democracies as well as the older, established democracies of Germany, Japan, the United Kingdom, and the United States. Paolo Bellucci, Marco Maraffi, and Paolo Segatti examine information flows through secondary associations and their impact on electoral turnout and partisan preferences. Paul Beck and Bradley Richardson explore the extent to which flows of information through the media and face-to-face communications within personal networks are homogeneous and reinforcing of the views of political parties, as compared with intermediation processes that deliver heterogeneous, cross-cutting partisan messages. And the combined electoral impact of all of these intermediation processes (after taking into account the effects of other common determinants of the vote) is systematically analysed in Chapter 5 by Pedro Magalhães. Finally, the chapter by Richard Gunther and Kuan Hsin-chi on socio-political values presents dramatic evidence of the extent to which values can polarize electoral competition in certain political systems.

Before we examine the contents of these chapters in greater detail, let us briefly examine the distinguishing characteristics of four different approaches to the study of electoral behaviour. This discussion will highlight the strengths and weaknesses of each approach, and will help to make it clear how our return to the Lazarsfeld framework can enhance the empirical study of voting and its theoretical underpinnings.

Four Approaches to the Study of Voting Behaviour

Among the very first studies of electoral behaviour utilizing survey data were those undertaken in the 1940s by a group of scholars surrounding Paul F. Lazarsfeld at Columbia University (see Merton, Coleman, and Rossi 1979). Earlier empirical studies of electoral behaviour were based on different kinds of data, employed different analytical methodologies, and developed different explanatory paradigms. These included the 'electoral geography' approach of Siegfried ([1913] 1964) and Génique

(1921), the aggregate data analysis of Tingsten ([1937] 1971), the rudimentary use of survey data by Merriam (1926 [1925] and 1970), the electoral experiments studied by Gosnell (1927), and the pioneer analysis of non-voting undertaken by Merriam and Gosnell (1924). The development of modern survey research by Lazarsfeld and his collaborators at Columbia University's Bureau of Applied Social Research (see Glock 1979) enabled Lazarsfeld to depart dramatically from these earlier studies by directly analysing individual-level data concerning social-psychological and social-structural determinants of behaviour. Particularly innovative was Lazarsfeld's development of panel surveys, which made it possible to overcome the shortcomings of cross-sectional observations in the study of attitudinal formation and change (Glock 1979). *The People's Choice*, the first work utilizing the 'Columbia' approach, analysed changes in electoral preferences through a series of panel waves conducted between May and November of 1940 in Erie County (Ohio). The principal finding of this path-breaking study was that 'face-to-face contacts turned out to be the most important influences stimulating opinion change' (Lazarsfeld, Berelson, and Gaudet 1944: xxv). In contrast with the then widespread belief that newspapers exercised the greatest influence over the electoral behaviour of voters, the authors concluded that 'personal relationships are potentially more influential for two reasons: their coverage is greater and they have certain psychological advantages over the formal media' (Lazarsfeld, Berelson, and Gaudet 1944: 150). Particularly important was the role played by 'opinion leaders' in a two-step flow of political information through networks of family members, friends, and co-workers. These information sources were influential in large part because of the basic trust among members of these networks, their flexibility and pervasiveness, and their non-purposive nature with regard to political questions. 'In the last analysis', the authors conclude, 'more than anything else people can move other people' (Lazarsfeld, Berelson, and Gaudet 1944: 158).

This was followed by another important election study published in 1954 by Berelson, Lazarsfeld, and McPhee, *Voting*, which analysed the 1948 election utilizing interviews undertaken in Elmira, New York. Electoral intermediation was placed within a systematic framework that included social structures and processes (secondary organizations, social cleavages, social perceptions, and small groups) as well as more explicitly political factors (parties, candidates, issues, and the mass media). Ostensibly non-political secondary associations are seen as having a significant latent political impact in so far as their members tend, in the aggregate, to share a common partisan orientation or point of view: 'the organizations as such do little in the way of intentional political activity, yet membership does have an effect simply by bringing together people of like social position and interests' (Berelson, Lazarsfeld, and McPhee 1954: 52–3). The principal role of the mass communications media, in contrast, involves what was later labelled as agenda-setting: 'it is the role of narrowing down, of focusing, of defining what elections mean, and thus determining on what few dispositions, out of numerous possibilities, the political outcome of the election...will center' (Berelson, Lazarsfeld, and McPhee 1954: 251). But the greatest impact is exerted by small groups, based on their political homogeneity and congeniality (Berelson, Lazarsfeld, and McPhee 1954: ch. 6). In sharp contrast with the individualistic conceptions of the electoral process that are so prominent in democratic theory, these studies conclude that the principal political stimuli that influence voting decisions come from 'ordinary family, friends, co-workers, and fellow organization members with whom we are all surrounded. In short, the influences to which voters are most susceptible are opinions of trusted people expressed to one another' (Berelson, Lazarsfeld, and McPhee 1954: 115). Katz and Lazarsfeld subsequently (1955) elaborated on the importance of personal influence from a broader social-psychological point of view.

Thus, the Columbia approach included as important determinants of the voting decision the flow of politically relevant information in electoral campaigns through three distinctly different channels. These three intermediation processes involve (*a*) the direct transmission of political information through face-to-face contacts within personal networks, (*b*) the flow of messages through the mass communications media, and (*c*) indirect flows of political information through membership in secondary associations (trade unions, religious groups, fraternal organizations, etc.).[1]

Even though the Columbia approach introduced the study of intermediation processes into the very earliest survey-data based electoral studies, this concern with how voters receive information about politics virtually disappeared after the mid-1950s.[2] Neglect of these information flow processes was not based on any fundamental deficiencies of the Lazarsfeld approach, or on empirical evidence suggesting that these processes are unimportant. It was, instead, simply the result of the emergence of new paradigms that emphasized different kinds of variables and causal processes, leading successive cohorts of investigators to exclude the intermediation variables from their surveys.

One of these approaches dominated Western European studies of electoral behaviour for several generations. It was rooted in the notion that structural cleavages in society serve as the principal bases of voting decisions. To be sure, Berelson, Lazarsfeld, and McPhee had included 'social differentiation' among determinants of political opinions and the vote in their study—in particular, socio-economic cleavages involving occupation, income, and status, in addition to social cleavages rooted in religiosity, race, ethnicity, region, and urban–rural residence patterns. But electoral studies adopting the *social-cleavage approach* shifted the analytical focus in a manner set forth by Lipset and Rokkan (1967*a*). Lipset and Rokkan developed a historical and typological framework for the emergence of a distinctive structure of cleavages in Western European polities and stressed the importance of social class and religion as determinants of the vote, as well as ethnicity, regionalism, or nationalism in ethnically diverse countries. It is not difficult to understand why this social-cleavage approach to the study of electoral behaviour emerged in Europe and remained dominant for so many decades. To begin with, its origins in studies of voting behaviour based on ecological data (unavoidable, given the absence of survey data until the 1940s [Tingsten (1937) 1974; Goguel 1951]) led this approach to emphasize the importance of social-structural factors. Census data, combined with electoral returns within specific geographical districts, were widely available throughout the twentieth century, and these served as the basis of studies of voting behaviour based on ecological inferences. In addition, the Marxist orientation of the field of political sociology in its early years also contributed to the dominance of this tradition in Western Europe, especially with regard to its emphasis on social class as a determinant of the vote. This emphasis is clearly reflected in Lipset's oft-quoted description (1959*a*: ch. 7) of elections as 'the democratic expression of the class struggle'. It is also the logical outcome of the fact that the mass-based political parties that dominated politics in many Western European countries from the late nineteenth through the mid-twentieth centuries were organized along social-cleavage lines. Initially, these 'cleavage parties' were socialist or social democratic, and sought to mobilize working-class voters. They were joined by religious-based Catholic (and subsequently Christian Democratic) parties, whose clienteles were defined by specific religious beliefs and organizational affiliations. Under these circumstances, the explanation of the voter was a simple derivation from the patterns of electoral competition along the cleavage lines dominant in a given country.

The net result of these intellectual traditions was that most studies of electoral behaviour in Western Europe in the second half of the twentieth century were dominated by a concern with the impact of social cleavages on voting behaviour. The most frequently cited work in the school is without doubt the 1967 Lipset and Rokkan volume, *Party Systems and Voter Alignments*, and especially their concept of the 'freezing' of cleavages, according to which social divisions are seen as having a powerful impact on the vote even decades or generations after the cleavages which had originally given birth to a particular set of parties had waned as a result of processes of social change. As they pointed out, 'a crucial characteristic of Western competitive politics in the age of "high mass consumption" [is that] the party alternatives, and in remarkably many cases the party organizations, are older than the majorities of the national electorates. To most of the citizens of the West the currently active parties have been part of the political landscape since their childhood or at least since they were first faced with the choice between alternative "packages" on election day' (1967: 50)—'packages' that in most cases had been wrapped up between the turn of the twentieth century and the early 1930s.

While this claim was generally substantiated by empirical studies in the 1960s and 1970s, by the 1980s it was increasingly challenged by findings that these social-structural 'anchors' of the vote were weakening substantially. This empirical reality was a product both of fundamental processes of social change (increasing affluence and economic development, *embourgeoisement*, and secularization) and of party strategies that increasingly shifted to catch-all electoral appeals that entailed a progressive broadening away from the traditional core of supporters of what were once cleavage parties (cf. Kirchheimer 1966). Many scholars contended that the transformation of parties, their electoral strategies and social bases of support were culminating in political de-alignment and increased levels of electoral volatility (see, e.g. Dalton, Flanagan, and Beck 1984). Many studies within this tradition have confirmed that there has been a significant decline in the electoral impact of social cleavages in recent decades (e.g. Franklin, Mackie, Valen et al. 1992). Other studies have both criticized the implicit social determinism underpinning these explanations of the vote, which posit a direct relationship between the voter and the relevant social-structural cleavage (class, religion, national identity, and ethnicity) and emphasized the relevance of party elites as a critical intervening factor for activating, depolarizing, or shaping the divisive dimension of the cleavage structure (see, e.g. Przeworski and Sprague 1986; Gunther and Montero 2001b). In turn, these critiques have led scholars to shift their attention to an examination of other determinants of the vote.

In this volume, we continue to pay considerable attention to the cleavage-anchoring of electoral behaviour. We do not deny that the social origins of parties continue to have a substantial impact on the nature of their respective electorates, on the organizational forms adopted by parties, and on the electoral strategies that they employ to attract voters. But we depart in several important ways from the social-cleavage school of electoral studies. We reject the social-structural determinism implicit in causal processes and in that approach's inattention to more purely political actors and institutions. We also reject that approach's *assumption* that membership in a cleavage-based organization *per se* implies that individuals actively participate and interact with others inside the group, that they receive political information from the group, pay attention to that information, are effectively mobilized by the group, and therefore vote accordingly. We believe that it is important to empirically test each of these assumptions and analyse flows of information through organizations or informal social groups, as we do in the following chapters. In doing so, we combine a concern with the causal impact of social cleavages with a systematic examination of the intervening intermediation processes that convey cleavage-relevant messages to the voter. We also move beyond the study of *social-structural* determinants of the vote to explore the electoral impact of different kinds of cleavages that have emerged in many established democracies, particularly involving conflicting *socio-political values*.

Intermediation processes were also excluded from the second dominant approach which has guided studies of electoral behaviour over at least four decades. The so-called *Michigan school* had a dramatic impact on electoral studies in the United States following the publication of its seminal work, *The American Voter*, in 1960. Emerging from survey-based studies of electoral behaviour in the 1950s, this approach departed from the Columbia paradigm in at least four ways. First, its analysis was based on nationwide, cross-sectional surveys drawn from probability samples, in contrast with the Lazarsfeld et al. panel studies based on interviews within a single community. Second, the Michigan approach radically departed from the sociological processes so central to the Columbia school, and focused primary analytical attention instead on psychological orientations of individual voters as determinants of the vote. As Campbell, Converse, Miller, and Stokes themselves put it, their project 'represented a shift in emphasis from explanation in sociological terms to the exploration of political attitudes that orient the individual voter's behaviour in an immediate sense' (1960: 16). This alternative approach thereby sought to reconcile sometimes substantial shifts in the vote from one election to the next with the fact that social-structural characteristics (key determinants of the vote according to the social-cleavage approach) remained stable if not constant. Their approach also departed from the primacy assigned to social structures and processes by the Columbia school, which went so far as to assert that 'a person thinks politically as he is socially', since 'social characteristics determine political preference' (Lazarsfeld, Berelson, and Gaudet 1944: 27). While the authors of the Michigan approach did not deny that social-structural variables are relevant to electoral behaviour, they relegated them to the relatively minor role of contributing factors, temporally and causally distant from the vote at the base of a long 'funnel of causality'. They argued that attention should be paid instead to the attitudinal orientations of voters, most importantly their standing loyalties to political parties. As Campbell et al. (1960: 9, 17) added, 'our hypothesis is that the partisan choice the individual voter makes depends in an immediate sense on the strength and direction of the elements comprising a field of psychological forces, where these elements are interpreted as attitudes towards the perceived objects of national politics.... [I]dentification with a party... [is] a factor that is normally antecedent to these forces, yet susceptible at times to change by them.... The attitudinal approach directed more attention to political objects of orientation, such as the candidates and issues, which do shift in the short term.' Finally, their responses to problems associated with the cost of information, the complexity of politics, and utilization of the communications media further differentiate the Michigan from the Columbia approaches to electoral studies. For Lazarsfeld and his associates, personal contacts, membership in secondary associations, and interactions with opinion leaders reduce the severity of these problems, and exert considerable influence on the formation or reinforcement of electoral preferences. For protagonists of the Michigan approach, in contrast, the psychological function of party identification plays the key role in the interpretation of politics and for making electoral decisions with a minimal investment of time and information. As Campbell and his colleagues noted, 'our interest here centers primarily on the role of party as a supplier of cues by which the individual may evaluate the elements of politics.... Moreover, the complexities of politics and government increase the importance of having relatively simple cues to evaluate what cannot be matters of personal knowledge.... In the competition of voices reaching the individual, the political party is an opinion-forming agency of great importance' (Campbell et al. 1960: 128).

The appeal of the Michigan approach was fostered by the temporal and societal context within which it first emerged.[3] By the late 1950s, at the apex of the Eisenhower era, there was very little polarization of American society or politics along class or religious lines. Accordingly, an approach to the study of electoral behaviour which assumed that most voters were not well-informed about, actively mobilized by, or polarized along social-structural lines seemed to fit well with socio-political reality. At the same time, survey research had become a common tool of political analysis. This made it possible to analyse *attitudinal* data about ordinary citizens (which is clearly impossible using the aggregate data on which ecological studies are based), to develop a much broader array of empirical indicators, and to present them within a theoretically oriented framework in which variables are ordered by their level of importance in explaining electoral behaviour. Finally, as Manza and Brooks (1999: 15) note, the dominance of this approach was institutionalized when the protagonists of the Michigan school assumed control of the National Election Study, and thereby gained privileged access to research funding from the American National Science Foundation.

But this approach to the study of electoral behaviour has also been strongly criticized. Many scholars, particularly those rooted in the social-cleavage tradition, questioned the conceptual status of party identification, arguing that party ID is too close to the actual voting decision itself, and, rather than serving as a long-term determinant of the vote, may be an artefact of electoral choice per se. Empirically, it has often been noted that this indicator does not 'travel well', particularly to countries with fragmented multiparty systems, where a more generic self-placement of voters along a left–right continuum may serve as a more durable and common basis of electoral choice. Finally, it was noted that levels of party identification appeared to decline significantly even in the United States, such that other determinants of the vote assumed relatively greater importance. While some studies (e.g. Miller and Shanks 1996) have attempted to re-establish the basic elements of the Michigan approach, others (including those within the Michigan tradition) have since the late 1970s increasingly turned their attention to a variety of short-term factors that influence the vote, particularly the electorate's stands with regard to 'issues' and their evaluations of the personal attributes of candidates (e.g. Nie, Verba, and Petrocik 1979). As Beck (1986: 262) summarizes these trends, 'recent years have witnessed a decline in the hegemony of the Michigan Model.... Ideology, issues, social groups, and party loyalties adjusted in response to short-run factors are now integral parts of the conceptual lexicon of the student of voter behaviour. There is an increased tendency to view the voter as a rational decision maker weighing present performance rather as the committed partisan of the Michigan Model.'

The last of these analytical paradigms, the *economic approach* to the study of voting, builds on the notions of performance evaluation and limited information. It has taken on many different forms that are somewhat related to one another. The pioneering formulation by Downs (1957) explicitly assumed that voters would behave like individuals in a market, and would rationally choose to maximize their own utilities, however, those are defined. The economic approach to the study of voting sets aside both the sociological variables that are of central importance for the Columbia and social-cleavage approaches, as well as the political attitudes and psychological processes on which the Michigan model is based. Instead, it portrays voters as rational actors who base electoral choices on calculations of which candidate is more likely to deliver benefits to the voter on the basis of his or her preferred objectives. 'As a result', argues Downs (1957: 40, 49; emphasis in the original text), 'the most important part of a voter's decision is the size of his *current party differential*, i.e., the difference between the utility income he actually received in period *t* and the one he would have received if the opposition had been in power.... [These differentials] establish his preference among the competing parties.' Another substantial difference between the economic approach and the Columbia and Michigan schools of electoral study involves how they deal with the problem of the lack of information on the part of voters. Rather than constituting a troubling reality that is far from the democratic ideal, it is perfectly rational. As Downs put it (1957: 259), 'In general, it is irrational to be politically well-informed because the low returns from data simply do not justify their cost in time and other scarce resources. Therefore many voters do not bother to discover their true views before voting, and most citizens are not well enough informed to influence directly the formulation of those policies that affect them.' Both because of the collective nature of elections and because of the impossibility that a citizen can influence the results in a significant manner, the individual investment in acquiring information is a cost to be avoided. Rational voters can reduce the costs of information acquisition by attending to the flow of free information in all societies, coming primarily from the providers of information like advertisers, interest groups, political parties, and the government, as well as from those citizens who possess a certain level of information (Downs 1957: chs. 11 and 12).

Following in the footsteps of *An Economic Theory of Democracy*, two generations of scholars expanded on this approach by applying the specific analytical techniques that dominate the field of microeconomics. Thus, among others, rational-choice, formal-modelling, and game-theory approaches to the study of voting behaviour have become common, particularly in American political science. The publication of Edward Tufte's *Political Control of the Economy* in 1978 strengthened the link with the field of economics. The most commonly assumed utility was always defined in economic terms, and the electoral victories or defeats of incumbent governments were seen as rewards or punishments by voters for the manner in which they managed the economy. While substantial debates arose within this school among scholars exploring 'retrospective' and 'prospective' voting (i.e. concerning punishment of the incumbents for their previous economic policies, versus assessments of economic promises made in the course of campaigns), as well as 'egocentric' versus 'sociotropic' evaluations by voters (involving assessments of personal benefit, as contrasted with concern over the economic condition of society as a whole), they all conceived of elections as referenda on the state of the economy.[4] Another version of the economic approach to the study of voting has been called the 'Rochester model' by Weisberg (1986). Derived from the seminal works of William Riker (1982, 1990; also see Riker and Ordeshook 1968, 1973), the Rochester model is characterized by the heavy use of formal models and survey data in an attempt to demonstrate the superiority of rationalist (rather than psychological) explanations of voting behaviour. In Weisberg's view (1986: 300), 'the original versions of both [models] were oversimplistic, but both have been influential and both have furthered our understanding of voting.... What is most intriguing, from the standpoint of the history of science, is that the two models have coexisted for more than two decades, each providing a source of challenge to the others.' In contrast with the large number of variables and explanatory factors usually analysed by adherents of the Michigan school, the greater parsimony of the Rochester model is highly valued by its protagonists.

Detractors of several manifestations of the economic approach to the study of voting point to the inadequate empirical testing of its propositions, as well as the unrealistic and simplistic assumptions that underpin its application to the complex 'real world'. These shortcomings are particularly serious with regard to the paradox of voter turnout, spatial theories of party competition, and cross-national comparative studies of electoral behaviour.[5] One problem complicating its cross-national application is that the economic approach originally focused on competition between two individual *candidates*; its application to electoral competition between *parties* in a multiparty system is therefore problematic. Moreover, this approach emphasizes proximity between the position of an individual voter and those of competing candidates with regard to selected issues, taken one at a time; in so far as different voters are fundamentally concerned with different sets of issues, these assumptions can substantially impede the analysis of a multi-dimensional real world. Indeed, an investigator can only move beyond the analysis of one issue at a time by assuming that multiple issues are arrayed on a single conceptual dimension, and this is a highly problematic assumption.[6] The identification of those interests that have the greatest impact on the voter's electoral choice constitutes another recurrent problem. Given the origins of this approach in the field of economics, there is a strong temptation to assume that economic interests are paramount in determining voting decisions. But even if this temptation is avoided, outside investigators often have no adequate means of determining the proper 'preference ordering' of the voter, which is inherently subjective and varies from person to person, time to time, and culture to culture. Another problematic characteristic of this approach is that it assumes that voters have perfect information about the stands on those issues taken by candidates, and that they have a clear understanding of their own interests; many empirical studies, on the other hand, have demonstrated that most voters possess little accurate information about most issues most of the time. As we pointed out in the preceding discussion, both the Columbia and Michigan approaches were keenly aware of this reality and its implications for democratic theory. Indeed, the information-processing functions of intermediary networks and party identification directly address this problem of information deficits on the part of voters in those two approaches. Within the field of rational choice, a similar perspective appears to be emerging among those who have adopted a 'softer' methodological approach, in contrast with the more orthodox models of voting behaviour. The concepts of bounded or limited rationality (Simon 1982, 1995) allow citizens to rely on heuristic mechanisms for making reasoned and/or reasonable choices.[7] Among these heuristics are the aforementioned opinion leaders, personal contacts, social relationships, and the mass media, in conjunction with those related to party identification, spatial modelling on the basis of the left–right continuum, and simplified cues delivered in the course of the election campaign by parties and candidates.

The Comparative National Elections Project

The Comparative National Elections Project (CNEP) is a multinational project in which teams of scholars have studied important aspects of political communication and social structure within the context of election campaigns using compatible research designs and a common core of survey questions. The initial focus of this study was the 'intermediation process' through which citizens receive information about policies, parties, candidates, and politics in general during the course of election campaigns. Accordingly, survey questionnaires include batteries of questions dealing with flows of information through primary social networks (among family members, friends, neighbours, and co-workers), and secondary associations (especially trade unions, religious organizations, and political parties), as well as flows of information from the communications media.

The first phase of this cross-national project involved studies of the established democracies in Germany, Britain, the United States, and Japan in the early 1990s. The second wave of this ambitious collaborative project began with the incorporation of Spain into the project in 1993, and included the subsequent addition of two countries from each of the following world regions: South America, Southern Europe, Eastern Europe, and East Asia.[8] Having seen in the first phase of the project how useful the CNEP questionnaire and research design can be for tapping into the institutionalization and dynamic processes of democracy at the grass roots, it was decided to systematically apply this instrument to the study of newly established (or, in the case of Italy, substantially reconfigured) democracies. Added to the core questionnaire in CNEP II were several items specially suited for the measurement of mass-level attitudes underpinning regime consolidation and the nature and quality of democratic participation in new democracies, as well as the structure of basic values (concerning traditional religious beliefs, individual political and civil liberties, and preferences regarding the nature of the economy and public policies) that have often given rise to partisan political conflict in established democracies. This broadened focus on information-intermediation, democratization, and the structuring of politically relevant values was retained in all of the CNEP studies in countries which have undergone

15

transitions to democratic rule during the so-called 'third wave' of democratization (Spain, Chile, Uruguay, Greece, Bulgaria, Hungary, Indonesia, and Portugal) or taken halting steps in that direction (Hong Kong), or have undergone a profound transformation of its party system (Italy) or experienced a marked political polarization in recent years (the United States). It is thus possible to undertake a detailed study of the structuring of partisan politics in new or transformed democracies, and compare these emerging or evolving institutions and patterns of interaction with those of long-established democracies. (All of these survey data-sets, questionnaires, and information about sampling and other technical matters are available through the website: www.cnep.ics.ul.pt)[9]

In none of its three phases has the CNEP been a conventional 'election study'. While its questionnaires have included measures of standard determinants of the vote, they have also allowed for detailed analyses of electoral intermediation in old and new democracies, of political attitudes related to the political system in new democracies, and of electorally relevant socio-political values.

Electoral Intermediaries: Social Networks

From the very beginning, CNEP I was a broad study focusing on political intermediation processes and their impact on electoral politics. As we noted above, even though the importance of these information-flow processes has been widely acknowledged ever since the seminal work of Lazarsfeld and his collaborators (Lazarsfeld, Berelson, and Gaudet 1944; Berelson, Lazarsfeld, and McPhee 1954; Katz and Lazarsfeld 1955), these linkages were largely unexplored in American studies of electoral behaviour over the following three decades, when the dominance of the Michigan school of electoral behavioural research shifted the focus of most researchers to the study of attitudes and other psychological variables detached from their social context (e.g. Campbell et al. 1960). And the strong assumptions of most rational-choice approaches made unnecessary the analysis of these informational processes, regarding them as superfluous for the instrumentally rational voter. These information-flow mechanisms were also largely ignored by West European electoral researchers, even though their social-cleavage orientation could easily have accommodated empirical analysis of these grass-roots linkages between citizens and partisan politics. Most studies of the social-cleavage school stress the importance of cleavage-group membership and group interest, but simply *assume* that the crucial intermediation functions linking individuals to groups are being performed effectively. The neglect of these information-flow processes has led to incomplete understandings of the dynamics of voting choice in all three of these alternative approaches to the study of electoral behaviour. And this, in turn, has undermined our ability to monitor changes over time in the basic structures and electoral mobilization efforts of political parties.

Failure to explore these linkages has meant that important questions regarding both old and new democracies have remained unanswered or addressed by largely speculative interpretations. The rich and detailed data generated by the CNEP research design enable us to test key hypotheses in the electoral behaviour literature, particularly with regard to the important roles played by social networks and personal contacts. The CNEP questionnaires include an extensive battery of items dealing with informal discussions of politics within primary groups. Perceptions of the political loyalties and views of frequent discussion partners within stable interpersonal networks are solicited. Questionnaire items carefully distinguish among family members, friends, co-workers, neighbours, and fellow members of secondary associations as sources of political information, and ask respondents to describe any political biases exhibited by those information sources. In addition, in some countries, a complementary 'snowball sample' is generated by first asking the respondent to identify frequent discussion partners, and then by interviewing those individuals in an effort to corroborate the perceptions of the primary respondent, and gather additional information about these discussion partners.[10]

Electoral Intermediaries: Secondary Organizations

A substantial battery of items in CNEP questionnaires focuses on the nature and extent of involvement with secondary organizations. While virtually all election surveys have included items tapping membership in trade unions, and some have also touched upon membership in religious and other voluntary groups, past research has generally failed to examine the relevant intermediation processes in sufficient detail, relying, instead, on mere correlations between organizational membership and the vote. And yet it is obvious that a great deal of uncertainty surrounds the influence of group membership on attitude formation and electoral behaviour. The extent to which members actively participate in group activities or read an organization's literature are important variables that cannot be taken for granted. Merely nominal membership is distinct, in this respect, from frequent attendance at group functions and extensive conversations with fellow members. Even more fundamental is the extent to which the secondary organization is politicized, either formally (by adopting stands on salient political or social issues and disseminating information about those positions to members) or informally (by creating a pronounced climate of opinion favourable towards one partisan option or another).

Organizational membership is a crucial variable that differentiates one democratic system from another—separating most continental European democracies, where labour and religious organizations are often explicitly partisan, from the United States and some other countries, which had been characterized by more uneven patterns of politicization of secondary groups. This variable can also affect important changes over time: in Lenski's classic study (1961) and even as recently as the late 1970s (see McDonough, Barnes, and López Pina 1984: 662), religiosity was more weakly related to partisan orientations in the United States than in most other Western democracies. Yet it is clear that some religious denominations have become more substantially politicized since the 1980s (see Manza and Brooks 1999; Norris and Inglehart 2004: ch. 4). Only a detailed analysis of the nature of the organization and the individual's involvement with it could adequately capture a qualitative transformation of this kind. Our CNEP questionnaires measure the extent of involvement within a wide variety of groups, the nature and degree of partisan politicization information flowing from these organizations, readership of the group's publications, the frequency of political discussion within secondary associations, and the extent to which each group can be characterized by a pronounced climate of opinion concerning relevant political and social issues.

Electoral Intermediaries: Mass Media

Intriguing arguments have been advanced concerning the nature of electoral politics in modern societies, and in particular the impacts of television on voting behaviour and the quality of democracy. Robinson (1976) introduced the concept of 'media malaise'—a syndrome including low political trust, internal inefficacy, and distance and disaffection from involvement in democratic politics—as a consequence of dependence on television as a source of news. This argument, however, clashes with the more optimistic scenario of Inglehart (1971, 1990), Dalton (1984), and Dalton, Flanagan, and Beck (1984), who see the steady increase in the educational levels of modern electorates as improving the quality of electoral choice—that better-educated voters are more capable of making up their own minds about key issues and voting accordingly. But the somewhat problematic dimension of these latter arguments is that they do not usually take into consideration the possible impact of the communications media on the vote or the basic political attitudes of citizens. Accordingly, some scholars have speculated that there may be significant negative consequences of certain patterns of media exposure. Ranney (1983), for instance, suggested that an electorate's increasing dependence on television may culminate in an increased personalization and trivialization of electoral politics. Television, he argued, is a poor medium for the conveyance of detailed, extensive, or complex information about important public policy issues, but it is an excellent medium for the creation and manipulation of the public images of individual politicians. The quality of democracy could therefore be debased if voters were to shift their focus away from important programmatic issues and towards the highly personalized trivia and symbol manipulation that became such important features of campaign politics in the 1980s, particularly in the United States.[11] As Norris (2000a: 238) stated, 'television coverage of politics is thought to encourage viewers to become cynical and disenchanted with their institutions of government because its focus on exposing government scandals and corruption, revealing insiders strategies, and dramatizing political conflict'. At the same time, however, it has also been argued that there may be a positive relationship between media exposure (especially, in recent decades, to television) and the civic commitment of citizens. Newton (1999c) and Norris (2000b) suggest that media exposure may be linked in a 'virtuous circle' with greater political interest and information on the part of citizens, and with greater political involvement in general (which, in turn, includes higher levels of exposure to political news through the media). These contradictory and inconclusive findings make this an important but largely unresolved issue. We believe that the impact of television on voting behaviour and the quality of democracy in modern societies can best be examined through the kind of research design adopted by the CNEP.

The CNEP core questionnaire is also perfectly suited to examine the impact of media bias on electoral behaviour. Questionnaire items not only generate specific information concerning which television channels, radio programmes, and newspapers are watched, listened to, or read by respondents, but also include measures of their perceptions of the extent to which those media channels present disproportionately favourable coverage of candidates or parties. These data have greatly facilitated efforts to measure the impact of media bias as an agent of electoral mobilization (e.g. Dalton, Beck, and Huckfeldt 1998; Gunther, Montero, and Wert 2000; Beck et al. 2002). While media bias has been the object of scholarly analysis for decades, the emergence of new sources of bias in the flow of political information—such as 'narrow-casting' of information through intensely partisan and polarizing 'talk radio' in some democracies—has substantially revived interest in this line of research.

Attitudes Towards the Political System and Intermediation

This book goes beyond the original Columbia approach in our efforts to understand the nature of political support and related democratic attitudes in newly established democracies. Despite the importance of attitudes and evaluations of political institutions by citizens in new democracies, most cross-national research projects have failed to generate relevant and reliable data. If the established democracies can be said to have suffered from a general and apparently irreversible erosion of political support over the past few decades (Norris 1999a; Dalton 2004), the implications of these kinds of problems could be much more serious in new democracies. The CNEP II questionnaires included a series of questions that have enabled us to measure support for and satisfaction with democracy, as well as those associated with the 'political disaffection' syndrome. Our findings were remarkably consistent across all of the CNEP countries examined, and have culminated in the exploration of several hypotheses concerning the origins and behavioural consequences of these various types of attitudes towards democracy, as well as the role played by the development of such attitudes in the broader processes of democratic consolidation (see Torcal 1995, 2002a; Gunther and Montero 2006; Montero, Gunther, and Torcal 1997). As is often noted in the literature on democratic transition and consolidation (e.g. Linz and Stepan 1996), one of the key ingredients in the transformation of authoritarian or post-totalitarian political systems into stable and healthy democracies is the widespread holding of attitudes that acknowledge the legitimacy of the new system and encourage political behaviour that is consistent with fundamental democratic norms. Mass-level attitudes supporting democracy may therefore serve as the bedrock of democratic stability, particularly over the long term. Accordingly, much of the literature on democratic consolidation places considerable emphasis on the establishment and dissemination of democratic attitudes and values, on the one hand, and broader attitudinal support for democracy, on the other (see Bratton and Mattes 2001a; Bratton 2005). The items incorporated within the

CNEP II common core help us to understand and explain cross-national differences regarding the cultural underpinnings of democratic stability. In addition, we explore the varying relationships between fundamental attitudes towards democracy and preferences for specific parties.

Sociopolitical Values

The CNEP II has also gone beyond the original Columbia approach by including a systematic analysis of socio-political values that are believed to have a significant impact on electoral politics, particularly in the United States, where there has been considerable journalistic and popular discussion of the so-called 'culture wars'. Culturally rooted values relating to seemingly non-political domains of social life (such as religious beliefs, attitudes towards individual initiative in the workplace, and towards the environment) have often been politicized in the course of partisan conflict. Nonetheless, the literature is largely devoid of systematic, comparative efforts to 'map' the value clusters that often emerge as the bases of ideologies that help to structure institutionalized partisan conflict. Indeed, very few cross-national studies of public opinion and electoral behaviour include many comparable items dealing with values and attitudes, and they tend to focus their attention on social-structural variables instead. And those few attitudinal variables that cross-national research instruments typically contain are either abstract and generic (such as self-placement on the left–right continuum, or basic personality attributes), or are restricted to a narrow range of value orientations (such as those relating to 'postmaterialism' or support for democracy). In sharp contrast, most single-country 'election studies' include substantial numbers of attitudinal variables, usually dealing with issues that become salient during election campaigns, as well as voters' assessments of the personal qualities of the principal candidates for high office.[12]

We therefore developed for CNEP II a battery of questions pertaining to politically relevant (or potentially relevant) values. These new items were intended to help identify differing attitudinal domains that may underpin the left–right continuum, or may have political relevance independent of voter self-placement on the scale. They eschew the high specificity and ideographic nature of 'campaign issues' and seek to tap into more durable value orientations which would be stable over time and likely to affect electoral behaviour over several decades (not just in the context of a single election campaign) in several different countries. Instead, they involve normative orientations that have been embedded within political ideologies in many Western democratic systems. As we see, they have considerable impact on electoral behaviour in several democratic systems.

The Contents of this Volume

In the first substantive chapter of this volume, Richard Gunther, José Ramón Montero, and Mariano Torcal undertake a systematic examination of attitudes towards democracy. Many of these have been indiscriminately used in the literature for the purpose of making inferences about the legitimacy and overall level of popular support for democratic regimes. The authors, however, building on work that they had published earlier (using CNEP data), make an effort to discriminate among these attitudes, clarify their conceptual and dimensional characteristics, and analyse their different political implications. Employing a variety of methods (including exploratory and confirmatory factor-analysis techniques), they demonstrate that these commonly used survey items are of three entirely different types which are both conceptually and empirically distinct from each other. One of these does, indeed, measure general support for democracy. Accordingly, the two relevant CNEP survey items are found constitute an attitudinal dimension appropriately called *democratic support*. The second attitudinal domain includes satisfaction with the 'performance of democracy', satisfaction with the performance of the government, and satisfaction with the condition of the economy. These attitudes are found to be highly contaminated by partisanship, and are strongly correlated with a vote for or against the incumbent party. Accordingly, the authors create a separate scale of political attitudes relevant to this *political discontent* dimension. Finally, they deal with a third cluster of attitudes different from those in both the democratic support and discontent attitudinal domains. These involve *political disaffection*, a cluster of attitudes which includes a certain estrangement or detachment from politics and the public sphere, as well as a critical evaluation of core political institutions, elected representatives, and the political process in general. Previous studies of these orientations have found that they can be further subdivided into those referred to as 'internal efficacy' and 'external efficacy' (pertaining to the respondent's own perceptions of his or her personal competence relevant to political involvement, and to his or her assessments of the degree of responsiveness of political elites in the political system, respectively). Perhaps most importantly, this chapter explores the behavioural correlates of these three clusters of attitudes. Their findings reaffirm their empirical separability and their distinctly different implications for democratic systems. The behavioural consequences of political discontent are found to be entirely compatible with the proper functioning of democratic regimes as envisaged in democratic theory, particularly with regard to the capacity of voters to hold incumbent politicians accountable for their performance in office. High levels of political disaffection, in contrast, are seen as undermining the quality of democracy, particularly in so far as such orientations discourage voters from being sufficiently active in the political process as to cast their ballots in an informed manner. And in keeping with the bulk of the literature on the consolidation of new democracies, fundamental democratic support emerges as of considerable importance, particularly in so far as the absence of such support may lead voters to give electoral support to parties that pose a direct threat to the survival of the existing democratic regime. Finally, while the 'direction of causality' is far from clear, each of these sets of attitudinal orientations is closely linked to its own distinct 'intermediation story', particularly with regard to the crucial role played by secondary associations, thereby linking this analysis of orientations towards democracy to the Lazarsfeld framework which is the central concern of the CNEP. At the same time, this analysis finds no empirical support for a 'social capital' explanation of democratic support.

In Chapter 3, Rüdiger Schmitt-Beck and Katrin Voltmer also deal with attitudes towards and support for democracy, but they focus their analysis on the role of the media as the principal causal agents. To what extent does exposure to the broadcast and print media help to form fundamental political attitudes? Does a particular type of media exposure have an equal impact on the development of all kinds of political attitudes, or does it have a more substantial impact on certain kinds of orientations? In addressing these questions, the authors pay particular attention to the systematic testing of the aforementioned 'media malaise' hypothesis— that is, the assertion that frequent exposure to television broadcasts of political news tends to culminate in attitudes of cynicism towards and disaffection from politics. Against this hypothesis, Schmitt-Beck and Voltmer posit an alternative, in which exposure to political information through whatever medium will build citizen competency that facilitates participation and helps to secure loyalty for the political regime. They use a variety of dependent variables in their analyses, including support for democracy, interest in politics, political knowledge, political participation, and attitudes towards political parties. Utilizing multivariate analyses, they explore the impact on these democratic attitudes of various communications media and find that media exposure does have a sub-stantial multifaceted impact on the development of various kinds of attitudes generally positive with regard both to general support for democracy and for the development of citizen competence and political involvement.

In the remaining substantive chapters of this volume, we turn our atten-tion from attitudes towards democracy as a dependent variable to more overtly partisan and behavioural phenomena. All the following chapters deal to some degree or another with electoral mobilization—that is, the extent to which these intermediation channels can serve as 'transmission belts' of electoral support for political parties.

In Chapter 4, Paolo Bellucci, Marco Maraffi, and Paolo Segatti analyse secondary associations and address the question of the extent to which political participation, in general, is encouraged by membership in sec-ondary groups. They begin their study with a detailed cross-national com-parison of widely varying levels of membership by citizens in secondary organizations of different kinds. These differing levels of nominal organi-zational affiliation are paralleled by cross-national variations in the degree of intensity of organizational involvement. The authors then turn their attention to the extent of politicization of different types of associations in these countries, and to the varying degrees to which they explicitly endorse parties and candidates. Finally, they undertake extensive multi-variate analyses of the extent to which these groups succeed in mobilizing their members in support of parties or candidates. They find that, while secondary associations in general may politicize smaller segments of the electorate than they may have done during the alleged 'golden age' of mass-based partisan politics, they are still capable of 'encapsulating' many voters and channelling their votes in support of one or another party or candidate. Their findings also suggest that different types of associations have very different capacities for electoral mobilization, but that the ways in which secondary organizations politicize have basically remained the same as in the past. The authors also find that cross-national differences by far outdistance cross-sectional differences, and thus corroborate the previous finding that there is no common associational pattern that characterizes these countries. The impact of associational membership on electoral turnout and partisan mobilization is highly conditioned by specific features of intermediation processes and exposure to partisan political cues.

In Chapter 5, Bradley Richardson and Paul Allen Beck take the next logical step in this line of argument by systematically exploring the extent of partisan biases in the flows of political information through the other two major channels of intermediation explored in this volume— interpersonal discussions within social networks, and direct exposure to political information through the communications media. And in light of the 'two-step' flow of political messages from the media through 'opinion leaders' to voters within personal networks, it is important that these two seemingly distinct intermediation channels be analysed within the same chapter so that the interaction between their respective influences on partisan preferences can be systematically examined. To what extent are individuals exposed to information that systematically favours one party or the other, as compared to an overall exposure to mixed messages that are balanced in their partisan biases overall? To what extent do individuals choose specific intermediation channels that favour their partisan biases ('selective exposure'), thereby embedding themselves within partisan political contexts that reinforce their initial partisan predilections? If selective exposure to only supportive information is excessive in a particular political system, then this might have some negative implications for the quality of democracy, in so far as the ability of the voter to make an independent and informed choice at the polling place would be undermined. These questions are explored within both new and older established democratic systems.

In Chapter 6, Pedro Magalhães reaches 'the bottom line' of this progressively developing and cumulative argument by taking into consideration all three of these channels of intermediation and measuring both their individual and cumulative impact on the vote. He presents clear evidence that these intermediation processes have a substantial impact on partisan preferences. The intermediation channels that are taken into account in his analysis are not only those of discussants/social networks, secondary associations and the media (newspapers and TV networks), but also those of party contacts (personal or by phone, and by mail). Even after strict controls are imposed in multivariate logistic analyses to take into consideration the usual social-structural variables (sex, age, education, income, and religiosity) and party identification, the author finds that these channels of political communication and the partisan biases voters perceive in them exert a substantial impact on short-term attitudes and on the vote. He finds that interactive interpersonal communications are particularly important, above and beyond the influence exerted through organizational channels and the media. He also finds that the net impact of these intermediaries seems to be greater in presidential elections where partisan cues are less clear cut.

Finally, Richard Gunther and Kuan Hsin-chi build on all of the preceding analyses of electoral mobilization in their exploration of the impact of another set of variables that has been largely neglected in studies of electoral behaviour—socio-political values. Conceptually, these may be regarded as intermediate between the specific and often transient 'issues' that have been explored in numerous election studies, and the fundamental personality attributes that are often studied by political psychologists (with the 'basic human values' that constitute most of the variables in the World Values Surveys [WVS] located near the latter end of this specificity/abstractness continuum). Despite the fact that the value items analysed by Gunther and Kuan had been deduced from political ideologies that have served as the basis of partisan political conflict for decades (and, in some cases, centuries), their impact on the vote had never been systematically examined in a comparative manner prior to this study. As in the case of the intermediation variables analysed in the preceding four chapters, these values are found to have a powerful impact on the vote, even after controls are introduced to take into account the causal contribution of several individual-level determinants of the vote. As substantial as the impact of these values may be, however, it is important to note that when the intermediation variables explored by Magalhães are entered as the last steps of these multivariate equations, they are found to retain most of their causal impact. From this perspective, this chapter can be seen as subjecting those intermediation variables to the most severe empirical test, and the ultimate conclusion is that they remain robust in their contribution to our efforts to explain the vote.

Something Old, Something New...

As noted in the Preface, the CNEP was born as a study of four established democratic systems—those of Germany, Japan, the United Kingdom, and the United States. These analyses of electoral processes and behaviour, however, were clearly distinct from standard election studies of the types that predominated in both Europe and the United States in so far as they added to the standard socio-demographic and attitudinal questionnaire items a number of detailed measures of the channels through which voters receive information about parties and candidates during the course of election campaigns. They systematically restored to the centre of our analytical focus important facets of campaign politics and electoral behaviour that had been key components of the very first modern survey-based voting studies undertaken in the 1940s and early 1950s. In this sense, the second phase of this cross-national research project, CNEP II, is based on 'something borrowed'[13] from a research tradition established over five decades ago, but which had been displaced by other paradigms that were established in the late 1950s and early 1960s. It is important to note that we do not regard this current study as an effort to challenge these other paradigmatic approaches. Instead, we argue that by reincorporating these intermediation variables into our research design we can complement at least two of these alternative approaches—the social-cleavage and Michigan models of electoral behaviour—and systematically address a number of key theoretical and empirical issues that are implicit within them. And as the following analyses of electoral behaviour will clearly reveal (especially in Chapters 6 and 7 of this volume), the addition of these intermediation measures to multivariate equations that in some respects can be regarded as capturing the essence of both the social-cleavage and Michigan approaches (i.e. as measured by the use of four standard socio-demographic variables and party identification as control variables) greatly strengthens their explanatory power.

Following the incorporation within this project of a number of newly established 'third-wave' democracies (Spain, Chile, Uruguay, Greece, Bulgaria, and Hungary), a substantially restructured democratic system (Italy), and an electoral system set within a political regime undergoing an uncertain transition (Hong Kong) in CNEP II, it was clear that 'something new' had to be added to the CNEP research design in order to address key questions relevant to theories of democratic consolidation and to salient features of electoral politics that had come into sharp focus by the end of the twentieth century—clashes over 'values' that were every bit as deep and potentially divisive as the social-structural cleavages of the first half of the century. Accordingly, in the next two chapters we treat attitudinal support for democracy (a key aspect of democratic consolidation) as a dependent variable. But in addressing these questions, we discovered that in several ways they were strongly linked to the intermediation processes on which CNEP I was initially founded. Thus, the 'something new' that had been added because of the salience of these democratic attitudes for newly established democracies turned out to be more strongly affected by these intermediation processes than we had anticipated. In short, our understanding of the processes of democratic consolidation is greatly enhanced by carefully taking into account the roles played by secondary associations and the media—two of the three crucial sets of independent variables identified by Lazarsfeld and his colleagues in studies of electoral behaviour over five decades ago. With regard to the addition of a new battery of questions regarding socio-political values, what has been further strengthened is our ability to predict our respondents' electoral preferences—the principal dependent variable of analyses of voting behaviour since the Columbia studies of the 1940s and early 1950s. But whether they are treated as independent or intervening variables in this latest wave of survey-based analysis, intermediation processes emerge as of considerable importance.

We conclude this overview of the analyses to follow by urging that the political functions performed by these information-intermediation channels should not be ignored any longer. Their neglect cannot be justified on either conceptual grounds (indeed, they nicely complement the theoretical perspectives of both the social-cleavage and Michigan paradigms) or on the basis of empirical evidence, since, as we and the other authors in this volume demonstrate, they contribute very substantially to our efforts to explain voting behaviour. The electoral intermediaries voters use to remedy their lack of political information, the channels through which political information and partisan cues flow to voters during election campaigns, and the varying social contexts of these intermediation processes are worthy of study over the coming years.

2

Democracy and intermediation: some attitudinal and behavioural dimensions

Richard Gunther, José Ramón Montero, and Mariano Torcal[1]

The central focus of this book, and, indeed, the entire CNEP is the nature of intermediation in a wide variety of democratic systems, and the implications of differing patterns of intermediation for the nature of politics and the quality of democracy in those countries. As we see in the other chapters of this book, intermediation is profoundly affected by and, in turn, can have substantial impact on broader characteristics of societies and political behaviour in these countries. In this chapter, we pay special attention to attitudinal factors that are of considerable importance for new or recently re-established democratic systems in Southern and Eastern Europe, and in Latin America—basic attitudes towards democracy among the mass public.

In contrast with older established democracies (in this volume, the United States, the United Kingdom, Germany, and Japan), in new democracies it cannot be taken for granted that democratic politics has been successfully consolidated and the regime is regarded as legitimate by a broad consensus of opinion, that supportive behavioural norms are widely internalized, and that the quality of democracy is not impaired as a result of widespread disaffection and disengagement from the political process. Accordingly, we turn our attention in this chapter to various attitudes relevant to the performance and survival of newly established democratic systems, and to the relationships among these attitudes and intermediation processes. We pay particular attention to intermediation through membership in secondary organizations and through direct face-to-face contact with friends, family, neighbours, and co-workers. However, since the following chapter by Rüdiger Schmitt-Beck and Katrin

Voltmer thoroughly analyses the relationship between exposure to the communications media, on the one hand, and these same kinds of democratic attitudes, on the other, our examination of intermediation through the media will be rather brief.

Relevant attitudes towards democracy are of several different kinds, and have differing but significant impacts on democratic performance. Mass-level attitudes supporting democracy are often regarded as the bedrock of democratic stability and an important ingredient for the functioning of a healthy democracy, and much of the literature on democratic consolidation therefore places considerable emphasis on the establishment and dissemination of democratic attitudes and values (e.g. Przeworski et al. 1995: 59; Linz and Stepan 1996: 6). This chapter presents a detailed analysis of various attitudes towards democracy and the behavioural correlates of those attitudes in seven democratic systems that had emerged from the 'third wave' of democratization since the mid-1970s—in Bulgaria, Chile, Greece, Hungary, Portugal, Spain, and Uruguay.

In contrast with much of the earlier literature on these democratic attitudes, we argue that it is extremely important to clearly differentiate among different types of attitudinal orientations. In our previous work,[2] we found that such attitudes must be clearly separated into three different clusters, which we called *democratic support, political discontent,* and *political disaffection.* We begin this chapter by presenting a summary of findings demonstrating that these are three entirely separable and conceptually distinct attitudinal domains.

We then turn our attention to patterns of political behaviour that are associated with these attitudes and with the intermediation channels that are the principal focus of this book. As we demonstrate, these three sets of attitudes have quite different behavioural correlates or consequences: a lack of fundamental support for democracy is strongly associated with votes for anti-system parties; political discontent is clearly linked with votes against the incumbent party or governing coalition; and political disaffection is part of a broader syndrome of alienation and disengagement from active involvement in the political process. These orientations interact in varying ways with information flows through primary and secondary personal contacts, and from the communications media, but in some respects the direction of causality linking these attitudes to political intermediation is uncertain or reciprocal. We hypothesize that a lack of fundamental support for democracy may be the product of ties to specific parties, elites, and their supportive organizations at crucial stages in the transition to democracy (as we argue in our discussions of the 'transition and consolidation effect'); but once adopted, such attitudes may subsequently attract such voters to anti-system parties, reversing the direction of causality linking attitudes and behaviour. Two different kinds of 'intermediation story' link political discontent to opposition parties: on the one hand, discontent may lead to a vote against the incumbents; but, on the other hand, supporters of opposition parties may be predisposed to be critical of the performance of the rival party or parties in government. The politically disaffected tend strongly to be uninvolved with all three intermediation channels examined in this book; but it is unclear whether behavioural disengagement fosters disaffection, or disaffection simply leads to marginalization from most facets of organized politics. Finally, we conclude with speculative observations concerning the implications of these findings for both the existing state of theory in this realm of political science, and the real world of politics.

Three Concepts and Seven Countries

Most published studies of attitudes towards democracy share two characteristics. First, they tend to assume that attitudes towards the political system constitute one single attitudinal domain, or at most, two. In his seminal work on this subject, Easton (1965) argued that such orientations could be broken down into two categories, which he called *diffuse support* and *specific support* for democracy. Other studies did not even go this far and indiscriminately mixed a wide variety of attitudinal orientations into their analyses assuming that they occupied a common conceptual domain. This is, they argue, because Easton's original conceptualization was so vague as to lead invariably to research that is 'ambiguous, confusing, and non-cumulative' (Kaase 1988: 117) because the relevant measurement problems are insuperable (Loewenberg 1971), because this distinction is tautological and derived exclusively from the employment of an inferior methodology (Craig 1993), or because citizens are simply not capable of distinguishing between them (Muller and Jukam 1977).[3] Unfortunately, in our view, by including such seemingly distinct orientations as basic support for democracy and satisfaction with the current performance of governmental institutions within a single attitudinal domain, this literature has produced a plethora of inconsistent findings and a great deal of confusion about the impact of democratic attitudes on individual-level political behaviour and the overall performance and legitimacy of democratic systems. For that reason, we demonstrate why it is important to differentiate more clearly among these different types of attitudinal orientations.

A second claim often found in this literature posits a close (if not deterministic) relationship between citizens' levels of satisfaction with the performance of political institutions or the economy, and support for the democratic regime *per se*. Weatherford (1987: 13), for example, states that 'Over the long run, of course, legitimacy is wholly determined by policy performance'. And Przeworski (1991: 95) flatly asserted, 'As everyone agrees, the eventual survival of the new democracies [in post-Soviet Eastern Europe] will depend to a large extent on their economic performance. And since many among them emerged in the midst of an unprecedented economic crisis, economic factors work against their survival.' Some scholars have even suggested that the legitimacy of established Western democracies is increasingly dependent on their performance (see Fuchs and Klingemann 1995: 440).

In earlier publications (Montero, Gunther, and Torcal 1997; Gunther and Montero 2000, 2006; Gunther 2004), we tested some of these propositions and found no support for them. We found that the most commonly used indicators constituted three attitudinal domains that were both conceptually and empirically distinct from one another. And we found that fundamental support for democracy was not contingent on satisfaction with the performance of the economy, the incumbent government, or of democracy in general.

Two of the three clusters of attitudes towards democracy that emerged from our earlier analysis are roughly similar to Easton's distinction between diffuse and specific support. *Democratic support* pertains to citizens' beliefs that democratic politics and representative democratic institutions are the most appropriate (indeed, the only acceptable) framework for government. This is the key attitudinal component of regime legitimacy. Such beliefs focus on the political regime in the aggregate, and should be expected to be stable over time and immune from the influence of such factors as the popularity of the government and partisanship—specifically, the correspondence between the citizen's partisan preferences and the party of the incumbent government—and evaluations of concrete institutions and their performance (Hibbing and Theiss-Morse 1995).

In contrast, *political discontent* is based on 'peoples' judgments about the day-to-day actions of political leaders and the operation of governmental institutions and processes' (Kornberg and Clarke 1992: 20). In other words, political dissatisfaction arises from citizens' evaluations of the performance of the regime or authorities, as well as of their political outcomes (Farah, Barnes, and Heunks 1979). Distinct from fundamental support for democracy, it should thus be expected to fluctuate over time in accord with the government's performance, the condition of the society and economy, or the performance of key political institutions. And since it focuses on partisan political leaders and the governments they lead, it would not be surprising to find that, other things being equal, citizens supporting the same party as that of the incumbent government would be more positive in their assessments than those who voted for the opposition.[4]

The third cluster of attitudes that we shall explore, *political disaffection*, is conceptually distinct from both of those described above, although it is often indiscriminately lumped together with measures of citizen support for and satisfaction with democracy. Following DiPalma (1970: 30; also see Torcal 2002*a*: ch. 3, 2002*b*), we regard political disaffection as a certain estrangement of members of the polity from both its core political institutions and, more generally, from politics. As described by Torcal (2001, 2002*c*: 2–3) political disaffection refers to 'the subjective feeling of powerlessness, cynicism and lack of confidence in the political process, politicians and democratic institutions, but with no questioning of the political regime' (also see Montero, Gunther, and Torcal 1997: 136). Polit- ical discontent may be regarded as the result of a negative evaluation of the performance of incumbent authorities and political parties, although it might be accompanied by a positive orientation towards the democratic system as a whole. In contrast, political disaffection is a reflection of a fundamentally distrusting and suspicious vision of political life and the institutions and mechanisms of democratic representation. And unlike discontent (which our earlier analysis found to ebb and flow in accord with current assessments of the performance of incumbents or democratic institutions), we found that attitudes of disaffection are remarkably stable. In addition, while discontent is closely associated with partisanship (with supporters of opposition parties generally more critical of the performance of the government and dissatisfied with its policy outputs than those who identify with the incumbent party), disaffection is more far reaching and indiscriminate in its objects of negativity, although it does not entail a denial of the regime's legitimacy.[5]

Let us begin this exploration of attitudes towards democracy, their relationships with intermediation, and their behavioural consequences by examining the extent to which these attitudes fall into separable dimensions in six of the new democracies included within the CNEP, as well as in Portugal. Post-election surveys undertaken in Spain (1993),

Greece (1996), Uruguay (1994), Bulgaria (1996), Portugal (2002), Hungary (1998), and Chile (1993) included identical or very similar items measuring the three core concepts of democratic support, political discontent, and political disaffection. (In addition, the inclusion of some of these items in the 1985 Four Nation Study and the 1996 Italian and 2000 Chilean CNEP surveys makes it possible for us to test one crucial hypothesis, although so many of the other items were not included in those surveys as to preclude broader comparisons with the other countries in this initial dimensional analysis.) The geographical, institutional, and social diversity of the cases analysed in this study facilitates our efforts to test the generalizability of our initial findings concerning the separability of these three attitudinal domains (based heavily on our multi-method analyses of Spain). Moreover, their greatly different historical experiences and democratization trajectories enable us to speculate about the origins of these democratic attitudes in widely varying contexts, as well as to explore their behavioural consequences and implications for regime stability.

As can be seen in Table 2.1, these countries spanned the full range of democracies arrayed in accord with our core measures of democratic legitimacy, with Greece near the very top in terms of the extent of support for democracy, while support for democracy in Bulgaria is much lower. The Portuguese data (derived, as noted, from a 2002 survey that was not part of the CNEP project) utilized a response format that precludes a direct comparison of marginals with these others, but the overwhelming level of support for democracy in Portugal would have placed it near the top of this rank-ordering of countries.[6]

The surveys conducted in Spain, Uruguay, and Chile included as a measure of support for democracy the respondent's agreement or disagreement with the proposition that 'Democracy is the best political system for a country like ours', which is labelled *DemBest* in the following tables. The other surveys also included a second measure of democratic support, *DemAuth*, which asks respondents to choose among the following three sentences: 'Democracy is preferable to any other form of government'; 'Under some circumstances, an authoritarian regime, a dictatorship, is preferable to a democratic system'; and 'For people like me, one regime is the same as another' (with the latter recoded to fall between the other two as an intermediate category). Most of the CNEP surveys also included three different measures of what we hypothesize will fall into a separate 'discontent' cluster: these are *DemSat* (the respondent's degree of dissatisfaction with 'the way democracy is working in Spain [... Greece, Uruguay,

Table 2.1 Support for democracy in CNEP democracies, in comparative perspective: 1993–2000

	Agree	Don't know/It depends	Disagree
DemBest: 'Democracy is the best form of government for a country like ours'			
Uruguay (1994)	88%	7%	4%
Greece (1996)	87	9	4
Spain (1993)	79	14	7
Chile (1993)	79	11	10
Hungary (1998)	72	18	10
Bulgaria (1996)	57	24	19
Hong Kong (1998)	62	14	24

	Dem. always preferable	They're all the same	Sometimes auth. regime best	Don't know, no answer
DemAuth: 'Democracy is preferable to any other form of government'				
Denmark	93%	2%	5%	1%
Norway	88	2	5	5
Greece	85	3	11	1
Portugal	83	4	10	4
West Germany	84	5	8	3
The Netherlands	82	5	9	5
Spain	81	7	8	4
Italy	81	10	7	2
Uruguay	80	8	6	8
France	77	11	7	5
Great Britain	76	11	7	6
Argentina	71	11	15	3
Belgium	70	10	10	10
Bolivia	64	15	17	4
Chile (2000)	64	16	17	3
Ireland	63	21	11	6
Peru	63	14	13	10
Venezuela	62	13	19	6
Colombia	60	18	20	2
Bulgaria	59	14	25	2
Hungary	58	25	7	10
Chile	54	23	19	4
Mexico	53	17	23	7
Ecuador	52	23	18	7
Brazil	50	21	24	5

Sources: For DemBest in Bulgaria, Chile, Greece, Hong Kong, Hungary, Italy, Spain, and Uruguay, as well as DemAuth in Bulgaria, Greece and Hungary CNEP surveys; and for DemAuth in Latin American and European countries, Lagos (1997) and Eurobarometer 37, 1995.

etc.]'); *PolitSit* (the level of discontent over 'the political situation of the country'); and *EconSit* (the extent of dissatisfaction with 'the economic situation of the country'). Three variables that we regard as indicators of disaffection were also included in the questionnaires administered in each of these countries: *PolComp* reflects agreement or disagreement with the statement, 'Generally, politics seems so complicated that people like me cannot understand what is happening'; *DontCare* is the respondent's agreement or disagreement with the proposition that 'Politicians do not worry much about what people like me think'; and *NoInflu* taps into the respondent's belief in or rejection of the idea that 'People like me do not have any influence over what the government does'.[7]

Preliminary examination of the other sets of attitudes that we are analysing in this chapter presents a very different picture. With regard to levels of dissatisfaction with the economy, the political situation of the country and with the functioning of democracy vary considerably from one country to another, and these cross-national patterns do not correspond with the levels of support for democracy presented in Table 2.1. Respondents in Portugal and, especially, Bulgaria are by far the most negative in their assessments of the state of the economy (with 64% and 96%, respectively, describing it as 'bad'; this compares with 60% in Greece, 58% in Spain, 50% in Uruguay, and just 14% in Chile). These assessments of the economy closely parallel those of the political situation of the country, with Bulgarians once again by far the most negative (81% describing conditions as 'bad') and Chileans most positive (only 26%), with respondents in the other countries in between (with between 52% and 60% evaluating political conditions negatively). When asked to describe the functioning of democracy in their countries, respondents were substantially more satisfied, but again Bulgarians anchored the negative end of the continuum (46% 'bad'): this stood in sharp contrast with Chile (11%), Uruguay (12%), Spain (13%), Portugal (15%), and Greece (19%). There were far fewer cross-national differences with regard to the attitudes associated with disaffection. The range of respondents agreeing with the 'politics is complicated' item was from 43 per cent in Bulgaria to 56 per cent in Greece; while national scores on the 'politicians don't care' item ranged from a low of 60 per cent to high of 75 per cent. Only with regard to the 'no influence' item is the range of national-level responses more substantial (from a low of 56% in Uruguay to a high of 80% in Hungary).

Dimensional Analyses of Democratic Attitudes

Tables 2.2–2.4 present the results of two different approaches to analysing the dimensional structures underpinning the clustering of these attitudes and behaviours in these countries. Measures of bivariate association (tau-b) among all of these items appear in the matrices composed of the first five, six, or seven columns of these tables. The final two or three columns in these tables display the loadings that emerged from an exploratory factor analysis of all of these items following a Varimax rotation of the principal component solution. For all countries except Chile a similar latent structuring emerges that clearly reflect three distinct attitudinal dimensions: democratic support, political discontent, and political disaffection.

It is clear from the data for Spain, Uruguay, and Greece in Table 2.2 that Factor 1 is made up of items involving *political discontent.* As we hypothesized, all three measures of dissatisfaction belong to this cluster; the magnitude of the factor loadings, the percentage of variance explained by this factor (ranging between 24.1% and 29.4%[8]), and the bivariate measures of inter-item association are all strong and statistically significant (at the .001 level or better). It is also noteworthy that the degree of satisfaction with the functioning of democracy in all three countries was strongly linked to assessments of the economic and political conditions of the country. In sharp contrast, basic support for democracy, as measured by *DemBest* and (when available) support for non-democratic alternatives, as measured by *DemAuth*, is, at best, weakly related to dissatisfaction with the economic or political situation of the country. In Uruguay, there is no statistically significant relationship between support for democracy and either of these two measures of discontent, while in Spain and Greece the relationships are quite weak (ranging between tau-b scores of −.06 and −.11). Dissatisfaction with the performance of democracy (*DemSat*) is moderately associated with our measures of democratic support (with tau-b scores ranging from −.14 to −.22), but the factor analyses indicate that support for democracy and the three discontent measures are not part of the same attitudinal domain. In Spain, support for democracy (*DemBest*) simply fails to fit with the other items in the discontent cluster, while in both Uruguay and Greece the two measures of democratic support constitute their own separate attitudinal dimension. It is also clear that, as hypothesized above, the disaffection items cluster together to make up a third distinct attitudinal dimension, although the small percentages of variance explained by this factor (just barely above what would have been produced by random chance) indicate that the variables in this cluster are rather loosely associated with one another. Overall, however, the most noteworthy finding regarding the disaffection measures is that they are not at all statistically linked to democratic support items, and in Spain and Uruguay, are very weakly associated with indicators of political discontent, as well.[9]

Table 2.2 The dimensionality of attitudes towards democracy: factor loadings and tau-b correlations

	EconSit	PolitSit	DemSat	DemBest	DemAuth	PolComp	NoInflu	Factor 1	Factor 2	Factor 3
Spain 1993										
EconSit	—							**.762**	-.035	-.126
PolitSit	.43**	—						**.802**	-.016	.014
DemSat	.28**	.31**	—					**.687**	-.125	.359
DemBest	-.06*	-.10**	-.14**	—				.306	.348	**.934**
PolComp	.00	.01	.05	.00		—		.021	**.639**	-.092
NoInflu	.06*	.06	.08*	.04		.17**	—	-.056	**.651**	.186
DontCare	.14**	.13**	.21**	.08*		.25**	.28**	-.247	**.728**	-.028
Percentage of variance explained								28.1	19.9	14.6
Uruguay 1994										
EconSit	—							**.811**	.076	
PolitSit	.36**	—						**.767**	-.108	
DemSat	.25**	.21**	—					**.609**	-.018	
DemBest	.00	-.07	-.14**	—				.028	.050	
PolComp	.08*	-.01	.00	.03		—		.106	**.752**	
NoInflu	.01	.06	.00	.04		.19**	—	-.052	**.615**	
DontCare	.04	.11**	.03	.00		.32**	.22**	-.100	**.760**	
Percentage of variance explained								24.1	21.9	
Greece 1996										
EconSit	—							**.823**	-.094	.009
PolitSit	.47**	—						**.849**	-.072	.021
DemSat	.29**	.34**	—					**.612**	-.217	.314
DemBest	-.08	-.11**	-.22**	—				.130	.032	**.788**
DemAuth	-.08	-.09*	-.19**	.29*	—			.025	-.090	**.802**
PolComp	.13**	.08*	.16**	-.01	-.08	—		-.040	**.730**	-.052
NoInflu	.12**	.12**	.15**	-.02	-.08	.22	—	-.090	**.677**	-.011
DontCare	.19**	.17**	.21**	-.05	-.08	.32**	.28**	-.173	**.729**	-.027
Percentage of variance explained								29.4	16.0	14.3

* Denotes significance (2-tailed) at .01; ** Denotes significance (2-tailed) at .001 or better.

In order to subject these hypotheses to more rigorous empirical tests, a 'confirmatory factor analysis' was performed using these same variables clustered in accord with the three latent factors described above.[10] The results of these analyses confirmed the same dimensional structure for all three countries. All of the individual variables were found to be linked to one another as in the initial clusters that emerged from the exploratory factor analysis whose results are presented in Table 2.2.[11] Moreover, the correlations among latent factors further revealed that these clusters are independent of one another: these inter-factor correlations ranged between .00 and .19. Given our particular interest in the relationship between discontent and fundamental support for democracy, it is most noteworthy that these correlations were negligible in all three cases: .07 for Spain, .04 for Uruguay, and .07 for Greece. Overall, the Root Mean Square Error of Approximation (RMSEA) 'goodness-of-fit' statistic reveals that these three-factor models adequately capture the nature of the relationships among these variables: the RMSEA statistic for Spain is .055, for Uruguay is .067, and for Greece is .054.[12]

Similar patterns emerge from analyses of the underlying structure among these political attitudes in Portugal, Bulgaria, and Hungary, despite the fact that these three countries have suffered worse economic and/or political crises than the first three countries we have examined. In contrast with the relatively tranquil transitions to democracy in Spain, Uruguay, and Greece, the downfall of the Salazar/Caetano dictatorship in Portugal was followed by over a year of revolutionary chaos and tumult. Indeed, it was not until a year and a half later that a counter-coup by more moderate military officers set Portugal on the path towards democracy and ultimate regime consolidation. Nonetheless, as can be seen in Table 2.3, the pattern of relationships among these individual variables and dimensional factors is precisely the same as we saw earlier. There is no statistically significant relationship between dissatisfaction with the condition of the economy or the performance of the incumbent government, on the one hand, and a measure of support for democracy (which is quite similar to *DemBest*),[13] on the other. And the degree of association between basic support for democracy and dissatisfaction with the performance of democracy ($-.09$) is significantly weaker than we saw in Spain, Uruguay, and Greece. Similarly, the two disaffection measures included in this survey were not substantially associated with either the democratic support or political discontent measures. Confirmatory factor analysis of these data is supportive of these findings: while the absence of some key variables and slight differences in item wording lead to weaker closeness-of-fit with the

Table 2.3 The dimensionality of attitudes towards democracy: factor loadings and tau-b correlations

Portugal 2002	EconSit	GovPerf	DemSat	BestDem	PolComp	Factor 1	Factor 2	Factor 3
EconSit	—					**.767**	.037	.117
GovPerf	.30**	—				**.741**	.005	.012
DemSat	.17**	.19**	—			**.588**	.015	-.342
DemBest	.01	-.02	-.09*	—		.002	-.004	**.947**
PolComp	.00	-.03	.00	-.02	—	-.101	**.812**	-.081
DontCare	.08**	.07**	.03	-.01	.27*	.148	**.791**	.075
Percentage of variance explained						25.8	21.1	17.1

Bulgaria 1996	EconSit	PolitSit	DemSat	DemBest	DemAuth	PolComp	NoInflu	Factor 1	Factor 2	Factor 3
EconSit	—							-.035	**.799**	-.071
PolitSit	.39**	—						-.019	**.790**	-.005
DemSat	.20**	.18**	—					.526	.480	.001
DemBest	.05	.03	-.21**	—				**.822**	-.087	-.073
DemAuth	.01	.01	-.24**	.47*	—			**.822**	-.008	-.022
PolComp	-.05	-.02	.03	-.17**	-.10**	—		-.199	.187	.578
NoInflu	.10**	.08*	.02	.01	-.05	.14	—	.036	-.105	**.731**
DontCare	.11**	.04	.04	-.01	.01	.13**	.34*	.031	-.125	**.737**
Percentage of variance explained								22.5	19.0	16.7

Hungary 1998	EconCon	RespCon	DemBest	DemAuth	PolComp	NoInflu	Factor 1	Factor 2	Factor 3
EconCon	—						**.889**	.024	-.062
RespCon	.60**	—					**.884**	.071	-.041
DemBest	-.05	-.07	—				-.047	-.004	**.769**
DemAuth	-.08*	-.09*	.21**	—			-.043	-.100	**.752**
PolComp	-.02	.02	-.05	-.20**	—		-.100	**.738**	-.139
NoInflu	.07*	.10**	-.05	-.05*	.27**	—	.103	**.699**	.130
DontCare	.09*	.10**	-.09*	-.15*	.30**	.24**	.101	**.690**	-.131
Percentage of variance explained							25.9	20.2	16.0

* Denotes significance (2-tailed) at .01; ** Denotes significance (2-tailed) at .001 or better.

three-factor model than we have observed above (the RMSEA statistic is .090), and the factor loadings among items within each cluster are lower than we observed in analyses of Spain, Greece, and Uruguay,[14] the correlations among the discontent, disaffection, and democratic support factors are extraordinarily low, ranging between −.01 and +.01. Among these findings, the latter data relating to the separability of the three dimensions are the most significant theoretically.

In the light of the severe economic crisis and the collapse of law and order that accompanied the transition to democracy in Bulgaria, it is not surprising to find that the aggregate level of support for democracy in that country is lower than is to be found in most other democratic systems at the same time that it has the highest levels of political discontent and disaffection, as we saw in the presentation of marginals above. The data presented in Table 2.3, however, indicate that, despite some coincidence at the aggregate level, at the individual level the relationships between dissatisfaction with the economic and the political situation of Bulgaria, on the one hand, and two measures of support for democracy, on the other, are not only statistically insignificant, but they are of the wrong sign! And the correlation between the latent factors of discontent and democratic support that were generated by the confirmatory factor analysis was just .02—a figure that was lower than comparable statistics for Spain, Uruguay, and Greece. As we saw in Spain, Greece, Uruguay, and Portugal, dissatisfaction with the performance of democracy (*DemSat*) in Bulgaria has somewhat stronger bivariate linkages with each of our two measures of democratic legitimacy, but these relationships (tau-b scores of −.21 and −.24) are still only of moderate strength (Table 2.3). Perhaps most importantly, the factor loadings reveal that support for democracy and satisfaction with the political and economic situation of the country constitute two distinctly different attitudinal domains, with dissatisfaction with the performance of democracy (*DemSat*) straddling the two dimensions. Given the logical overlap between the face content of that item (satisfaction with the performance of democracy) and our measures of democratic legitimacy (the belief that democracy is the best form of government for the country), this empirical overlap is not surprising. Accordingly, the RMSEA statistic for the three-factor model in Bulgaria (.081) reveals that the model fits these patterns of relationships among variables somewhat less well than we saw above in the Spanish, Uruguayan, Greek, and Portuguese analyses, but that this model still provides a reasonable mapping of these relationships. It is important to note, however, that the correlations among the three latent factors that

resulted from the confirmatory factor analysis (ranging between −.03 and
.02) are even lower than we saw in those three other countries, reflecting
an even higher level of independence among those dimensions, and the
factor loadings among the variables within each cluster are acceptably
strong.[15] The overall conclusion to be drawn from these data is that the
link between support for democracy in Bulgaria and assessments of the
economic situation is surprisingly weak.[16] The Bulgarian data also reveal
that those attitudes that we hypothesized would fall within a distinct
political disaffection cluster do, indeed, inhabit a separate attitudinal
domain, and are only weakly (or not at all) associated with those making
up the political discontent and democratic support. This can be seen
in the results of the exploratory factor analysis presented in Table 2.3,
and also in the extremely low correlations between disaffection and the
two other latent factors in the confirmatory factor analysis: −.01 with
discontent and −.03 with the democratic support cluster.

The case of Hungary provides another opportunity to explore the
dimensionality of democratic attitudes in a post-communist country that
also had to confront serious economic difficulties (although by no means
as severe as in Bulgaria) simultaneous with democratization. In this case,
however, the key elites of the non-democratic predecessor regime initiated
and willingly collaborated in far-reaching processes of economic and
political liberalization, as well as with the early stages of the democratization process itself. Accordingly, we can take advantage of this fundamental difference in the transition process to effectively manipulate one of
our central explanatory variables—the formative role of political elites. As
can be seen in Table 2.3, the results of the exploratory factor analysis and
the bivariate measures of association clearly indicate that the two items
in this satisfaction/optimism cluster[17] are dimensionally distinct from
those dealing with democratic support. The independence of these two
clusters of attitudes is further reflected in the extremely low correlation
between these two latent factors that was generated by the confirmatory
factor analysis (.02). The clustering of attitudes constituting the disaffection dimension is also clear cut and quite consistent with our earlier
findings. The latent factor of disaffection items correlates with those of
democratic support and discontent at extremely low levels—.04 and .02,
respectively. And neither the discontent nor disaffection item clusters
is strongly related to the two measures of democratic legitimacy, which
clearly constitute a third attitudinal dimension in the factor analysis.
Thus, the three-dimensional structure of these attitudes found in Spain,
Uruguay, Greece, Portugal, and Bulgaria also emerges from our analysis

of Hungary. Indeed, the RMSEA statistic for Hungary (.044) indicates a closer fit with the three-factor model than in the first three countries we analysed.[18]

It is important to note that these findings are highly significant for theories of democratic consolidation: despite bold predictions to the contrary by several prominent scholars,[19] in none of these countries is dissatisfaction with the political or economic situation of the country strongly associated with fundamental support for democracy. Even the bivariate link between democratic legitimacy and the broader measure of dissatisfaction with the 'performance of democracy' is only of moderate strength, and is not located in any of these factor analyses within the same attitudinal domain as support for democracy.

It is only in the case of Chile in 1993 that we encounter evidence suggesting that support for democracy is significantly linked with the items in the discontent cluster. As can be seen in Table 2.4, the bivariate measures of association (tau-b) linking the belief that democracy is the best form of government for Chile and dissatisfaction with the economy, with the political situation of the country, and with the performance of democracy range between $-.12$ and $-.24$, and the exploratory factor analysis placed support for democracy (*DemBest*) in the same cluster as those satisfaction measures.

A confirmatory factor analysis testing our three-dimensional model, however, produced strikingly different results. While the correlation between the latent factors of democratic support and discontent is slightly higher (.10) than we found with the other cases, the overall pattern of correlations among latent factors (summarized in Table 2.5) definitely reveals the same clustering of items as in the other countries. Most striking

Table 2.4 The dimensionality of attitudes towards democracy: factor loadings and tau-b correlations

Chile 1993	EconSit	PolitSit	DemSat	DemBest	PolComp	NoInflu	Factor 1	Factor 2
EconSit	—	—	—	—	—	—	**.642**	−.250
PolitSit	.39**	—	—	—	—	—	**.718**	−.220
DemSat	.27**	.34**	—	—	—	—	**.736**	−.024
DemBest	−.12*	−.19**	−.24**	—	—	—	**.604**	.190
PolComp	.16**	.15**	.10*	−.02	—	—	−.119	**.696**
NoInflu	.10**	.11**	.04	.01	.20**	—	.005	**.629**
DontCare	.17**	.16**	.09**	.01	.33**	.26**	−.071	**.759**
Percentage of variance explained							30.1	19.3

* Denotes significance (2-tailed) at .01; ** Denotes significance (2-tailed) at .001 or better.

Table 2.5 Correlations among latent factors and RMSEA statistics from confirmatory factor analysis

	Correlation discontent/ dem. support	Correlation dem. support/ disaffection	Correlation discontent/ disaffection	RMSEA statistics
Spain	.07	.02	−.12	.055
Uruguay	.04	.19	.00	.067
Greece	.07	−.02	−.11	.054
Portugal	.01	−.01	.00	.090
Bulgaria	.02	−.03	−.01	.081
Hungary	.02	.04	−.02	.044
Chile	.10	.04	−.08	.031

Note: The Root Mean Square Error of Approximation (RMSEA) is a goodness-of-fit statistic that is sensitive to the complexity (i.e. the number of estimated parameters) in the model. Values less than .05 indicate very good fit, values as high as .08 reflect reasonable errors of approximation, and values above .10 indicate poor fit.

in this regard, the RMSEA statistic produced by the Chilean confirmatory factor analysis (.031) indicates *better* fit with the three-factor model than in those other countries!

Why are the findings of the exploratory and confirmatory factor analyses for Chile inconsistent? One potential explanation lies in the combination of certain unusual characteristics of Chile's transition to democracy and the particular alignment of political forces at the time of the Chilean election survey. As we argue later in this chapter, these attitudinal patterns are to some extent the product of a deep cleavage in the Chilean polity separating those on the centre and left with strongly pro-democratic attitudes, who tended overwhelmingly to vote for parties belonging to the Concertación coalition, from those on the right, who harboured reservations about the merits of democracy, favourably evaluated the economic accomplishments achieved under the military dictatorship, and gave their electoral support to candidates and parties that are generally sympathetic towards the Pinochet regime (Tironi and Agüero 1999; Torcal and Mainwaring 2003). Political discontent, as noted earlier in this chapter, is strongly associated with one's partisan preferences: supporters of the incumbent party (in any democratic system) tend to be much more satisfied with the political and economic conditions of the country than are those who support the opposition party (for similar findings, see Huneeus and Maldonado 2003). Accordingly, we contend that the link in Chile between low levels of support for democracy *and* dissatisfaction with various performance indicators is an artefact of the particular alignment of political forces at the time of this survey. More broadly, these findings suggest that the roles played by competing sets of political elites can have a substantial and lasting impact on fundamental support for democracy among their respective sets of followers.

Intermediation, Attitudes Towards Democracy, and Political Behaviour

To what extent are these attitudes towards democracy related to social or political processes involving intermediation? In this and the following sections of this chapter, we systematically explore the relationships linking attitudes towards democracy to the three sets of intermediation channels that are the central foci of this book—membership in secondary associations, direct face-to-face contacts with individuals in different types of social networks, and exposure to the media—as well as to patterns of political behaviour that are central to the functioning of democratic systems. In doing so, we will test a variety of hypotheses in which attitudes towards democracy and patterns of political behaviour are treated variously as causes or consequences of flows of political information through intermediation channels.

An examination of the correlates of these attitudes, especially those involving overt political behaviour or with proto-behavioural implications, is important for several reasons. First, such additional data can strengthen (or undermine) the construct validity of the concepts that we delineated in the preceding section of this chapter. Second, these data speak directly to the most devastating of questions in the social sciences: 'so what?' If we were to find that those holding one set of attitudes behaved in a manner indistinguishable from those with the opposite orientations, the very value of studying these aspects of political culture might be called into question. Third, and most importantly, empirical data concerning these behavioural or proto-behavioural correlates makes it possible to explore some of the implications of such attitudes for the quality, the performance, and perhaps even the survival, of democratic regimes.

Having determined the dimensional clustering of these various attitudes, we can simplify the following steps in this analysis by constructing scales measuring political discontent and disaffection. The *Discontent* scale was constructed out of dissatisfaction with the economic situation (*EconSit*), with the political situation (*PolitSit*), and with the function of democracy (*DemSat*).[20] A second scale was created by adding together responses to the three *Disaffection* measures, *PolComp* ('Politics is too complicated'), *NoInflu* ('People like me do not have any influence'), and *DontCare* ('Politicians don't care'). Support for democracy is operationalized as responses to the *DemBest* item.

We begin this exploration of the attitudes towards democracy and their correlates with various forms of behaviour and political intermediation by testing one hypothesis that is currently most popular among political scientists in which democratic attitudes may be formed or otherwise affected by one important set of intermediation channels involving membership in secondary associations.

The 'Social Capital' Hypothesis

It has been frequently argued that the development of attitudes related to a strong 'civil society' and the development of 'social capital' are essential for the health of democratic politics. Central to both of these sets of hypotheses is a high level of affiliation with secondary organizations. The most prominent proponent of this view is Putnam (2000), who argues that social capital (which is developed through embeddedness in social networks and participation in private voluntary organizations) is conducive to the health of democratic politics in many ways. First, active membership in organizations instils 'in their members habits of cooperation and public spiritedness, as well as the practical skills necessary to partake in public life' (Putnam 2000: 338). 'Voluntary associations are places where social and civic skills are learned: [they are] "schools for democracy." [They] serve as forums for thoughtful deliberation over vital public issues' (ibid. 338–9; also see Almond and Verba 1963).

Several scholars have explored the relationship between membership in secondary associations and social trust, but to what extent is organizational membership related to attitudes towards democracy? Putnam (1993, 2000) has inconclusively explored some of these relationships. Norris (1999*a*, 1999*b*: 21–2) and Newton (1999*a*: 17), while not strong advocates of the social capital approach, have broadened the social capital argument to include not only to citizens' trust in each other,[21] but also to their confidence in representative institutions. As Newton (1999*b*: 179) put it, political confidence and social trust are considered to be 'different sides of the same coin'. From this perspective, *political* confidence is at least to some extent a by-product of *social* trust, and is exogenous to the political system (cf. Mishler and Rose 2002: 31). Other scholars have demonstrated that not all secondary associations may produce the same beneficial effects (Stolle and Rochon 1998). Accordingly, and on the basis of preliminary analyses of these data, we found that it is important to separate membership in those organizations that are explicitly political (such as political parties and, in the European context, trade unions) from those that are at least ostensibly non-partisan (e.g. religious organizations and business or professional groups) or are almost certainly uninvolved in political matters (sports associations, youth groups, etc.). Separate scales were therefore created to capture membership in one or more of each of these two types of organization.[22]

The bivariate relationships (tau-b) between membership in each of these two types of organization, on the one hand, and each of our three clusters of attitudes towards democracy, on the other, are presented in Table 2.6. As can be seen, the statistical associations are weak or non-existent with regard to both support for democracy and political discontent.[23] In only two countries (Spain and Bulgaria) is the linkage between membership in political organizations and support for democracy statistically

Table 2.6 Correlations (tau-b) with organizational membership

	Democratic support	Political discontent	Political disaffection
Political organizations[a]			
Spain	.06*	.04	−.08**
Greece	.04	−.03	−.13**
Uruguay	.01	−.01	−.09**
Chile	−.05	−.03	−.04
Hungary	.00	.03	−.06*
Bulgaria	.10**	−.06*	−.10**
Portugal	−.02	.06*	−.08**
Non-political organizations[b]			
Spain	.03	−.04	−.03
Greece	−.03	−.05	−.13**
Uruguay	.00	.05	−.06*
Chile	−.02	.00	−.04
Hungary	.03	−.05	−.16
Bulgaria	.05	−.06*	−.08**
Portugal	.06	.03	.00

* Correlation is significant at the .05 level (2-tailed); ** Correlation is significant at the .01 level (2-tailed).

[a] Includes membership in political parties and trade unions (except in Portugal, where respondents were not asked about party membership).

[b] Includes membership in professional, religious, cultural, ecological, youth, sports, feminist, and neighbourhood associations, parent–teacher organizations, and others (except in Portugal, where it included only those belonging to business, farmer, and professional associations).

significant, but even in these cases the relationships were quite weak, and were further weakened in a subsequent round of analysis in which education was introduced as a control. And in no country was there a statistically significant relationship between membership in non-political organizations and support for democracy. Similarly, the linkage between aggregate levels of membership in secondary organizations and political discontent is also weak or non-existent in the great majority of these countries.

This is not to say, however, that membership in specific organizations has no impact on political discontent. As we noted in our earlier analysis, political discontent is highly contaminated by partisanship, such that individuals supporting opposition parties or groups are predisposed to be more dissatisfied with the performance of government and democracy in general than are supporters of the governing party or parties. While measures of organizational membership in the aggregate are not linked to political discontent, membership in organizations that are highly politicized, if not closely linked to political parties, is associated with political discontent in a statistically significant manner. In the cases of Spain and Portugal, for example, affiliation with trade unions (which are dominated by communist and/or socialist parties) correlates significantly with measures of political discontent.

Not surprisingly, there was a stronger association between political disaffection and organizational membership, particularly with regard to membership in political organizations. But this statistical association begs the important question of direction of causality. Since disaffection involves a general estrangement from society and its institutions, one could argue that individuals with disaffected attitudinal predispositions simply choose not to join organizations, particularly of the political variety. The reverse direction of causality could also be posited, however, in which organizational membership fosters attitudes that are the opposite of those associated with disaffection and societal estrangement. Clearly, these cross-sectional data cannot resolve that question of direction of causality. (However, we shall present evidence consistent with one speculative interpretation of this relationship later in this chapter.)

The frequency of face-to-face discussion of politics with family, friends, neighbours, or fellow workers, however, is more substantially associated with each of these three sets of democratic attitudes, at least in some countries, as can be seen in Table 2.7. Support for democracy is positively associated with frequency of political discussion in Spain and Bulgaria:

Table 2.7 Correlations (tau-b) between frequency of discussion of politics (with family, friends, neighbours, or fellow Workers) and attitudes towards democracy

	DemBest	Discontent	Disaffection
Spain	.10**	−.04	−.14**
Greece	.01	−.10**	−.14**
Uruguay	.05	.06	−.24**
Chile	−.11**	−.17**	−.16**
Hungary	.03	.01	−.25**
Bulgaria	.18**	−.03	−.11**

those who are more supportive of democracy in these countries tend to discuss politics more frequently. Again, it is not clear if the supportive attitude towards democracy encourages political discussion, or if talk about politics is conducive to positive attitudes towards democracy. In Chile, however, the direction of this relationship is reversed, although the relationship is rather weak. A mixed pattern of findings is also revealed with regard to the relationship between frequency of political discussion and political discontent. This relationship is significant only in Greece and Chile, where dissatisfaction with the performance of government, economy, and/or democracy itself is negatively associated with the frequency of political discussion.

Much stronger and more consistent findings are found with regard to the link between frequency of political discussion and disaffection. In all of the countries examined, political disaffection is moderately or strongly associated with the avoidance of political discussion. Interpretation of this relationship, however, is greatly complicated by questions regarding the direction of causality. It is quite likely that those who are politically disaffected choose to avoid discussion of politics with family, friends, neighbours, or fellow workers; it is less plausible to argue that infrequent discussion of politics 'causes' political disaffection. Moreover, the introduction of other 'control' variables, such as education, somewhat weakens this relationship.

Overall, the most consistent finding from this phase of our analysis is that there is little evidence to support an assertion that fundamental support for democracy is rooted in widespread membership in secondary associations. Even when an elaborate multiple regression analysis was performed, with democratic support as the dependent variable, only in the case of Bulgaria did a statistically significant relationship emerge.[24]

Organizational membership may (as we see in subsequent chapters) play a crucial role in efforts to mobilize the electorate during election campaigns, but it does not have the decisive importance that advocates of civil society or social capital sometimes assert with regard to core attitudes relevant to the legitimacy of democratic regimes.

'Throw the Bums Out': The Behavioural Consequence of Discontent

Having found little support for the social capital hypothesis, which casts intermediation (in the form of organizational membership) as a cause of fundamental attitudes towards democracy, let us turn our attention to the behavioural consequences of those attitudes. This analysis begins with the creation of two new variables that one might suspect can be affected by such attitudinal orientations. *Vote* distinguishes between ballots in favour of the incumbent party, on the one hand, and support for all other parties, or blank ballots, on the other. And *Involve* is a scale dealing with the respondent's degree of involvement with politics. It is made up of one item measuring the frequency with which the respondent tries 'to convince friends, relatives, or co-workers to share [his/her] point of view'; a second, which is itself a multi-item scale, gauging the respondent's ability to correctly identify prominent and not-so-prominent political figures; and a third, tapping into the respondent's self-reported level of interest in politics. The tau-b correlations among these scales provide a general indication of the behavioural consequences of two of these clusters of political attitudes.

Table 2.8 presents the results of this analysis for Spain, Uruguay, and Greece. The results are remarkably similar for all three countries. Consistent with the theoretical delineation of concepts with which we began this study, satisfaction with the performance of democracy/the political situation of the country/the condition of the economy is highly partisan in character, and is clearly associated with support for the incumbent government (as was also reported in many studies, such as Anderson and Guillory 1997; Anderson and Tverdova 2001; Linde and Ekman 2003). As cognitive consistency theory would hypothesize, those who cast ballots in favour of the governing party are much more likely to assess these conditions favourably than are those who supported opposition parties. One cannot, however, determine the direction of causality of this relationship on the basis of these data alone: it is not clear if the respondent's prior partisan predilections (which should be strongly linked to the decision to vote for the governing party or the opposition) colour his or her feelings

Table 2.8 Behavioural correlates (tau-b) of attitudes towards democracy

	Discon	Vote	DemBest	DemAuth	Disaffect.
Spain 1993					
Discontent	—	—	—	—	—
Vote	.36**	—	—	—	—
DemBest	−.12**	.02	—	—	—
Disaffect.	.11**	.08*	.04	—	—
Involve	.01	.14*	.12*	—	−.24**
Uruguay 1993					
Discontent	—	—	—	—	—
Vote	.27**	—	—	—	—
DemBest	.05	−.04	—	—	—
Disaffect.	−.01	.01	.04	—	—
Involve	.04	−.07	−.01	—	−.27**
Greece 1996					
Discontent	—	—	—	—	—
Vote	.33**	—	—	—	—
DemBest	−.16**	−.13**	—	—	—
DemAuth	−.13**	−.16**	.29**	—	—
Disaffect.	.20**	.04	−.04	−.10**	—
Involve	−.17**	−.04	.06	.08*	−.18**

* Denotes significance (2-tailed) at .01; ** Denotes significance (2-tailed) at .001 or better.

of satisfaction with the performance of the government/economy, etc. or whether dissatisfaction with the state of the polity or the economy leads the individual to cast a vote to 'throw the bums out', as classic democratic theory would dictate. In either case, it is quite clear that discontent (with the situation of the economy, with the political situation of the country, and/or with the performance of democracy) is strongly associated with a vote against the incumbent party. And, consistent with the results of the earlier item-by-item analysis, the discontent scale is not strongly associated with support for democracy (with tau-b figures ranging between .02 and −.16).

Also in accord with our conceptualization of these three clusters of attitudes towards democracy, the principal proto-behavioural correlate of the disaffection scale is a low level of involvement in politics—both in the attitudinal sense (as measured by self-reported interest in politics) and behaviourally (as measured by the frequency of efforts to convince others of the wisdom of one's political preferences, and by the respondent's actual level of political information). In the concluding section of this chapter, we more extensively explore the nature of this relationship, particularly with regard to its interaction with the intermediation channels that are the principal concern of this book.

Table 2.9 Behavioural correlates (tau-b) of attitudes towards democracy

	Discon	Vote	DemBest	DemAuth	Disaffect.
Portugal 2002					
Discontent	—	—	—	—	—
Vote	.24**	—	—	—	—
DemBest	−.04	.01	—	—	—
Disaffect.	.04	−.01	.00	—	—
Involve	−.09**	.00	.15**	—	−.24**
Hungary 1998					
Discontent	—	—	—	—	—
Vote	.27**	—	—	—	—
DemBest	−.07*	−.04	—	—	—
DemAuth	−.10**	.01	.20**	—	—
Disaffect.	.07*	−.07	−.08*	−.19**	—
Involve	−.01	−.07	.02	.18**	−.23**

* Denotes significance (2-tailed) at .01; ** Denotes significance (2-tailed) at .001 or better.

The data presented in Table 2.9 reveal precisely the same patterns of association among these attitudinal dimensions in Portugal and Hungary. In both countries, discontent is strongly associated with a propensity to vote against the incumbent party, while disaffection is equally strongly associated with low levels of political involvement. And in neither of these countries is there a close association between discontent and support for democracy: no statistically significant relationship between variables in these clusters can be found in Portugal, while in Hungary the association between discontent and our two measures of democratic support are weak (as indicated by tau-b coefficients of −.07 and −.10).

Political discontent is primarily a negative reaction rooted in dissatisfaction with the performance of the incumbent and/or the economy. This dissatisfaction is a product of the flows of political information through the three different types of intermediation channels that are systematically explored in this book. In passing through these channels, information is coloured or distorted as a product of media bias or the political orientation of secondary associations; it is perceived through 'partisan-coloured glasses', and is evaluated or processed in conjunction with the opinions expressed by family, friends, neighbours, and/or co-workers. And its principal behavioural consequence is a vote against the incumbent party, which is affected by the electoral mobilization efforts of parties and their supported organizations in society. Since these themes are much more extensively dealt with in other chapters of this book—which analyse the role of intermediation in electoral mobilization processes—we shall not further analyse the behavioural consequences of discontent here.

Support for Democracy: Another 'Intermediation Story'

To this point, we have seen that analysis of data from Spain, Uruguay, Greece, Portugal, and Hungary reveals strong relationships linking discontent with voting against the governing party, and disaffection with low levels of political involvement. But no behavioural correlates of low levels of support for democracy have been identified. In Table 2.10, however, some more intriguing and suggestive patterns begin to emerge. The most striking findings are that support for democracy in Bulgaria and Chile is strongly linked to votes cast for or against parties closely identified with the non-democratic predecessor regime. In contrast, support for the Socialist (former Communist) Party of Hungary is not at all linked to one's attitudes regarding the legitimacy of democracy, as reflected in statistically insignificant tau-b correlations of $+.01$ and $-.04$ with the two democratic support measures. How can we explain cross-national differences of this kind?

These differing patterns, we contend, can be accounted for by the 'transition and consolidation effect' hypothesized by Torcal (2002c)—that is, the strategies and behaviour of prominent political elites and organizations during particularly salient stages in the democratization process

Table 2.10 Behavioural correlates (tau-b) of attitudes towards democracy in Bulgaria and Chile

	Discon	Vote	DemBest	DemAuth	Disaffect.
Bulgaria 1996					
Discontent	—	—	—	—	—
Vote	.00	—	—	—	—
DemBest	−.06*	.28**	—	—	—
DemAuth	−.09**	.29**	.47**	—	—
Disaffect.	.06*	.02	−.10**	−.07*	—
Involve	.05	−.07	.20**	.11**	−.17**
Chile 1993					
Discontent	—	—	—	—	—
Vote	.12**	—	—	—	—
DemBest	−.23**	−.17**	—	—	—
Disaffect.	.18**	−.05	.02	—	—
Involve	−.28**	.15*	.07*	—	−.25**

* Denotes significance (2-tailed) at .01; ** Denotes significance (2-tailed) at .001 or better.

may have a major impact on the political attitudes of their respective sets of followers.[25] In both Bulgaria and Chile, the leaders of the former non-democratic regime resisted the democratization process (at least initially), and this had a lasting impact on attitudes towards democracy among supporters of their successor parties, even long after the latter had gone to great lengths to demonstrate their loyalty to the new democratic regime. In the other countries, in contrast, figures prominently associated with the former dictatorships either became completely irrelevant to the conduct of partisan politics in the democratic era (e.g. the military officers who dominated the Greek and Uruguayan juntas), or actively collaborated with the transition to and construction of the new democracy (e.g. political elites of the authoritarian regimes in Portugal and Spain who became leaders of democratic conservative parties and did loyally participate in the new democratic system).

The decision to vote against the Bulgarian Socialist (former Communist) Party (BSP) is more strongly associated with support for democracy than it is with any of the three items in the discontent cluster. One interpretation of this finding is that the stubbornly anti-democratic stance of the Bulgarian Communist Party (BCP) and that party's extremely late democratic transformation, have had a lasting impact on attitudes towards democracy among both its loyal supporters and opponents. Bulgaria's pre-democratic regime remained harshly authoritarian until shortly *after* the fall of the Berlin wall. Despite pressures from below and from sectors within the Communist Party itself, the government of Todor Zhivkov refused to allow significant political liberalization, even, in 1988, to the extent of purging from the Politburo several prominent proponents of the kinds of reforms introduced in the Soviet Union by Mikhail Gorbachev. Indeed, no significant progress towards political liberalization or democratization occurred until after Zhivkov's ouster from power on 8 November 1989. It was only after his replacement by more moderate and reformist communist leaders (who subsequently won Bulgaria's first democratic election) that rapid liberalization and a pacted transition to democracy could take place (see Karasimeonov 1990). What is most surprising is that the negative relationship between attitudes towards democracy and support for the former Communist Party remained strong in the mid-1990s, by which time the BSP had established a consistent record for loyal competition within and support for the democratic regime; in contrast, its principal rival, the UDF (which grew out of the anti-communist opposition), has sometimes engaged in disruptive semi-loyal behaviour (Vassilev 2000). Despite the BSP's commitment to democracy, the reluctance of UDF elites to accept the legitimacy of a 'formal democracy' governed by the BSP, and its semi-loyal strategies pursued during critical states of the transition to democracy appear to have had a lasting impact on the political attitudes of Bulgarians.

The Chilean data reveal a pattern similar to that found in Bulgaria: support for the presidential candidate most closely associated with the regime of the Chilean dictator, General Augusto Pinochet, was strongly associated with a lack of attitudinal support for democracy (see Torcal and Mainwaring 2003). This is not surprising, given the extremely unusual trajectory of the Chilean transition to democracy, particularly in its early stages. From the very beginning, the transition to democracy was only reluctantly tolerated by Pinochet, who continued to cling to positions of power for nearly a decade following the 1989 election. Pinochet had never intended to liberalize the political system, and only initiated the transition to democracy inadvertently, by unexpectedly losing a plebiscite that he had anticipated would further strengthen his grip on power. Even after the first democratic elections and the election of a civilian president (Patricio Aylwin), he retained control over the armed forces, which enabled him to constrain government policy decisions and crudely threaten the democratic regime from time to time—all of which led Linz and Stepan (1996: 206) to describe Chile's transition as 'the most democratically "disloyal" transfer of [any of their] Southern European and Southern Cone cases'. Throughout the first decade of Chile's restored democracy, the party system was deeply divided by a cleavage separating parties that were fully democratic in their ideologies and behaviour (the parties that made up the governing Concertación alliance—including the Christian Democrats and Socialists), on the one hand, and those that were semi-loyal and (until 1999) pro-Pinochet (Tironi and Agüero 1999; Torcal and Mainwaring 2003) on the other. It is likely that the extremely high salience of this political cleavage helps to explain the abnormal pattern of relationships among the attitudinal variables analysed in Table 2.4, as well as the association between vote and support for democracy in Table 2.8. In accord with this interpretation, non-democratic rightists looked favourably on the rapid economic development of the Pinochet era, and disparaged the economic slowdown of the early 1990s (under governments of the anti-Pinochet Concertación coalition). Conversely, supporters of the incumbent Concertación parties perceived the economic and political situation more favourably. Accordingly, we contend that the stronger linkage between satisfaction with economic and political conditions, on the one hand, and support for democracy, on the other, is at least in part a product of this constellation of partisan forces.[26]

The Chilean case is also unusual in so far as political discontent is also linked to political disaffection and levels of involvement with politics. In Table 2.8, the bivariate relationships between discontent, on the one hand, and disaffection and involvement, on the other (with tau-b coefficients of .18 and −.28, respectively), are much stronger than these same bivariate relationships in other countries. And as in the case of Bulgaria, the durability of the impact of elite behaviour during the transition on attitudes towards democracy is striking. By the time of the 1999–2000 election (over a decade after the first democratic elections), General Pinochet was under house arrest in London and under indictment for human rights abuses, and the presidential candidate of the conservative party, Joaquín Lavín, had taken great strides towards moderating his party's ideology, programmes, and public image, as well as to distance himself from Pinochet as much as possible.[27] And yet, as we see later in this chapter, the strong association between partisan preference and support for democracy remained a distinguishing characteristic of Chilean electoral behaviour.

The behaviour of key political elites and parties in the other countries surveyed here was quite different.[28] The Hungarian Communist Party, for example, played a role greatly different from its Bulgarian counterpart both prior to and during the transition to democracy. In Hungary, economic reforms had been introduced by the Communist Party decades before the abrupt collapse of Eastern European communism in 1989, and even prior to the appearance of Mikhail Gorbachev in Russia, the Communist government of Hungary allowed for more civil liberties and organized pluralism than was to be found elsewhere in the Soviet Bloc (except, perhaps, for Poland at certain times). The pace of reform accelerated in the 1980s, culminating in a series of round-table negotiations between the Communist government and representatives of the non-Communist opposition in 1989 (prior to the fall of the Berlin Wall) that paved the way for free democratic elections (see Linz and Stepan 1996: 296–316). Thus, in contrast with the BCP, which remained a conservative force firmly opposed to democratization until the collapse of Eastern European communism appeared inevitable, the Communist Party of Hungary had initiated significant economic, social, and political reforms, and played an active and positive role in the transition to democracy (see Elster 1996; Tökes 1997). Hence, it is not surprising to see that supporters of its successor Socialist Party are no less committed to democracy than are those who cast ballots for rival parties.[29]

Similarly, in Spain and Greece the principal parties of the right played leading roles in the dismantling of right-wing dictatorships and the founding of new democratic regimes. This was particularly noteworthy in Spain, since the leaders of the major conservative parties (Adolfo Suárez of the centre-right Unión de Centro Democrático and Manuel Fraga of Alianza Popular [AP], which transformed itself into the Partido Popular [PP] in 1989) had both served as high-ranking officials under the Franco regime. They and their parties were, nonetheless, unstinting in their support for democracy throughout the transition, and Suárez served as the principal orchestrator of the democratization process. In Greece, as well, Constantine Karamanlis (a prominent conservative politician in the semi-democratic regime that pre-dated the Colonels' coup in 1967) played an overwhelmingly dominant role in liquidating the right-wing regime and establishing a fully democratic system. In both cases, the parties of the right, which had traditionally been sceptical or downright hostile to democracy, established reputations as fully loyal democratic competitors at earlier stages in the transition, and their most prominent leaders as the founding fathers of new democracies.[30] And in Portugal, individuals who had been involved with Marcelo Caetano's half-hearted regime liberalization (such as Francisco Sá Carneiro and Francisco Pinto Balsemão) re-emerged during the revolutionary period as opponents of the left-wing junta which had seized power following the collapse of the Salazar/Caetano regime, and played key roles in establishing a new democratic regime in the course of Portugal's 'second transition'. In short, in these countries political leaders with roots in the predecessor authoritarian or semi-democratic regime were able to lead democratic parties and to become staunch supporters of the democratization process. As a result, the parties which they founded or joined could not be regarded as 'anti-system' or 'semi-loyal' in their commitment to democracy.

The 'transition and consolidation effect' hypothesis receives additional confirmation through analysis of mass-level behavioural measures, such as vote for anti-system or semi-loyal parties. In most established democracies, testing these relationships is difficult if not impossible: support for democracy is so widespread as to be taken for granted, the democratic regime is not under any real threat, and support for anti-system parties is so low as to preclude analysis using survey data based on samples of 1,000 to 1,500 respondents. Fortunately (from a purely methodological standpoint, that is!), two of the countries we have examined above are faced with or have previously confronted serious challenges to their survival.

One of these CNEP countries is Spain, whose new democracy was not fully consolidated until about 1982 (more than five years after coming into existence). In the general election of 1979, a coalition of extreme-right-wing anti-system parties received sufficient electoral support to send one of their own (the diehard *falangista* Blas Piñar) to the Congress of Deputies. Just two years later, moreover, a coup attempt came frighteningly close to seriously interrupting the consolidation process and perhaps terminating Spain's democratic regime. As can be seen in Table 2.11, a substantial plurality of those who voted for ultra-right-wing parties or coalitions in the 1979 Spanish election (Unión Nacional, Fuerza Nueva, the Falange Española, etc.) explicitly rejected the statement that 'democracy is the best form of government for a country like ours', while less than a quarter of those extreme-right-wing voters endorsed democracy. This was very substantially divergent from the pro-democracy stance of

Table 2.11 Relationship between support for democracy and vote for anti-system party

	Agree	It depends	Disagree	N
Spain 1979, DemBest: 'Democracy is the best form of government for a country like ours'.				
Vote for FN, UN, falange, etc.	24%	33%	44%	46
Vote for other parties	68	24	9	4,940

	Democracy preferable	They're all the same	Sometimes authoritarian best	N
Chile 1989 (2000 survey), DemAuth: 'Democracy is preferable to any other form of government'.				
Vote for Hernán Büchi	35%	12%	53%	97
Vote for other candidates	78	14	8	392
Chile 1999 (vote in first round), DemAuth: 'Democracy is preferable to any other form of government'.				
Vote for Joaquín Lavín	44%	16%	40%	201
Vote for other candidates	84	11	5	302
Italy 1983 (1985 survey), DemAuth: 'Democracy is preferable to any other form of government'.				
Vote for MSI	30%	13%	57%	53
Vote for other parties	78	9	13	1,344
Italy 1996, DemAuth: 'Democracy is preferable to any other form of government'.				
Vote for Alleanza Nazionale	73%	5%	22%	306
Vote for other parties	87	5	8	1,668

Sources: For Spain in 1979, DATA 1979 post-election survey; for Italy in 1985, The Four Nation Study; and for Italy in 1996 and Chile, CNEP surveys.

the overwhelming majority of voters (see Morlino and Montero 1995: 247).[31] While the overall level of support for these anti-system, extreme-right groups was quite low (reaching a peak of 2.1% of the vote in 1979 and virtually disappearing in subsequent elections), the mix of attitudes held by the largest party on the right, AP, also seemed to pose a potential challenge to the legitimacy of Spanish democracy, particularly since the AP surged in its share of the vote from 6.1 per cent in 1979 to 26.5 per cent just three years later, becoming the second largest party in Spain. In the late 1970s, 69 per cent of Spanish voters regarded the AP as *franquista*, and another 47 per cent believed that it was not a democratic party (Linz et al. 1981: 472; Montero 1993). In a 1979 survey, the mean 'feeling therm-ometer' evaluation of Franco among AP voters was a strongly favourable 7.5 (as compared with a hostile 1.9 among PSOE voters), and even as late as 1982, it was 6.7. Finally, its levels of support for democracy in their responses to the *DemAuth* ('democracy is preferable') item were a relatively low 48 per cent of its voters in both the 1979 and 1986 elections.[32] Over time, however, these potentially anti-system attitudes progressively declined, such that by the time of our 1993 survey, those who cast ballots for the Partido Popular (following the 'refounding' of the AP as the PP) held attitudes that were almost indistinguishable from those of the PSOE's electorate (Gunther and Montero 2001*a*). This evolution of opinion provides strong evidence of the importance of elite strategies and behaviour of party elites, and was due, in this specific case, to a substantial ideological moderation and explicit embrace of democracy on the part of the leaders of the AP/PP (see Alexander 2002: ch. 5).

The case of Chile provides further clear evidence of the strong rela-tionship between democratic support and preferences for parties and candidates who played sharply contrasting roles in democratic transition processes (Huneeus and Maldonado 2003). As can be seen in Table 2.11, only 35 per cent of CNEP survey respondents who claimed to have voted in the 1989 presidential election for Hernán Büchi, General Pinochet's former finance minister, while fully 53 per cent of pro-Pinochet voters openly embraced the notion that 'under some circumstances, an authori-tarian regime, a dictatorship, is preferable to a democratic system'. In sharp contrast, Chileans who voted for other candidates were about as supportive of democracy as citizens in fully consolidated democratic regimes, as can be seen in Table 2.1. What is most intriguing about support for democracy in Chile is that there has not been much of an increase in aggregate levels over the course of the first decade of democratic rule (see Table 2.1), and there remains a sizeable bloc of 'undemocratic' voters on the right.[33] This unusual pattern, we contend, was a product of Chile's unusual political trajectory throughout this period, particularly in so far as the former dictator did not unequivocally relinquish power and vanish from the scene following the convening of the first democratic elections. Instead, he remained a highly visible, polarizing political figure over the following decade, and used his position at the pinnacle of the armed forces hierarchy as a platform from which to issue menacing threats against the new democracy and its government. Given his anti-system stance and the continuing loyalty of a substantial segment of the Chilean electorate, the widespread lack of democratic support among voters on the right remained an important feature of Chilean political culture until at least as recently as the 1999–2000 presidential election. Despite the fact that Joaquín Lavín went to great lengths in the course of his presidential campaign to distance himself from Pinochet, he was unable to disso-ciate himself from that authoritarian legacy. Accordingly, an extraordi-narily low percentage of voters supporting him unequivocally supported democracy (similar findings are reported by Huneeus and Maldonado 2003).

Finally, the Italian case provides further corroboration of this pattern. While the 1996 Italian CNEP survey included too few of the 'discontent' and 'disaffection' variables as to have allowed for a parallel factor analysis, both that survey and one conducted in the mid-1980s did include the 'democracy is preferable' (*DemAuth*) item. Thus, we can explore the prin-cipal behavioural correlate of democratic support in a political system in which an explicitly anti-system party had received a sizable (and therefore analysable) number of votes.[34] The 1983 Italian election was held in the aftermath of a very turbulent period in the history of Italy's post-war democracy, in which the country's former prime minister, Aldo Moro, was kidnapped and murdered by anti-system terrorists of the left, and terrorist bombings by an anti-system faction on the right had killed or injured scores of Italian citizens. And at that time, the neo-fascist Movimento Sociale Italiano (MSI), which received 12.4 per cent of the vote (making it the third-largest party, behind only the Christian Democratic (DC) and the Communist PCI) was explicitly anti-system in its stance. The data in Table 2.11 show clearly that a substantial majority of MSI voters endorsed the proposition that 'under some circumstances, an authoritarian regime, a dictatorship, is preferable to a democratic system', while fewer than one-third selected the pro-democratic response option, in sharp contrast with over three quarters of those who supported other parties. Thus, the case of Italy in the early 1980s corroborates our findings from Spain and Chile that a lack of support for democracy is closely associated with electoral support for anti-system parties.

An examination of CNEP data from Italy over a decade later provides even clearer evidence consistent with this argument. By 1996, the MSI had been converted into a loyal democratic party, Alleanza Nazionale (AN), provoking a schism in which hard core neo-fascists departed to form the tiny Fiamma Tricolore-MSI. In large measure, this conversion was motivated by a realization that, in the aftermath of the breakdown of the long-standing party system following the election of 1994, and within the context of a consolidated democracy, an anti-system stance will alienate most voters and consign a party to permanent and powerless opposition status. Accordingly, the AN's leaders markedly altered their language and image, as well as the programmatic stands of the party, to cast themselves in the role of loyal democratic competitor. This strategy was remarkably successful: in 1992, the old MSI received just 5.4 per cent of the vote; but in the 1994 election, the new AN increased its share of the vote to 13.5 per cent (subsequently rising to 15.7% two years later), and was included in a coalition government for the first time in postwar Italian history (see Ignazi 1993; Tarchi 1997; Caciagli and Corbetta 2002). It is most important to note that the percentage of its supporters explicitly endorsing democracy (in response to an identical survey item) increased from 30 per cent of MSI voters in 1983 to 73 per cent of AN supporters in 1996. Again, it is not at all clear whether the respondent's fundamental attitude towards democracy affects or determines his or her voting choice, or if loyalty to a particular party induces respondents to learn and internalize new or different attitudes in accord with messages disseminated from above. But these data certainly indicate that there is a strong statistical association between the holding of anti-democratic attitudes and the casting of ballots for anti-system parties. Moreover, the marked change in attitudes towards democracy of supporters of the MSI/AN further suggests that political elites have some ability not only to modify their images and electoral appeals, but also to modify the attitudinal orientations of their supporters (see Slomczynski and Shabad 1999).

It is important to note that the preceding analysis of the behavioural correlates of a lack of support for democracy in some countries (i.e. voting for anti-system parties) and our speculative interpretation of widespread support for democracy in the others are both 'intermediation stories'. They assign to the most prominent and visible leaders of those secondary associations that are most directly relevant to democratic politics—political parties—a key role as points of reference and as agents of (re)socialization. While this does not involve active membership and participation on the part of most citizens, we strongly suggest that these elites and the partisan organizations that they lead have played important roles in fostering support for new democratic regimes in most of these cases, or in polarizing society into pro-democracy and anti-democratic or semi-loyal camps.

Intermediation and the Behavioural Consequences of Disaffection

To this point, we have focused our attention on the behavioural consequences of political discontent (i.e. voting against the incumbent party) and low levels of basic support for democracy (electoral support for anti-system parties). We now turn our attention to the correlates of disaffection, operationalized by constructing a scale out of responses to the 'politics too complicated', 'no influence', and 'politicians don't care' items whose interrelationships with the other types of attitudes towards democracy have been analysed earlier in this chapter. In Tables 2.8–2.10, we saw that disaffection was generally associated with a low level of 'involvement' with politics. In addition, the literature on 'social capital' referred to earlier in this chapter further suggests that membership in secondary organizations should also be expected to encourage involvement in politics. Thus, we shall examine the impact of both of these factors on individuals' predispositions towards active involvement in politics. However, the extensive research literature on political participation has repeatedly demonstrated that political involvement is a function of a number of other social attributes and experiences as well. In particular, in most countries better-educated citizens tend to participate more actively in politics than the uneducated or poorly educated; the young are typically much less involved in democratic politics than those in middle age; and women in many countries are less politically active than men. Thus, an analysis of the causal impact of disaffection, per se, as well as of membership in 'intermediary' secondary organizations on political involvement (conceptualized as interest in and knowledge about politics, as well as frequent discussion of politics with family, friends, neighbours, and co-workers) must introduce simultaneous controls for the impact on political behaviour of these other potentially causal variables as well. Accordingly, it is necessary to begin our exploration of the impacts of disaffection and various forms of intermediation on political involvement by including those other relevant factors as independent variables in multiple regression equations analysing, as the dependent variable, the

Table 2.12 Correlations (tau-b) with involvement in politics

	Age	Gender	Education	Disaffection	Non-political org. member	Political org. member
Spain	−.06**	−.21**	.28**	−.25**	.10**	.14**
Greece	−.10**	−.04	.01	.05	−.08*	−.14**
Uruguay	.03	−.11**	.26**	−.27**	.08**	.13**
Chile	.08*	−.13**	.07**	.02	.00	.02
Hungary	.13**	−.12**	.24**	−.17**	.12**	.07**
Bulgaria	−.01	−.16**	.42**	−.13**	.07**	.28**
Portugal	−.02	−.12**	.15**	−.24**	.09**	.11**

* Denotes significance (2-tailed) at .01; ** Denotes significance (2-tailed) at .001 or better.

level of an individual's involvement in politics. But before that multi-variate analysis can be undertaken, the zero-order correlations (tau-b) between political involvement and each of these potentially causal variables should be examined. These bivariate relationships can be seen in Table 2.12.

Consistent with the findings of a multitude of studies of political participation (for classic examples, see Nie, Powell, and Prewitt 1969; Milbrath and Goel 1977), education is positively and strongly associated with involvement in politics in most countries. Only in Greece is there no statistically significant relationship between education and involvement, while in Chile the relationship is weak, and in Portugal is only of moderate strength. Gender is also quite consistent as a predictor of political interest, information, and discussion: in all of these countries, women are less involved in politics than men, although, as we will see in the following round of multivariate analysis, the introduction into the equation of other independent variables—especially education—weakens this relationship, and in Hungary and Bulgaria those controls actually reverse it. Finally, with regard to the last of the sociodemographic control variables included in our analysis, it should be noted that age exerts a decidedly mixed influence on involvement in politics, and nowhere do we find the moderately strong positive relationship that is found in most established democracies. Contrary to the United States, for example, where the young exhibit very low levels of involvement in conventional forms of political involvement, in Greece and Spain young people are significantly more engaged in politics. Unlike in many established democracies, socialization experiences of the older age cohorts (such as the trauma of civil wars in both countries, and the political repression and anti-democratic propaganda under their authoritarian regimes) have discouraged active involvement in politics and encouraged much higher levels of political disaffection among older citizens (cf. Montero, Gunther, and Torcal 1997; Torcal, Gunther, and Montero 2002).

Disaffection is strongly and negatively associated with political involvement in all of these countries except Greece and Chile. These same two countries stand out as puzzling exceptions when we examine the relationship between organizational membership and involvement: in Chile, there is no statistically significant relationship with membership in either political or non-political organizations, while in Greece, belonging to both types of secondary associations actually leads to *lower* levels of involvement in politics. In all other countries, however, there are statistically significant relationships in the predicted direction. It is also noteworthy that in all of those countries except Hungary there is a stronger positive impact of membership in political organizations (parties and trade unions) than in non-political organizations, with which these correlations are relatively weak or of moderate strength. The difference between membership in political and non-political organizations is particularly strong in Bulgaria. From one perspective, the relationship between affiliation with political organizations and involvement in politics (operationalized here as reflecting interest in, knowledge about, and frequent discussion of politics) is obvious, verging on the tautological. From another perspective, however, these findings have significant implications for commonly stated claims growing out of the 'social capital' literature. It appears that the *type* of organization to which one belongs has an important bearing on whether group membership leads to higher levels of involvement in politics. When a member is surrounded by other individuals who are politically interested and motivated, and when the nature of the organization tends to channel consistent messages reinforcing one particular political view, then the mobilizational impact of group membership can be quite substantial. However, when the recruitment of group members is more random with regard to political viewpoint, and/or the basic purpose of the organization is irrelevant to politics (e.g. bowling leagues), then the positive relationship between group membership and political involvement is much weaker.

How do these bivariate relationships hold up when simultaneous controls for the impact of other variables are introduced? Table 2.13 presents the results of multiple regression analyses of political involvement (with the involvement scale serving as the dependent variable) and all of the aforementioned variables introduced as independent variables. The ability of these equations to predict respondents' levels of involvement

Table 2.13 Regression analysis of involvement in politics: Standardized beta coefficients[a] (and T scores)

	Spain	Greece	Uruguay	Chile	Hungary	Bulgaria	Portugal
Age	.13 (4.7)	-.13 (-3.7)	.11 (3.3)	.10 (3.1)	-.09 (-3.6)	.15 (4.7)	.12 (3.5)
Gender	-.14 (-5.7)	-.10 (-2.9)	.05 (1.5)	-.14 (-4.0)	.28 (10.6)	.14 (4.5)	-.08 (-2.8)
Education	.33 (11.7)	-.03 (.8)	.25 (7.4)	.13 (3.5)	.28 (9.9)	.47 (14.3)	.16 (4.6)
Disaffection	-.21 (-8.8)	.05 (1.5)	-.21 (-6.5)	.06 (1.8)	-.10 (-3.7)	-.08 (-2.5)	-.24 (-8.4)
Non-political org. member	.07 (3.0)	-.08 (-2.2)	.02 (.6)	-.06 (-1.7)	.04 (1.4)	.00 (.1)	.06 (1.9)
Political org. membership	.09 (3.8)	-.13 (-3.7)	.09 (2.8)	.00 (.3)	.00 (.1)	.16 (5.2)	.06 (2.0)
R	.462	.213	.392	.201	.394	.554	.342
R²	.213	.045	.153	.040	.155	.307	.117

[a] For unstandardized coefficients and standard errors, see Appendix.

in politics in Chile and Greece is very weak (explaining just 4% and 5%, respectively) of variance in political involvement. This may help to account for some puzzling sign reversals regarding the beta (β) scores for some key independent variables. We shall therefore focus our attention on the results for the other countries, whose R scores are much more robust, ranging from .342 to .554.

In Spain, Uruguay, Hungary, Bulgaria, and Portugal, political disaffection is consistently associated with low levels of political involvement, and in three of those countries the relationships are quite strong. In Spain, Uruguay and, especially, Bulgaria, membership in a politically relevant organization is substantially more strongly associated with political involvement, while in Portugal, membership in political and non-political organizations are roughly of equal strength. It is only in Hungary where the positive impact of both types of organizational membership largely vanishes when controls are imposed capturing the causal impact of other variables. Overall, however, it can be said that both political disaffection and organizational membership remain as statistically significant determinants of involvement in politics even after other variables (including the extremely powerful impact of education) are taken into account.

To this point, we have dealt with the impact of political disaffection in very general terms, using as the hypothetical dependent variable an aggregate scale of involvement with politics. Let us conclude this analysis of the consequences of disaffection by breaking down political involvement into several specific manifestations that are more directly linked to the three intermediation channels that are the principal focus of this book. As we shall see, this more detailed investigation leads to an intriguing and somewhat surprising conclusion regarding the *quality* of political participation of the disaffected.

The first column of figures presented in Table 2.14 clearly reveal that political disaffection is strongly (with the partial exception of Bulgaria) correlated with low levels of interest in politics, as measured by the respondent's self-report. This lack of interest is reflected in a strong propensity of the disaffected in all of these countries to read about politics in the newspapers less frequently (column 2). The same tendency is also reflected in exposure to news about politics through radio broadcasts (column 3), although the relationship is significantly stronger in some countries than in others. A much weaker and more variable association between disaffection and exposure to political news can be seen in the data presented in column 4: with the single exception of Hungary, the

Table 2.14 Correlations (tau-b) of disaffection scale with . . .

	Interest in politics	Newspaper reading	Listen to radio news	Watch news on television	Political information
Spain	−.27***	−.18***	−.13***	−.09***	−.18***
Uruguay	−.28***	−.15***	−.05	.00	−.20***
Greece	−.19***	−.19***	−.08**	−.01	−.17***
Portugal	−.28***	−.20***	−.18***	MD	−.10***
Hungary	−.28***	−.17***	−.11***	−.17***	−.19***
Bulgaria	−.10***	−.17***	−.03	−.03	−.10***
Chile	−.24***	−.18***	−.06**	−.11***	−.22***

Notes: No asterisk, not statistically significant.
* Significant at .05 level; ** Significant at .01 level; *** Significant at .001 level or better.

tau-b measuring the association between disaffection and an item measuring the frequency with which respondents follow political news on television is much weaker than is the case with regard to newspaper reading (Spain and Chile), or is not even statistically significant (Uruguay, Greece, and Bulgaria). In short, the disaffected are much less likely to regularly follow politics through newspaper reading than are other citizens, but in most countries are not so averse to television coverage of politics.

Given their lack of interest in politics and less frequent exposure to it through the newspapers, the disaffected are substantially less informed about politics than are other citizens. In all of the countries analysed in this study, the disaffected were less likely to correctly identify prominent political figures in a four-item 'information test' that was embedded in the CNEP questionnaires (see the data in column 5 of Table 2.14). This finding, in conjunction with those concerning exposure to specific sources of political information presented in columns two through four of this table, is consistent with an argument frequently set forth in the literature on the media and politics: as Ranney (1983), Sartori (1998), and Gunther and Mughan (2000a) have argued, television does a much poorer job than newspapers in conveying a large volume of policy-relevant information to citizens (with few exceptions, such as Great Britain). Thus, even though the disaffected are not much less likely to watch the news on television than other citizens, this exposure is insufficient to offset the 'information deficit' that results from their markedly less frequent newspaper readership.

Political disaffection is also consistently associated with a propensity to avoid involvement in discussions of politics, and are less likely to try to convince others to agree with their political views and support their preferred candidates (see the first two columns of Table 2.15). Thus,

Table 2.15 Behavioural correlates (tau-b) of disaffection

	Discuss politics	Convince others	Organization membership	Attend rallies	Work in campaign	Vote
Spain	−.25***	−.17***	−.05*	−.06*	−.06*	−.02
Uruguay	−.25***	−.15***	−.15***	−.13***	−.11***	+.09**
Greece	−.16***	−.11***	−.16***	−.04	−.10**	−.02
Bulgaria	MD	−.13***	−.12***	−.17***	−.16***	−.04
Hungary	MD	−.25***	−.13***	.11***	−.08**	−.16***
Portugal	−.25***	−.11***	−.06*	MD	−.13***	−.08**
Chile	−.23***	−.18***	−.04	−.09**	−.07*	−.02

Notes: No asterisk, not statistically significant.

* Significant at .05 level; ** Significant at .01 level; *** Significant at .001 level or better.

exposure to political stimuli through primary, face-to-face interpersonal networks is significantly lower among the disaffected. So, too, is the propensity to belong to one or more secondary associations (political or not). The tau-b statistics presented in column 3 of Table 2.15 indicate that this relationship holds up in all of these countries, although it is weaker in Chile, Portugal, and Spain. Not surprisingly, the disaffected are less likely in all countries to have attended a political rally during the election campaign and to have engaged in volunteer work on behalf of a party or candidate.

At the same time, it is noteworthy that the disaffected (except in Hungary and Portugal) are no less likely to participate in elections than are other citizens, and in Uruguay they actually vote with *greater* regularity. The consistent finding, across all countries, that the disaffected are less interested, less exposed to and informed about political news, less engaged in face-to-face discussions of politics and less likely to belong to a secondary association of any kind, while at the same time (except in Hungary and to a lesser extent in Portugal) they vote regularly in elections raises interesting questions about the *quality of democratic citizenship* in those countries where political disaffection is high.

Theoretical and Substantive Implications

The findings of this comparative analysis provide powerful and consistent evidence that fundamental support for democracy, satisfaction with the performance of the system, and attitudes and behavioural patterns reflecting disaffection from politics make up attitudinal domains that are both conceptually and empirically distinct from one another. Only in the case of Chile did we encounter evidence of a substantial overlap between items otherwise falling into the separate democratic support and discontent dimensions. But this statistical association, we argued, was an artefact of the particular alignment of partisan forces in Chile throughout all of the elections examined in this study, with the anti-system party serving as the principal party of opposition.[35] With regard to all other countries, as we saw in Tables 2.2 through 2.5, the relationships between measures of satisfaction with the political situation of the country and the economic situation, on the one hand, and support for democracy, on the other, were very weak. The link between dissatisfaction with 'how democracy works' in the respondent's country (which factor analyses indicated is associated with the economic and political satisfaction items in every country examined here) and measures of democratic legitimacy is somewhat stronger, but the strength of these bivariate relationships (tau-b statistics ranging from $-.09$ to $-.24$) is surprisingly modest given the logical overlap between the 'face content' of the two items. It is clear that support for democracy is not strongly linked to discontent in anything remotely approaching a deterministic relationship.

Our aggregate measure of discontent was much more strongly linked in most countries to a form of behaviour that is perfectly in keeping with the ground rules and the spirit of democracy. Excluding the aberrant cases of Bulgaria and Chile, there was a strong tendency for those who are dissatisfied to vote against the incumbent party, in accord with the basic tenets of democratic accountability.

Without exception, the principal behavioural correlate of the three-items making up the disaffection scale was a low level of involvement in politics. These strong and consistent empirical findings strengthen the construct validity of our concept of political disaffection, and they provide evidence of the autonomy of that attitudinal dimension from other types of democratic attitudes. In no country did either the exploratory or the confirmatory factor analyses place disaffection in the same attitudinal domain as support for democracy or political discontent, and bivariate measures of association between disaffection and attitudes belonging to the other two attitudinal domains were generally weak or, at best, moderate in strength.

Cross-sectional analysis of survey data collected at a single point in time does not make it possible to ascertain the causal origins of these sets of attitudes. Hence, we cannot go beyond mere speculation about how the flows of political information through various intermediation channels might have affected the acquisition of such orientations. Moreover, the very nature of these sets of concepts begs the fundamental question of direction of causality: for example, does a low level of exposure to political information through the media or face-to-face discussions with friends, family, etc. lead to the development of political disaffection; or does disaffection lead individuals to shun such exposure to political information? Accordingly, we cannot rely on these data to advance arguments about the origins of such political attitudes. But we can examine zero-order correlations between exposure to intermediation channels, on the one hand, and these sets of political attitudes, on the other, to determine if any empirical linkage exists, and on that basis undertake a preliminary assessment of the plausibility of some common hypotheses.

Frequent assertions concerning the crucial role played by membership in secondary associations and the underlying health of democracy appear, on this basis, to be exaggerated. In no country does membership in a non-political organization have a statistically significant zero-order relationship with fundamental support for democracy. Somewhat surprisingly, democratic support and affiliation with a political organization (party or trade union), *per se*, are only weakly linked in Bulgaria and Spain, and not at all associated in the other countries examined here. This is not to say that political organizations are unrelated to the development of attitudes supporting legitimacy, on the one hand, or challenges to the legitimacy of a democratic system, on the other. When we examine this relationship at the level of specific political parties we find that an anti-democratic orientation by a party's leaders is reflected in low levels of support for democracy in those countries with significant anti-system parties or movements. Again the question of direction of causality makes it impossible to go beyond the realm of speculation: it is possible that individuals who hold (for whatever reason) anti-democratic attitudes make their electoral choices on that basis and cast their votes for anti-system parties. But we suggest that a more plausible interpretation is that the roles played by party leaders and their supportive organizations during crucial stages of the transition to democracy have a lasting impact on fundamental support for democracy among their respective electorates. Moreover, we find that this causal hypothesis is very consistent with cross-national variations in patterns of support for democracy. Where a significant segment of the elite of the authoritarian predecessor regime opposed democratization and resisted pressures for political reform until at least the early stages of the regime-transition process, followers of those political leaders retained their anti-democratic orientations. And when this occurs (as in the cases of the BCP, General Pinochet, or Italian fascists), attitudes can be forged that are stubbornly resistant to change, even after the leaders of the party in question have abandoned their previous anti-democratic stance. Conversely, when prominent political elites of the predecessor regime are either completely neutralized (as in the cases of the Uruguayan military or 'the Colonels' in Greece) or play active and constructive roles in the democratization process (as in Spain, Hungary, Portugal, or Karamanlis in Greece), their respective sets of supporters can be re-socialized to fully and unequivocally embrace democracy. While this hypothesis cannot be directly tested with survey data collected in the 1990s, it is given considerable credence by the consistency of the cross-national patterns of variation examined in our analysis in conjunction with the differing regime-transition trajectories followed by these countries. And although it is not directly comparable to the analyses of the impact of organizational membership on politics that appear elsewhere in this book, we regard this interpretation as very much an 'intermediation story'.

We are thus presented with a mixed picture concerning the ability of political elites to alter their political images and, accordingly, their electoral fortunes. To some considerable degree (as in Spain and Italy), elites have been able to divorce themselves and their parties from anti-democratic stands with which they had previously been associated. However, the inability of comparable parties and elites in Bulgaria and Chile to distance themselves from the authoritarian past also suggests that these historical legacies may be difficult to erase from the minds of voters, despite their considerable efforts to embrace democracy. The linkage between the mass and elite levels of the political system thus appears to be substantially affected by a certain time lag that can serve as a constraint on elites' abilities to mould public opinion and behaviour.

These findings further suggest that the manner in which democratic consolidation has been conceptualized in previous work is consistent with political reality, and holds together as a coherent and politically meaningful concept. In that work (see, e.g. Gunther, Diamandouros, and Puhle 1995; Linz and Stepan 1996; Merkel 1998; Morlino 1998: ch. 2; Diamond 1999: ch. 3), it is argued that the concept of democratic consolidation is multidimensional, and has at its core the widespread acknowledgement of the legitimacy of democratic institutions at both the elite and mass levels. It was also asserted that the absence of significant support for anti-system parties could be used as one of several possible operational indicators of consolidation. Some critics have subsequently attacked the notion that the presence or absence of significant anti-system parties can or should be used in this manner (e.g. Encarnación 2000: 489). In this empirical study of support for democracy at the mass level in several new democratic systems, however, we have shown that support for anti-system parties and a lack of attitudinal support for democracy are closely interrelated. Thus, the empirical findings presented in this chapter reaffirm our initial conceptualization of democratic consolidation. They also suggest that the development of support for democracy at the mass level is an important task facing political elites and party leaders in new democracies. While the absence of fundamental support for democracy among large numbers of citizens may not, by itself, be sufficient to place the survival of a new democracy in doubt, the growth of an organized political group under the leadership of political entrepreneurs with an anti-system political agenda may pose a real threat to the regime. As we have seen, the absence of support for democracy at the mass level may be a prerequisite or facilitating condition for the development of an organized anti-system party with the capacity to pose a threat to the stability or even survival of a new democratic regime. Within the theoretical framework of this book, this appears as yet another intermediation story in which the political impact of an anti-democratic subculture is contingent on the emergence or prior existence of a political organization with the capacity to mobilize popular resistance against a regime.

Political discontent also emerges as a highly conditional variety of intermediation story. While aggregate levels of organizational membership have no consistent or significant impact on dissatisfaction with the performance of democracy, the incumbent government or the economy, membership in certain kinds of partisan groups is very strongly linked to this concept. Indeed, as we hypothesized at the beginning of this chapter, assessments of these conditions are filtered through strong partisan lenses. Long-standing supporters of the incumbent party are much more likely to favourably evaluate these dimensions of government performance, while those who identify with the opposition are predisposed to negatively assess the political situation of the country, the condition of the economy and, more broadly, the performance of democracy. The principal behavioural correlate of political discontent—vote against the incumbent party—is also explicitly focused on a particular intermediation channel, although in this context it serves very much as a 'dependent variable'.

Perhaps the most important finding derived from the preceding analysis for the stability and prospects for survival of new democracies is that dissatisfaction with current economic and/or political conditions is unrelated to fundamental support for democracy. This finding, in turn, provides reassuring evidence that voters, and citizens in democratic systems more generally, are more sophisticated than some one-dimensional approaches to the study of politics would suggest. They suggest that economic-reductionist arguments about individual behaviour and regime survival may be predicated on excessively simplistic models of human behaviour. By positing, for example, that dissatisfaction with the current state of the economy or with the performance of the incumbent government will undermine support for democracy, per se, they do an injustice to the somewhat more sophisticated responses that are reflected in these data. In accord with democratic theory, discontent leads citizens to cast ballots in a manner intended to replace the incumbent government with a new set of elected officials. But there is little evidence here that dissatisfaction with economic performance, with the performance of the incumbent, with the political situation of the country, or even with the way democracy is working at that particular time leads citizens to withdraw their support for democratic forms of governance in general or for the current democratic regime, in particular. In short, most citizens who are angry about how the current government is running the country tend to respond by voting to 'throw the bums out', rather than by rooting for the colonels and their tanks to overturn democracy and replace it with an authoritarian regime. Citizens, in these democratic systems at least, are not that simplistic and illogical.

But the preceding analysis has also shown that not all citizens are alike, and that some may take the responsibilities of voters as portrayed in 'civics textbooks' more seriously than others. Conversely, those whose political orientations fall within the political disaffection syndrome are less engaged in political life in a number of ways that are directly relevant to intermediation processes. They are less interested in politics, and follow political news less frequently through the media—especially through the normally more 'information-dense' print media. Accordingly, they are much less well informed about politics. They are also less involved in various forms of political and quasi-political activities, including discussion of politics, membership in political organization, work for political campaigns, and attendance in political rallies. Seen from one perspective, their self-marginalization from most aspects of political life means that their lack of political knowledge may not have adverse impact on the functioning of the democratic system. There is, however, one form of political participation that may have a marked impact on the broader political system: the disaffected and uninformed vote as regularly as other citizens in Chile, Greece, Spain, and Bulgaria, and in Uruguay they vote with greater regularity than those who are not disaffected. Their systematic uninvolvement in every other participatory mode may undermine the quality of democracy by strengthening the inequality of governmental outcomes, broadening the gap between citizens and representatives, and weakening the accountability and responsiveness of democratic governments.

3

The mass media in third-wave democracies: gravediggers or seedsmen of democratic consolidation?

Rüdiger Schmitt-Beck and Katrin Voltmer

Beginning in the mid-1970s, a 'third wave' of democratization (Huntington 1991) brought into existence a large number of new democracies, first emerging in Southern Europe and Latin America, and eventually spreading to Eastern Europe. However, the stability and viability of many of these new democracies still remains fragile and vulnerable. Democratic consolidation is a complex process with many dimensions, one of the most crucial being the establishment of widespread popular support. Since citizens' experience with their political system is to a large extent a mediated experience, the way that the mass media perform this intermediation role can be of decisive importance.

Some observers assert that the media exert a negative influence on the stabilization of democracy. Bennett (1998), for example, states that the media may have contributed to the breakdown of the former autocratic regimes, but are rather obstructive to the consolidation of the new order. Drawing on assumptions that have been claimed by the 'video malaise' theory (Robinson 1976), it is hypothesized that especially in new democracies, where citizens lack any lasting experiences with the working of democratic politics, the negativism of media reporting may feed distrust and alienation. Paradoxically, even media that perfectly perform their democratic role may contribute to alienating new democracies' citizens from this regime, since these citizens lack the necessary experience with democratic politics that would enable them to cope with the picture of politics that is provided for them by news media serving as watchdogs of the democratic political process (Scammell and Semetko 2000).

However, in the established democracies of North America and Western Europe, the notion of media 'malaise' has in recent years been challenged by a more optimistic view that puts the emphasis on the information function of the mass media. The alternative hypothesis states that the mass media have 'democratized' political information, making it access-ible to all citizens regardless of class and education. The positive effects of the media on democratic orientations, most notably on cognitive com-petence and mobilization, have recently been corroborated in empirical studies conducted in Western democracies (Newton 1999c; Norris 2000c). In the context of new democracies, the information function of the media can be assumed to be of even higher relevance as old values have lost their validity and alternative agents of socialization are notoriously weak.

In this chapter we aim to find evidence whether and, if so, in which way the media matter for the emergence of a political culture that is supportive for the consolidation of new democracies that have emerged at various stages of the third wave of democratization. Do the mass media in these countries contribute to the emergence and stabilization of political cultures that are congruent to these nations' recently inaugurated demo-cratic institutional orders? Or are they, to the contrary, undermining the cultural foundations of these fledgling democracies? Is the impact of the media the same for orientations towards different components of political systems, or does it vary? Further, it is of great interest whether, with respect to these questions, similar trends are visible in all new democra-cies, or whether we find instead a variety of country-specific relationships. In particular, the stage of the transformation process may make a differ-ence; perhaps the media play a different role in new democracies that just recently adopted democratic regimes, and in countries that for a longer period have travelled the road of democratic consolidation. One might also hypothesize that differences in the nature of the autocratic systems from which the process of democratization originated create specific tra-jectories with regard to the importance of the media for democratic con-solidation. Of similar interest is the role of different media: Do patterns of relationships vary, depending on what type of media we are looking at? Are some media more important than others? Are there counterbalancing forces at work with regard to mass media, where some media exert positive effects, while others have more problematic consequences for democratic attitudes?

We address these questions by analysing data from nationally representative surveys of voters in six new democracies of the 'third wave' of democratization: Greece, Spain, Uruguay, Chile, Hungary, and Bulgaria, collected in the situational context of national parliamentary or presidential elections during the 1990s.[1] In our empirical analysis, we concentrate on those mass media that usually are considered the most important: the daily press and television news. To prepare the ground for these analyses, the following sections review the debate on the relationship between political culture and mass communication in the light of research from established Western democracies—with special attention to the specific conditions of new democracies—and discuss the specificities of media systems and media politics in new democracies. We then present the findings and implications of our empirical analyses.

Mass Media and Political Culture

Drawing on Almond and Verba's seminal work, we may define the political culture of a country very generally as 'the particular distribution of patterns of orientations towards political objects among the members of the nation'. Such orientations refer to different aspects of these objects and can be of cognitive, evaluational, or affective content (Almond and Verba 1963: 14–15). The particular political culture of a country can be supportive of its institutional order or can be antithetical to it. In the first case, the stability of this political order is assumed to be sustained, whereas the latter case represents a situation of tension, where the existing institutional architecture rests on uncertain foundations and may quickly be called into question and erode if serious challenges arise.

Although political culture research over the last decade has seen a renaissance, not the least spurred by the recent wave of democratization of formerly autocratic political systems (Almond 1993; Diamond 1993; Kaase 1994), one of the main problems which has plagued this research paradigm from the beginning still remains unsolved. Political culture research lacks a systematic and agreed-upon notion of its core concept that clearly demarcates which individual orientations are to be considered relevant for political culture and which are not, and how they combine into a coherent political culture (Kaase 1983; Reisinger 1995). Yet, as Reisinger (1995) notes, studying specific dimensions of political culture is a worthwhile effort in its own right.

The analyses presented by Gunther, Montero, and Torcal in the preceding chapter underline the importance of focusing on political culture as a multi-dimensional concept. They distinguish three important dimensions of political culture: Democratic Support, roughly corresponding to Easton's (1965, 1975) notion of diffuse support and relating to the new regime's legitimacy; Political Discontent, measuring degrees of satisfaction with the performance of the political system; and Political Disaffection, tapping into a general disengagement from politics. In this chapter, we push this dimensional perspective somewhat further, by making distinctions among six separate orientations of citizens towards aspects of political systems and their elements, including their own role as members of these political systems. While fully compatible with the Gunther–Montero–Torcal classification, we apply a more item-specific analytical framework.

As a starting point for our analyses we use a heuristic distinction drawn by Almond (1990), which in turn is based on Almond and Verba's classical taxonomy of objects of orientation (Almond and Verba 1963: 15–16). Almond conceived of three broad classes of orientations that he considered relevant building blocks of the political cultures of societies: 'system culture', consisting of orientations towards the political system as a whole; 'process culture', that is, orientations of citizens towards the self as political actor, as well as towards organized and institutional political actors involved in the process of generating demands for the political system and of transforming these into policy outcomes; and finally 'policy culture', that is, orientations towards this policy output itself (Almond 1990: 153). Another useful conceptual framework is Easton's distinction among three different, hierarchically ordered levels of political objects at which citizens' political orientations can be directed: the 'authorities', that is, the incumbents currently occupying the political roles within a particular political system; the political 'regime', that is, the specific institutional order as it exists in the political system and its fundamental values and norms, and the political 'community', consisting of the members of a political system that are bound together by a political division of labour (Easton 1965: 171–219). Closely connected to this notion of hierarchically ordered objects is the distinction between 'specific support', concerning satisfaction with a political system's performance and referring especially to the office-holders and the structure of the political regime, and 'diffuse support', which refers to the general evaluation of the abstract notion of a democratic political order and the 'higher' levels of the political system (Easton 1975).

Consequences of Mass Media for Political Culture: Malaise or Mobilization?

So far, political scientists studying democratic transitions have largely ignored the role of the media in processes of regime change and the subsequent consolidation of democracy. Gunther and Mughan's volume (2000*a*) is one of the few exceptions that not only contrasts the role of the media in new and established democracies, but also employs an interdisciplinary approach integrating findings from both communications studies and political science. However, there is still a marked lack of empirical research on the relationship between mass communication and individual orientations towards the newly established democratic regime. Hence, it remains an open question whether media influence can be expected to be beneficial or detrimental to the consolidation of a democratic political culture in new democracies. This problem is by no means confined to new democracies. On the contrary, the question as to whether the apparent erosion of public confidence in political institutions and declining civic engagement has been caused by the media has recently re-entered the academic discussion in established democracies. Putnam (1995*a*, 1995*b*, 2000), like many other observers, blames the media as at least partly responsible for the erosion of social capital, in so far as they foster individualization and the tendency to withdraw from public life. With regard to the media in the United States, Patterson (1993, 1998) claims that media reporting is characterized by a massive anti-political bias. Severely distrusting politicians, and competing with their news management activities in order to maintain control of news content, reporters resort to an aggressive style of 'attack journalism' that is assumed to be one of the major sources of increasing cynicism about democratic institutions and public officials among citizens of established democracies (also see Zaller 1998). Others claim that modern media create an unrealistic image of politics that resembles horse races and game shows rather than the endeavour to solve the problems that plague modern societies, again contributing to increased political distrust (Cappella and Jamieson 1997). Yet another strand of argument focuses on the behaviour of politicians as presented by the media. Current styles of covering the news give greater visibility to aggressive attacks among politicians rather than to constructive deliberations on the part of political elites, creating an image of politics that has more to do with fighting for its own sake than with finding solutions to the problems that face modern societies (Kepplinger 1998).

When it comes to empirical evidence, however, the existing literature provides much less unequivocal results than these assertions may suggest. While some studies find negative effects, others find only positive relationships or no effects at all. Most of these inquiries are single-country studies of American voters. Robinson (1976) was one of the first scholars who empirically investigated the negative link between media coverage and political trust, which he termed video malaise. Based on laboratory experiments and representative surveys he found that persons who rely mainly on television for political information reveal significantly lower degrees of internal efficacy and institutional trust than those whose media diet was more varied. While Robinson only used exposure measures, Miller, Goldenberg, and Erbing (1979) were able to specify the exact amount of negative coverage that any single respondent was exposed to by linking content analysis data with survey data. Their results support the general assumption of media malaise, though media-induced distrust was confined to specific policies—that is, the output of the political system—while the evaluation of political institutions remained unaffected. Recently, Cappella and Jamieson (1997) systematically varied format characteristics of television news in experiments and found significant negative effects on individual political competence and on trust in the political process and political actors. They argue that framing politics in terms of a tactical manipulation of political discourse contributes to the alienation of the public from politics.

The malaise hypothesis has recently been challenged by proponents of a mobilization theory that assumes positive effects of the media on political involvement. In fact, as an extensive review of the existing literature reveals (Wolling 1999), most empirical studies find a beneficial impact of the media on political attitudes. Mobilization theory emphasizes the importance of information for mass politics. Never before have citizens had access to such an amount and scope of information as today. What media critics view as a negative feature of media information—for example, the trivialization of politics—supporters of the mobilization hypothesis regard as an opportunity for 'low-salience learning' that enables even normally passive and apathetic citizens to get involved in politics (Neuman 1986: 132–57). Dalton (1996) shows that a remarkable 'cognitive mobilization' of mass publics can be observed in advanced Western democracies over the last decades along with the spread of mass media, especially television.

Using British survey data, Newton (1999c) scrutinizes the empirical evidence regarding media malaise and media mobilization. His results largely support the latter. Following the news, whether on television or in newspapers, increases the cognitive competence of the respondents, while there are no, or only weak, negative effects on orientations towards the political system. Norris (2000*a*, 2002*b*) reports similar results for a wide range of established European and non-European democracies. She assumes a 'virtuous circle' at work, arguing that the causal relationship between use of the news media and civic engagement is more likely to be interactive rather than unidirectional. Information stimulates the appetite for more information, which increases the motivation to actively take part in the political process. No comparable vicious circle, involving negative reinforcement of the inactives, could be found. Studies that distinguish among types of media seem to suggest that different media have different effects. In particular, highly informative, more serious media seem to increase citizens' political self-confidence and involvement and thus have a mobilizing effect, whereas more entertaining ways of presenting political content have no or perhaps even detrimental effects on political attitudes (Holtz-Bacha 1990; Schmitt-Beck 1998; Aarts and Semetko 2003).

These contradictory empirical results are puzzling. Taking a closer look at the design of various studies in this field, it becomes clear that operationalizations of both dependent and independent variables vary considerably, which might contribute to the incoherent picture.

With regard to the *dependent variables* operationalized in these studies, it soon becomes clear that a wide range of different concepts have served as indicators for malaise or mobilization, respectively. Among these are internal and external efficacy, participation, knowledge, democratic legitimacy, satisfaction with government, evaluation of candidates, and a variety of idiosyncratic constructs (see Wolling 1999). One could argue, however, that the impact of the media, both in terms of strength and direction (positive/negative) of effects, differs depending on whether it is related to cognitive, attitudinal, or behavioural variables. Many authors inspect only one particular type of effect and then wrongly generalize their results to any other dimension of political orientations. Hence, most of this research addresses various media effects in a piecemeal fashion and does not attempt to systematically place it within a more elaborate, multidimensional concept of political culture. On the whole, the literature is characterized by a certain arbitrariness in the selection of dependent variables, and by a low degree of theoretical and conceptual integration.

Closer inspection of the literature reveals that the malaise hypotheses have mostly been proposed with reference to specific orientations towards aspects of the political regime—that is, the institutional order,

Objects of orientations	Direction of effects	
	Negative	Positive
Self as political actor	Apathy	Mobilization
Political regime	Malaise	Support

Figure 3.1 Media effects on orientations towards aspects of political culture

and its basic values and normative foundations. Mobilization hypotheses, in contrast, have mostly concerned people's views and feelings towards their own role as citizens such as political involvement and participation. Figure 3.1 classifies these hypotheses into a simple two-dimensional framework, defined by the objects of political orientations and the direction of the proposed media effects. It becomes clear that, in principle, two more hypotheses may be proposed which so far have not attained similar importance within the literature. The combination of the two dimensions of political orientations and possible positive or negative media effects logically yields two sets of opposing hypotheses concerning the impact of the media on political culture: With regard to citizens' orientations towards their own political competencies, a positive role of mass media would contribute to their mobilization into the political system, as maintained by the literature referred to above. In addition, there is also the possibility of a negative role, leading to depoliticization and apathy. With respect to the regime as the object of political attitudes, it has mostly been hypothesized that media reporting may contribute to political malaise and alienation. But by implication there is also the alternative possibility that the media contribute to a strengthening of political support.

When we turn our attention to the *independent variables* that have been included in these studies, it turns out that the literature holds different assumptions as to which media-related factors are responsible for changes in political orientations. The video malaise hypothesis claims that it is the specific format in which the media depict politics that causes political cynicism. Accordingly, political coverage is characterized by negativism, sensationalism, and conflict while the substance of political issues is largely neglected. Political actors are portrayed as corrupt and unresponsive to the needs of ordinary citizens while political institutions appear as inefficient and biased towards the privileged classes. By presenting political news in this manner, the media contribute to popular disenchantment, mistrust, and withdrawal from active participation. These media formats are closely linked to so-called news values—that is, professional standards of the media as to how to select and present political events. While news values are general criteria underlying the news production of all media, it is assumed that television news is more strongly characterized by negative characteristics than is political coverage in print media. The potential difference between audio-visual and print media is therefore another aspect that has to be considered when analysing their effects on political orientations.

However, it may be difficult to blame the media for the way in which they portray political matters since media formats can partly be traced back to the normative assumptions of the media's role in democratic societies. Journalists regard themselves—and are viewed by their audience as such—not only as information providers, but also as watchdogs whose task it is to control the government and to bring any abuses of power to the attention of the public (Janowitz 1975; Weaver 1998). This view is deeply rooted in democratic theory that locates the media within the system of checks and balances (Kelley and Donway 1990). From a normative point of view it is hard to draw the distinction between, on the one hand, investigative journalism that provides citizens with information that enables them to oust an obviously ineffective government, and, on the other hand, destructive negativism that systematically undermines the legitimacy of democratic institutions. These considerations apply even more to new democracies. Under autocratic rule, the media's role was restricted to providing the regime with public support, while freedom to publish unfavourable news and to criticize politicians is one of the main gains of democratic transformation. It is therefore unclear how citizens in new democracies regard journalistic negativism, given their previous experiences with political repression and heavy-handed efforts to manipulate public opinion. Accordingly, critical news reporting might be widely interpreted as an indicator of the working of the democratic system rather than of its deficiencies.

The alternative approach of conceptualizing the media as a force that shapes political orientations places greater emphasis on the *content* of political coverage. Authors who found empirical evidence for the mobilization hypothesis typically argue that media information enables citizens to acquire valuable knowledge about political matters regardless of the format in which the information is presented. This knowledge fosters the feeling of having control over the environment and empowers people to take an active part in politics. Holtz-Bacha (1990) looks at the other side of the coin in expanding the analysis to include the effects of entertaining media content. Distinguishing between information-seeking and entertainment-seeking media users, she finds that video malaise effects are caused by a high exposure to entertainment programmes rather than by exposure to political news as had been argued by Robinson.

Finally, there is a third argument regarding the media's role helping to shape the political culture of a society. This involves the particular historical and societal *context* in which political communication and political opinion formation take place. Usually, political orientations are acquired in a long-term process of political socialization in which the media are only one of several socialization agents, most importantly primary groups and intermediary political organizations. This argument becomes important when taking into account that media consumption can be seen as a process of actively making sense of received content rather than of passively absorbing it. If the meaning of media messages is to some degree constructed by the audience (and, thus, in the eye of the beholder), then the experiences of this audience become a crucial intervening variable for media effects. Obviously, the experiences of citizens from old and new democracies differ dramatically, with potentially important implications for the role of mass communications in shaping political culture. In new democracies, the continuous process of political socialization is dramatically interrupted by the breakdown of the old regime involving not only a change of the institutional structure but also the erosion of the value system on which the old system has been resting. Bennett's argument (1998) quoted in the introduction of this chapter refers to the unique and highly volatile situation in democratic transitions. While in established democracies the media might have only little impact on political orientations of citizens, new democracies are assumed to be much more vulnerable to detrimental media influences because democratic values and beliefs are still malleable, and few individuals have had experience to draw on to check and evaluate negativistic and critical media messages.

Media and Media Policy in Third-Wave Democracies

As Gunther and Mughan (2000*b*) argue, the degree to which the media are able to fulfil their democratic role must be conceptualized as a complex interaction between macro- and micro-level conditions. In order to understand the impact of the media on the consolidation of a democratic political culture, it is therefore important to clarify the similarities and differences of the specific structural contexts in which political communication takes place. In this section, we survey the countries in our sample with the objective of providing crucial background information on the transformation the media systems of third-wave democracies that has taken place in the course of democratization. Indeed, as we see, both the nature of democratic transitions and the structures of media systems in these countries have differed considerably.[2] One important distinction regarding the type of predecessor autocratic regime involves systematic differences between the Latin American and Southern European cases, on the one hand, and the Eastern European cases on the other hand (Linz and Stepan 1996; Offe 1997). Although in each of these non-democratic regimes the media were submitted to strict state censorship, the function assigned to the media under communist rule differed systematically from that under military dictatorship or corporatist-authoritarian regimes. The different functional roles of the media were reflected in the institutional arrangements through which political communication took place. These differing historical trajectories would continue to affect media policy even after democratic regimes were set in place.

With regard to the East European predecessor regimes, it is evident that the revolutionary aspirations of communism entailed massive indoctrination efforts that went far beyond mere suppression of deviant opinions. In fact, the legitimacy of communist regimes depended heavily on the mobilization and politicization of the population. Lenin's famous dictum of the press being not only a 'collective propagandist and collective agitator', but also a 'collective organizer' (Inkeles 1951: 153–74) expresses the extent to which communist leaders employed the media to establish and maintain the regime. Therefore, both the press and broadcasting were owned by the state, the Communist Party or its subordinate mass organizations to allow for direct interference with news coverage. Since the goal of communist propaganda was to re-educate the masses and to mobilize active support for an ideology that proclaimed a new society and the ideal of a new communist personality, it went far beyond the mere stabilization of the existing power structure. Hence, media content was constantly highly politicized both in terms of the amount of political information and in its attempt to interpret current events in the light of Marxist-Leninist ideology. However, with the increasingly apparent failure of the system to deliver economic wealth and human development the ideological manipulation of the media yielded unexpected side effects (Gunther and Mughan 2000b). The more people became aware of the contrast between their own day-to-day experiences and the idealized picture portrayed by the media, the more they lost their faith in the regime and its official ideology. As a consequence, governments gradually loosened their grip on the media coverage and allowed for more entertainment content, especially in broadcasting, to meet the not quite so revolutionary needs of the audience (Jakubowicz 1995).

After the collapse of communist regimes in Eastern Europe, rapid privatization of the press was largely undisputed among policymakers. Countries that promised to create thriving consumer markets, such as Hungary, attracted international media tycoons who acquired considerable parts of the press. In contrast, in economically less successful countries, like Bulgaria, the press remained highly dependent on state subsidies (Splichal 1992; Bruck 1993; O'Neil 1997). Western media companies also introduced a newspaper type that had been unknown in Eastern Europe so far: the tabloid press. Tabloids have been especially successful in Bulgaria, but also account for about a quarter of the circulation in Hungary (Gulyas 1998). Although journalistic professionalism has clearly improved over the last decade, news reporting is frequently criticized for not meeting basic quality standards. The norm of separating facts and opinion is widely unknown so that the news is often openly biased in favour of particular political parties or politicians. Furthermore, journalists are blamed for having adopted an excessively critical and polemical style of dealing with politicians (Johnson 1998; Voltmer 2000).

In contrast with the transformation of the press, broadcast regulation became one of the most controversial policy areas in post-communist countries. Politicians found themselves almost entirely dependent on the media to communicate to voters, in large measure due to the fact that decades of one-party rule had made intermediary organizations (which can serve as an important channel of information flow between political elites and citizens) notoriously weak. At the same time, broadcast media were determined to liberate themselves from state control and the firm grip of political instrumentalization. The widely used term 'media war' reflects the intensity of this struggle. In Hungary, it took five years for the parliament to agree on a new broadcasting law; in Bulgaria, the struggles concerning a new regulatory framework for the broadcasting media went on even longer and included several unsuccessful attempts to enact a new legislation (see Gergely 1997 and Sükösd 2000 for Hungary; Tzankoff 2002 for Bulgaria; Jakubowicz 1996 and Milev 1996 for other post-communist countries). Even under the new regulations, broadcasting remains highly vulnerable to political interference (Popescu and Tóka 2002). The newly licenced private stations could have provided a counterbalance, but they chose to offer overwhelmingly commercialized entertainment programming. In sum, media systems in post-communist countries are characterized by a coincidence of almost untamed market forces in the press and governmental dominance in broadcasting (Splichal 1994: 32).

Turning to the Southern European and Latin American countries that had been subjected to 'rightist' forms of authoritarian rule, we find a different pattern of relationship between the media and the political system. Unlike communism, these autocratic regimes lacked coherent ideologies and had no revolutionary aspirations to create a new society. Thus, state propaganda, although frequently employing strong anti-communist rhetoric, was largely confined to the legitimization of the status quo. Depoliticization and acquiescence rather than broad mass mobilization was the preferred strategy to secure power (Linz, Stepan, and Gunther 1995). Consequently, censorship and state control over mass communications were primarily used to exclude oppositional and critical viewpoints from the public agenda while at the same time lowering citizens' involvement in politics (Fox 1988; Gunther, Montero, and Wert 2000).

In Southern Europe, where the transition to democracy took place before the emergence of new communication technologies that paved way for the proliferation and commercialization of broadcasting, the government retained considerable control over public television even after democratization. Particularly in Spain, political coverage tends to be biased in favour of the political party in power, although the private stations are no less one sided with regard to the same or to other parties. In Greece and Spain, the Southern European countries of our sample, television is now highly commercialized. Due to its close relationship with the government and the subsequent erosion of credibility, public television has lost substantial audience shares in both of the two countries (Rospir 1996; Papathanassopoulos 2000).

The situation in Latin America is somewhat different. Here the modernization and privatization of the media, in particular television, took place under autocratic rule, and in fact was even promoted by the regime (Tironi and Sunkel 2000). However, similar to ideological manipulation in communist countries, the commercialization of the media yielded unintended consequences in the long run. The media's participation in a globalized market has led to the importation of much foreign programming, particularly from the United States. Although this was limited to entertainment shows, the commercialization of the media made it more difficult for the regime to maintain control over the content disseminated to the audience. Hence, the lack of ideology and private ownership of the media can be assumed to have contributed to a gradual pluralization of ideas in the public sphere. Since commercialization of the media took place under the old regime, the institutional structure of the media remained largely unchanged throughout the transition to democratic, thereby avoiding the devastating conflicts over media policy which characterized the transformation of media institutions in post-communist countries. However, this is not to say that Latin American media are free from state intervention. Threats issued against critical media outlets and 'negotiated' news coverage remain recurrent problems of political communication.

While private ownership might have facilitated the erosion of the old regime and the transition process itself, some authors argue that the excessive commercialization of mass communication constitutes a severe obstacle to institution building and successful consolidation of Latin American democracies (Skidmore 1993; Waisbord 1995). Television programming consists almost exclusively of entertainment, at the cost of providing political information to the public, and even news programmes devote a good deal of time to non-political topics. There has also been a growing obsession of the media with political scandals and corruption, reflecting an alarming 'consolidation of a muckraking ethos' (Waisbord 1995: 221). This journalistic practice suits the media's need for sensational stories while at the same time allowing them to portray themselves as the guardians of democracy, protecting the people from power-hungry politicians. As similar trends in the new democracies in Eastern Europe suggest, in a situation where years of censorship and media manipulation has undermined their credibility, the media try to establish themselves as an independent political force by emphasizing an adversarial rather than a mediating role in the political process.

Furthermore, election campaigns are increasingly characterized by massive 'Americanization', involving the professionalization of media strategies, the decline of partisan messages, and growing personalization (Espindola 2002). The latter, in particular, may contribute to further aggravating the problem of weak institutionalization of key political structures such as political parties and parliament. Over the past decade, Latin American countries have seen the rise of numerous populist candidates who managed to win elections without the support of political parties. However, it has to be kept in mind that the two countries of our sample, Chile and Uruguay, differ from most other Latin American countries in that party politics still persists and political parties are still able to mobilize broad popular support (Tironi and Sunkel 2000).

This brief overview of the processes of media transformation in the differing contexts of democratization demonstrates that both the institutional structure of the media, in particular broadcasting, and the quality of political information imparted to the citizens varies depending on the media's role under the old regime. However, in spite of the path dependency of media transformation there is also a general pattern of highly adversarial and sensational news reporting evolving across different countries. This development can be attributed to a coincidence of a general acceleration of commercialization and globalization of the media industry over the past two decades, on the one hand, and the specific situation journalists find themselves in after the demise of authoritarian rule, on the other hand. While the former is a worldwide trend that affects virtually every country, the latter evolves from the particular conflicts of the transformation of political communication in new democracies when a new balance between state interests and press freedom has to be negotiated.

The Design of the Study

In the following section, we analyse whether, to what extent, and in what direction political orientations of the citizens of these six new democracies vary in relation to the intensity and patterns of these individuals' contacts with mass media's political reporting. We base this analysis on data collected from surveys conducted in the context of national parliamentary or presidential elections that took place in the late 1990s. All countries used the same core questionnaire items to ensure comparability. Minor deviations are confined to national particularities or additional questions.

The principal aim of this study is to determine whether mass media are relevant for the development of political culture in new democracies: Is exposure to mass media of any import for new democracies' citizens' orientations towards their political systems? Our main concern is, of course, to determine if the role of the media is beneficial or detrimental for the creation of a political culture supportive of democratic institutions and practices, as suggested by the media malaise and mobilization hypotheses discussed earlier.

Our dependent variables are six different types of orientations towards the political system and the roles of citizens. We are also interested in intervening factors that moderate this role of the media. They involve the extent to which the patterns of influence are the same in all new democracies, or whether there are systematic differences between countries. Finally, we shall examine the extent to which the type of communications medium may also be of relevance.

The Dependent Variables: Six Orientations Towards Political Systems

In order to overcome the methodological shortcomings and inconsistent findings discussed earlier, some of which resulted from the arbitrary selection of dependent variables, we will focus our analysis on six specific orientations taking into account their status in a general conceptual framework of political culture (see Appendix 3.2 for details of operationalization). Four of these orientations are closely related to the three general dimensions of Democratic Support, Political Discontent and Political Disaffection discussed in the chapter by Gunther and Montero. Seen from a different perspective, three of these orientations concern citizens' orientations towards their own political roles, while the other three involve evaluations of various aspects of the political regime.

Citizens' political engagement is an important correlate of the Political Disaffection dimension (as analysed in the preceding chapter) and a crucial aspect of the viability of democracy. Hence, we shall explore the extent to which citizens' media exposure affects their passive and active involvement in political affairs. Citizens' *interest in politics* is a passive form of involvement. Interested citizens are eager to keep informed and closely monitor political life (van Deth 1990; Gabriel and van Deth 1995). We operationalize this variable by means of a measure of respondents' self-reported level of interest. *Political knowledge* is another form of cognitive involvement. Individuals who are unaware of what is going on in politics and lack sufficient understanding of their political system and its functioning, cannot properly perform their roles as democratic citizens (Delli Carpini and Keeter 1996). To measure respondents' political knowledge, a test of their ability to correctly identify a number of political office-holders is used.

While interest and knowledge are essentially passive forms of involvement, *political participation* is the means by which individual citizens can voice demands and hold political elites accountable and responsive. We focus here on activities concerning that mode of political participation which even in established democracies is by far the most widespread, and that during processes of democratization marks the decisive watershed where active citizen involvement first finds its institutionalized

Table 3.1 Political participation (in %; N in parentheses)

	Greece	Spain	Uruguay	Chile	Hungary	Bulgaria
Voted	95.3 (921)	88.4 (1,209)	97.1 (607)	90.5 (815)	68.0 (1,015)	82.0 (995)
Attended meetings	24.9 (241)	8.8 (120)	38.9 (198)	8.2 (74)	6.1 (91)	16.8 (201)
Worked for party	12.6 (122)	2.5 (34)	11.7 (79)	4.1 (37)	1.0 (15)	5.3 (64)

form: voting and other activities related to the institution of general elections (Milbrath and Goel 1977; Verba, Nie, and Kim 1978; Norris 2002). Specifically, we measure respondents' levels of electoral participation by means of an additive index, combining respondents' self-reports about their participation in elections, attendance of parties' campaign meetings, and participation in campaign activities of a party. Cross-national variations in its components are displayed in Table 3.1. Not surprisingly, voting is everywhere the most widespread activity, although there are sizeable differences between countries. In the two East European countries, participation in elections is considerably lower than in both the Latin American and the Southern European new democracies. With great regularity, in all six countries attending meetings is a more frequent form of participation than working for parties. However, again we see huge differences. In Uruguay and Greece, the shares of citizens that take part in campaign meetings are far larger than in the other four countries. Actively supporting parties is also more widespread in these two countries.

With regard to the political regime as the object of these orientations, we consider two sub-dimensions of orientations, namely attitudes towards political parties, as part of what Almond referred to as process culture, and support of democracy, a component of system culture. *Political parties* in the context of a competitive party system fulfil a number of vital tasks for representative democracy. Among others, they provide individual citizens with opportunities for political participation; they articulate the demands of social groups; and they perform as socialization agents for elites and mass public alike. By organizing socio-political conflict in a peaceful way they contribute to the integration of the political system as a whole (Neumann 1956). Since it is difficult to conceive of a functioning democracy without political parties, a broad foundation of support for the institution of competitive parties seems a necessary aspect of a democratic process culture. It is important to note that we are not referring here to citizens' electoral support of particular parties but to the general legitimacy of parties and partisan conflict as an institutionalized form of democratic politics. Citizens should accept the notion that parties are a necessary element of democracy, they should find at least one party of those their party system is composed of acceptable, and they should perhaps even develop lasting affective ties to one of these parties (Lipset 1994: 14–15; Fuchs and Roller 1998; Rose, Mishler, and Haerpfer 1998: 155–7; Torcal, Gunther, and Montero 2002).

Finally, we analyse two aspects of system culture, both of which were analysed in the preceding chapter—Democratic Support and Political Discontent. Easton (1975) distinguished between two types of orientation towards the political system that he referred to as 'diffuse' and 'specific' support. Gunther, Montero, and Torcal confirmed the conceptual distinctiveness of those two sets of attitudes, referring to them as Democratic Support and Political Discontent, or its antonym 'satisfaction'. The Democratic Support dimensions concerns the general evaluation of the abstract notion of a democratic political order, and is a key component of regime legitimacy. Its points of reference are the norms of democracy as opposed to other, non-democratic forms of government. To measure respondents' support for democracy we use an additive index, counting agreement with the following statements: 'Democracy is the best system for a country like ours'; and 'Democracy is preferable to any other form of government' (this variable is only available in Greece, Hungary, and Bulgaria), the same two items analysed in the preceding analysis. Discontent, which we refer to by its antonym as 'Satisfaction with Democracy', in contrast, refers to the performance of the democratic regime as it has actually been implemented in the political systems of new democracies. We tap into this dimension by using the item measuring satisfaction 'with the way democracy is working in... [the respondent's country]' (the variable referred to as '*DemSat*' in the previous chapter).

The analysis presented in the next section seeks to reveal to what extent and in which ways these orientations of new democracies' citizens towards aspects of their political systems vary in dependence on the intensity with which these citizens attend to the political reporting of mass media.

Media Dependency and the Selection of Countries

According to the theory of media dependency, the likelihood that media messages will alter the audience's beliefs and behaviour increases the more an individual relies on media information resources. This dependency is heightened in periods of rapid social change as the subjective feeling of uncertainty increases the need for information and orientation (Ball-Rokeach and DeFleur 1976). For citizens in new democracies, the breakdown of the old political order implies not only a cognitive challenge, since they have to become familiar with a new institutional environment, but also the erosion of old values, beliefs, and ideologies. At the same time, key channels of information in the intermediary system—political parties, interest groups, whose function it is to provide this kind of guidance—are still very weak in most of the new democracies. To rebuild the organizational landscapes, left flattened after decades of autocratic rule, takes a long time—if it can be achieved at all. Many signs indicate that the new democracies bypass the organizationally well-developed mass-based type of party, with their allied secondary organizations, and 'leapfrog' directly into the age of postmodern politics, where political elites rely on the media, especially television, instead of organizational channels to communicate to the electorate, and where elite-directed opinion polls instead of grass-roots organizations assume the function of expressing societal demands and interests (Swanson and Mancini 1996; Pasquino 2001; Popescu and Tóka 2002).

Consequently, citizens in these new democracies depend heavily on the mass media when making up their mind about political matters. As Table 3.2 shows, rates of organization membership are considerably lower in new democracies than in established democracies.[3] Many more people in new democracies attend to the mass media for political information than are embedded into networks of organizational communication. We can therefore assume that media dependency is generally high in new democracies—a contextual condition that favours media effects. If anything, it appears more likely that we will find media effects on citizens' orientations towards their political system in the countries examine here than in older, established democracies. The data in Table 3.2 also reflect substantial cross-national differences with regard to the extent to which citizens follow the news through the print media. Some countries (Japan, the United States, and Germany) have relatively high levels of newspaper readership, while in others (Hungary, Spain, Chile, Greece, and, especially, Uruguay) relatively few citizens read newspapers on a regular basis. Conversely, overwhelming majorities of the population in each of these countries follow the news through television broadcasts, ranging between 97 per cent in the United States and United Kingdom to 82 per cent in Chile, with only Bulgaria (74%) as an outlier on the low-exposure

Table 3.2 Media penetration, political media exposure, and organization membership in established and new democracies (%)

	Greece 1993	Spain 1993	Uruguay 1994	Chile 1993	Hungary 1998	Bulgaria 1996	West Germany 1990	East Germany 1990	Britain 1992	USA 1992	Japan 1993
Daily newspaper circulation (per 1,000 people, 1990–9)[a]	153	99	293	98	186	254	311		331	212	578
Television receivers (per 1,000 people, 1990–9)[a]	240	409	239	215	435	394	567		521	806	686
Quality press	34.4	20.9	3.1	18.0	17.5	19.7	11.0	—	16.0	13.6	71.2
'Middle market' press	11.4	30.9	31.7	32.0	34.0	18.6	54.2	85.1	26.5	77.4	30.3
Tabloid press	2.3[b]	—	0.3	11.0	5.4	23.4	28.2	43.5	35.0	—	12.3
Party press	—	—	—	—	—	12.8	—	—	—	—	—
Total daily newspapers	40.4	45.3	32.4	43.9	48.9	52.5	73.0	90.0	66.3	83.8	96.2
Public stations' TV news	17.0	62.1	10.0	56.6	60.8	73.4	93.5	97.0	93.4	—	58.1
University stations' TV news	—	—	—	48.9	—	—	—	—	—	—	—
Private stations' TV news (national)	93.4	50.5	68.8	34.0	54.3	—	38.2	—	88.8	86.9	73.3
Private stations' TV news (local or regional cable broadcasters)	—	—	14.9	—	5.0	4.9	—	—	—	95.4	—
Total TV news	93.5	86.7	86.7	82.1	83.2	74.2	95.5	97.0	96.8	97.0	91.9
Membership in organizations[c]	19.3	23.1	28.8	43.7	19.9	26.1	39.4[d]	51.4[e]	n.a.	87.0	69.8
(N_{min})	(966)	(1,328)	(712)	(900)	(1,500)	(1,216)	(1,323)	(676)	(2,303)	(1,293)	(1,253)

[a] *Source:* United Nations InfoNation database (http://www.un.org/Pubs/CyberSchoolBus/infonation/e_infonation.htm).

[b] Local press.

[c] Including political parties, excluding sports clubs.

[d] N = 449 (second panel wave).

[e] N = 253 (second panel wave).

end of this range. We discuss these varying patterns in media exposure below.

While a high degree of media dependency can be seen as a typical feature of new democracies in general, there may also be some variation between new democracies. In countries where the regime transition has just been completed, citizens have a particularly high need for information and guidance. They are forced to adapt to a rapidly and fundamentally changing political, social, and, in the case of former communist countries, economic environment. Uncertainty about the new conditions of life is pervasive. Media dependency can thus be assumed to be extraordinarily high. In contrast, citizens of 'older new democracies', where the rules of the democratic game had been established for a more considerable time, have already adjusted to the new conditions. Their immediate need for information can therefore be assumed to be lower. Their media dependency, while higher than among citizens of established democracies, can nonetheless be expected to be lower than immediately after the regime turnover.

To be able to take account of these differences among new democracies we have selected six countries that not only represent different historical and political contextual backgrounds of third-wave democracies, but also different stages of democratic consolidation: transition from military rule, having taken place in Greece in the mid-1970s and in Latin America in the 1980s (Chile and Uruguay), transition from a civilian authoritarian system in Spain in the mid-1970s, as well as democratization after the breakdown of communism in Eastern Europe in 1989 (Bulgaria and Hungary). Thus, our sample consists of three pairs of countries, with the two Southern European countries looking back to the longest period of democratic development after the demise of the authoritarian regime, and the Eastern European countries being the most recent cases of democratization. The Latin American cases fall in between. These differences can be expected to have important implications for the strength of media effects. It can be expected, as discussed above, that media dependency will lead to stronger media effects in younger and less consolidated democracies than in those with longer democratic experience. Different levels of media dependency can also be expected as a result of varying trajectories of system transformation, due to differences in the nature of the autocratic regimes from which the countries in our study started their journey towards democracy, particularly in so far as Hungary and Bulgaria underwent massive transformations of their economic systems in addition to the political changes that have characterized all of these cases.

The Independent Variable: Media Exposure

Our central independent variable is exposure to the political reporting of various mass media. Given the cross-sectional survey data on which this study is based, our analysis has certain obvious limitations. For instance, we must neglect the conceptual distinction between exposure and reception as differing dimensions of media contact (Chaffee and Schleuder 1986; Price and Zaller 1993), and rely only on exposure measures, assuming that these capture both exposure and reception of media messages. We also have no way of looking into the 'black box' of the process by which media recipients actively make sense of the content they encounter in the media. We lack independent measures of the content actually conveyed by the media, so that we have no way to distinguish systematically between the conveyed content, and channel characteristics of the various media. We are measuring effects of individual respondents' contact to mass media on their political orientations. But we are not able to determine precisely what exactly it is about the media that produces these effects. Lastly, given that we are using cross-sectional data, although we use the language of causality it goes without saying that what we are basically talking about is correlational evidence. Only longitudinal data would allow for truly causal analysis.

Classifying Media

Mass media differ with regard to how information is transformed and moulded into the recognizable shape and form. Thus, the same topics dealt with by various media may reach the audience in substantially different forms. These differing media formats define the way media-represented political reality is experienced by their respective audiences (Altheide and Snow 1988). Most media research take these differing formats into account by distinguishing between print media, such as newspapers, and broadcast media, especially television. We are primarily concerned with the extent to which these formats affect the 'quality' of the information conveyed, particularly with regard to the amount of information disseminated and the degree of 'intellectuality' in their style of presentation. The first aspect concerns the number and range of topics covered, and the second, the depth, complexity, and 'seriousness' with which each topic is treated (Kleinnijenhuis 1991). We assume that the format of the respective medium will affect the strength and direction of media effects on political orientations. In particular, we expect that information-oriented media have a higher potential for enhancing their audience's mobilization and support for democracy than do media with a focus on entertainment (Holtz-Bacha 1990; Newton 1999c; Aarts and Semetko 2003). In addition, due to its higher demand in terms of cognitive involvement, the press may generally be more advantageous for political culture than television.

The specific and detailed data collected through the use of CNEP II surveys provide us with a unique opportunity to analyse the influence of these differing formats. Instead of using simple, generic indicators like the frequency of newspaper reading or TV watching in general, the use of open-ended questions determined which particular newspaper each respondent habitually read and which news programmes they watched on TV. Following the specific identification of each channel of information flow, the frequency of exposure to that medium was measured. These media were then categorized (based on published information and descriptions provided by country experts[4]) according to various format dimensions. This format classification began with the traditional distinction between the press and television. Specific media outlets within these two general types were then broken down into separate categories in accord with assessments of the 'quality of information' conveyed. In some cases, the political leanings of the respective media were also taken into account.

With regard to newspapers, our principal classification distinguishes among the 'quality press', 'tabloids', or the 'popular press', and a middle stratum of dailies. The *quality press*, as conceptualized in many studies of media systems, is characterized by comprehensiveness of coverage, background reports, in-depth news articles and analysis, and a lack of 'sensationalism'. Such papers are often produced by journalists of high professional reputation and cater to the information needs of the national elite. They often occupy an opinion-leader role within national media systems (Merrill and Fischer 1980: 3–23). At least one such paper exists in each of the countries selected for our study. At the other end of the information-quality continuum is the *tabloid or popular press*. The tabloids' mode of presentation is emotional, sensationalistic, and simplistic. Personalization is an important stylistic device, and high emphasis is placed on visual appearance. Articles are typically very short and written in easy-to-understand everyday language. The thematic spectrum of tabloids is more varied than that of the serious press and presents politics along with sex, crime, and sports. Tabloids thus cater more to entertainment than to information needs (Bruck and Stocker 1996: 9–33). Such dailies exist in most, but not all countries of our sample (see Appendix 3.1 for details). Bracketed between the quality and tabloid press we usually find a *middle stratum* of dailies which cover fewer topics than the quality press, and whose reporting does not achieve the same analytic breadth and depth, although they clearly strive for more 'seriousness' than the tabloids. Unlike the quality press, which is usually distributed nationwide, the dailies of the middle stratum often concentrate on local and regional information that the national quality press does not deliver.

Regarding television, the distinction between *public* and *private* broadcasters can be expected to be of some consequence with regard to the quality of disseminated political information (Pfetsch 1996; Aarts and Semetko 2003). Commercial television organizations are usually more dependent on audience markets than public television organizations. Therefore, the private stations' dominant motive behind programming decisions is mass attractiveness. This general rationale also influences the amount and type of news offered to the audience. In contrast, public television stations are usually at least to some degree kept free from market pressures by means of public subsidies or audience fees. At the same time, they are to varying degrees dependent on political actors like governments or political parties, whereas commercial broadcasters are usually more autonomous from such partisan influences (albeit with prominent exceptions in recent years, such as Silvio Berlusconi's television networks and Fox News in the United States).

Public broadcasters exist in all countries of our sample. And in every country except Bulgaria a liberalization of the television market has been initiated, so that several national commercial broadcasters controlled by private investors compete with each other and with public television for the attention of the audience. In addition, in some countries we find private broadcasters operating on local or regional levels. This category is a mixed bag, as some of these stations are operating in legal 'grey' zones, and are sometimes closely linked to local power elites. An unusual characteristic of the Chilean television system is that a number of stations are operated neither by the state nor by private investors but by universities—a heritage of the early days of Chilean television in the 1960s, when only universities, as educational institutions, were allowed to run television stations, while the state was not yet active in the field of broadcasting (Delgado Rühl 1994).

While in West European countries most newspapers subscribe to the principle of objectivity and have abandoned close 'press-party parallelism' (Seymour-Ure 1974), media in new democracies often have well-defined ideological orientations. However, in so far as this concerns their stances with regard to the issues of the day, we are not assuming this to be of any consequence for the more general orientations of their readers towards their political systems and towards democratic politics as such. Only when newspapers took clear stands with regard to the political transition itself will we take these newspapers separately into account. In our sample, this concerns primarily the Bulgarian party press, which has few counterparts in the other countries. Although most newspapers have party-political leanings, none of those with a significant mass readership are genuine party outlets. But in Bulgaria, both the Socialist Party, heir to the Communist Party of the old regime, and its main opponent, the Union of Democratic Forces, publish their own newspapers, and these are read by substantial portions of the citizenry. Two quality newspapers in Chile took opposing stands during the transition to democracy, with *La Epoca* favouring democratization and *El Mercurio* maintaining a very conservative posture, they are not party papers.[5]

Patterns of Media Exposure

Table 3.2 presented data concerning the size of the audience for each of these media outlets. Given that media influences can only be exerted on individuals actually exposed to the mass media, what becomes most immediately apparent is the small share of citizens in all of the new democracies under study who regularly follow the news through the printed daily press. In stark contrast to countries like Germany, the United States, or, above all, Japan, where newspapers are habitually read by at least three out of four citizens (Schmitt-Beck 1998), in the more recently established democracies at least half of the citizenry do not pay any attention to the daily press as a source of political information. Belated processes of socio-economic modernization contributed to the historic weakness of the press in these countries (Deutsch 1961; Braga de Macedo 1983: 56–60). In more recent times, the competition of television, but also rather mundane aspects of media economics, like inefficient distribution systems, prevented the emergence of a mass readership. In many countries, subscription to newspapers is uncommon. Instead, they must be purchased, copy by copy, at street news-stands. In Uruguay, the dailies' importance is especially low, apparently a result of market pressures and the concerted efforts of the authoritarian regime to destroy the press. Newspaper readership had been considerably higher before the authoritarian period, but now only one out of three citizens ever reads a newspaper in Uruguay.

These countries vary substantially with regard to exposure of their citizens to these differing types of newspapers. In most countries, roughly one out of five citizens follows the news through the quality press, with Greece and especially Japan being outliers at the high end of this range and Uruguay falling far below that level. Some countries have relatively high percentages of citizens who read tabloids (Germany, Britain, and Bulgaria), while others (Spain, Greece, Uruguay, and the United States) are generally devoid of those low-quality news outlets.

In all of these countries, television reaches far more citizens than daily newspapers. Large majorities of citizens are exposed to at least some political information through television news programmes. Thus, although to a somewhat lesser degree than in established democracies, television appears as an almost ubiquitous source of political information, capable of linking people to the world of politics that would not otherwise be reached by any political information mediated by mass media (Schmitt-Beck 1998). Below this level of generally high attention for television news, striking peculiarities emerge, however. Of particular interest is that the importance of public television as a source of political news varies substantially. In many countries (Greece, Uruguay, and the United States being noteworthy exceptions), only small minorities are never exposed to the news of public broadcasters. Commercial news broadcasts also vary in importance. While they reach only a third of Chileans, viewership is considerably greater in the other countries.

Backgrounds of Media Exposure

These cross-national variations in media exposure are due in part to the differing availability of certain types of outlets. In some countries, quality papers published in large cities, if not the capital itself, may be difficult to obtain in rural regions. Television stations are sometimes unable to reach all parts of the country with their broadcasts. But the socio-demographic characteristics of the audience also appear to affect the frequency of exposure to these media as a source of political news. As can be seen in Table 3.3, regularly reading newspapers is more closely linked to the respondents' socio-demographic features than watching the news on television. Factors like the respondents' gender, age, levels of formal education, and material well-being also help to predict patterns of newspaper readership. In every country except Uruguay, the quality press

Table 3.3 Correlates of media usage (β coefficients)

	Greece	Spain	Uruguay	Chile	Hungary	Bulgaria
Quality press[a]						
Gender	.15**	.14**	.01	.06***	.07**	.13**
Age	.03	−.01	−.07	.03	.05*	.04
Education	.13**	.25**	.02	.25**	.26**	.20**
Affluence	.13**	.11	.18**	.14**	.16**	.14**
Left–right identification	−.06*	−.06*	.07	.05***	−.10**	.02
Adj. R^2	.071**	.123**	.030**	.115**	.136**	.078**
Middle-stratum press						
Gender	.04	.17**	.02	.05***	.03	.02
Age	−.18**	−.02	.03	.01	−.01	−.01
Education	.07***	.09**	.12**	.06	.03	−.01
Affluence	.08*	.12**	.16**	.16**	.16**	.10**
Left–right identification	.11**	−.06*	−.10*	−.02	.00	.02
Adj. R^2	.042**	.067**	.066**	.037**	.029**	.007*
Tabloid press						
Gender	.03	—	.02	.11**	.03	.07*
Age	.03		.02	−.08*	−.02	−.12**
Education	−.00		−.04	−.14**	.03	.13**
Affluence	.02		.04	.05	.00	.14**
Left–right identification	.05		−.06	−.05	−.01	.01
Adj. R^2	.00		−.003	.029**	−.001	.067**
Public TV news						
Gender	.08*	.02	.02	.01	.09**	.04
Age	−.19**	.21**	.01	−.00	.24**	.13**
Education	−.01	.02	−.02	.05	.16**	.13**
Affluence	−.02	−.02	−.02	.05	.09**	.19**
Left–right identification	−.02	−.03	−.07	−.09**	−.03	.06*
Adj. R^2	.039**	.042**	−.004	.009*	.081**	.071**
University stations' TV news						
Gender	—	—	—	−.04	—	—
Age				.13**		
Education				.06		
Affluence				.19**		
Left–right identification				.07*		
Adj. R^2				.060**		
Private TV news (national)						
Gender	−.01	.03	−.08*	−.05	−.02	—
Age	−.04	−.07**	.04	.03	−.16**	
Education	−.01	.04	.02	−.00	−.04	
Affluence	−.11**	.12**	.15**	.02	.07*	
Left–right identification	.06***	.01	−.05	−.00	−.03	
Adj. R^2	.011**	.027**	.030**	−.002	.026**	
Private TV news (local or regional cable broadcasters)						
Gender	—	—	.05	—	.03	−.02
Age			.01		−.04	−.04
Education			.04		−.01	.04
Affluence			−.07		.10**	.05***
Left–right identification			.11*		.04	.02
Adj. R^2			.010***		.011**	.006*
(N_{min})	(949)	(1,322)	(568)	(897)	(1,419)	(1,196)

* $p < .05$; ** $p < .01$; *** $p < .10$.

[a] For Bulgaria inclusive of party press.

is used more often by educated citizens, but affluence may additionally increase the likelihood of reading such papers, independently of the higher levels of education that are correlated with higher socio-economic status. The likelihood of reading a middle stratum paper also generally increases with rising affluence, but is substantially affected by the respondent's level of education only in Uruguay and Spain. In Bulgaria, even tabloids are read more often by the relatively well-to-do. Taken together, these patterns suggest that newspaper readership is often characterized by a strong socio-economic component: Readership of the more demanding quality papers appears to require higher levels of education, and material well-being facilitates the regular purchase of a newspaper. In addition, consumption of quality dailies is clearly connected to gender, with men in most countries reading them more often than do women.

In contrast, tabloids seem to be a rather indistinct medium in terms of these socio-demographic characteristics. Only in Chile does the impression emerge that tabloids cater more to the taste of the less educated. In addition, both in Chile and in Bulgaria, younger people also appear somewhat more interested in the tabloid press. Political ideology is weakly and inconsistently related to usage of newspapers: in Spain, newspapers are read somewhat more often by those identifying with the left; in Uruguay, a similar patterns applies to the middle stratum press; while in Hungary the same is to be observed with regard to the quality press. In Greece, readers of the quality press lean towards the left, while readers of the middle stratum press are characterized by a distinctly conservative orientation.

With respect to television news, the most pronounced patterns emerge with regard to public networks in the two post-communist countries, and concerning university stations in Chile. Exposure to public broadcasting also has a distinct socio-demographic profile in the Southern European countries, with public television news followed more frequently by older viewers in three of the four European countries. Surprisingly, in Greece, exactly the opposite relationship emerges, while in Latin America no pattern is apparent except that news broadcast by Chilean university stations seems particularly attractive to older viewers. The second variable often associated with the frequency of television news exposure is affluence, although the nature of this relationship varies from country to country. The more affluent tend to be more regular viewers of public television channels in Bulgaria, university networks in Chile, and private-sector television news in Spain, Uruguay, and Hungary. While this relationship is most inconsistent, it suggests that the cost of purchasing TV sets may in some countries still be responsible for introducing an upward bias in the reach of mediated political information, thus widening the social knowledge gaps already observed with regard to differential usage of the press. Only in Greece do the less affluent tend to be exposed to television news more regularly, and, in this case, only with regard to private-sector broadcasts. In Eastern Europe, watching the news on public television is a behaviour more typical of older and better educated persons, regardless of their material standard of living. Finally, there appears to be no consistent and significant relationship between television viewing, *per se*, and ideological predisposition towards the left or right.

Logic of Analysis

In analysing how mass media in new democracies influence citizens' orientations towards their political systems, we proceed in two steps. Given the limitations of our data, we aim at a conservative test of the impact of the mass media on political culture. Significant relationships between media exposure and political orientations will only be accepted as indications of genuine media effects if they prove robust even in the presence of powerful controls. For each of the six dependent variables described above, we will run blockwise multiple regression analyses. The first step will be a model containing the full set of control variables. In the second step measures of respondents' media exposure will be added (see Appendix 3.2 for details of operationalization). If the addition of these media-exposure variables in the second step improves the explanatory power of the equation, we will examine the extent to which 'negative' effects support the 'apathy' and 'malaise' hypotheses or, conversely, positive relationships give credence to the mobilization and support hypotheses, and the degree to which this can be attributed to specific media rather than others.

As explained above, the dependent variables in these multivariate analyses will be Democratic Support, satisfaction with the performance of democracy, the respondent's level of interest in, knowledge about, and participatory involvement in politics, and attitudes towards political parties. The socio-demographic 'control' variables include the respondent's age, gender, and level of formal education (cf. Newton 1999c) and left–right identification. Not only are such factors often incorporated into multivariate analyses of political behaviour, but in new democracies they may have significant impact for additional reasons: Age may capture both generation-specific socialization experiences and changes related to the life cycle, and these may be substantially affected by systematic changes in the political context, particularly regarding substantial differences between democratic and non-democratic regimes (see Torcal 2002c). Gender seems worth taking into account since the transition processes may have affected men and women quite differently. Formal education serves as a proxy for a whole range of factors, like cognitive capabilities, social status, and again differing socialization experiences. Several studies indicate that citizens' relationships to their political order may also be influenced by their ideological identifications. With varying signs, depending on whether democracy was achieved in succession to right-wing or to leftist authoritarianism, it may make a difference for orientations towards democracy and its elements whether respondents are leaning towards the political left or the right (Morlino and Montero 1995; Wessels and Klingemann 1998). In addition, since (as we have seen) these variables are in differing patterns linked to media consumption, we must take them into account in order to control for selectivities in media usage.

We shall also consider Holmberg's 'home team' hypothesis (Holmberg 1999: 117; also see Gunther, Montero, and Torcal in this volume), which posits that citizens' attitudes towards political institutions and regime structures may be influenced by their partisan preferences: supporters of governing parties are believed to be more favourable not only to the current government, but also to more general aspects of the architecture of governance that are not inherently related to party competition. In autocratic regimes, the issue of replacing office-holders is inherently coupled to the issue of change in the power structure itself, and it is difficult for citizens to evaluate elites and the political structures within which they are positioned independently of each other. While democracy can be seen as an institutionalized technique for changing leaders without altering the structure of the political system itself (Schumpeter 1962), in new democracies the possibility must be taken into account that the supporters of current minority parties that are relegated to the opposition benches may rather quickly generalize their discontent from the level of the incumbent government to the level of the regime itself (Tóka 1995; Wessels and Klingemann 1998). We therefore include, as an independent variable, a measure indicating whether respondents have been on the winning or on the losing side at the previous election. Finally, for the two dependent variables that pertain to the democratic political system as a whole, we add to these equations a number of subjective and objective measures of economic well-being, including evaluations of personal and general economic situation, household affluence, personal employment status. These are variables that some (e.g. Lipset 1959*a*, 1959*b*, 1994) have argued are essential for successful democratization, and others (e.g. Gunther, Montero, and Torcal in this volume) have demonstrated are closely linked to satisfaction with democracy.

In constructing these multivariate models, we must keep in mind that orientations towards the political system and its component parts may not be fully independent of each other, and that variables concerning conceptually 'neighbouring' objects may be related to each other in reciprocal patterns. For instance, political interest certainly contributes to a higher level of political knowledge, while knowledgeable people are especially eager to learn even more about politics (Converse 1990; Delli Carpini and Keeter 1996: 178–217). Similarly, a hierarchical logic may be assumed to be important. For instance, citizens who are knowledgeable and thus understand the workings of their political systems, or who are in favour of the idea of a competitive party system can also be expected to be more positively oriented towards the general notion of a demo-cratic political system. Including orientations towards political objects according to this hierarchical and transactional logic implies a modelling strategy that seeks only to reveal *direct* effects of media consumption on political orientations. However, in addition to these direct effects there may also be hidden *indirect* effects, mediated through other intervening orientations. The further we proceed to the more general orientations, the more important this possibility gets, because more orientations towards component parts of the political system enter the models as control variables. Thus, in addition to the conservative estimates of the media's direct influences (in which 'neighbouring' as well as hierarchically subor-dinate attitudinal orientations are included as control variables), we also want to estimate their overall impact, including both direct and mediated influences. Accordingly, after submitting these hypotheses to the most 'conservative' and demanding tests, we also compute estimates of the media's overall importance for each of the six political orientations by not controlling for other dimensions of political culture.

Findings

Let us begin with a discussion of the direct impact of media exposure on orientations towards process culture—that is, political involvement (the respondent's self-professed interest in politics, political knowledge, and participation in politics)—and system culture—that is, evaluations of the political system (including attitudes towards political parties and democracy in general, and satisfaction with the performance of democracy in the respondent's country). Each of these will be treated as dependent variables in multivariate regression equations, and our summary measure of the impact of media exposure on these orientations will be operationalized as the incremental increase in R^2 (commonly understood as 'percentage of variance explained') resulting from the introduction of our media-exposure variables as a bloc into each equation after the impact of the control variables has been taken into account. For the sake of brevity and in the interest of a clearly focused analysis, we will not enter into a very detailed discussion of the role of the control variables for political culture. Only particularly interesting findings will be discussed. The interrelationships between various dimensions of political culture will also be dealt with only in a few instances. (Complete data from each of these regression equations are presented in Tables A1–A6 in Appendix 3.3.)

Figure 3.2 presents a summary of 'the most conservative' estimate of the impact of media exposure on each of these six dimensions of political

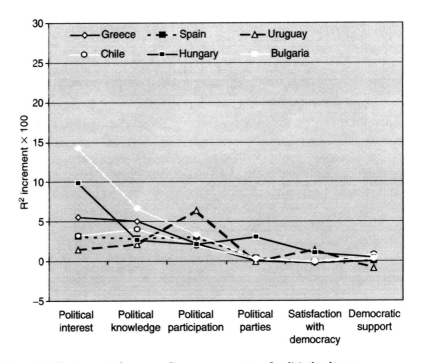

Figure 3.2 The impact of mass media on components of political cultures

culture in Greece, Spain, Uruguay, Chile, Hungary, and Bulgaria. For each of these six orientations, it presents in graphic form the incremental contribution to R^2 resulting from the addition, as a bloc, or measures of exposure to the quality press, tabloids, and middle-stratum newspapers, as well as of following the news on public- and private-sector television. In each equation, controls for the impacts of education, gender, age, left–right orientation, and support for government versus opposition parties had been introduced through the inclusion of those variables in the previous step of the regression analysis. In addition, in order to subject these media effects to the most severe test, we conservatively estimate their impact after controls had also been introduced to eliminate the impact of interactions with neighbouring concepts. That is, the equation analysing 'political interest' also includes 'political knowledge' as a control; the analysis of political knowledge controls for the impact of political interest; and so on.[6] Remarkably, with few exceptions, respondents' media use significantly enhances the predictive power of our models to explain political orientations. However, the data summarized in Figure 3.2 also make it clear that the magnitude of the media-induced increases in the models' explanatory power differs strongly both among countries and, even more strikingly, from one of these aspects of political culture to the other.

With regard to differences among the six countries in our sample, the patterns apparent in Figure 3.2 are consistent with our hypothesis concerning stronger media effects under conditions of higher media dependency within a less consolidated political environment. Particularly high incremental R^2 statistics can be observed in the two youngest democracies, Bulgaria and Hungary, indicating that in these countries exposure to political media coverage tends to have the strongest impact on political orientations. This is especially true of political interest. In addition, the impact of media exposure on political knowledge is strongest in Bulgaria, while Hungary shows particularly strong relationships with regard to assessments of political parties and satisfaction with democracy. In contrast, there is little impact of media exposure on any of these orientations in Spain and Uruguay, two of the oldest among the new democracies studied here. These findings strongly support our hypothesis concerning the strength of media effects and the 'age' of the new regime.

When we focus our attention on the various types of democratic orientations, the most striking finding is that media effects are not uniform. Generally speaking, the more closely the orientation relates to the respondents' own roles as political actors, the higher is the probability of media influence. Conversely, orientations concerning system culture are generally only very weakly connected, if at all, to the mass media's political reporting and to citizens' exposure to it. The fact that these patterns can be observed in all six countries suggests that similar psychological processes are at work, independent of the specific structural context in which people are forming their opinions.

In all six countries, the extent to which citizens are motivated to follow the political process and keep informed, as well as the degree to which they are knowledgeable about political matters are highly dependent on their patterns of media usage. While in most countries these linkages are of similar strength for both orientations, media influence on political interest surpasses the impact on political knowledge by a sizeable margin in both of the new Eastern European democracies, with the additional explanatory power of media effects reaching 9.9 per cent in Hungary and 14.2 per cent in Bulgaria. The corresponding figures for political knowledge are 2.7 per cent in Hungary and 6.7 per cent in Bulgaria. Only Uruguay deviates from the otherwise dominant pattern of stronger effects for political interest and knowledge than for other orientations; in that country, the media's impact on both political interest (1.5%) and political knowledge (2.1%) is smaller than their influence on political participation.

In contrast to these two passive forms of political involvement, active involvement in the form of election-related participation is usually somewhat less responsive to media habits. The only exceptions of this regularity are Spain, where this correlation does not differ in size from those found for political interest and political knowledge; and Uruguay, where political participation is, as mentioned, in fact more dependent on media exposure than any other orientation. With the exception of the latter relationship, the R^2 increments of media use remain below 3.5 per cent for all of the other dependent variables. Moving away from citizens' own political self leads almost everywhere to sharp decreases in the importance of their media contacts. Only in Hungary are citizens' orientations towards political parties significantly related to media exposure. The Hungarian case is also deviant in so far as this relationship is even stronger than the impact of media exposure on political participation (with an incremental R^2 of 2.7% for attitudes towards parties and 2.3% regarding participation).

Turning to system culture, in most countries satisfaction with the performance of democracy is unrelated to media exposure. Only in Hungary and Uruguay do the media exert any influence over citizens' evaluations of the functioning of their political regimes (with incremental impact of only 1%), and in Uruguay this relationship is not statistically significant at the .05 level. Instead, mirroring the findings of Gunther, Montero, and Torcal, these orientations appear highly sensitive to citizens' perceptions of the economy, especially with regard to 'sociotropic' (Kiewiet 1983) assessments of the state of the national economy (as compared with personal well-being). With the single exception of Chile, where the government–opposition divide has an even stronger effect, the respondent's assessment of the general state of the economy is the most important factor 'explaining' satisfaction with democracy, with β coefficients ranging between .12 (Chile) and .26 (Greece; see the tables in Appendix 3.3). In Bulgaria, Spain, and Chile, democratic satisfaction is also strongly connected to whether people are supporters or opponents of the incumbent governments (β = .12, .19, and .38, respectively). These findings are consistent with the 'home team' hypothesis of Holmberg (1999: 117).

With regard to Democratic Support as the dependent variable in the analysis, no substantial media effects can be observed. In no country does the addition of the media exposure variables increase the predictive power of the multivariate equation by as much as 1 per cent, and in most countries there is no statistically significant relationship at all.

The Direction of Media Effects: Beneficial and Detrimental Influences of Media Exposure

The preceding analyses suggest that exposure to the mass media does, indeed, have an important influence on new democracies' political cultures, but almost exclusively with regard to process cultures and the extent of citizen involvement in politics, and in a manner that varies from one country to another. They did not, however, tell us in which ways the media influence these citizens' orientations towards their political systems. Does the political information provided by the media make a positive contribution to consolidation of these new democracies, or has it undermined support for democracy and citizen involvement in democratic politics? In short, do they contribute to apathy and malaise or to mobilization and support? To obtain answers to these questions, we need to reexamine our findings in more detail. The signs of the β coefficients for media effects tell us whether the intensity of media usage goes along with a strengthening or a weakening of the various aspects of political culture that we are looking at in this chapter. Positive signs indicate that media exposure is healthy for democratic political culture, while the reverse is true for negative signs.

As can be seen in the data presented in Appendix 3.3, with very few exceptions (most of which hardly attaining conventional levels of statistical significance), the direction of the effects exerted by mass media on citizens' orientations is positive. Indeed, in only three cases can we find negative β coefficients whose statistical significance exceeds the .05 level. In Uruguay, watching private local television stations' news seems to diminish rather than increase their viewers' political knowledge, albeit rather weakly ($\beta = -.08$). Our findings also suggest that watching Chilean university television channels leads to significant decreases in recipients' readiness to vote and participate in parties' campaign activities ($\beta = -.11$). Finally, readers of *El Mercurio*, a right-wing outlet that occasionally still favours Chile's old authoritarian order, express a considerably lower general esteem for democratic government as such, independently of how they evaluate the actual functioning of democracy in their country ($\beta = -.09$). Aside from these deviant cases, all relevant media effects are in a positive direction, suggesting that mass media in new democracies perform a constructive rather than destructive role in the process of democratic consolidation.

Types of Media and Media Formats: Not All Media Are Alike

The fine-grained analysis undertaken for this study allows us to go beyond general assessments of the role of the media by asking if particular media are of special importance for democratic consolidation. Although our results are fairly complex, some regularities do nonetheless emerge when looking at the patterns of significant β coefficients in our tables (cf. Appendix 3.3).

Both the quality press and newspapers of medium levels of information quality generally fulfil the crucial role of drawing citizens into the political process by motivating them to follow public affairs, enhancing their factual knowledge, and increasing their likelihood to participate. This applies without qualifications to Spain (where all βs for both quality and middle-stratum newspapers are significant, ranging from .07 to .14), Hungary (where statistically significant βs range from .06 to .17), and Greece (where only the relationship between political knowledge and reading middle-stratum papers fails to achieve statistical significance at the .05 level). Curiously, reading the middle-stratum press in Uruguay has a much stronger positive impact on political interest and participation than does reading the quality press (for which positive βs are statistically insignificant). But political knowledge in Uruguay is significantly facilitated by exposure to the quality press in that country. In Chile, reading the high-quality (but right-wing) *El Mercurio* substantially enhances political knowledge, and political interest and participation are stimulated by reading *La Epoca*, while middle-stratum papers have a significant positive impact on both interest and knowledge. In Bulgaria, reading the quality press contributes to both political interest and knowledge (β = .08 and .14, respectively), while exposure to the middle-stratum newspapers is only significantly associated with interest in politics (.10).

Not surprisingly, given the much lower information content of their coverage of politics (such as it is), tabloids exert a much less consistent and positive influence on these three dimensions of citizen involvement in politics. To be sure, our ability to draw general conclusions from these data is limited by the fact that this type of publication is found in only four of our six countries (Bulgaria, Chile, Hungary, and Uruguay). Nonetheless, the general lack of positive and statistically significant associations between tabloid readership and political interest, knowledge and participation, stand in sharp contrast to what we observed regarding the impact of exposure to the high-quality and middle-stratum press. The sole exceptions to this lack of statistically significant relationships between tabloid reading and these three citizen-oriented orientations are the following: In Chile, tabloid readership is related to higher levels of political participation (β = .09); in Hungary, it is weakly linked to interest in politics (.05); and in Bulgaria, it is associated with higher levels of both political interest and knowledge (.13 and .09, respectively). Indeed, the status of the tabloid press in Bulgaria is somewhat anomalous, in so far as it appears to be more strongly linked with higher levels of political interest and knowledge than is readership of middle-stratum newspapers. Aside from these few exceptions, we can conclude that exposure to tabloid news coverage plays neither a positive nor a negative role with regard to developing the citizenship skills tapped by our first three dimensions of political culture.

While reading both quality and middle-stratum newspapers are rather consistently and significantly associated with high levels of political interest, knowledge and participation, and tabloid readership is generally irrelevant to those orientations, attitudes towards political parties and towards democracy itself are rarely directly affected by newspaper reading. Indeed, among all of the newspapers in these six countries for which we have data (including high- and medium-quality papers, as well as tabloids), only two newspapers are associated with orientations towards parties, support for democracy, or satisfaction with its performance at a level of statistical significance exceeding .05. In Chile, readers of the right-wing *El Mercurio* are less disposed to support democracy in the abstract ($\beta = -.09$), while in Bulgaria, readers of the pro-UDF (anti-communist) *Demokratia* are slightly more disposed to support democracy than other respondents in the sample ($\beta = .07$). With regard to all the other newspapers in these countries for which we have data, there is no statistically significant relationship between readership and support for parties or democracy in the abstract, or satisfaction with democratic performance.

Television is often believed to be an especially influential medium, capable of becoming a powerful weapon in the hands of political entrepreneurs. As discussed above, in many new democracies the issue of who controls public television has been hotly contested, and governments have usually been very reluctant to loosen their grip on public broadcasting networks and their programming. Despite this precarious position of public television in new democracies, its role with regard to political culture is, according to our results, nonetheless often a positive one. In the majority of countries, watching public television news contributes to citizens' political interest and propensity to participate in electoral politics. And in no country is viewing public television news negatively associated with the three dimensions of democratic citizenship under examination in this paper. Concerning political interest, significant β values for watching public television range from .07 in Chile to .30 in Bulgaria. Only in Uruguay, where public television reaches a small audience (only 10% of our respondents, as we saw in Table 3.2), do we not find a significant and positive relationship with political interest. With regard to citizens' propensity to participate in the electoral process, following the news on public television exerts a positive influence in most countries. Beta coefficients linking public TV news exposure and the respondent's level of political participation range between .07 and .17 in Greece, Spain, Bulgaria, Hungary, and Uruguay. Only in Chile do we fail to find a statistically significant relationship between participation and public TV viewing.

In contrast, after controlling for respondents' political interest, watching public television rarely has a discernible impact on how much people know about politics. Only in the two young Eastern European democracies do we find such effects ($\beta = .09$ in Hungary, and .18 in Bulgaria). This suggests that despite its programming philosophy—nicely captured in the first part of the BBC's decades-old mission statement 'to inform, educate, and entertain'—public television has only a limited capacity to actually educate its audience in matters of politics, at least in new democracies. Only in the two Eastern European countries do we find relationships that indicate that viewers may become more politically knowledgeable by watching political programmes on public television. On the whole, however, as demonstrated above, citizens' needs for gaining factual political knowledge seem to be better served by the press than by television—a result well in line with numerous studies from established democracies (Weaver and Buddenbaum 1980; Schönbach 1983; Robinson and Levy 1986; Schmitt-Beck 1998). This finding has somewhat negative implications for the countries included in this study, however, since in none of them the press is widely read.

Attitudes towards political parties are only significantly influenced by following the news through public television in Chile and Hungary (β = .06 and .15, respectively). Likewise, only in these same two countries does public television news seem to significantly enhance recipients' support for democracy (β = .08 in both countries). Given that almost no other media are relevant in a positive way for this very basic orientation in any of the six countries, it seems no exaggeration to state that, as far as mass media are concerned, public television bears the potential to be the single most important factor of democratic consolidation. In sum, although somewhat less clear-cut than the 'serious' press, public television appears as an important source of democratic consolidation. Yet since political culture is an aggregation of myriad individual orientations, its real impact on the shape of this crucial aspect of system culture can only be adequately assessed when taking additionally into account how many people are actually reached by this medium. Here, we observe a cleavage between Greece and Uruguay on the one hand, and the other countries on the other: whereas in the latter four countries, public television is attended to by more citizens than any other medium, Uruguayan public television is actually watched by barely one in ten citizens, while less than one in five Greeks take note of public television news—clearly not enough to make a substantial difference in terms of these countries' political cultures.

Commercial television does not adequately fill the gap created by public broadcasters' lack of attractiveness to the Greek and Uruguayan television audiences. Taken together, the news programmes of private broadcasters seem to fulfil a less valuable role for political culture, although they are not irrelevant. In some countries and for some orientations, their effects are very similar to those of public television. In Spain and Hungary, for instance, political interest is enhanced not only by public television but also by watching private broadcasters' news ($\beta = .08$ and $.16$, respectively). In Hungary, there is also no difference between the two types of broadcasters with regard to their importance for orientations towards political parties ($\beta = 15$ in both cases). Furthermore, in Hungary and in Bulgaria not only public but also private television contributes to citizens' political knowledge, albeit to a lesser extent (β for private television = $.06$ and $.07$, respectively; corresponding values for public television: $.09$ and $.18$, respectively). In Greece, where public broadcasting attracts the attention of only a small share of the television audience, the private channels' role is similarly important with regard to political participation ($\beta = .09$; corresponding value for public television: $.08$), which in all other countries is only stimulated by public television, and it is actually more important with regard to political knowledge ($\beta = .12$; no significant effect for public television). In both Latin American countries, however, private television seems inconsequential with regard to any of the citizens' orientations towards their political systems. This is perhaps due to the exceptionally strong commercialism in these broadcasters' programming. Finally, Chilean university television does seem to be of some consequence, although in a paradoxical way: while discouraging active involvement among its viewers ($\beta = -.11$), it stimulates their passive involvement ($\beta = .08$ for political interest and $.09$ for political knowledge).

Overall Impact: Taking Mediated and Transactional Processes of Media Influence into Account

Models including political culture variables as controls produce very conservative estimates of the direct effects of media exposure on citizens' orientations towards components of their political systems. Omitting such controls gives us a less conservative view of the overall importance of mass media for these various aspects of political culture. At the same time, by keeping all other control variables in the models (age, gender, education, left–right identification, support for government vs. opposition parties, as well as, for attitudes towards democracy, evaluations and experiences with the economy), we maintain a safeguard against the danger of grossly overestimating the media's importance. As with our preceding analysis of the direct impact of the media, we use the incremental contribution to R^2 resulting from the entry of the media variables into the equation as our indicator of the impact of media exposure on these orientations. The R^2 increments of these less conservative estimates are displayed in Figure 3.3. The numerical results, along with levels of significance appear

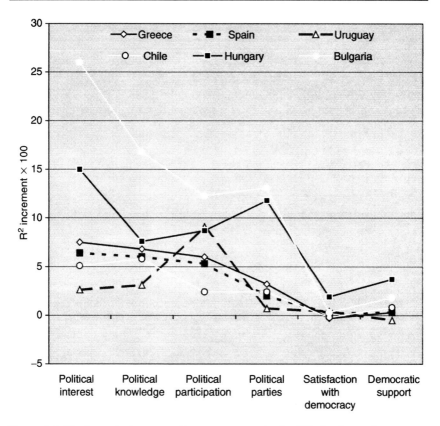

Figure 3.3 The impact of mass media on components of political cultures (less conservative estimates)

in the tables in Appendix 3.3.[7] Comparing Figures 3.2 and 3.3 suggests something like an 'amplified elevator effect': in almost every case the registered impact of the media on each of our dependent variables is increased when the complicated relationships of mediation and transaction between the political culture variables are ignored. Almost all R^2 increments are higher in Figure 3.3 than they were in Figure 3.2. And the greater the impact of the media apparent in Figure 3.2, the more it further increased in Figure 3.3.

The empirical findings presented in Figure 3.3 are consistent with those from the preceding 'conservative' estimation of media effects. Even more clearly than in the previous analysis, the most recently established democracies in our sample, Bulgaria and Hungary, are those in which the impact of the media on political culture is particularly strong. This finding supports our earlier hypothesis that 'media dependency' is greater in contexts characterized by greater uncertainty and malleability of institutions and behavioural norms.

More generally, these data indicate that the strength of media effects is magnified (as compared with our more conservative models) when we eliminate controls for interactions among conceptually neighbouring orientations. This is especially noteworthy with regard to the three orientations that most directly involve the respondent's political involvement—that is, the two passive orientations, political interest, and political knowledge, as well as active participation in electoral politics. With regard to political interest, for instance, the greatest increase in the apparent strength of media effects is found in the two countries where the media's role had already appeared as the strongest in the more conservative analysis discussed above. In Bulgaria, the R^2 increment almost doubles, from 14.2 per cent (see Figure 3.2) to an impressive 26 per cent; and in Hungary, it increased from 9.9 per cent (in the equation where the potentially causal impact of 'political knowledge' had been included as a control) to 15 per cent. In contrast, the smallest shift is detected in Uruguay, where the media's incremental impact on political interest increases only from 1.5 to 2.6 per cent. An even more striking pattern emerges for political knowledge. The explanatory power of our media variables more than doubles in Bulgaria (from 6.7% to 16.8%), but barely changes in Uruguay (from 2.1% to 3.1%). Thus, for those dimensions of political culture for which the data presented in Figure 3.2 (and Tables A.1–A.6) suggested a particularly important role of the media, the strength of media effects was magnified by setting aside the possible impact of these various political orientations on each other, resulting in a substantially widened gap between the most recently established democracies and countries that had been democratized at earlier stages of the third wave.

When we turn our attention to the two system culture variables largely unaffected by media exposure in the more conservative models—Democratic Support and, especially, satisfaction with the performance of democracy—we find that the removal of these controls has little impact on the strength of these relationships. Media effects were negligible in the data presented in Figure 3.2, and, with the partial exceptions of Bulgaria and Hungary, they remained negligible in the 'less conservative' models. Only in Hungary is there a statistically significant impact of media exposure on democratic satisfaction, which increased slightly from 1 per cent of explained variance to 1.9 per cent following removal of controls for the other cultural orientations. And only in Hungary and Bulgaria do either of these two rounds of analysis indicate the presence of media effects on fundamental support for democracy of statistical significance accounting for as much as 1 per cent of explained variance. The R^2 increments of 3.7 and 1.8 per cent estimated for Hungary and Bulgaria (respectively) in the less conservative models are small, but not entirely trivial. We may thus conclude that there is no impact of media exposure on Democratic Support in four of these six countries, and even in the two most recently established democracies, Hungary and Bulgaria, they are quite weak, even in the less conservative analyses of this relationship.

With regard to evaluations of political parties, our findings are more mixed. As we saw in Figure 3.2, there was no substantial impact of media exposure on attitudes towards parties in all countries except Hungary (where it explained 3% of the variance in these conservative models). When controls for the interactive influences of political interest, knowledge, and participation are removed, however, powerful media effects become apparent in both Bulgaria and Hungary (where the share of explained variance increased by 12.8% and 8.8%, respectively). Eliminating these control variables from equations estimating media effects on attitudes towards parties also increased their apparent impact in Greece, Chile, Spain, and Uruguay, but by much more modest magnitudes (3.2%, 2.1%, 1.6% and 0.6%, respectively).

The theoretical perspective that underpins our understanding of the impact of the media on these dimensions of political culture acknowledges that these media effects may be partly mediated through webs of hierarchical and transactional interconnections among these orientations. Accordingly, we began our multivariate analysis by introducing into the equations (in a stage prior to the entry of the media variables) controls for potential influence of these cultural orientations on each other. This was intended to calculate the most conservative estimate of media effects—that is, with the incremental R^2 reflecting only the 'direct' impact of media exposure on each respective dependent variable, and excluding the mediated flow of such influences through related (conceptually neighbouring) cultural orientations. As we have seen in this section, in which our multivariate analysis did not include such controls, the conservative estimates, as anticipated, understate the overall impact of the media on these democratic orientations. In no instance did this different analytical approach fundamentally alter our conclusions, but they did amplify the strength of those empirical findings: relationships that were strong and statistically significant in the first round of analysis became stronger, while weak or non-existent relations remained weak or statistically insignificant. In the aggregate, we conclude that the media exert some influence over each of these cultural dimensions, and in a generally positive manner that is conducive to democratic consolidation and the quality of democracy. But the strength of these relationships varies greatly depending on which cultural dimension is analysed, and from one country to another. The three process culture variables that directly involve the respondent's citizenship role—interest in and knowledge about politics, and political participation—are substantially affected by media exposure, especially in the most recently established democracies, those of Bulgaria and Hungary. Conversely, media effects with regard to Democratic Support and satisfaction with the performance of democracy are much weaker or statistically insignificant, even after controls for the influence of the other democratic orientations have been removed. Our most uneven pattern of empirical findings involves orientations towards political parties. Exposure to the media has a strong and uniformly positive impact on evaluations of parties in Bulgaria and Hungary, while these media effects are much weaker (but still uniformly positive) in the other countries examined in this chapter. Finally, in conformity with our 'media dependency' hypothesis, it should be noted that the impact of media exposure on these orientations tends to be much stronger in the more recently established democracies of Eastern Europe than in our Southern European and Latin American cases.

Conclusion

Transition to democracy is a fragile and highly complex process, the success of which is dependent on a number of interrelated factors. In this chapter we have argued that a congruent political culture is a vital precondition for the consolidation of the new institutional order, and that this culture of citizen involvement and support is affected by the media's representation of political matters. This argument draws its significance from the fact that the media are the main, often the only, source from which citizens learn about politics. Hence, the media can be regarded as a crucial intermediary between the macro and micro levels of democratic consolidation, linking the institutional dimension with the attitudes and beliefs held by the public. However, many observers have raised concern about the role of the media in democratic transition, arguing that the media are actually undermining the psychological foundations of popular involvement and support that these new regimes so desperately need. Indeed, the actual performance of the media in many new democracies is characterized by aggressive criticism, negativism, and bias. Rather than strengthening a democratic political culture, such patterns of behaviour suggest that the media may actually undermine citizens' trust in the new institutional order.

To what extent are these assumptions supported by empirical evidence? Based on representative opinion surveys from six new democracies in Southern Europe, Eastern Europe, and Latin America, our study explored the impact of the media on democratic orientations during times of regime change and the subsequent period of consolidation. The wide variety of relevant data gathered under the auspices of the CNEP enable us to explore in great detail the impact of the media's role in the development of a democratic political culture within several different historical, social structural, and political contexts. Let us conclude by drawing on our empirical findings in addressing the four key questions with which we began this chapter.

DO THE MEDIA MATTER?

Scholars disagree over the extent to which the media exert a significant influence on individuals' attitudes which cannot be attributed to other pre-existing orientations. In our analysis of the strength of media effects on political culture, we began with a strictly conservative logic of analysis, followed by a less rigid (but probably more realistic) approach. The conservative approach was designed to measure only the 'direct' impact of the media on these orientations, excluding any intervening or interactive influences of these orientations on one another. The less rigid approach sought to estimate the overall power of the media, taking into account both direct and indirect effects that are mediated through other political orientations. Both procedures resulted in findings that refuted the 'minimal effects' hypothesis. On the contrary, the incremental R^2 that resulted from the introduction of media exposure variables into multivariate equations that had previously controlled for the influence of other potential determinants of these democratic orientations increased the explanatory power of our regression models by up to 14 per cent using the conservative approach, and by as much as 26 per cent when both direct and indirect media effects are taken into consideration.

GRAVEDIGGERS OR SEEDSMEN OF DEMOCRACY?

Having determined that the magnitude of such media effects is substantial, and in some instances very powerful, we turn our attention to the extent to which this impact is beneficial or detrimental to the consolidation of new democracies. In our review of the relevant literature, we

119

identified four different patterns potentially linking media exposure to specific dimensions of political culture, relating both to one's own role in politics and orientations towards the political regime. The media malaise hypothesis, despite its plausibility in light of certain common features of media coverage, was not supported by empirical data analysed in this study. In spite of the media's hunger for scandals and other unseemly aspects of politics in some countries, media exposure in the aggregate does not seem to affect people's evaluations of political actors or, more importantly, democracy itself in a negative way. While the statistical association between media exposure and Democratic Support is quite weak, those findings that are statistically significant are almost exclusively positive. Only regular readership of Chile's right-wing *El Mercurio* are substantially lower in their support for democracy than the average Chilean respondent.[8] All other significant relationships (at the .05 level or better) between Democratic Support and media exposure—be it readership of quality, tabloid or middle-stratum newspapers, or viewing public or private television—are positive, indicating that higher levels of media exposure contributes to the strengthening of support for democratic institutions. Interestingly, this effect is most evident in Hungary, the country which underwent fierce 'media wars' over the autonomy of public broadcasting from government interference.

When we turn our attention to aspects of democratic culture that cast the individual citizen as the principal protagonist, our findings are more dramatically positive. Rather than media-induced political malaise, the overwhelming majority of our empirical findings supports the 'media mobilization' theory, which sees active citizenship as facilitated by media exposure. Accordingly, the media are seen as playing an important part in the cognitive mobilization of individuals by stimulating political interest and enhancing political knowledge. In turn, the cognitive competence of the electorate and their ability to make intelligent choices contribute significantly to the quality of democracy. Seen from this perspective, the media play a crucial role in helping citizens to learn about the functioning of their new political environment and to keep abreast of the day-to-day political events. The media even promote active participation in terms of voting turnout and campaign-related activities, albeit to a markedly lesser degree than passive forms of cognitive involvement. Hence, media exposure (as we saw in the previous chapter) is negatively associated with political disaffection, two key manifestations of which are apathy and a general withdrawal from politics. In this chapter, we focused our analysis on three aspects of democratic culture that are the antithesis of the disaffection syndrome, interest in and knowledge about politics, and political participation, and we found that media exposure is strongly, positively, and consistently associated with the development of citizen competence, particularly in the newest and most uncertain democratic environments, in Bulgaria and Hungary.

It is important to note that, while our exploration of correlational evidence is cast in terms of a causal relationship portraying media effects as one of the determinants of these democratic-citizenship orientations, we acknowledge that the actual interpretation of the relationship between media exposure and individual political orientations is a rather ambiguous one. The single-wave survey analysis on which our analysis is based does not make it possible to address doubts about the proper direction of causality inherent in these relationships. Thus, rather than thinking of the audience as passive recipients of messages, it would be preferable to conceptualize media effects as an interactive process in which the audience plays an active part by selecting the amount and content of information they pay attention to. In this perspective, the positive impact of the media we found in our study can be assumed to be to a certain degree audience-induced effects that are dependent on the individual's motivation to learn about political matters. In this way, a dynamic reciprocal process—a virtuous circle (Norris 2000c)—may be set in motion. A person who is generally interested in public affairs usually spends more time with reading the newspaper or watching news programmes than a less interested person, for example, which in turn stimulates political interest and increases the demand for more information (Früh 1991). Similarly, people who are involved in some kind of political activity have a higher demand for political information, which in turn may provide them with new facts that convince them of the necessity to expand their political activism. It must be noted, however, that a virtuous circle of this type can have a dark side. Those individuals who are less politically involved are left farther and farther behind so that the gap between the haves and haves-not of political competencies is growing larger.

DOES THE MEDIUM MATTER?

Although we most frequently refer to the media in a rather generalized way, it is obvious that 'all media are not created equal' (Zukin 1977: 245). They employ different formats of presenting political information, and they are faced with differing pressures in their efforts to establish the proper balance between information and entertainment. Our findings suggest that it is primarily the information-rich media, especially high-quality and middle-stratum newspapers, that make the most positive contribution to the health of a political culture and, in turn, the quality of democracy. Tabloids, due to their sensationalist style, personalism, and low-information content, are often assumed to exert a negative influence on the political process. Our empirical analysis, however, does not reveal any significant effect of exposure to tabloids—neither positive nor negative.[9] Bulgaria is an interesting exception, in so far as its tabloids have a stronger positive impact on cognitive mobilization than does the quality press.

With regard to audio-visual media, it is mainly public television that performs a beneficial role, although its level of impact is consistently lower than that of newspapers. The picture for commercial television is more mixed. It must be borne in mind, however, that newspaper readership in most of the countries in our sample is generally low so that a relatively small proportion of the population benefits from the high quality of information provided by the printed press.

DOES THE CONTEXT MATTER?

Finally, we were interested in determining whether the media's impact on political orientations differs across countries. In accord with the assumptions of media-dependency theory, the role of the media is found to be particularly strong in the youngest of the new democracies investigated in this study, suggesting that the media's relevance is highest in the early phases of democratic consolidation. During this period of regime change the need for orientation and information on the side of the citizens is extraordinarily high, as old certainties and familiar procedures are no longer valid. These empirical findings, however, are also compatible with arguments involving the macro-level of politics, particularly relating to the 'flattened landscape' hypothesis advanced by Juan Linz and Alfred Stepan (1996). Post-totalitarian Bulgaria prior to the collapse of communism was characterized by the absence of secondary organizations independent of the state or party. This stood in contrast with the 'limited pluralism' that characterized the Southern European and Latin American authoritarian regimes. Accordingly, it could be argued that media dependence was greater in Bulgaria than in those other world regions due to the absence of these alternative sources of political influence and socialization. Moreover, the transitions that unfolded in both Bulgaria and Hungary were more far-reaching than the purely political transformations that the Southern European and Latin American countries underwent. They included substantial changes in fundamental economic and social structures and relationships. Arguably, this created a particularly high need for orientation which, again, worked in the direction of stronger media effects in these two countries. This finding confirms Gunther and Mughan's hypothesis of the 'contingent nature of media effects' (2000b: 20) according to which the degree of media influence on citizens' political attitudes and behaviour is, at least to some extent, contingent on processes going on at the macro-level society of politics.

On the whole, our observations from six very different new democracies show country-specific differences, but at the same time underline a clear general pattern of media effects across countries regardless of their specific historical and institutional peculiarities. In addition, our results are surprisingly consistent with what has been found in recent studies from established democracies. There is now a large body of accumulated evidence beyond the particularities of specific countries or situational contexts that provides us with reasonable confidence that the media contribute to mobilization rather than malaise in democratic politics.

Nevertheless, the juxtaposition of apparent deficiencies in political reporting, on the one hand, and generally positive effects of exposure to political media content, on the other, seems to be a puzzling paradox. How can information that is characterized by bias and negativism translate into active citizenship and even support for democracy? In particular, in new democracies where, depending on the nature and duration of autocratic rule, large segments of the citizenry do not have any first-hand experience with democratic practice, one would have expected a higher degree of vulnerability to the way in which the media typically present political matters. Although our data do not allow us to further explore this problem empirically, some tentative considerations might help to shed light on the underlying processes.

First, as mentioned above, audience members do not necessarily take at face value what they encounter in the media, but rather interpret what they see, hear, and read in an active effort to make sense of a complex world. To some extent, the media messages' meaning emerges only in the eye of the beholder. It would be a mistake to assume that citizens in new democracies are inexperienced with regard to interpreting complex political messages. On the contrary, having lived under political circumstances where public communication has been subjected to extensive manipulation and censorship has probably equipped citizens with extraordinary skills for 'reading between the lines' and carefully selecting the information they need to make sense of the political environment. From this perspective, citizens in new democracies can be assumed to be perfectly capable of identifying the relevant bits of information while refusing to put too much weight on the day-to-day drama of pseudo events and scandals.

Second, from a normative perspective it can be argued that emphasizing conflict and uncovering negative information is actually in line with the media's democratic function. Besides providing information about daily political events, the media are also expected to act as a public watchdog that holds government and political authorities accountable. Hence, what is often regarded as a threat to the evolving civic culture in new democracies is in fact part of the media's democratic role, even though it might be difficult to draw the line between negative information that undermines trust and constructive criticism that keeps democracy alive. The watchdog role is of particular significance in the transition period following the breakdown of an autocratic regime, when the media struggle for autonomy from the government in order to get into a position of being able to criticize, control, and attack political authorities. So far, we know very little about how individuals who experience these fundamental changes in the nature of public communication interpret the new adversarial style of the media. It can well be that after decades of autocratic rule, where the media's role was confined to serving as a mouthpiece of the ruling elite, citizens welcome unfavourable news and critical accounts of politicians as an indicator of the working of democracy rather than a flaw of the new order. The results of our study point in this direction.

Finally, it has to be kept in mind that, as yet, there are no systematic content analyses of media coverage in new democracies that would allow us to come to a precise judgement of the media's performance and professionalism. Existing evaluations of the quality of political reporting stem from concerned observers who might exaggerate, or even misinterpret, the nature of political conflicts. Nonetheless, there are reasons for concern with regard to the quality of political information. Since the media in many new democracies are desperately short of sufficient and reliable income streams, they increasingly choose strategies of commercialization and tabloidization which appear as a guarantee for attracting larger audiences. However, unlike in established democracies, these developments usually take place within a communication culture lacking a viable public service tradition that could provide for a counterbalance to the marginalization and trivialization of politics in some segments of the media system. These developments may eventually contribute to a weakening of the high-quality information that we found to be most valuable for the consolidation of political culture in new democracies.

Classification of Media

	Greece	Spain	Uruguay	Chile	Hungary	Bulgaria
Quality press (high information quality)	*Eleftheros Tipos* *Nea* *Eleftherotypia* *Ethnos* *Vima* *Kathimerini* *Ependytis*	*ABC* *Ya* *El Mundo* *Vanguardia* *Diario 16* *El País*	*El Observador*	*El Mercurio* *La Epoca*	*Népszabadság* *Magyar Nemzet* *Magyar Hírlap* *Népszava* *Napi Magyarország* Business newspapers	*Trud* *Kontinent* *Kapital*
Middle-stratum press (medium information quality)	*Apogevmatini* *Adesmeftos Tipos* *Rizospastis*[a] *Mesimvrini* *Estia* *Avriani* *Ependytis* *Pontiki* *Avgi* *Naftemboriki* *Niki*[a] *Proinos Tipos* *Neoi Kairoi* *Thessaliki* *Neos Agonas* *Eleftheria* *Thessaloniki*	Local and regional press	*El País* *La Mañana* *La República* Local and other newspapers	*La Segunda* *La Tercera* *La Nacion* *Las Ultimas Noticias*	Regional newspapers	Local and other newspapers

Cont.

	Greece	Spain	Uruguay	Chile	Hungary	Bulgaria
Tabloid press (low information quality)	Local newspapers		El Diario	La Cuarta	Mai Nap Kurir Blikk	24 chasa Standart
Party newspapers						Demokratia (UDF) Duma (BSP)
Public TV news	ET-1, -2, and -3	TVE 1 and 2	Channel 5 (SODRE)	Channel 7 (TVN)	MTV 1 and 2 Duna TV	Channels 1 and 2
University broadcasters' TV news				Channel 5 (UCV) Channel 11 (CHV) Channel 13 (TVUC)		
Private TV news (national)	Antenna Mega Star Sky	Antena 3 Tele 5 Canal plus	Channel 4 Channel 10 Channel 12	Channel 4 (La Red) Channel 9 (Megavisión)	RTL Klub TV 2	
Private TV news (local or regional cable broadcasters)			Local channels		TV 3 Sziv TV M Sat Other local cable stations	Nova TV TV 7 days Regional stations

Note: [a] Rizospastis and Niki are party papers (of the Communist Party and the PASOK, respectively), but subsumed to the category of middle-stratum papers, due to small numbers of readers.

Overview of Variables

Dependent variables

Political interest
: Self-assessment of general interest in politics (scale from 0 = no interest to 3 = strong interest).

Political knowledge
: Additive index, based on count of correctly answered knowledge questions regarding names of political office-holders (chairpersons of trade unions or interest organizations, ministers, chairpersons of national parliaments, a.o.); range differs between countries, due to varying numbers of knowledge questions asked.

Political participation
: Additive index, counting number of activities actually performed by respondents, out of the following three election-related activities: voting; attending campaign meetings of parties; actively participating in campaign activities of a party (range: 0–3).

Political parties
: Additive index, counting pro-party orientations out of the following list of orientations: Agreement with statement 'Without parties there can be no democracy'; positive evaluation of at least one party on closeness scales; party identification (range: 0–3).

Democracy: specific support
: 'In general, are you very satisfied, somewhat satisfied, not very satisfied, or not at all satisfied with the way democracy is working in [country]?' (range: 0 = not at all satisfied to 3 = very satisfied).

Democracy: diffuse support
: Additive index, counting agreements with the following statements: 'Democracy is the best system for a country like ours'; only in Greece, Hungary, and Bulgaria: 'Democracy is preferable to any other form of government' (range: 0 to 1 resp. 2).

Independent variables

Intensity of exposure to daily newspapers
: Additive indices based on frequency of habitual reading of newspapers per week. Initial measurement was on the level of specific newspaper titles (up to two titles per respondent); where several titles were combined into a class of newspapers, the mode of combination was additive. Measurement was in days per week, with the exception of Greece and Hungary, where less fine-grained scales were used (range: 0 = non-reader to 7 [Greece and Hungary: 4] = reading a specific title every day, resp. 14 [Greece and Hungary: 8] = reading two newspapers of a particular class every day).

Intensity of exposure to TV news
: Additive indices based on frequency of habitual watching of TV news per week. Initial measurement was on the level of specific channels (Greece, Spain, Chile: up to three channels, other countries: up to two channels); where several channels were combined into a class of broadcasters or aggregated to the level of a single broadcaster in the case of public stations with more than one channel, combination was additive. Measurement was in days per week, with the exception of Hungary, where a less fine-grained scale was used (range: 0 = no news-watching to 7 [Hungary: 4] = watching the news of a specific [one channel] broadcaster every day, resp. 14 [Hungary: 8; Greece, Spain, Chile: 21] = watching the news of a particular class of broadcasters [or a broadcaster with two resp. three channels] every day).

Cont.

Control variables

Support for government vs. opposition parties resp. candidates	1 = voting for winning party resp. presidential candidate in previous election (Greece: Nea Demokratia; Spain: PSOE; Uruguay: Nationalist Party; Hungary: FIDESZ or FKgP; Bulgaria: Stojanow), −1 = voting for losing party resp. presidential candidate in latest election, 0 = other categories: non-voters, do not know, refused, etc. (first-wave measurements in Greece, Spain, and Uruguay, where pre-post-panel design was used in data collection). Chile: performance rating of government of president Aylwin (range: −2 = bad to 2 = good).
Left–right identification	Ten point left–right scales (to save cases missing data are assigned to scale midpoint, in accordance with findings reported by Inglehart/Klingemann 1976).
Age	In years.
Gender	1 = male, 0 = female.
Education	1 = completed secondary education, 0 = less (for lack of genuine comparable instruments like the CASMIN scale [cf. König et al. 1988] in the CNEPII surveys, this dichotomization is the only way to achieve comparability of educational levels between nations).
Evaluation of general economic situation	−2 = very bad, to 2 = very good (Hungary: question referred to expected situation in one year).
Evaluation of personal economic situation	−2 = very bad, to 2 = very good (Hungary: question referred to expected situation in one year).
Affluence	Greece, Spain, Hungary, Bulgaria: interviewer assessment of quality of respondents' housing; Uruguay, Chile: household income. Ranges: 1–3 for Chile; 1–4 for Greece, Spain, Bulgaria; 1–5 for Uruguay and Hungary.
Unemployment	First dummy: 1 = unemployed vs. 0 = else; second dummy: retired, students, housewifes, etc. vs. 0 = else (implied reference category: gainfully employed).

APPENDIX 3.3

Table 3.3A1 Media exposure and political culture: Greece (β coefficients)

	Political interest	Political knowledge	Political participation	Political parties	Satisfaction with democracy	Democratic support
Quality press	.12**	.18**	.08*	.05***	−.02	.06***
Middle-stratum press	.16**	.05	.10**	.00	−.00	−.03
Local press	−.00	.06*	.00	−.01	.02	.03
Public TV news	.14**	.03	.08*	−.00	−.02	.02
Private TV news	.04	.12**	.09**	.04	−.00	.02
Political interest		.14**	.14**	.20**	.04	−.02
Political knowledge	.15**		.03	.11**	.08*	.03
Political participation				.19**	.05	.03
Political parties			.19**		.10**	.02
Satisfaction with democracy						.26**
Support for government vs. opposition parties	−.01	.02	−.05	−.07*	−.08*	.05
Left–right identification	−.04	−.05	.06	.13**	.06	−.16**
Age	−.16**	−.08*	.06***	−.14**	.03	−.07***
Gender	.04	.26**	.06*	−.06***	−.04	−.03
Education	.08*	.07*	−.15**	−.05	−.01	.03
Evaluation of general economic situation					.27**	−.02
Evaluation of personal economic situation					.09*	.00
Affluence					.03	.02
Unemployed (vs. gainfully employed)					−.01	.04
Retired etc. (vs. gainfully employed)					.03	−.02
Adj. R^2: full model	.157**	.210**	.157**	.183**	.144**	.081**
Adj. R^2: increment media	.056**	.050**	.022**	.000	−.003	.000
(N)	(948)	(948)	(942)	(942)	(929)	(921)
Not controlling for other dimensions of political culture[a]						
Quality press	.15**	.20**	.14**	.13**	.01	.07*
Middle-stratum press	.17**	.07*	.14**	.07*	.02	−.02
Local press	.01	.06*	.01	−.00	.03	.04
Public TV news	.15**	.06***	.11**	.05	−.01	.03
Private TV news	.06***	.13**	.12**	.09**	.02	.03
Adj. R^2: full model	.139**	.193**	.092**	.090**	.122**	.024**
Adj. R^2: increment media	.075**	.068**	.060**	.032**	−.003	.003
(N)	(948)	(949)	(949)	(943)	(932)	(930)

* $p < .05$; ** $p < .01$; *** $p < .10$.

[a] Coefficients for other control variables not shown in this and following five tables.

Table 3.3A2 Media exposure and political culture: Spain (β coefficients)

	Political interest	Political knowledge	Political participation	Political parties	Satisfaction with democracy	Democratic support
Quality press	.11**	.15**	.07*	−.05***	.03	.01
Middle-stratum press	.10**	.10**	.14**	.01	.02	.02
Public TV news	.08**	.02	.11**	.05***	−.00	−.05***
Private TV news	.08**	.05*	.04	.07*	.00	−.00
Political interest		.27**	.09**	.18**	.03	−.00
Political knowledge	.29**		.06***	.11**	.06*	.09**
Political participation				.13**	.01	.01
Political parties			.13**		.14**	.19**
Satisfaction with democracy						.11**
Support for government vs. opposition parties	−.00	−.07**	−.03	.08**	.19**	−.04
Left–right identification	−.07*	−.05***	−.08**	−.01	−.08**	−.06*
Age	−.07**	.12**	.05	.08**	.04	−.04
Gender	−.02	.20**	−.01	−.00	−.02	−.01
Education	.13**	.15**	−.00	−.02	−.01	.05
Evaluation of general economic situation					.24**	.03
Evaluation of personal economic situation					.04	.03
Affluence					.00	.03
Unemployed (vs. gainfully employed)					.03	.00
Retired etc. (vs. gainfully employed)					.07*	−.02
Adj. R^2: full model	.227**	.288**	.110**	.102**	.181**	.087**
Adj. R^2: increment media	.031**	.028**	.030**	.004*	−.002	.000
(N)	(1,302)	(1,302)	(1,242)	(1,242)	(1,229)	(1,223)
Not controlling for other dimensions of political culture						
Quality press	.16**	.19**	.09**	.01	.04	.03
Middle-stratum press	.14**	.14**	.16**	.07*	.03	.06*
Public TV news	.09**	.05***	.13**	.09**	.02	−.03
Private TV news	.10**	.08**	.06*	.11**	.03	.02
Adj. R^2: full model	.163**	.231**	.072**	.036**	.161**	.029**
Adj. R^2: increment media	.064**	.060**	.053**	.020**	.002	.003
(N)	(1,302)	(1,304)	(1,304)	(1,243)	(1,287)	(1,282)

* $p < .05$; ** $p < .01$; *** $p < .10$.

Table 3.3A3 Media exposure and political culture: Uruguay (β coefficients)

	Political interest	Political knowledge	Political participation	Political parties	Satisfaction with democracy	Democratic support
Quality press ('El Observador')	.01	.07*	.04	−.09***	−.08	−.04
Middle-stratum press	.14**	.07***	.20**	−.04	−.09	.01
Tabloid press ('El Diario')	.00	.03	−.02	−.01	.01	.04
Public TV news	−.00	.01	.17**	−.01	.00	.07
Private TV news (national)	.06	.06	−.07	.03	−.05	.02
Private TV news (local)	.01	−.08*	−.02	.08	.10***	.02
Political interest		.19**	.26**	.17**	.15**	−.00
Political knowledge	.20**		.00	.02	.05	−.01
Political participation				.11*	−.03	.01
Political parties			.10*		.05	.05
Satisfaction with democracy						.13*
Support for government vs. opposition parties	−.01	−.03	.02	.04	.02	.13*
Left–right identification	−.11**	−.12**	.04	−.02	.03	−.02
Age	.05	.16**	−.07	.16**	.08	.05
Gender	−.06***	.08*	.03	−.01	−.00	.05
Education	.13**	.15**	.00	.01	.04	.10
Evaluation of general economic situation					.26**	−.09
Evaluation of personal economic situation					.19**	.13***
Affluence					−.09	−.04
Unemployed (vs. gainfully employed)					−.00	.03
Retired etc. (vs. gainfully employed)					.02	.03
Adj. R^2: full model	.143**	.167**	.160**	.064**	.175**	.013***
Adj. R^2: increment media	.015**	.021**	.064**	−.001	.014***	−.009
(N)	(658)	(658)	(407)	(407)	(336)	(336)
Not controlling for other dimensions of political culture						
Quality press ('El Observador')	.02	.08*	.03	−.03	−.05	−.05
Middle-stratum press	.16**	.11**	.25**	.05	−.05	−.01
Tabloid press ('El Diario')	.01	.04	−.03	.02	−.08***	.03
Public TV news	−.00	.00	.16**	−.06	−.00	.05
Private TV news (national)	.08***	.07***	−.06	.06	.00	−.00
Private TV news (local)	−.01	−.08*	−.02	.10*	.05	.01
Adj. R^2: full model	.110**	.134**	.093**	.055**	.150**	.007***
Adj. R^2: increment media	.026**	.031**	.091**	.007***	.004	−.005
(N)	(658)	(662)	(417)	(648)	(548)	(555)

* $p < .05$; ** $p < .01$; *** $p < .10$.

Table 3.3A4 Media exposure and political culture: Chile (β coefficients)

	Political interest	Political knowledge	Political participation	Political parties	Satisfaction with democracy	Democratic support
'El Mercurio'	−.00	.16**	.04	−.01	.01	−.09**
'La Epoca'	.08**	−.03	.07*	.03	.03	.02
Middle-stratum press	.13**	.09**	.01	−.00	.02	−.03
Tabloid press ('La Cuarta')	.02	.02	.09*	−.02	.02	.03
Public TV news	.07*	.03	.04	.06*	−.02	.08*
University TV news	.08*	.09**	−.11**	.03	−.03	.00
Private TV news	.01	.01	−.02	.05***	−.03	−.03
Political interest		.18**	.10**	.26**	.11**	−.02
Political knowledge	.21**		.11**	.15**	−.03	.01
Political participation				.10**	−.05	−.02
Political parties			.11**		.10**	.12**
Satisfaction with democracy						.17**
Support for government vs. opposition parties	.13**	.09**	.02	.11**	.38**	.08*
Left–right identification	−.12**	−.08**	−.03	.02	−.01	−.11**
Age	−.02	.15**	.13**	.02	.05	.01
Gender	−.01	.19**	−.07*	−.06***	.03	.06***
Education	.17**	.25**	−.03	−.01	−.05	−.03
Evaluation of general economic situation					.12**	.07***
Evaluation of personal economic situation					.08*	.06
Affluence					−.04	.02
Unemployed (vs. gainfully employed)					.01	.02
Retired etc. (vs. gainfully employed)					.01	.02
Adj. R²: full model	.224**	.314**	.090**	.183**	.258**	.102**
Adj. R²: increment media	.032**	.040**	.019**	.003	−.002	.008*
(N)	(895)	(895)	(890)	(890)	(877)	(877)
Not controlling for other dimensions of political culture						
'El Mercurio'	.03	.16**	.06***	.03	.01	−.09*
'La Epoca'	.07*	−.01	.08*	.06	.04	.03
Middle-stratum press	.15**	.12**	.04	.06***	.04	−.02
Tabloid press ('La Cuarta')	.03	.02	.09*	.00	.02	.03
Public TV news	.08**	.05***	.06***	.10**	−.01	.08*
University TV news	.10**	.10**	−.07*	.06***	−.02	.00
Private TV news	.01	.02	−.01	.06***	−.02	−.02
Adj. R²: full model	.195**	.289**	.054**	.082**	.238**	.067**
Adj. R²: increment media	.051**	.058**	.024**	.024**	−.002	.008*
(N)	(895)	(897)	(897)	(892)	(882)	(890)

* p < .05; ** p < .01; *** p < .10.

Table 3.3A5 Media exposure and political culture: Hungary (β coefficients)

	Political interest	Political knowledge	Political participation	Political parties	Satisfaction with democracy	Democratic support
Quality press	.17**	.15**	.09**	.01	.01	−.01
Middle-stratum press	.14**	.06*	.10**	.04	.07*	−.04
Tabloid press	.05*	.01	.01	.02	−.02	.04
Public TV news	.19**	.09**	.09**	.15**	.05***	.08**
Private TV news (national)	.16**	.06*	.03	.15**	−.02	.02
Private TV news (local or regional cable broadcasters)	.05*	.01	−.01	.08**	.08**	.03
Political interest		.24**	.13**	.22**	.04	.06***
Political knowledge	.22**		.11**	.07**	−.00	.03
Political participation				.19**	.00	.03
Political parties			.20**		.11**	.29**
Satisfaction with democracy						.17**
Support for government vs. opposition parties	−.02	−.04***	−.04	.05***	−.04	.00
Left–right identification	.03	−.04	.05*	−.01	−.02	−.02
Age	.00	.17**	.06*	−.10**	−.10**	−.00
Gender	.07**	.09**	.00	−.03	−.02	.09**
Education	.18**	.16**	.07*	.04***	−.03	.12**
Evaluation of general economic situation					.13**	.01
Evaluation of personal economic situation					.09**	.01
Affluence					.01	.08**
Unemployed (vs. gainfully employed)					−.07*	−.02
Retired etc. (vs. gainfully employed)					.06***	.00
Adj. R^2: full model	.326**	.255**	.228**	.266**	.091**	.275**
Adj. R^2: increment media	.099**	.027**	.021**	.030**	.010**	.005*
(N)	(1,440)	(1,440)	(1,381)	(1,381)	(1,353)	(1,346)
Not controlling for other dimensions of political culture						
Quality press	.22**	.20**	.15**	.10**	.03	.05***
Middle-stratum press	.16**	.09**	.15**	.11**	.08**	.01
Tabloid press	.06*	.02	.03	.04	−.02	.05*
Public TV news	.22**	.15**	.18**	.25**	.09**	.19**
Private TV news (national)	.18**	.10*	.10**	.21**	−.02	.09**
Private TV news (local or regional cable broadcasters)	.06*	.02	−.01	.10**	.09**	.08**
Adj. R^2: full model	.289**	.216**	.150**	.177**	.078**	.155**
Adj. R^2: increment media	.150**	.076**	.087**	.118**	.019**	.037**
(N)	(1,443)	(1,441)	(1,431)	(1,397)	(1,414)	(1,405)

* $p < .05$; ** $p < .01$; *** $p < .10$.

Table 3.3A6 Media exposure and political culture: Bulgaria (β coefficients)

	Political interest	Political knowledge	Political participation	Political parties	Satisfaction with democracy	Democratic support
'Demokratia'	.07**	.05*	.05***	.03	−.02	.07*
'Duma'	.09**	.03	.18**	.01	−.03	.03
Quality press	.08**	.14**	−.00	.00	−.04	.03
Middle-stratum press	.10**	.02	−.01	.04	.03	.01
Tabloid press	.13**	.09**	−.03	.04***	−.04	.03
Public TV news	.30**	.18**	.07*	.05	.03	−.06***
Private TV news (local or regional cable broadcasters)	.00	.07**	−.01	.03	−.01	.00
Political interest		.23**	.10**	.27**	.02	.08*
Political knowledge	.22**		.07*	.11**	−.07*	.10**
Political participation				.27**	.06***	.01
Political parties			.30**		.14**	.15**
Satisfaction with democracy						.16**
Support for government vs. opposition presid. candidate	−.04	−.07**	.013**	−.04	.12**	.12**
Left–right identification	.06*	.01	−.08*	.02	.15**	.20**
Age	.07**	−.00	.05***	−.01	−.00	−.01
Gender	.10**	.09**	.02	.02	.01	−.01
Education	.02	.22**	−.01	−.04	−.01	.08**
Evaluation of general economic situation					.20**	.01
Evaluation of personal economic situation					.06***	.03
Affluence					.09**	.07*
Unemployed (vs. gainfully employed)					−.01	−.05***
Retired etc. (vs. gainfully employed)					.02	−.05
Adj. R^2: full model	.365**	.338**	.245**	.306**	.134**	.296**
Adj. R^2: increment media	.142**	.067**	.033**	.003	−.001	.003
(N)	(1,173)	(1,173)	(1,096)	(1,096)	(1,067)	(1,047)
Not controlling for other dimensions of political culture						
'Demokratia'	.08**	.07**	.09**	.09**	−.02	.09**
'Duma'	.11**	.05***	.24**	.10**	−.02	.06*
Quality press	.12**	.17**	−.04	.07*	−.04	.04
Middle-stratum press	.11**	.05***	−.05***	.07**	.04	.05***
Tabloid press	.16**	.12**	−.02	.11**	−.02	.07*
Public TV news	.36**	.27**	.19**	.25**	.06*	.03
Private TV news (local or regional cable broadcasters)	.02	.08**	.00	.04	−.01	.02
Adj. R^2: full model	.338**	.303**	.148**	.156**	.116**	.220**
Adj. R^2: increment media	.260**	.168**	.123**	.131**	.003	.018**
(N)	(1,208)	(1,174)	(1,175)	(1,162)	(1,175)	(1,155)

* $p < .05$; ** $p < .01$; *** $p < .10$.

4

Intermediation through secondary associations: the organizational context of electoral behaviour

Paolo Bellucci, Marco Maraffi, and Paolo Segatti

Political intermediation between political elites and voters can take several forms in contemporary democracies. Politicians can interact directly with public opinion through mass media; state institutions can be the locus of eventful encounters among elites, bureaucracy, and citizens; governments usually enact policies interacting with bureaucracy and interest groups representing different segments of the electorate; etc. In this chapter, we focus our attention on the associational context of political participation. In particular, we are interested in the extent to which non-political voluntary associations serve as channels through which the citizens are involved in mass politics, especially in so far as they politicize their members, structure their perception of political stimuli, mobilize them for active participation, and influence their voting decisions. We explore these processes in contemporary democracies that vary considerably with regard to their respective political histories, patterns of economic development, and cultural legacy. Before moving on to these more demanding analytical tasks, we describe the patterns of secondary association membership across the CNEP countries.

Regrettably, interest in the study of secondary association within the field of electoral behaviour research has declined over the past few decades. Earlier research on political behaviour had traditionally placed great emphasis on the social context in which political participation and voting take place. As the editors noted in the Introduction to this volume, the so-called sociological approach to political behaviour—which lay at the heart of both the European (Rokkan 1999) and Columbia (Lazarsfeld, Berelson, and Gaudet 1944) research traditions begins with the premise that 'people vote in groups'. Accordingly, political parties and movements mobilized citizens along the lines of social, economic, cultural, and ethnic cleavages. They integrated individuals and communities into the larger polity, structured group identities, and articulated interests in a manner intended to guide their electoral behaviour and other modes of political involvement. In Europe, in particular, these processes tended to encapsulate sectors of the electorate, isolating their supporters from outside influences, through the development of parallel organizations, eventually leading to the development of distinctive and separate political subcultures. Accordingly, *organizational membership* is an important analytical dimension of the Rokkanian cleavage concept, along with objective location within the social structure and subjective identification with the social group (Bartolini and Mair 1990; Bartolini 2000).

Later research moved away from social group theory, placing greater emphasis on the individual voter and on psychological processes underpinning the calculus of electoral choice. In part, this trend was a reflection of transformations of the social and economic structures of contemporary democracies, the erosion of traditional religious and class cleavages, and the ensuing processes of individualization of political behaviour. The crucial point of the 'Michigan approach' is the mediating role of long-term political predispositions—captured by the concept of party identification—in orienting electoral behaviour (Dalton and Wattenberg 1993). This paradigm shift, augmented by more recent research on rational and cognitive behaviour, has greatly enriched our comprehension of mass political behaviour, and has successfully challenged the assumption of a homogeneous within-social-group electorate. Unfortunately, it has also discouraged research on the social context of political behaviour in general and voting in particular, leaving the study of the political role of secondary associations to students of pressure groups politics and policymaking. We believe that it is still important to study the political ramifications of class, ethnic, regional, cultural, and gender cleavages in society, but we also believe that we should move beyond the original Rokkanian approach by systematically examining the mediation processes linking voters to their respective societies and political systems. Since these intermediation processes have largely been ignored by scholars in the field of electoral behaviour between the mid-1950s and the early 1990s, relatively little is known about the structural elements of socio-political intermediation. And yet linkages between political and civil societies are of central importance in both old consolidated and new or transitional democracies.

Over the past decade, there has been a resurgence of interest in and research into the connections between associations and democracy. This research lies at the intersection of sociology, political science, and democratic theory. By addressing the general question, 'How do associations enhance democracy?' scholars have brought civil society and groups back into the normative and empirical investigation of democracy, broadening in this manner the research focus from the previous concentration on how secondary associations were linked to political and electoral behaviour, but at the same time making them less salient (Edwards, Foley, and Diani 2001).

The Intellectual Background

Following Tocqueville, a high degree of societal pluralism is seen as a requisite for a viable and responsive democratic decision-making process and institutions in two ways. First, as the pluralist and neo-functionalist traditions both emphasized, organizational pluralism allows for the articulation of citizens' interests and, through linkages to parties and political institutions, for the aggregation of disparate interests into more coherent inputs into democratic decision-making (Almond and Powell 1978). Second, social participation through membership in voluntary associations is assumed to increase citizens' political awareness and sense of efficacy by providing them with political information, imbuing them with political skills, and developing their civic values. Overall, as Putnam (1993, 1995) has argued, associational life nurturing an ethic of reciprocity enhances democratic governance.

Fung (2003) lists six ways in which associations can enhance democracy: 'through the intrinsic value of associative life, fostering civic virtues and teaching political skills, offering resistance to power and checking government, improving the quality and equality of representation, facilitating public deliberation, and creating opportunities for citizens and groups to participate directly in governance.' For Warren (2001: 94), these contributions are not all mutually compatible with one another, and different forms of associations have differing impacts on democracy according to 'the degree to which an association is voluntary or nonvoluntary; the kind of (associative) medium—social attachment, money or power—within an association is embedded or towards which it is oriented, and the...purposes of the associations'. In sum, the basic tenet of the current wave of variations on a theme by Tocqueville suggests that secondary associations are the two pillars of democratic competition, either directly, through the experience of being a member, or indirectly, through exposing individuals to a variety of viewpoints which help to educate them as members of a pluralistic community.

But to what extent do such descriptions accurately reflect the workings of political institutions and processes within contemporary democracies? Some scholars argue that public confidence in political institutions appears to be declining (Pharr and Putnam 2000), while voluntary activism and social participation seem to be increasingly detached from political participation and political decision making. Moreover, other scholars have contended that civil and political societies have tended to separate as cleavage parties based on class and religion decline in contemporary societies, as the cognitive capabilities of electorates are supposedly increasing, and as individual voters depend less on group identities. Most importantly, pressure groups are entering more directly into the political arena, while cartel parties (Katz and Mair 1995) are, to a certain extent, less dependent on society's support. In the end, parties no longer have deep roots with organized groups in society.

To be sure, these trends are less than definitively established. Other scholars have argued that democratic support is not eroding (Klingemann 1999); that political behaviour and civic involvement do not depend directly on social capital (Newton 1999a); that there is no steady cross-national decline of membership in intermediary organizations (Norris 2002); and that membership in intermediary organizations is not becoming de-politicized, at least as far as unions are concerned (Aarts 1995). Also, cross-national comparative studies have found a positive correlation between civic engagement and indicators of democratization and good governance (Norris 2002). Finally, the rise of 'critical citizens' (i.e. those dissatisfied with the performance of their political systems) might end up promoting political reforms rather than de-legitimizing democracy (Norris 1999*d*).

Most importantly, alternative approaches claim that not always or everywhere is the vibrancy of association conducive to democracy. There is a 'dark side' of social capital, as exemplified by the mafia and other criminal organizations. Moreover, the proliferation of politicized mass-membership organizations may be less an indicator of a healthy democracy than it is of polarization within a vulnerable democratic system in crisis, as was true of Weimar Germany (see Allen 1965; Linz and Stepan

1978). 'Bridging' or 'bonding' networks (Putnam 2000) can have widely varying impacts on culture and society at large. More telling in this context, however, is the argument that the nature, democratic or not, of associations' effects depends on distinctive features of that society's political and institutional context. For Berman (1997*a*: 427), 'many of the consequences of associationism stressed by neo-Tocquevillean scholars can be turned to antidemocratic ends as to democratic ones. Perhaps, therefore, associationism should be considered a politically neutral multiplier—neither inherently good nor inherently bad, but rather dependent for its effects on the wider political context' (see also Berman 1997*b*).

We assume this claim as a basic premise for our inquiry, admitting, however, that relatively little is known about the relationships among social, political, and electoral involvement. We lack extensive, cross-national analyses of how civic and social involvement is connected to organized politics at the grass-roots level. We need to ascertain the way voluntary associations politicize their members, translating their organizational involvement into political behaviour. In short, we need to know if secondary associations still play a significant political intermediation role in contemporary consolidated democracies.

We begin this exploration, therefore, by examining cross-national patterns of associational membership. One issue that needs to be addressed is whether these patterns reflect prior characteristics of non-democratic regimes. Linz and Stepan (1996) have argued that a legacy of 'limited pluralism' might emerge in democracies which evolved from post-authoritarian regimes, while no societal pluralism (a 'flattened landscape') might be associated with post-totalitarian societies.

A second consideration is whether the development of secondary organizations in new democracies can be characterized by 'leapfrogging'. Gunther, Puhle, and Diamandouros (1995), Pasquino (2001), and Morlino (1995) have suggested that parties in new democracies might reveal features of 'modernity' or 'the new campaign politics' more clearly than do parties in long-established democratic systems. In old democracies, most parties were created and institutionalized in the early twentieth century or in the immediate aftermath of the Second World War, when the mass-based cleavage party model was still dominant. In so far as the institutionalization of parties perpetuates key organizational features and electoral strategies of that earlier era, they may evolve towards new party models slowly and through processes involving considerable intra-party conflict (as exemplified by the British Labour Party's struggle over the retention of Clause IV in its charter). In contrast, parties created 'from scratch' in the late twentieth century are less institutionally constrained, and can more quickly and thoroughly take on the organizational forms and strategic orientations of newer party models, such as the catch-all party—characterized by personalization of politics through an enhanced role of leaders, direct appeal to voters through mass media, no mass membership, broad, inter-class electoral and programmatic appeals, and lacking close links to mass-organized groups and secondary organizations (see Kirchheimer 1966; Gunther and Diamond 2003).[1]

In short, we need to compare and analyse how secondary associations provide the organizational context of political behaviour in contemporary democracies. This chapter is a step in that direction.

The associational context of political participation can be addressed from two different perspectives: that of the association and the individual. These perspectives reflect the complexity of the notion of mobilization. As Bartolini (2000: 11) argues, mobilization includes processes of hetero-mobilization and self-mobilization, of 'mobilizing' and of 'being mobilized'. In accord with this distinction, our research first explores the extent of associational politicization from the point of view of the organizations themselves, and then analyses the process of politicization at the individual level, particularly with regard to how organizational membership and level of involvement mobilize individuals for active electoral participation.

Our initial expectation is that the extent of political intermediation by secondary associations varies according to the political history of the country and to association types. Some organizations, such as unions and religious associations, have traditions of political activism, especially in Europe—functioning as collateral agencies of political parties, organizing their members, and channelling their electoral support. Other types of associations, such as civic non-religious groups, have been more detached from explicit political action. The constellation of such roles across countries depends on the historical pattern of development of political cleavages (Lipset and Rokkan 1967a; Rokkan 1999; Bartolini 2000). Time and space constraints would not allow for analyses of complex historical patterns of cleavage formation and structuring. Instead, we analyse the extent to which secondary organizations in the 1990s still played a political role in contemporary democracies—often characterized as lacking structured links between parties and organized societal groups, and as composed of individuals rather than social groups—and whether old and new democracies are alike in this regard. While our study does not deal with the 'strong' concept of political mobilization—that is, of integrating former 'subjects' into the political system, as appears to be taking place in the post-communist countries of Central Europe (Enyedi 2003; Markowski 2003)—but it will analyse efforts by political organizations to activate members as voters in elections.

Neither will we explore the interest-articulation roles performed by secondary associations in the manner conceptualized by Verba and Nie. As they observed (1972: 175), organized groups increase

the potency of the citizenry vis-à-vis the government in a number of ways. Organizations through their paid officials speak *for* their members.... [Individuals] can gain access to the government *through* the organization.... [O]rganizations may have an impact on political life in a society through the influence they have on the participatory activities of their members. Citizens may participate directly *because* of their affiliation with an organization.... A rich political participant life may rest on a rich associational life.

The problem with this approach is that the distinction between social and political participation at the individual level does not have clear boundaries. Associations seemingly unrelated to politics, such as sports and leisure clubs, can be strongly connected with a party. There is no doubt that in such contexts members are exposed to a number of political stimuli. They might be exposed to information flows or to cues indicating support for the party which their organization was linked to. Even within these groups, reception of information and political cues might be not uniform across individuals. Some members could be more responsive to the political stands of their organization and successfully politicized, others less.

We regard the degree of receptiveness to political messages from organizations as crucial to the process of politicization. In turn, an individual's receptivity to these messages is a function of the level of organizational involvement—over and above other factors, such as level of education, social status, age, political interest, and so on (Verba and Nie 1972; Baumgartner and Walker 1988; Verba, Schlozman, and Brady 1995). We analyse this relationship across CNEP countries and across different types of associations.

We also examine the behavioural consequences of organizational involvement, such as with regard to turnout, carefully controlling for other determinants of the level of electoral participation (e.g. social status, political interest, sense of political efficacy, and party strength [Verba, Nie, and Kim 1978; Norris 2002]). Another relevant behavioural consequence is voting for one party or another and the extent to which the individual's partisan choice is consistent with the cues and recommendations of the politicized secondary association. In doing so, we analyse what studies in the social-cleavage tradition referred to as 'encapsulation', that is, the ability of some organizations to create an 'external closure' of their members from outside pressures (Bartolini and Mair 1990). Bartolini and Mair seem also to suggest that, among the three components of a cleavage—social, normative, and organizational—it is associational membership that contributes most to the political closure of social relationships. Their aggregate-level study found that organizational density, operationalized as the density of union membership and the ratio of party voters to party members, has had a particularly strong impact, stabilizing partisan preferences and reducing the level of electoral volatility over more than a century of European electoral history. With the benefit of cross-nationally comparable survey data, we test this relationship at the individual level, and expand the range of organizations to be analysed beyond unions and parties. These cross-sectional data, unfortunately, do not allow us to fully explore the *dynamic* factors affecting the formation of political preferences (Zaller 1992). But we undertake a cross-national comparison of the share of the electorate in each country that is 'encapsulated', as well as an attempt to determine the impact on this encapsulation process of such factors as the type of association, the extent of active involvement within the organization, the degree of exposure to its political messages, and perceptions of bias in that flow of information.

The polities included in the CNEP study reflect a wide array of political development trajectories, levels of social and economic development, and organizational structures. This variation will greatly facilitate our analysis and provide a unique research opportunity. In this chapter, we focus on ten countries (Bulgaria, Chile, Greece, Hungary, Hong Kong, Italy, Spain, Uruguay, and the United States), which vary substantially in their patterns of association membership, aggregate levels of involvement, and the development of social capital and democratic legitimacy.

The United States, previously regarded as the paradigmatic example of a democratic polity nurtured by a diffuse texture of social participation, has experienced a decline of social capital, and an acceleration in the personalization of politics and in the individualization of voting behaviour. Italy's fifty-year-old democracy, with a record of intense partisan cleavages, underwent in the 1990s a radical change of its party system which substantially altered relationships between parties and other secondary associations (with the Christian Democratic collapse undermining the political relevance of religious associations). Japan also underwent similar changes in the early 1990s. Spain and Greece, in contrast, consolidated their democratic institutions without developing the close links between parties and other organizations that were forged in Italy in the 1940s. Bulgaria and Hungary are post-communist systems with no significant prior democratic experience, and whose civil societies are considered less vibrant than those in countries with long democratic histories. Chile and Uruguay, at the time of the 1993 and 1994 surveys, represented yet a different political, social, and economic pattern, with Chilean democratic consolidation still a work in progress. Hong Kong stands alone, since it is not a democratic regime, and its future political trajectory is still very much in doubt. These widely differing political trajectories will make it possible to compare the political roles of secondary associations in new democracies with those in older, long-established democratic systems.

This chapter is organized as follows. In the second section, an analysis of patterns of membership in voluntary associations is presented, and an explanatory model of social participation is discussed. In the third section, we explore how countries differ as to the degree of politicization of their secondary associations. We also discuss factors that affect our respondents' perceptions of stands taken by their respective associations, and influence electoral turnout and partisan choice. In the fourth section, we analyse, cross-nationally and across different types of secondary association, the extent of electoral encapsulation.

Voluntary Associations: Patterns of Membership

We begin our analysis by considering the patterns of social participation among our group of countries, employing three standard indicators of joining propensity: the membership rate, measured by the share of citizens who belong to at least one association; the density rate, that is the individual multi-membership in voluntary associations; and active membership, that is the percentage of citizens who participate actively in the life of associations. The three measures together describe the 'joining propensity' of civil society, although each taps a different dimension of social involvement.

Being an Association Member

As expected, membership in voluntary associations varies quite considerably across countries. The overall membership rate for each country is

143

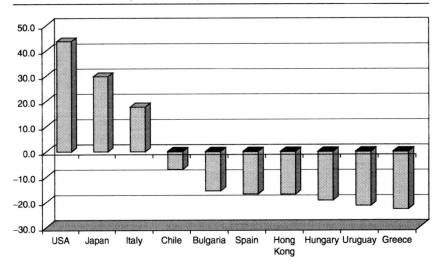

Figure 4.1 Overall associational membership (Percentage difference against average value)

presented in the second-to-last row of Table 4.1. In terms of overall membership, on average, more than 40 per cent of the citizens in our countries belong to at least one association. But there is considerable cross-national variation, from a peak of 85 per cent in the United States to less than 20 per cent in Greece. In general, it can be said that longer-established democracies exhibit a higher 'joining propensity' than younger democratic polities, with the United States as an unequivocal leader and Japan and Italy not far behind. A clearer picture of the differences between the new and old democracies can be seen in Figure 4.1, which presents a graphic image of each country's deviation from the pooled average.

These findings lend support to the hypothesis that liberal democratic institutions encourage a wider range of associations and deeper associational activity than do less liberal polities. Nonetheless, it should be noted that one study (Paxton 2002) found that the impact of democracy on secondary associations (i.e. that more associations would be expected to exist when governments allow them to exist) was relatively modest following the introduction of controls for other variables.[2] Our data also show that the nature of the previous non-democratic regime does not seem to affect the joining propensity. In Greece and Spain, both previously authoritarian regimes, the overall membership rate is actually lower than that of Bulgaria, which had a post-totalitarian regime.

Table 4.1 Membership in voluntary associations (percentage of total population)

	USA	Japan	Italy	Chile	Bulgaria	Spain	Hong Kong	Hungary	Uruguay	Greece
Labour unions	14.1	8.4	24.7	5.6	13.7	6.8	8.4	12.3	8	2.3
Political parties	—	4.9	6.2	3.1	10.3	1.7	0.2	1	7.7	6.6
Professional associations	27.3	6.8	15.8	4.3	0.3	2.8	4.8	2.4	2.1	5.5
Farmers' associations	4.3	13.3	—	—	—	—	—	—	—	—
Religious associations	52.7	4.7	5.1	22	2.1	3.2	6	2.5	8.6	0.9
Cultural associations	—	—	—	3.7	0.7	2.3	1.1	0.9	4.5	2.5
Public interest groups	14.8	—	—	—	—	—	—	—	—	—
Fraternal associations	16.6	—	—	—	—	—	—	—	—	—
Environmental associations	11.3	0.6	4.5	1	0.4	0.8	0.8	0.1	0.6	1
Youth associations	—	—	3.5	2.4	0.5	0.7	1.4	0.4	1.8	0.7
Sports associations	17.1	11.4	16.9	13.7	0.8	5	0.7	1.4	5.9	4.5
Feminist associations	4.3	0.5	—	1.1	0.4	1	1.3	—	1	0.1
Neighbourhood associations	22.2	47.3	—	10.1	0.5	5	4.2	0.8	3.5	—
Parents' associations	—	—	11.6	7.9	0.4	4.3	4.2	—	2.5	2.3
Voluntary associations	—	—	—	—	—	—	—	—	—	—
Veterans' associations	9.3	1.5	—	—	—	—	—	—	—	—
War bereaved associations	—	0.5	—	—	—	—	—	—	—	—
Civic groups	20.5	—	—	—	—	—	—	—	—	—
Ethnic/racial associations	5.1	—	—	—	—	—	—	—	—	—
Support groups	14.1	—	—	—	—	—	—	—	—	—
Livelihood cooperatives	—	9.8	—	—	—	—	—	—	—	—
Young/old man/woman associations	—	13.1	—	—	—	—	—	—	—	—
Groups of service to public	—	2.8	—	—	—	—	—	—	—	—
Hobby clubs	—	13.3	—	—	—	—	—	—	—	—
Other associations	—	—	12.1	2.2	0.6	1.7	1.2	2.8	1	0.6
Overall membership	**85.4**	**71.5**	**59.5**	**34.7**	**26.2**	**25.0**	**24.9**	**22.5**	**20.4**	**19.0**
No. of cases	1,318	1,333	2,502	1,305	1,216	1,448	988	1,500	1,005	966

The rows above the Overall Membership rate in Table 4.1 present the percentages of the population belonging to each type of organization.[3] These data reveal large variations cross-nationally with regard to the *type* of voluntary association. To be sure, cross-national differences are quite modest among types of associations with generally low-membership levels (e.g. feminist, youth, and cultural groups). But for other types of organizations (e.g. professional, sports, union, neighbourhood, and religious associations) the range is quite considerable, with cross-national variations running up to 52 per cent of respondents for religious groups. Particularly noteworthy is the extraordinarily high level of membership in religious organizations in the United States (and, to a lesser extent, in Chile). In the American context, this high level of affiliation (53% of population) may in part be a supply-driven consequence of a competitive sectarian market (Curtis, Douglas, and Grabb 1992; Chaves and Gorski 2001), which boosts the participation rate.[4] In Japan, the joining propensity is particularly marked by a high level of involvement in neighbourhood associations (47% of population), a peculiar feature of Japanese society not found elsewhere.[5] However, it is not only membership in religious associations which sets the United States apart from other countries. Civic non-religious associations—which in the aggregate have the largest membership in our sample (22% of the total)—are a case in point. Here again, apart from Japan, the huge lead of American citizens goes unchallenged. Thus, our findings seem to support the claim by Lipset (1990: 74–89) that the strong American orientation to religious voluntarism extends and spills over to voluntary community or civic activity in general.

Yet this gap between the United States and the other countries shrinks significantly when other types of associations are taken into account. This trend is already well visible in the case of unions and professional associations; sport associations are another example.[6] Finally, when we look at the propensity to join a political party, Americans are outpaced by citizens of several countries: noticeably, though little surprisingly, Bulgarians, but also Italians, Greeks, and Uruguayans. In addition, it should be noted that differences *across countries* increase, pointing to the working of some specific local factors.

One explanation of these cross-national variations that has been put forward is that membership rates are related to a country's level of economic development: *ceteris paribus*, the higher the income per capita, the higher the propensity to join an association. On the whole, this relationship receives some support (Pearson's r = .74): the United States, Japan, and Italy are almost perfectly aligned on the polynomial regression line. But at lower levels of associational involvement, Hong Kong and Bulgaria are widely off it, though in opposite directions, as are Spain and Chile. Clearly, other factors impinge on associational propensity other than a country's level of economic development (see, among others, Curtis, Douglas, and Grabb 2001).

The data we have examined to this point are based on objective measures of organizational affiliation. Let us turn our attention to a more subjective notion of associational membership. Our CNEP questionnaire asked respondents to identify 'the most important' organization to which they belong. We aggregated these responses by type of association, and present the percentage mentioning each type in each country in Table 4.2. The resulting typology distinguishes among professional associations, labour unions, political parties, sports groups, religious organizations, and a residual category (which we call 'civic non-religious') in which we include community groups, social welfare organizations, cultural associations, etc. Seen from this perspective, it becomes apparent that there is no common associational pattern. Rather, each country exhibits a distinct 'associational configuration', clearly indicating that associational membership is remarkably context- and path-dependent. A typical example of this dependence is union membership, both for formerly socialist countries and also for countries with closed-shop practices. Other examples are religious associations in the United States and Chile, or neighbourhood associations in Japan. If we exclude political parties from the analysis (as we do throughout the remainder of this chapter), so as to concentrate on (ostensibly) non-political voluntary associations, the picture does not change significantly, except for Bulgaria, Greece, and Uruguay, where political parties are an important component of the country's associational landscape (see Table 4.2).

We now move to an analysis at the individual level utilizing a 'pooled' data-set in an effort to assess those factors leading to membership in voluntary associations. As can be seen in Table 4.3, taking into account membership in *any* voluntary association, characteristics commonly associated with 'social centrality' appear to foster higher levels of social participation (Milbrath and Goel 1977): in particular, being male, employed, and better educated makes it more likely to join a voluntary association of some kind.[7] Only the age factor seems to have a different impact, in the sense that all age groups have a higher probability of associational membership vis-à-vis the youngest cohort considered (18- to 29-year old).

However, the most interesting result of the analysis is the huge impact that the variable country has on membership propensity, even controlling

147

Table 4.2 Membership by type of voluntary association and country (most important group as percentage of total association members)

Type of association	USA[a]	Japan	Italy	Chile	Bulgaria	Spain	Hong Kong	Hungary	Uruguay	Greece	Overall
Civic non-religious	13.7	61.2	33.8	18.7	6.1	33.3	36.9	20.5	20.2	21.7	30.1
Union	2.1	8.5	23.2	10.4	45.9	26.5	27.4	51.2	21.6	12.0	18.4
Professional	2.8	16.6	17.4	7.3	1.3	10.0	13.3	9.9	5.3	23.9	11.3
Religious	11.2	5.2	5.0	40.5	7.3	11.2	21.2	8.1	26.9	4.9	11.0
Sport	1.6	7.9	16.1	18.7	1.0	14.2	0.8	5.1	9.6	13.0	9.2
Party	0.4	0.6	4.5	4.4	38.5	4.7	0.4	5.1	16.3	24.5	5.9
Multi-member	68.1	—	—	—	—	—	—	—	—	—	14.0
Total	100.0	100.0	100.0	100.0	100.0	100.0	100.0	100.0	100.0	100.0	100.0
No. of cases	1,130	950	1,412	385	314	339	241	332	208	184	5,495

[a] Since most important association is not recorded, associations' membership (re-coded in mutually exclusive categories plus a multiple membership category) is used.

Table 4.3 Logistic model of membership in voluntary associations (pooled analysis)[a]

	All associations	Civic non-religious	Religious	Sport	Union and professional	Parties
Age (18–29)						
30/45	0.406*	0.437*	0.067	−0.489*	0.902*	0.503*
46/59	0.408*	0.452*	0.194***	−0.750*	1.023*	0.704*
60+	0.438*	0.469*	0.408*	−1.136*	0.851*	1.103*
Not working						
Work	0.422*	−0.030	−0.098	−0.014	1.197*	0.169
Education (less than secondary)						
secondary completed	0.374*	0.499*	0.036	0.206*	0.276*	0.559*
Gender (male)						
female	−0.349*	−0.045	0.134***	−1.057*	−0.511*	−0.697*
Country (USA)						
Spain	−2.616*	−2.183*	−3.538*	−1.359*	−1.610*	−0.541**
Italy	−1.286*	−1.439*	−2.975*	−0.081	−0.123	0.632*
Chile	−2.241*	−2.038*	−1.774*	−0.830*	−2.176*	−0.368
Bulgaria	−2.752*	−3.961*	−3.973*	−3.163*	−1.371*	1.068*
Greece	−3.149*	−3.100*	−4.785*	−1.560*	−2.156*	0.649*
Hong Kong	−2.806*	−2.380*	−2.826*	−3.380*	−1.638*	−2.801*
Uruguay	−2.999*	−2.758*	−2.774*	−1.616*	−2.291*	0.541*
Hungary	−2.858*	−3.281*	−3.719*	−2.590*	−1.101*	−1.096*
Japan	−0.824*	0.025	−3.137*	−0.470*	−0.741*	−0.809*
Constant	1.093*	−0.232**	−0.103	−0.722	−1.880	−4.057
No of cases	13,459	13,459	13,459	13,459	13,459	13,459
χ^2	3,353.39	3,312.87	2,199.59	1177.80	2,418.98	441.90
p	0.000	0.000	0.000	0.000	0.000	0.000
Pseudo R^2	0.297	0.334	0.320	0.192	0.262	0.112

* $p < .01$; ** $p < .05$; *** $p < .10$

[a] Dependent variable: member of voluntary association (1); non-member (0).

for socio-demographic factors. Using the United States as the reference category, citizens of all other countries exhibit a much lower propensity to join a voluntary association. Only the Japanese are not so vastly outdistanced by the Americans as far as membership propensity is concerned. Again a note of caution is appropriate at this point: this picture might have been different if other countries (such as Britain, Canada, Australia, and Scandinavian countries) were compared with the United States.[8]

Somewhat different findings result from analyses using specific types of associations as the dependent variable. For example, employment status disappears as a significant determinant of joining propensity except for membership in union and professional associations. And the impact of other variables (age, gender, and education) also varies, but in a rather predictable fashion.[9]

Networks of Involvement

Absolute membership rates, however, are less relevant than the existence of an articulated network of associations in which individuals are involved. In this respect, the countries we analyse exhibit a highly differentiated level of associational density (Table 4.4). On the whole, more than half of association members belong to a single association, a quarter of them to two organizations, and a fifth to three or more. Differences across countries appear large, with the United States being

Table 4.4 Density of membership (multiple membership) in non-political voluntary associations (excluding political parties)[a]

Country	Number of associations					Total	Mean	Standard deviation	N
	1	2	3	4	>4				
USA	25.2	26.5	19.9	11.5	16.9	100	2.87	1.83	1,126
Japan	43.4	33.6	15.1	5.0	2.8	100	1.92	1.08	953
Italy	57.6	28.4	10.0	2.9	1.0	100	1.61	0.87	1,459
Uruguay	65.6	21.9	8.2	3.8	0.5	100	1.54	0.94	183
Chile	65.9	22.2	9.4	1.8	0.7	100	1.49	0.80	446
Spain	72.7	19.3	6.0	1.4	0.6	100	1.38	0.75	352
Greece	73.8	20.1	6.0	0.0	0.0	100	1.32	0.58	149
Hong Kong	74.3	19.2	4.9	0.4	1.2	100	1.37	0.87	245
Hungary	86.0	11.0	2.4	0.6	0.0	100	1.18	0.48	328
Bulgaria	88.7	9.5	1.8	0.0	0.0	100	1.13	0.39	221
Total	54.5	25.2	11.4	4.4	4.4	100	1.83	1.26	5,462

[a] The table refers only to association members. Non-members are excluded from calculations.

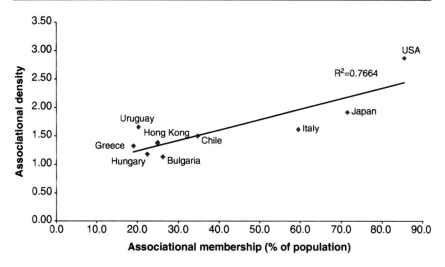

Figure 4.2 Association membership and association density

a noteworthy outlier: only a quarter of those Americans who belong to an organization belong to just one, while 17 per cent belong to more than four associations—a percentage which vastly exceeds those of the other countries in this survey. On average, Americans belong to 2.9 associations (standard deviation 1.83). In this respect, it is not inaccurate to speak of American exceptionalism (Putnam 2000; Putnam and Feldstein 2003). All the other countries appear to be in a different league altogether, with the partial exception of Japan. By contrast, at the other end of the spectrum, the overwhelming majority of Bulgarian and Hungarian respondents who belong to a group limit their membership to a single association (mostly, unions), confirming the poor civic articulation of these post-communist societies.

In terms of explaining the density of associational affiliation, by far the best predictor is the country's aggregate level of membership. As can be seen in Figure 4.2, the higher the membership rate of a country, the higher also its associational density. The strength of this linear relationship is quite impressive (R^2 = .77).

Membership Versus Active Participation

The growing literature on social capital has emphasized the importance of distinguishing between people who are simply members of associations and those who are actively involved in the workings of the organizations they join (see Newton 1999*a*). If participation is limited to mere formal membership and check-writing rather than active involvement with these groups, the positive internal effect of membership—on communication and organizational skills, socialization, political efficacy, etc.—are weak or non-existent. From this viewpoint, the third measure of social participation we take into account is *active membership*.[10] Overall, almost 40 per cent of association members appear actively involved in the life and work of their organization. Of course, this is an average value; cross-country differences are indeed noticeable. In fact, the 'involvement index' (the ratio between active and passive members) ranges from 1.37 in the United States and a meagre 0.18 in Italy, as can be seen in Table 4.5.

It is noteworthy that, seen from this perspective, the relative rankings of countries are quite different from what we observed above: Uruguay and Greece, which ranked lowest in terms of overall membership rate, are second and fourth in terms of the involvement index. At the other end of the spectrum, we find Hong Kong and, especially, Italy, where the overwhelming majority of association members is uninvolved with the activities of their organizations. These changes in relative rankings notwithstanding, there is a very strong positive correlation ($r = .87$) between overall membership and active membership. In other words, the degree of involvement is a positive linear function of the size of associational membership in our countries. The propensity to activism (better, the factors leading to it) among association members is roughly similar in all countries examined, with the exception of Italy.

The type of organization is another factor explaining the intensity of participation. It is to be expected that different kinds of associations entail different commitments of time, anticipated costs, problems of availability, etc., which in turn influence the depth of individual involvement in the groups activities. We can explore this dimension by examining the distribution of active members according to the typology of non-political voluntary associations we have elaborated taking into account 'the most important organization' mentioned by our respondents mention (see above). As can be seen in Table 4.6, there are, indeed, substantial differences among types of groups with regard to the intensity of involvement. Religious groups show the highest rate of activism (55% of whose members participate always or often in group activities), followed, as one could perhaps have foreseen, by sport groups (49%). Civic non-religious

Table 4.5 Intensity of participation in activities of voluntary non-political associations by country (percentage of total population, excluding political parties)

Intensity of participation	USA	Uruguay	Chile	Greece	Japan	Spain	Bulgaria	Hungary	Hong Kong	Italy	Overall
Non-member	19.4	84.7	67.9	85.1	31.4	77.9	84.6	78.6	75.2	43.8	61.6
Passive involvement[a]	34.1	6.9	14.6	6.8	35.6	14.7	11.0	15.4	18.9	47.5	23.7
Active involvement[b]	46.5	8.4	17.5	8.0	32.9	7.5	4.5	6.0	5.9	8.7	14.7
Total	100.0	100.0	100.0	100.0	100.0	100.0	100.0	100.0	100.0	100.0	100.0
No. of cases	1,318	971	1,288	921	1,327	1,432	1,095	1,483	987	2,438	13,260
Involvement index[c]	1.37	1.22	1.20	1.17	0.92	0.51	0.41	0.39	0.31	0.18	0.62

[a] Passive involvement: members participate never or sometimes to activities of association.

[b] Active involvement: members participate often or always to activities of association.

[c] Ratio between active and passive involvement.

153

Table 4.6 Intensity of participation in activities of voluntary non-political associations by type of association and country (percentage of active members; countries are ranked according to overall activism from highest to lowest)

Type of association	USA	Uruguay	Chile	Greece	Japan	Spain	Bulgaria	Hungary	Hong Kong	Italy	All countries
Religious	63.4	68.0	49.0	a	53.1	67.6	47.8	55.6	52.9	38.0	54.5
Sport	a	a	64.3	91.3	69.9	48.9	a	a	a	31.1	49.2
Civic non-religious	39.0	66.7	62.7	59.0	43.2	34.8	a	45.6	25.8	17.8	35.3
Professional	25.0	a	18.5	42.9	56.9	15.2	a	9.1	0.0	4.5	23.3
Union	22.7	26.3	80.0	27.3	42.3	17.0	25.2	15.9	7.6	5.2	18.6
Multi-member	63.1	—	—	—	—	—	—	—	—	—	—
All associations	57.7	55.0	54.6	54.0	48.0	33.8	29.0	28.0	23.7	15.5	38.3
No. of cases	1,062	149	414	137	910	317	169	318	245	1,371	5,092

Note: Entries are active members as a % of total members.
a N < 20.

groups (35%) and, especially, professional associations (23%) and labour unions (19%) show significantly lower rates of activism.

When these patterns of organizational affiliation are examined cross-nationally, three different groups of countries can be distinguished. A first cluster, made up of the United States and Japan, is characterized by higher-than-average levels of involvement for all types of associations. In a second group of countries—Uruguay, Chile, and Greece—some types of associations (different for each country) show an extraordinarily high level of members' activism, pushing their overall percentage above the average value. In the last, and largest, group of countries—including Spain, Bulgaria, Hungary, Hong Kong, and Italy—the level of active involvement for some types of associations is so low as to depress significantly their average level of activism. On the whole, the observed differences among countries' 'working' memberships appear to depend both on the association's specific involvement capacity and on the varying combinations of voluntary associations within countries.[11]

The data we have presented to this point clearly reveal that membership in voluntary associations varies quite considerably across countries, although this point should not be overemphasized: certain types of associations are characteristic of a specific country, and if we leave these national peculiarities outside general analysis, cross-country differences in membership rate decrease considerably. Second, what appears more important than rates of membership is the fact that there is no common associational pattern among the countries we analyse. Rather, each country exhibits a specific 'associational configuration', implying that associational membership is remarkably *context- and path-dependent*. This also appears at the individual level with regard to factors pushing towards associational membership. Third, there is no obvious pattern in membership density among our countries, except for its strong linear correlation with the overall membership rate. Fourth, shifting to active participation in the life of associations, our data reveal that the degree of involvement is a linear function of the size of associational membership in our countries: the more widespread that associational affiliation is, the higher the degree of individuals' involvement. Unions show the smallest rate of activism and religious associations the highest. Finally, the observed differences among countries' working memberships appear to depend both on the different configuration of voluntary associations within countries and, especially, on the association's *specific* involvement capacity. Significant interaction effects between country and types of association were found.

Political Intermediation by Voluntary Associations: Associations' Efforts and Individual Resources

In this section of the chapter we analyse the linkages between political and civil societies by looking at the pattern of group politicization, that is, the involvement of various associations in the electoral process through the mobilization of their members. We analyse this relationship from a dual perspective: first, that of the association, and then that of the individual. In the last section, we then discuss the extent to which politicized secondary associations succeed in channelling their members' electoral support, and help to shape their voting preferences.

The Web of Associations' Political Contacts

We begin our analysis by examining the extent to which civil societies are involved in the electoral process. To gauge these group activities, we consider the respondents' reported political contacts at time of elections by associations to which respondents belong.[12] Table 4.7 shows the percentages of members of each type of group contacted. Overall, about 30 per cent of group members reported that they were contacted at time of elections by associations passing on information about the upcoming election, with Japan showing the highest level of group politicization (58%) and Hungary the lowest (11%).

What is most noteworthy in this table is the high percentage of political contacts among organization members in Asia. This is best seen if we look at the ratio of informed to uninformed members, as is presented in the second row of data. This indicator reflects the associations' capacities to distribute political information to members. In Japan and Hong Kong, these ratios are 1.39 and .98, respectively. Much lower ratios are found in other countries, ranging from about .4 in the United States and Uruguay to .18 and .13 in Spain and Hungary, respectively. Italy and Chile share a low score of .22: for every 100 uninformed members, only 22 were exposed to political information from the (most important) organizations which they belong to. Overall, it is clear that the degree of politicization of voluntary associations varies considerably from one country to another, and that this variation is not correlated with the aggregate level of organizational membership in each country. Higher levels of membership are not accompanied by higher propensities of groups to get politically involved.

Table 4.7 Non-political voluntary associations' electoral contacts by country and according to type of association (countries ranked according to percentage of informed members)

Type	Japan	Hong Kong	Uruguay	USA	Bulgaria	Greece	Chile	Italy	Spain	Hungary	All	All (weighted[b])
Informed members (% of members)	58.2	49.6	28.7	28.3	25.4	25.2	20.3	18.0	15.5	11.4	29.9	32.0
Ratio of informed/not informed	1.39	0.98	0.40	0.39	0.34	0.33	0.22	0.22	0.18	0.13	0.42	0.46
Type of association												
Professional	74.1	40.6	*a*	12.5	*a*	15.9	*a*	23.3	12.5	9.1	36.1	39.0
Union	60.5	68.2	51.1	70.8	27.1	54.5	38.5	30.8	37.8	15.3	35.7	38.2
Sport	45.3	*a*	15.0	*a*	*a*	20.8	11.4	9.3	4.4	*a*	15.7	17.7
Religious	65.3	29.4	25.0	22.8	4.3	*a*	14.8	16.9	11.1	11.1	23.2	23.8
Civic non-religious	54.6	44.9	19.0	22.6	31.6	25.0	23.8	10.7	6.7	5.9	30.2	33.6
Multi-member (USA)				30.0							30.0	30.0
Base (N)	944	240	174	1,126	193	139	202	1,348	291	315	4,972	4,603

Note: Entries are informed members as a % of members of associations.

[a] N < 20.

[b] Data weighted to equal sample size by country.

One possible explanation of these varying patterns involves the type of organization. We hypothesize that the nature of the intermediary organization may exert some influence on its perceived political activism. The percentage of members reporting that they received electoral information for each type of group is presented in Table 4.7. Indeed, different kinds of organizations vary with regard to political contacts reported by their members, with unions and professional organizations perceived as the most politicized, and sport associations the least politically involved.

Labour unions are the most heavily involved in vote-mobilization efforts in all countries except Bulgaria, where community organizations appear slightly more politically active. This does not come as a surprise, given unions' historical record of engagement in electoral politics. Seen from this historical perspective, however, unions are actually weaker in their electoral contacts than one might have assumed. With the exception of Japan and Hong Kong, where over two-thirds of union members report having received electoral information, the range is from a high of about 50 per cent in Uruguay and Greece to a low of 15 per cent in Hungary. In Italy and Spain, only between three and four out of ten union members received political information. And in both of our post-communist countries, Bulgaria and Hungary, unions exhibit a very low propensity to engage in electoral politics. With regard to the United States, which shows a very high propensity to be active at election time, these data must be interpreted with some caution, since this variable is constructed in a manner that differs from those in the other questionnaires.[13] The dissemination of political information by the other economic-based organizations—professional associations—is less common, except in Japan, Hong Kong and, to a lesser extent, Italy. In these somewhat 'corporatist' countries, membership in a professional organization may be a requisite to practise a profession, meaning that joining may not be a fully voluntary activity, which might, in turn, affect receptivity to these messages.

Civic non-religious associations are the next most frequent disseminators of political information. This is a significant finding. Closest to the 'model' of civic engagement, these associations politically mobilize their members at a rate (34%) only slightly lower than that of unions (whose weighted average is 38%). One could speculate that a weakened political role of unions has been counterbalanced by a rise of political engagement of civic associations, although we have no diachronic data to test this hypothesis. The overall trend appears to be one in which union and civic group membership reinforce each other: countries with higher union political involvement show also a more intense civic association political activity. This is not a uniform finding, however: in Spain and Italy, where unions are significant sources of political information for their members, civic associations do not appear to be politicized, while the exact opposite is true in Bulgaria and Chile.

Religious organizations exhibit an intermediate propensity to engage in politics. On average a quarter of their members in our panel were contacted at election time. Again, Japan stands out as exceptionally high (65%), although the relatively small share of our respondents who belong to such groups (5%) suggests that not too much should be made of this finding, since only about 3 per cent of the electorate received political information through this channel. The reverse is true of our interpretation of data from the United States: while only 23 per cent of religious group members received such communications in the course of the 1992 election, they amount to fully 12 per cent of our respondents.[14] Findings for other countries are mixed. In Chile and Italy, political involvement of religious organizations appears lower than one might have predicted on the basis of the strong Catholic subcultures in both countries. Spain's low level of political involvement of religious organizations in 1993 (11%) reflects the prudence shown by the Church during the transition to democracy (Linz and Stepan 1996: 93), while the low scores for post-communist Bulgaria and Hungary are most likely a legacy of restrictions on religious practice under the previous communist regimes.

The overall levels of exposure to political communications through secondary associations (presented in the first row of Table 4.7) can be regarded as the aggregated product of highly differentiated patterns of politicization of the various types of groups in these countries. And each country's particular associational configuration is, in turn, a product of highly path-dependent processes of institutional evolution of these groups with regard to both overall levels of organizational membership and varying levels of group politicization. Accordingly, the low rates of both information diffusion and political involvement of secondary associations in former communist countries is explained by the fact that the relatively low level of politicization of trade unions (the organizational type with the highest membership rates), coupled with the overall weakness of other types of organizations. Similarly, surprisingly low level of dissemination of political information by organized groups in Italy, a country with relatively high levels of organizational membership, is explained by the weak partisan links of those groups following the complete restructuring of the Italian party system in the mid-1990s and the predominance of catch-all-type parties. It is likely that these scores would have been much higher a decade earlier when the Italian party system was dominated by mass-membership parties with strong links to allied secondary associations. This same configuration is also generally characteristic of the United States, which has a very high level of organizational membership but a relatively modest level of group politicization. Again, we must interpret these data in light of the specific political context of the 1992 elections. At that time, religious organizations were characterized by relatively low levels of partisan involvement (Verba, Schlozman, and Brady 1995: 63; in future research, we will be able to examine the extent to which the politicization of religion over the following decade and a half has altered this partisan/associational configuration in the United States). The exact opposite configuration can be seen in Uruguay and Hong Kong, which are characterized by low levels of organizational membership but high politicization of those groups (especially unions and religious groups in Uruguay and unions and civic associations in Hong Kong).

Organizations' Explicit Partisan Support

To what extent is the political information disseminated by organizations explicitly supportive of a party or a candidate? Secondary organizations can take positions on many political issues, and inform their members of their positions. But does this information explicitly endorse candidates and parties? Some organizations, such as unions, have a long and established tradition of political and party involvement (though our data reflect some recent retrenchment). In other cases, partisan involvement is more recent, such as the recent politicization of the fundamentalist right in the United States. Other groups, in contrast, may adopt non-partisan stands on a number of political issues.

With the striking exceptions of Bulgaria and Hungary, which stake out the two extreme ends of the continuum, we find surprisingly little cross-national variation in the extent to which our respondents report having received information explicitly endorsing a party or candidate (see Table 4.8). For most of the countries examined in this chapter, the percentages reporting such contacts range between 16 per cent (in Spain) to 26 per cent (Japan). The two post-communist countries, in contrast, are extreme and puzzling outliers, with only 8 per cent of Hungarian respondents reporting such contacts, while fully 79 per cent of Bulgarians having received such information. What is most striking about the Bulgarian case is that all three of the predominant types of organization (trade unions,

Table **4.8** Non-political voluntary associations' electoral support by country and according to type of association (percentage of association members who report electoral support by organization; countries ranked according to percentage of those members perceiving support)

Type	Bulgaria	Japan	Greece	Hong Kong	Uruguay	USA	Chile	Italy	Spain	Hungary	All	All[a]
Members perceiving associations' electoral support (% of all members)	78.8	25.7	25.2	21.3	21.3	19.2	17.8	16.8	15.8	8.3	21.5	22.5
Ratio support/ not support	3.76	0.34	0.33	0.27	0.27	0.24	0.19	0.20	0.19	0.09	0.27	0.29
Type of association												
Professional	b	41.8	27.3	25.0	b	6.3	b	10.6	19.4	3.0	21.9	24.9
Trade union	79.2	60.5	59.1	47.0	28.9	62.5	30.8	35.7	44.6	7.6	41.4	43.9
Sport	b	8.0	12.5	b	5.0	b	11.4	6.6	2.2	b	7.5	7.9
Religious	87.0	63.3	b	0.0	19.6	11.0	9.9	14.1	5.4	14.8	19.0	19.0
Civic non-religious	73.7	15.7	15.0	13.5	21.4	11.0	21.4	12.4	3.8	11.8	14.2	14.7
Multi-member (USA)						21.4					21.4	21.4
Base (N)	193	944	139	240	174	1,126	202	1,348	291	315	4,972	4,604

[a] Data weighted by sample size per country.
[b] N < 20.

religious groups, and civic non-religious associations) are all highly politicized in an explicitly partisan manner. Post-communist Hungary and Bulgaria stand then in sharp contrast with one another, with the former having a relatively non-partisan civil society, but secondary associations in the latter being highly politicized and partisan. Given the presence of a strong post-Communist Party in Bulgaria, this pattern might be regarded as a legacy of the former regime's non-democratic mobilization from above rather than as an autonomous and lively civil society.

What explains the relatively narrow variance in the extent of partisan political involvement of secondary associations in the aggregate? An answer to this question requires an examination of the level of partisan politicization of each type of group. One pattern is clearly evident: in every country (except for Bulgaria and Hungary) unions are the most partisan organizations. Only in Hungary (8%) is the percentage of union members receiving explicit endorsements of parties and candidates below 30 per cent, and in four of these countries the percentage substantially exceeds 50 per cent. On average, 44 per cent of union members report that their trade organization explicitly favoured one party or candidate during the previous election campaign. If we also include professional organizations (25% of whose members report a political support), it is then evident that economic associations show the most pronounced political bias.

After unions and professional associations, religious groups would appear at first glance to be the next most politicized type of organization. Its average level of reported partisan contact (19%) is inflated by the very high figures for Bulgaria (87%) and Japan (63%). In the other countries, religious organizations actually appear to be generally non-partisan. Only in Japan, Hungary, and Bulgaria are religious organizations perceived as taking sides more than any other kind of organization. And with the exception of Bulgaria, and to a much lesser extent Uruguay and Chile, civic non-religious groups are generally non-partisan.

In general, then, economic secondary associations are clearly more strongly committed to partisan politics than are non-economic organizations. This has a substantial impact on the aggregate level of partisanship with which we began this discussion. Where traditional economic organizations are well developed, secondary associations have their greatest impact on the electoral process, in large measure because they tend to be more politicized and explicitly partisan. This finding implies that, from a social capital perspective, associations are not all alike in their impact on the political involvement of their members. Most strikingly, civic non-religious organizations—the very model of civic engagement—have a relatively modest impact on the flow of partisan information to their members, despite their relatively high levels of membership and their 'importance' to their members.

Individual-Level Effects of Association Involvement on Exposure to Political Information

The aggregate-level data we have discussed to this point have revealed that about 30 per cent of all members of secondary associations (or about 11% of the total population) across these ten countries report having received political information from those groups during the course of the previous election campaign. The average percentage of respondents reporting that organizations explicitly supported a party or candidate was about 8 per cent, or 21 per cent of those who belonged to at least one secondary association. The conventional wisdom, from Michels on, is that people highly involved in the association's life are more likely than less active members to perceive the political stands of their organization. In other words, organization involvement has an impact beyond those of individual-level factors such as education, social status, and political interest. Several recent studies have confirmed this observation. Baumgartner and Walker (1988: 923), for example, found in their analysis of American National Election Studies pilot-survey data that 'only 28.5 per cent of those who are contributors only or report that they are inactive members believe that the groups they are affiliated with are engaged in public affairs, while 43.5 per cent of those who describe themselves as active members report political activity by their groups'. They also found that active membership affects the awareness of the group's involvement in public affairs, 'regardless of the type of group with respondents are affiliated'. Additionally, Verba and Nie (172, 194) found that 'affiliation with manifestly non-political organizations does increase an individual's [political] participation rate but only if there is some political exposure within the organization'. In 1995, Verba, Schlozman, and Brady found new evidence of the strong relation between level of involvement and perception of the political stand of the association, showing also the crucial role played by the perception of association political stands in fostering the individual's political participation level. Contrary to Baumgartner and Walker, however, Verba and Nie (1972: 194) claimed that 'the groups differ in the opportunities they afford for activity and in the political exposures that takes place in them'. Thanks to the CNEP research design, we are able to test these hypotheses and determine whether these American-based findings also hold in other countries and across different types of organization.

In our earlier analysis of the correlates of organizational activism, we also found that the level of involvement varies according to the type of association, even after individual-level socio-demographic characteristics and country effects are controlled. The level of activism in an organization is greater among members of secular-voluntary and religious organizations than among union members. Even sport and recreational groups seem to offer more opportunities for individual activity than unions and professional associations. But we also found that these economic associations were more clearly perceived as disseminating partisan-biased information to their members than were other types of groups. What, then, is the net impact of these two seemingly contradictory influences on the politicization of members? While unions and professional associations allow for less active involvement, do these more partisan types of organizations have larger effects on perception of information and partisan support than do other organizations?

Finally, in the previous discussion we also pointed out that, at the aggregate level, the frequency of political contacts by non-political secondary associations appears to have been affected by each country's previous political evolution, particularly with regard to how its society was politicized. Not unexpectedly, in the majority of CNEP countries labour unions have been the most common associational sources of partisan information flowing to their members. But in other countries, other types of groups have also played this role.

Let us now turn our attention to an individual-level analysis of the effects of level of involvement in each type of association.[15] In the following analysis, the dependent variables represent (a) the probability that group members perceive having received political information from their respective associations and (b) the probability that they perceive having received explicit endorsements of a party or candidate. The independent variable is the type of secondary association to which the respondent belongs.[16] In the first two columns of Table 4.9, the zero-order probability of perceiving either of the two types of political communication is presented separately for both passive and active members.[17] In the next two columns, predicted probabilities generated by a logistic regression are presented for these same two types of group members after controls were introduced for demographic characteristics (gender, education, and age) and 'country'. Our expectation is that passive or rarely active union

Table 4.9 Zero-order probability and predicted probability of political cues and perception of partisan support

	Zero-order probability			Predicted probability after controlling for countries and socio-demographic factors		
	Non- or rarely active members (Col. 1)	Often active members (Col. 2)	Difference (Col. 3)	Non- or rarely active members (Col. 4)	Often active members (Col. 5)	Difference (Col. 6)
Perception of political cues						
Union (n)	0.34 (811)	0.46 (169)	0.12**	0.42	0.53	0.11*
Professional association (n)	0.28 (470)	0.63 (139)	0.35**	0.29	0.56	0.27**
Civic non-religious (n)	0.26 (1,069)	0.38 (538)	0.12**	0.22	0.29	0.07*
Religious association (n)	0.18 (242)	0.28 (238)	0.10*	0.16	0.25	0.09*
Perception of party's support						
Union (n)	0.38 (811)	0.59 (169)	0.21**	0.35	0.58	0.23**
Professional association (n)	0.16 (470)	0.42 (139)	0.26**	0.16**	0.32	0.16**
Civic non-religious (n)	0.14 (1,069)	0.14 (538)	0.00	0.14	0.13	−0.01
Religious associations (n)	0.20 (242)	0.19 (238)	−0.01	0.16	0.15	−0.01

Notes: Entries in columns 1 and 2 are the zero-order probability of perception of political cues and party support across levels of involvement within different secondary associations. Entries in columns 4 and 5 are predicted probabilities across levels of involvement within the secondary associations, setting the control variables at their mean value. Predicted probability scores are estimated through a logistic regression for each type of association. Control variables include gender, education, age, and country (all as dummy variables). Entries in columns 3 and 6 are differences between the probability of perception among the most active and the less- or non-active members.

(n) is the number of cases.

* Mean difference between levels of involvement significant at p < .10.

** Mean difference between levels of involvement significant at p < .05.

and professional association members perceive more political cues and partisan endorsements than do members of other types of groups.

The data in the first column show that the probability of perceiving a flow of political information from the organization is, indeed, somewhat higher among passive union members than among the inactive within other types of groups. Passive members of professional associations, however, are not substantially more likely to perceive such information flows than are members of civic non-religious and religious groups. The data in the second column reveal that active members of all types of organizations are substantially more likely to perceive political cues than are passive members, although these perceptions are by far the most common among active members of professional associations. In short, the level of active involvement with the group plays a powerful intervening role, particularly among members of professional organizations, as the data in column four indicate. With regard to perceptions of explicit partisan endorsements, the picture that emerges is somewhat different, in so far as level of involvement increases this probability only among members of union and professional associations. Active members of religious and civic non-religious organizations are no more likely than the inactive to perceive such partisan support by their respective groups. These same findings hold true even more strongly after controls are introduced for gender, education, age, and country, as can be seen in the data in column six.

Two conclusions emerge from this analysis. First, the extent to which partisan politics permeates organized groups varies from one type of association to another, with unions being more overtly politicized than the others. Secondly, within each type of organization more active members are more likely to perceive political cues than passive or rarely active members. The interactive effect of level of involvement is especially strong within professional associations. This finding is particularly interesting in light of the fact that opportunities for activism are generally greater among religious and civic non-religious groups than they are among the more elaborately institutionalized and hierarchical unions and professional associations.

The Impact on Turnout

Single-country studies of electoral participation tend to explain turnout rates on the basis of two main approaches. One perspective interprets voting turnout as a product of the skills and resources of individual citizens (in turn, a function of education, socio-economic status, etc.), while the other regards mobilization as the key to high rates of electoral participation.[18] The two approaches are in fact complementary. Mobilization may indeed contribute to compensate for the lack of resources and individual incentives (Verba, Nie, and Kim 1978). From this perspective, parties, their organizations and the psychological attachment they are able to build across the electorate, are considered the principal agencies of mobilization. The impact of non-political secondary associations on turnout has received less attention than that of parties, except in the work of Verba and his associates (1972, 1995), but even in their view electoral participation does not seem to be affected by associational involvement by itself. In *Voice and Equality*, Verba, Schlozman, and Brady (1995: 358) found that non-political organization membership had virtually no effect. More important were attitudes relating to political engagement, such as political interest, political information, political efficacy, and partisanship.[19] A contrary view is presented by Radcliff and Davis (2000: 137), who found that labour unions have a significant impact. Analysing turnout levels in the fifty American states in the 1980s, they found that unionization had a significant impact. Cox, Rosenbluth, and Thies (1998: 448), moreover, following the strategic elite model in explaining turnout, show that in Japan participation is 'an interactive function of closeness [in electoral competition] and social capital'—that is, a dense web of associations and social networks. It must be noted, however, that neither study includes in its analysis the effects of individual attitudes like political interest, political efficacy, and political information.

Comparative studies of electoral participation are able to undertake both cross-national and cross-sectional comparative analyses. On this basis, they have noted that cross-sectional turnout rate differences are generally less wide than cross-national differences in electoral participation. In Table 4.10, data summarizing average national turnout rates from 1961 to 1999 are presented for our sample of CNEP countries. These figures range from a high of 90 per cent in Italy to 52 per cent in the United States.

In order to explain these differing rates of turnout we need to consider other explanatory factors, such as the level of a country's socio-cultural development and institutions which shape the electoral process. Franklin (1996) and Norris (2002) consider the voters' instrumental motivation as largely determined by the institutional and political context in which elections take place.[20] By institutional and political context they mean to refer to a large set of factors, among them the salience of elections,

Table 4.10 Average electoral turnout in CNEP countries 1961–99

Italy (10)	90	Bulgaria (3)	73
Uruguay (7)	86	Japan (12)	69
Chile (7)	83	Hungary (6)	57
Greece (11)	82	USA (9)	52
Spain (7)	74	Hong Kong	NA

Data sources: Franklin (1996) and www.idea.int website (Uruguay data). In parentheses the number of elections.

the use of compulsory voting and postal voting, and the presence of a highly competitive party system. All these factors, plus the rules of the electoral system, may 'provide the most plausible explanation of cross-national differences in voting turnout because these influence the cost and the benefits of casting a ballot' (Franklin 1996: 148). Both the Norris and Franklin studies undertake comparative analysis of a large number of countries and generate evidence that these variables are powerful predictors of cross-national differences in voting turnout.

It is clear, however, that even this approach overlaps somewhat with the other two. For instance, party competitiveness can be considered part of the mechanism through which political mobilization takes place. Moreover, neither approach denies in principle that its central factors may interact with those of the other approaches. Anduiza Perea (1999), for example, in her detailed analysis of European countries' turnout rates, shows that taking into account the interaction between individual incentives and institutional variables increases powerfully the ability to predict both individual- and national-level differences in voting turnout.

This short summary of the main tenets of the explanatory theories of electoral participation helps us to frame our own analysis of the non-political association effects on turnout decision. First of all, we need to distinguish among four different dimensions of involvement with non-political association: being member of some voluntary non-political groups, a multi-membership density index (the number of associations to which respondents belong), the type of organization (professional associations and unions, on the one hand, and the civic non-religious, religious, and sports groups, on the other), and awareness of the association's political stands (both in the generic sense of receiving political information from the group and perceiving that it favours one particular candidate or party). The rationale for these distinctions is based on the notion that each of them relates to different aspects of the mobilization and resource theories. The density of organizational involvement could affect voting turnout because those who belong to multiple organizations may already have a participatory 'inclination' that can be easily transformed into voting behaviour. The type of association relates to the previously noted distinction between 'economic organizations' like unions and professional associations, which tend to be more permeated by politics, and other types of organized groups. These groups, therefore, have an inherent interest in encouraging their members to vote in order to advance their respective political interests. With regard to organizational membership, *per se*, one could further hypothesize that involvement with any association can increase the opportunity for political exposure. Finally, awareness of an association's political stands is linked directly to the subjective dimensions of mobilization.

In order to estimate the impact of these various dimensions of associational involvement, we must first control for individual resources and incentives, as well as institutional- and political-context variables commonly regarded as powerful predictors of within- and between-country differences in turnout. In carrying out this analysis, we have constructed two models. In the first (Model A), which includes nine of ten CNEP countries (excluding Hong Kong), our control variables include measures of individual-level resources (gender, age, education, and employment status), as well as institutional and political context measures: two country-level variables (the presence or absence of mandatory voting requirements, and of proportional electoral system). An additional independent variable was the ability of the respondent to place himself or herself on the left–right spectrum, able to indicate whether an individual shares the most important political representation of the party competition space.[21] In the second model (Model B), for the seven countries for which we have comparable data (Spain, Italy, Greece, Bulgaria, Hungary, Uruguay, and Chile), we included as additional controls political interest and political efficacy among the measures of individual resources. Table 4.11 presents the results of these two logistic regression analyses.

As can be seen, in both models the institutional and political context control variables (mandatory vote, electoral rules, and the ability to self-locate on the left–right continuum) have a large impact. In Model A, age and education also have an important effect. In Model B, not unexpectedly, political interest and political efficacy are important. These results largely confirm previous studies. Turning our attention to the impact of our associational variables, we see that simple membership and membership in multiple organizations have tiny effects, except for the American case as the category of multi-membership shows very clearly.[22]

Table 4.11 Effects of association mobilization, individual resources, psychological involvement, and institutional context on turnout (logistic regression, pooled analysis)

	Model A			Model B		
	B	S.E.	T score	B	S.E.	T score
Gender: man	0.05	0.05	1.0	−0.19	0.07	−2.7
Age (18–29)	ref.	—	—	ref.		
30–45	0.39**	0.06	6.5	0.46**	0.09	5.1
46–59	0.60**	0.07	8.6	0.82**	0.11	7.5
>60	0.76**	0.08	9.5	0.78**	0.11	7.1
Education: secondary completed	0.25**	0.05	5.0	0.02	0.08	0.3
Working	−0.10*	0.05	2.0	−0.08	0.08	−1.0
Mandatory vote	0.98**	0.05	19.6	1.07**	0.11	9.7
Electoral system: proportional	0.65**	0.05	13.0	0.51**	0.08	6.4
Left–right ideological awareness	1.5**	0.06	25.0	1.21**	0.09	13.4
Political interested	n.a.	n.a.	—	0.72**	0.09	8.0
Political efficacy (low)	n.a.	n.a.	—	ref.	ref.	
Medium	n.a.	n.a.	—	0.22**	0.08	2.8
High	n.a.	n.a.	—	0.42**	0.11	3.8
Perceive political information and support (No)	ref.	—	—	ref.	—	—
Only political information or support	0.00	0.09	0.0	0.32*	0.19	1.7
Both political information and support	0.47**	0.14	3.4	0.77**	0.32	2.4
Association member	0.11	0.22	0.5	0.12	0.39	0.3
Number of associational affiliations	−0.02	0.08	−0.3	−0.03	0.18	−0.2
Type of association (not members)	ref.	ref.	—	ref.	ref.	—
Union and professional	0.30	0.21	1.4	−0.10	0.34	0.3
Others (civic non-religious, religious, and sport)	0.22	0.20	1.1	−0.08	0.32	−0.3
Multi-membership	1.38**	0.24	5.8	n.a.	n.a.	—
Constant	−0.66**	0.08		−0.84**	0.13	
χ^2 Improvement	1,521.10**	—	—	696.63**	—	—
df	16	—	—	18	—	—
Nagelkerke R^2	0.18	—	—	0.17	—	—
N	11,619	—	—	6,208	—	—

* $p < .05$; ** $p < .01$.

Notes: Model A: 9 countries, only individual resources; Model B: 8 countries, political efficacy and political interest included. Dependent variable is respondent turn-out (scored 1 for yes and 0 for no). Independent variables: Association membership (ranging from 0 for not affiliated to 2 for membership in more than 1 association); Type of association (includes four categories [three in Model B]—not affiliated, professional and union, civic non-religious, religious, and sport, and, in the United States, multi-member); Political interest (ranging from 0, for 'somewhat' or 'no', to 1 for 'enough' to 'a lot'); Political efficacy (an index i.e. the sum of NoInflu, DontCare, PolComp, ranging from 0, for no efficacy, to 3, for disagreement with all three items); Political interest (a dummy variable with 0, for below average to 1, for above average); Mandatory vote (ranging from 0 to 1, where vote is mandatory); Electoral system (with 1 indicating proportional representation and 0, for 'Not PR'); and Ideological awareness (with 0 for those unable or unwilling to self-locate on the left-right continuum, and 1 for those who do).

T scores are the ratio between B values and their error standard. They provide a rough metric making possible comparisons across categories of variables.

In contrast, being aware of the association's political stands does matter. In fact, in both models, being aware of the political information flow and of which party is supported by the group increases the turnout probability significantly, even after controlling for factors commonly regarded as strong determinants of electoral participation.

Our data therefore suggest that what fosters electoral turnout by individuals belonging to secondary associations is whether they are aware of the group's political stands. Given the generally small percentage of members who are aware of the political stands of their associations, this limits the impact of organizational membership on electoral turnout. But it does provide a clearer insight into the specific dynamics of electoral mobilization, suggesting that groups can affect electoral participation by their members *if and only if* they are able to increase their members' subjective perception of their political orientations.

The Encapsulation of the Electorate

Having explored the impact of associational involvement on electoral turnout, let us extend this analysis a step further by exploring the extent to which politically committed secondary organizations are able to channel their members' political behaviour in support of a specific party or a candidate. In the following discussion, we also examine factors that may explain at the individual level the alignment between secondary associations and the partisan preferences of their members.

As we discussed in the introduction to this chapter, students of political cleavages refer to 'encapsulation' as the process through which parties and their collateral agencies create an external 'closure' of their members from outside pressures (Bartolini and Mair 1990). This process tends to stabilize electoral loyalties and provide a close connection between organized groups in society, political parties, and policymaking. However, a diffuse interpretation is that in contemporary democracies these linkages have been radically weakened by, among other factors, the transformation of parties as political institutions, and by the impact of social and cultural change on the cohesion of social groups. Partisan de-alignment, declining party identification, individualization of electoral behaviour, and unfreezing of cleavages are the result (Dalton and Wattenberg 2000). In the following section, we intend to examine the extent to which secondary organizations still play an active and successful partisan-political role, influencing the electoral choice of their members, and encapsulating their behaviour.

As we have seen, a portion of joiners ranging between 11 per cent in Hungary and 58 per cent in Japan were electorally mobilized by secondary organizations, which contacted their members about elections, and provided information, advice, and political orientations. Analogously, between 8 per cent (Hungary) and 26 per cent (Japan) perceived a political bias in the flow of information from the voluntary organization to which they belong. Lacking evidence for earlier periods, it is hard to determine from these figures whether there has been a decline in the capacity of organized movements to encapsulate sectors of the electorate, to isolate their supporters from influence of competing groups, and to eventually mould political subcultures and enclaves. But we can assess the current impact of efforts by these voluntary associations to politically mobilize their members by analysing their electoral preferences. Matching information on voting choice, association membership, and perceived organization political bias, we are able to provide a typology of electors in our countries.

As can be seen in Table 4.12, an average of 7 per cent of our respondents are members of voluntary organizations, perceived a political leaning from their organization, and voted for a party or a candidate *supported by their* organization. We label these individuals *coherent voters*, in so far as they voted according to the partisan line of joined organization. These are citizens fully politically encapsulated by their politicized voluntary association. Analogously, 3 per cent of the population are members of associations, but voted for party or candidate other than the one supported by his or her organization. We label them *incoherent voters*, as to underline that their electoral choice deviates from secondary organization's political stance. The vast majority of organizational members, however—27 per cent of the population—perceived no political bias from the association they belong to, either because the association itself was politically uncommitted (did not support any candidate or party) or because members failed to perceive a clear political leaning. These joiners cast a ballot without any reference to or constraint originating from her or his secondary association membership. Finally, 4 per cent of population is composed of joiners who did not show up at the polls.

How should these results be interpreted? On the basis of these figures alone, one would conclude that the political encapsulation of secondary associations' members' stand is quite weak. However, as previously noted, lacking data for earlier 'golden age' periods, we cannot definitively

Table 4.12 Political encapsulation of the electorate (country ranking according to percentage of members voting coherently)

Type[a]	Japan	Bulgaria	United States	Italy	Uruguay	Greece	Chile	Spain	Hungary	Hong Kong	All
Not voting—not joiners	6.0	15.6	5.2	1.7	5.8	3.7	7.9	15.4	27.0	22.0	10.8
Not voting—joiners	3.9	2.9	12.4	1.7	2.2	1.3	2.6	3.1	5.0	6.1	4.1
Voting—not joiners	20.5	58.5	8.7	40.5	63.5	77.1	62.7	61.2	50.8	49.6	47.7
Voting—joiners—no support	48.5	3.5	59.0	43.7	19.0	9.5	21.3	15.9	15.1	16.0	27.0
Joiners—incoherent voting	7.8	8.6	4.3	2.8	1.9	1.3	1.4	1.8	0.7	5.3	3.4
Joiners—coherent voting	13.3	11.0	10.4	9.5	7.5	7.1	4.3	2.6	1.5	1.0	7.0
Total	100	100	100	100	100	100	100	100	100	100	100
Base (N)	811	1,177	1,213	2,033	625	902	814	1,276	1,375	619	10,845

Note: Missing data on 'vote' variable excluded from the analysis.

[a] Definition of variables.

— Not voting—not joiners: not members of non-political voluntary associations, and did not vote;

— Not voting—joiners: members of non-political voluntary associations who did not vote;

— Voting—not joiners: non-members of non-political voluntary associations who voted;

— Voting—joiners—no support: members of non-political voluntary associations who voted and whose association either did not support candidate/parties or members who did not perceive a clear political leaning;

— Joiners—incoherent voting: members of non-political voluntary associations who voted for a party or candidate other than the one supported by his or her organization;

— Joiners—coherent voting: members of non-political voluntary associations who voted for the party or candidate supported by his or her organization.

conclude that the capacity of voluntary organizations to channel the political support of the citizenry has indeed declined. We simply cannot tell if the level of encapsulation we have observed is as low (or high) now as it has always been. Seen from a different perspective, however, the ability to orient the political choice of 7 per cent of the electorate, which corresponds to 12 per cent of 'joiners', is quite a powerful tool in the hands of organized groups. Moreover, to fully appreciate the relevance of these data it is useful to compare the aggregate percentage of encapsulated joiners (13%) to the share of joiners who received political information from their respective organizations (30%). The ratio of these two figures (.42:1) gives us a general indicator of the success with which organizations' flows of contacts and information translated into political behaviour: 40 per cent of joiners who have been contacted actually turned out to vote according to their associations' political stands. From this perspective, while the absolute level of encapsulated voters may be low, the processes which lead to it could be interpreted as a substantial achievement for the organizations. After all, if a television advertisement were able to convince 40 per cent of viewers to purchase the product, we would regard that as a great success.

There is of course notable variation across countries relative to the extent of voter encapsulation, from a low of 1 per cent in Hong Kong and 2 per cent Hungary, to 10 per cent in Italy, 10 per cent in the United States, 11 per cent in Bulgaria, and 13 per cent in Japan. The ranking is somewhat surprising, since it places the pluralist and participatory United States closest to post-totalitarian Bulgaria. It should be borne in mind in interpreting this seemingly puzzling finding that the highest levels of affiliation with organized groups in established democracies is with politically uncommitted secondary organizations, which do not seek to channel the electoral support of their members. Accordingly, the data in Table 4.12 indicate that established democracies have *both* the largest share of encapsulated *and* uncommitted group members while, with the exception of Bulgaria, more recently established democracies have significantly smaller shares of encapsulated voters *and* the lowest overall levels of organizational affiliation. This would imply that, at country level, political encapsulation rises with increasing social participation rate.

The data presented in Figure 4.3, however, tell a somewhat different story. There is no linear relationship across countries between the extent of political encapsulation and membership rate. Instead, the relationship appears to be curvilinear: political encapsulation rates are high among countries at either end of the range with respect to the overall level of

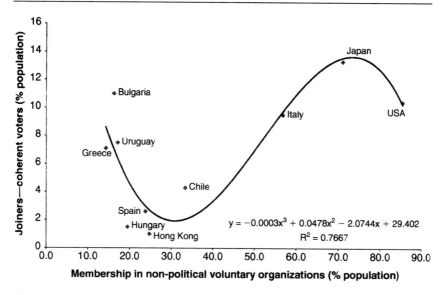

Figure 4.3 Association membership and political encapsulation of the electorate

organizational affiliation, while they are lowest in countries with moderate levels of social participation. We might attempt to explain this aggregate-level pattern by invoking the political histories of these countries. But this graphic presentation of these data does not reveal a close correspondence between the level of encapsulation, on the one hand, and the length of democratic experience or the nature of the predecessor regime (authoritarian or post-totalitarian), on the other. A complex of factors must be evoked in an attempt to explain these patterns, relating both to the associations and to the joiners.

As for the associations, we have noted a great deal of country-by-country variation in both joining propensities and the associations' political involvement. But we also found some patterns: though both economic and non-economic associations are relatively successful in disseminating political information to their members, civic non-religious organizations are perceived as less politically committed than are unions or professional associations. These factors translate into varying capacities of associations to encapsulate their members. As Table 4.13 shows, different types of associations differ greatly as to their rate of success in channelling their members' voting choices: on average, across all 10 countries, only 12.5 per cent of all joiners vote according to the political cues offered by their associations. Labour unions are the most successful in moulding the

Table 4.13 The political encapsulation of joiners by type of association (countries ranked according to percentage of joiners voting coherently)

Type of association	Bulgaria	Japan	Greece	Uruguay	Chile	Italy	United States	Spain	Hungary	Hong Kong	All
Professional	[a]	24.8	14.5	[a]	[a]	4.7	3.3	3.3	3.3	8.7	10.0
Trade union	19.4	36.5	52.4	20.0	20.8	32.3	25.0	22.5	2.6	6.7	22.0
Sport	[a]	2.4	4.8	[a]	11.8	3.7	[a]	0	[a]	[a]	4.4
Religious	21.7	56.1	[a]	13.5	9.5	10.0	7.1	5.7	7.7	0	12.9
Civic non-religious	[a]	10.2	5.4	14.3	20.0	9.5	6.4	2.1	4.9	1.6	8.6
Multi-member (USA)							13.9				13.9
All	18.9	17.7	16.4	14.8	13.2	12.9	12.1	8.1	3.5	3.4	12.5
Base (N)	185	592	128	162	189	1,120	1,045	284	278	174	4,167

Note: Percentage of members of non-political voluntary associations who voted for the party or candidate supported by his or her organization. (Respondents missing data on the vote variable are excluded from the analysis.)
[a] N < 20.

political preferences of their members (with 22% categorized as 'coherent voters'), while sports associations influence only 4 per cent of their affiliates. Between these two extreme values are religious and civic associations, with 14 per cent and 9 per cent of their members reporting votes for candidates or parties endorsed by the associations. There are of course country-specific variations in these patterns—such as the stronger capacity of civic groups to politicize their members in Latin America, not to mention the remarkable level of encapsulation by religious groups in Japan—but the overall trend is one in which organizations based on 'traditional' (economic and religious) cleavages are still more politically committed and more successful in mobilizing their members than other types of organization.

With regard to the joiners, we have seen that active membership is higher in religious and civic non-religious organizations than economic organizations. However, greater individual involvement in secondary associations explains political awareness in economic organizations but not in civic non-religious ones.

We conclude this analysis of political encapsulation by undertaking a multivariate logistic analysis, in which the dichotomous dependent variable is 'coherent voters' versus all other group members. The independent variables in these equations include the standard sociodemographic variables (age, employment status, education, and gender), group-membership characteristics (the degree of active involvement in the organization, and association type), exposure to political information from association, and a series of interactions aimed at testing the possible conditional impact of active membership and mobilization across different types of organizations. Two models are tested: a first one to assess the direct impact of factors assumed to be related to political encapsulation, and the second including the variable 'country', in an effort to control for the specific features of the polity. These two models are presented in Table 4.14.

These data indicate that politically encapsulated (coherent) group members tend to be socially peripheral (not working, and with only primary education), male and active members of their associations. Union membership is a very strong predictor of coherent voting as is, to a lesser extent, religious-group membership. There is a progressive lesser likelihood of being encapsulated among members of civic non-religious, professional, and sport associations, respectively. As expected, exposure to political information flowing from associations is a crucial predictor of political encapsulation. The direct effects of these variables are strong, as

Table 4.14 Logistic models of political encapsulation by associations (pooled analysis of members who vote coherently vs. all other members)

	Mod. 1			Mod. 2		
	B	S.E.	T score	B	S.E.	T score
Age (18–29)						
30/45	.12	.17	.72	.11	.17	.65
46/59	.03	.18	.15	.06	.18	.32
60+	.34***	.21	1.67	.33	.20	1.61
Not working						
Work	.33**	.13	2.43	.30**	.13	2.27
Education (less than secondary)						
Secondary completed	.14	.12	1.12	.23***	.13	1.67
Gender (male)						
female	.34*	.11	−2.99	−.29*	.11	2.52
Association membership (passive)						
active	.40***	.23	1.74	.32	.24	1.35
Political information (no)						
yes	1.14*	.19	5.96	1.17*	.20	5.81
Association (union)						
Professional	−1.42*	.36	−3.84	−1.59*	.37	−4.28
Sport	−2.67*	.64	−4.14	−2.84*	.64	−4.43
Religious	.62**	.29	−2.11	.70**	.31	−2.22
Civic not religious	1.06*	.22	−4.64	−1.19*	.24	−4.84
Multi-member	.76**	.30	−2.51	.73**	.39	−1.86
Interactions						
Active member*Professional	.26	.43	.61	.08	.45	.19
Active member*Sport	.13	.61	.21	.11	.62	.18
Active member*Religious	.31	.39	.79	.19	.39	.47
Active member*Civic	.38	.32	−1.18	.36	.33	−1.09
Active member*Multi-member	.69**	.34	−2.04	.62***	.34	−1.80
Political information*Professional	.53	.45	1.17	.60	.46	1.31
Political information*Sport	1.75*	.60	2.88	1.59**	.61	2.57
Political information*Religious	31	.37	.86	.29	.37	.79
Political information*Civic	−.01	.29	.05	.10	.31	.34
Political information*Multi-member	1.19*	.32	3.72	1.15*	.32	3.55
Country (USA)						
Spain	—	—	—	.19	.33	.58
Italy	—	—	—	.34	.27	1.26
Chile	—	—	—	.21	.35	.60
Bulgaria	—	—	—	.44	.33	1.32
Greece	—	—	—	.65	.34	1.91
Hong Kong	—	—	—	−1.58*	.49	−3.17
Uruguay	—	—	—	.05	.15	.87
Hungary	—	—	—	−1.20*	.43	−2.75
Japan	—	—	—	.37	.29	1.28
Constant	−1.15*	.23	−4.86	−1.12*	.37	−3.03
N	3,568	—	—	3,568	—	—
χ^2 (df)	324 (23)	—	—	370 (32)	—	—
P	.000	—	—	.000	—	—
Pseudo R^2	.14	—	—	.17	—	—

* p < .01; ** p < .05; *** p < .10.

Note: Data weighted by sample size per country.

Definition of dichotomous dependent variables:

— Joiners—coherent voting: members of non-political voluntary associations who voted for the party or candidate supported by his or her organization;

— Other joiners: members of non-political voluntary associations who voted a party or candidate other than the one supported by his or her organization or whose association either did not support candidate/parties or members did not perceive a clear political leaning.

revealed by the fact that the interactive variables—aimed at ascertaining a differentiated influence of active membership and political exposure according to different associations—generally have little impact, with the exception of information exposure from sport associations and multiple membership. This underscores the importance of the associations' mobilization efforts, since coherent voting increases with exposure to political information even from associations which exhibit the lowest propensity to get politically involved (such as sports organizations). Even after country is introduced as a control variable (see Model 2), all of these variables except 'active involvement' retain their strength as predictors of voter encapsulation, with Hong Kong and Hungary confirming their low propensity.

These findings help to explain the curvilinear relationship—at the country level—between political encapsulation and joining propensities depicted in Figure 4.3. The intervening variable between the extent of societal involvement and encapsulation is the differing mobilization capacities of associations. Those countries with a moderate level of social participation have low levels of political encapsulation not because of their citizens' medium level of involvement, but because their associations fail to mobilize their members. An additional explanatory factor is that different types of associations, with differing levels of political commitment, predominate in different countries. Spain's low encapsulation rate, for example, results from the predominance of civic non-religious group membership (amounting to one-third of all joiners), and these associations were only able to mobilize 7 per cent of their members. Likewise, Hungarian unions, with which 51 per cent of all of that country's were affiliated, mobilized only 15 per cent of their members. By contrast, in 'social-capital-poor' Greece, the two predominant types of association (professional and civic non-religious) were capable to reach out 16 and 25 per cent of members, respectively, resulting in a higher encapsulation rate than Spain or Hungary.

Thus, aggregate data and individual-level findings tell a similar story. Membership in non-political voluntary organizations helps turnout (as we saw earlier in this chapter) and forge electoral alignments (as we have just seen) to the extent that associations are willing and able to disseminate information and mobilize their members. Across our ten polities, secondary organizations differ in their capacity to do so. Economic associations, due to their historical contiguity with partisan politics, are still more capable of performing these roles. Religious and civic non-religious groups lag slightly behind in this respect, reaching one-third of their members on average. What makes the difference is then the capacity of secondary organizations to inform and persuade their members.

We conclude by returning to one important finding: while their electoral impact is not insignificant, encapsulated voters are only a minority of voters in contemporary democracies. Far more numerous are joiners whose electoral choices are framed without cues from their organizations. However, secondary organizations, differing as they do with regard to their levels of involvement in electoral politics, are still very effective in performing the crucial task of channelling political information in a persuasive manner and influencing voting choices.

Summarizing the Main Results

The main objective of our analysis was to determine the extent to which secondary organizations provide a relevant context for political exposure and behaviour, in particular with respect to turnout and voting in accord with organizational political cues. The first step was to analyse associational membership patterns cross-nationally, both with regard to the overall joining propensity of a country's population, and with regard to the types of associations with which they were affiliated. Our data made it clear that membership in voluntary associations varies substantially across countries. We further concluded that each country's associational configuration is remarkably context- and path-dependent. In general, longer established democracies exhibit a higher joining propensity than we found in third-wave democratic polities. This finding therefore lends support to the hypothesis that a long history of liberal democratic institutions encourages a wider range of associations and deeper associational activity. However, in both established and new democracies associations differ with respect to the opportunity they afford members to be actively involved: religious and civic non-religious groups entail far more participation than economic organizations. Associations also differ in their levels of political commitment: though their affiliates show lower levels of involvement, unions and professional associations are far more effective in acting as political intermediators than religious or civic organizations. The latter may be effective in disseminating political information to their members, but they fail to clearly convey their partisan preferences to their members.

Exposure to partisan political cues emerges as the critical factor in the process of politically mobilizing group members, both with regard to encouraging high electoral turnout and in mobilizing the vote in support of a particular party or candidate. Even after controlling for the substantial impact of institutional type and political context on turnout, being exposed to political information and partisan cues from the organization significantly increases turnout. Electoral encapsulation shows a similar picture. Even though cross-national differences are large, when social and individual resources, organizational involvement, and type of association and countries are considered conjointly, country effects on encapsulation are very substantially reduced. This implies that voting in accord with the association's political stands is more strongly related to individual-level attributes of group members and characteristics of the organization than it is to the contextual effects captured by our country variables. Thus, we can argue that the causal processes underpinning political encapsulation are similar in both old and new democracies.

In contemporary democracies, different as their political histories may be, parties are still able to encapsulate segments of the electorate, even though the proportion may not be very large. Nonetheless, this finding contradicts the conventional wisdom that parties are increasingly losing their connections with civil society. Our findings also tend to refute the claim that in contemporary democracies associational life *by itself* is sufficient for the performance of the partisan-politicization role. On the contrary, although on a smaller scale than in the past, the process of politicization seems to follow a path similar to that of the previous era, in which the principal actors were mass parties and their affiliated organizations. Indeed, our analysis shows that secondary organizations based on traditional (economic and, to a lesser extent, religious) cleavages have higher capacities to encapsulate segments of the electorate than have any other civic groups.

This leads us to reconsider from a slightly different perspective most of the recent debate on the effects of civic engagement on democracy. Some of the participants in that debate assume a positive and direct effect of secondary organizations on democracy, while others stress that there could be a dark side of civic engagement (Fiorina 1999), impinging on democratic standards and practices. Our study suggests a more nuanced and conditional assessment of the role of secondary association membership on democracy. In so far as associations can still influence citizens' democratic participation, in accord with their ability to mobilize and encapsulate some of their members, the effects of a vibrant civil society on democracy appear to depend on two sets of interrelated factors:

1. The nature of the associations—specifically, to use Putnam's concepts, if they are of the *bonding* or *bridging* type. Bonding voluntary organizations are 'inward looking and tend to reinforce exclusive identities and homogeneous groups' (Putnam 2000: 22) and promote exclusive interactions and values. Bridging organizations are 'outward looking and encompass people across social cleavages' (Putnam 2000), promoting inclusive multiple identities. Although both types of associations may be beneficial to democracy, bonding associations have higher risks of producing out-group hostility: reinforcing in-group solidarity need not necessarily be matched by civic involvement and political participation.

2. The nature of the values and attitudes that political elites might attempt to convey through the still efficient intermediation channels provided by associations. Both democratic and non-democratic ends can be fostered by involvement in organizations, depending on the nature of the organization itself.

In some cases, the interaction of these two sets of factors could lead to the mobilization of 'extremists', whose political values and policy preferences do not reflect those of the majority of the electorate, with the final outcome of distorting the political process and increasing mass alienation from democratic politics.[23]

In our study, we did not examine precisely what values or attitudes towards democracy or policy stands were actually flowing through these institutional channels, or the extent to which encapsulated voters were in this respect different from non-encapsulated citizens. We did find, however, that the organizational opportunities to implement political ideas, good or bad, are still there, and secondary organizations are very effective in translating political cues in voting behaviour. In many countries, they may be replaced by other channels of communication more diverse in their audiences, but secondary organizations are still powerful political weapons.

5

The flow of political information: personal discussants, the media, and partisans

Bradley Richardson and Paul Allen Beck

In contemporary elections, voters receive political information about candidates and parties from many different sources. Beyond the most local-level elections, very little of this information comes directly from the candidates and parties themselves, but is, instead, conveyed to voters by intermediaries.[1] As it flows through these intermediary channels, campaign information is processed in such a manner that it rarely reaches voters unchanged. Accordingly, differential exposure to various intermediary information sources, the kinds of information that are processed and communicated to voters, and the extent to which the resulting messages support the voter's personal political predispositions are all important characteristics of the political communication process during election campaigns. This flow of political information of course is not the only influence on the voting decision—as personal attitudes, values, interests, and perceptions have substantial impact, as demonstrated in most voting studies. Yet, at the margins, and as factors that may help to shape voters' predispositions in the first place, these information sources are important ingredients in what has been called the 'social calculus' of voting (Beck et al. 2002).

Among information sources, two stand out in modern political life. The mass media—newspapers since the nineteenth century and television since the 1950s—typically are the most visible sources of information about political campaigns. They have direct contact with the political world of candidates and parties, and they operate as information conduits from political elites to voters at the grass roots. So important are the mass media in conveying information about politics that they, especially television, often are accorded predominance in the modern flow of information that the other sources of information cannot rival.[2]

Voters rely on television and newspapers for information throughout the democratic world to a degree that makes us sometimes overlook the important role that personal networks play in supplying political information. From the beginning of democratic elections, a voter's personal contacts, her or his personal or social network, have been important information sources in election campaigns (Huckfeldt and Sprague 1995). Personal discussions about parties and candidates lie at the very foundations of a voter's political life, often communicating on a daily basis how like-minded others view the electoral landscape, and what is attractive or unattractive about the alternatives from other points of view (Granovetter 1973). Personal conversations are frequent with those closest to us, especially a spouse and the family, and often these conversations involve politics. They also extend beyond the family to friends, co-workers, and other contacts who sometimes are more intimate discussion partners than anyone in the family.

Voters of course are not passive receptacles for these political messages (Hovland, Janis, and Kelley 1953). To a considerable extent, they can actively search for information that will be most compatible with their own political predispositions. They can choose the television programmes they watch, the newspapers they read, and the people to whom they turn for information about politics. They can selectively perceive and filter the messages passed along to them from various information sources. When it comes to political information, the voters' own political predispositions, especially their partisan loyalties, can affect this information flow. Partisan voters may have a sense of which media and potential personal contacts are more or less sympathetic to their partisan 'side' and can select or 'correct for' these sources accordingly.

This chapter examines the political messages received by voters from personal discussants and the mass media in a dozen different countries, ranging from long-established democracies to new democracies, including some in which democracy has only the most tenuous hold.[3] Based on voter self-reports, it begins by addressing citizen exposure to political information from spouses, other personal discussants, newspapers, and television. We then turn to voter perceptions of the partisanship of the political messages they receive from each intermediary, or what we refer to as the partisan bias (or partisan direction) of the information. Finally, the chapter assesses how the voters' own partisanship is related to the information they seek and receive—the degree to which these political communicators and their communications, in short, are filtered through 'partisan lenses'.

With only twelve country cases, measured in but a single election in the 1990s, we must exercise great care not to generalize too readily from our data. Nonetheless, the cross-national similarities and differences we find in exposure to the flow of political information, and the bias thereof, and in how this may be modulated by the voter's own partisanship, can give us considerable insight into both the regularities and the country particularities of political communications in the democratic world.[4]

Exposure to Political Communication

At the level of the individual voter, the political communication process during an election campaign begins with exposure to political messages. Personal networks proliferate in all societies, and all democratic countries have sufficient media sources of information to offer their citizens the opportunity to rely on them to be informed. More variable is the extent to which different sources provide information about politics, and the extent to which individual voters turn to them for it. In the CNEP studies, we gauged exposure to political information by asking respondents if they read about the election campaign in newspapers, heard about the campaign on television news programmes, and discussed the campaign with spouses and/or other persons.

Table 5.1 presents the percentages of survey respondents' self-reported exposure to information about the election campaign from the different information sources—the two newspapers they read most often, the television news programme they watch most frequently, their spouse, and non-spousal personal contacts with whom they discuss important matters the most.[5] The cells in Table 5.1 contain the percentage of all respondents in each country who reported exposure to information about the candidates or parties[6] from each source.

Across the twelve CNEP countries, television news is usually the most common source of political information about the election campaign. At least two-thirds of adult citizens in every country relied on it to some degree, and it was eclipsed as an information source only in West Germany[7] and Japan, where newspaper readership is especially high. This result is hardly surprising, as television commonly is seen as the dominant

Table 5.1 Levels of exposure to different sources of information

	United States	United Kingdom	W. Germany	Spain	Italy	Bulgaria	Chile	Greece	Hungary	Uruguay	Hong Kong	Japan
Read first newspaper	84	66	78	46	71	59	81	40	49	34	75	96
Read second newspaper	35	23	26	18	44	27	24	21	12	17	43	33
Watch TV news	87	91	66	85	98	81	81	94	84	89	93	92
Talk politics with spouse	61	42	43	62	77	54	47	65	50	68	26	32
Talk politics with 1st discussant	72	53	65	25	47	27	42	32	24	23	16	27

Note: Figures in each cell are percentages of all respondents.

medium in modern times. Although the penetration of television into all households varies somewhat from country to country, as does the amount and kind of political content television carries, citizens across the democratic world rely heavily on television for their political information.

The pattern is much more variable for newspapers. While a majority of citizens read a newspaper for political information in most countries and over 20 per cent read a second newspaper in all but three countries, the percentage of readers ranges widely: from highs of 96 per cent in Japan and 84 per cent in the United States to 34 per cent in Uruguay and 40 per cent in Greece. With so few country cases, it is difficult to attribute the variations in newspaper readership to any single factor, but there are some possibilities to explore. Because literacy rates are virtually constant (ranging from 96% to 99%) across the twelve countries, they cannot explain variations in newspaper readership. Newspaper readership has, however, a significantly positive relationship to affluence as measured by both GDP ($r = .54$) and GDP per capita ($r = .54$) and an insignificant but positive relationship to income equality as measured by the GINI coefficient ($r = .29$).[8] These results show that affluence contributes to the use of newspapers to gain information about politics as a general rule, but that unique characteristics of each country also affect the extent its citizens' reliance on newspapers for political information. For example, in Japan schoolchildren were commonly taught that reading the newspaper was an important part of a citizen's duty.

The variation in political discussions with other people is considerable as well across the twelve CNEP countries: The two Asian cases in our study (Hong Kong and Japan) have the lowest incidence of discussion with both the spouse and the first-named discussant.[9] Whether this reflects different styles of interpersonal relationship in some generic 'Asian culture' is not determinable with only two cases, so we hesitate to even speculate about it. With this pattern of results, it is tempting to hypothesize that citizens in countries with a recent authoritarian past (the two former communist countries of Bulgaria and Hungary plus Chile, Greece, Spain, and Uruguay) have not yet had sufficient experience with democratic life to be comfortable about discussing politics where one's own partisanship may be revealed in interpersonal circles beyond the home. But this explanation of the results does not square with the fact that formerly fascist Italy and West Germany vie with the United States for the highest rates of personal discussion. Their experience may have occurred so long ago that it is no longer relevant for most voters in the post-fascist countries. Clearly, there is no obvious general explanation for the variations we observe in personal political discussion rates that does not require some reliance on unique country factors.

Differences among countries can also be examined from the perspective of multi-source patterns of political information gathering across the various sources. Television news is the most important medium conveying campaign information to which people are exposed in every country except West Germany and Japan, where newspapers are especially important. Beyond this observation, there are hints of a pattern that general cross-country factors rather than country uniqueness can explain. Television is especially predominant in the former communist countries, where interpersonal discussions of politics may have been suppressed not so long before and there is no tradition of an independent press. Television and newspapers together dominate the political communications landscape in the long-standing democracies with high levels of economic affluence and development (the United States and the United Kingdom). Drawing inferences from these hints, though, is not justified because of the paucity of cases and the multiplicity of possible causes.

The Partisan Bias of Political Communication

Exposure to a source of political information is only the first step in the political communication process. The next important step involves the nature of the message that is communicated. In an election campaign, the most important characteristic of a message is whether it regularly favours a candidate or party, and which candidate or party that may be.[10] Consequently, the CNEP survey in each country asked the respondents whether each source they used favoured a candidate or party, and then which candidate or party it favoured.[11] These responses are used to operationalize the concept, we call partisan 'bias'.[12]

Table 5.2 reports the country-by-country results of the perceived partisan bias of messages received from five different sources. In order to standardize the metrics across countries, here and in subsequent tables using this measure, we estimate the percentage of respondents in each country who report being exposed to partisan messages from each source from a base of all respondents. Thus, the measure of partisan bias employed combines both exposure to and perceptions of bias. Those who are not exposed to a particular source or who do not receive political information from it do not, by definition, receive biased messages from it, so they need to be included in determining the country's score on the variable.

Table 5.2 Perceived partisan bias in different information sources

% Bias	United States	United Kingdom	W. Germany	Spain	Italy	Bulgaria	Chile	Greece	Hungary	Uruguay	Hong Kong	Japan
First newspaper	44	76	53	10	39	16	9	27	7	7	8	26
Television news	32	23	6	18	31	11	13	14	10	10	2	24
Spouse	68	40	30	46	55	51	40	61	37	41	24	27
First discussant	66	48	44	38	40	44	42	56	38	51	11	13

Note: Figures in each cell are percentages who perceive a vote preference in the row information source out of all respondents.

The main storyline of Table 5.2 involves the contrast in bias of political messages between the media, on the one hand, and personal discussants, on the other. With few exceptions, voters report receiving fewer partisan messages from the media than from personal discussants. Television appears especially free from partisan bias across all nations—and comes as close to following a universal pattern as is seen in this chapter. Even where perceived as relatively high in partisan bias, such as in the United States and Italy, or to a slightly lesser degree, in the United Kingdom and Japan, television's partisan bias levels are viewed as below the partisan bias of personal discussants in virtually every case. The exception is Japan, where twice as much partisan bias is perceived in television (and newspapers and spouses) than among primary discussants. Moreover, Spain is the only case where voters perceive exposure to partisan bias more from television than from newspapers where the bias levels of both media attain double digits. The American 'outlier' in perceived television partisanship may be a result of a drumbeat of criticism from ideological conservatives there about the allegedly 'liberal media', even though objective content analysis of American television coverage of the 1992 election showed its messages to be balanced rather than partisan (Dalton, Beck, and Huckfeldt 1998). The relatively high partisan-bias score for Italy may be the result of concentrated private ownership of the media and its use in political campaigns—as evidenced in the 1996 Italian election by Silvio Berlusconi's use of his media empire on behalf of his own political ambitions.

Citizens of the democracies we studied did not see newspapers as heavily biased either, although they are not viewed as unbiased as is television. Despite the partisan origins of many newspapers in the older democracies, epitomized by the archetypally partisan reputation of the British press to this day, a majority of respondents reported that they faced a partisan-biased press in only two countries—West Germany and the United Kingdom. Nonetheless, though inferences must be tentative with so few cases, there is a hint of a pattern of exposure to newspaper bias: except for Greece, perceived newspaper bias is considerably lower in the democracies that experienced authoritarian interludes in the several decades before the 1990s (e.g. Bulgaria, Chile, Hungary, Spain, and Uruguay) than in the longer-standing democracies. Dissenting newspapers were heavily constrained during the authoritarian periods in most of these nations, and that legacy of newspaper non-partisanship may have been internalized by the time authoritarian rule was lifted.

As mentioned earlier, the principal exceptions to the perceived partisan neutrality of the mass media are newspapers in the United Kingdom and

West Germany, where a majority of voters reported reading a partisan press. The exceptionalism of these two countries reflects a tradition that has included a politicized press almost from its beginnings. In contemporary times, this press partisanship may be sustained where citizens have ready access to a range across the partisan spectrum of nationally distributed papers, such as are available in the United Kingdom and West Germany. The partisan stance of these national newspapers may be related to competition and market distinctiveness. Where most newspapers are localized and monopolize the local market (as in the United States), they have a powerful incentive to eschew partisan attachments or reputations. Rather than aim for a segment of their market through their partisan distinctiveness, local monopolistic newspapers aim to appeal to everyone by not taking sides on matters that divide their readership. Where there is substantial competition, by contrast, newspaper partisanship is one way to develop a distinctive niche in the marketplace. Whether newspaper markets are nationalized or localized and competitive, therefore, may play an important role in determining their partisan bias.[13]

The other near-universal pattern of perceived bias across our cases appears for personal discussants: substantial numbers of voters in almost all countries report facing partisan bias within their personal discussion networks.[14] With the exceptions of Hong Kong and Japan, where discussant bias is almost negligible and spouse bias is at its nadir, between one-third and two-thirds of spouses and first discussants are seen as having a partisan bias. This number is even more impressive in light of the limited number of personal discussants considered in this analysis and their initial identification without any explicit reference to political discussions. If we penetrate more deeply into discussion networks, the data we have collected suggest that the amount of bias increases significantly, especially with regard to the last-named discussant (who was explicitly to be one with whom the respondent discusses politics). It is likely easier for respondents to identify political bias where the content of the information is connected with daily life and cues about partisan content may be reinforced by continued interaction. Such is the case of political discussions within families, among kin, and in relationships with friends compared with television and newspapers.

Up to this point, we have explored bias in the source of political information, as perceived by the recipients of this information. The next step in our analysis is to turn to the relationship in partisan bias between the source and the recipient, that is, to the *congruence* between the vote preferences communicated by the intermediaries and the vote preferences of our respondents. Table 5.3 shows the percentage of respondents in each country whose information sources are biased in agreement with their own candidate or party preference, thus supporting their own vote choice.[15]

The most obvious inference to draw from the figures in Table 5.3, approaching a uniform pattern across all of the countries, is that personal discussants are usually more likely than the media to have congruent partisan biases with the respondent. Despite the CNEP project's initial assumption of a possible decline in personal network effects relative to 1940s research findings (Lazarsfeld, Berelson, and Gaudet 1948; Berelson, Lazarsfeld, and McPhee 1954), respondents' personal discussion networks clearly continue to play a larger role in the transmission of partisan bias, and conformity thereto at election time, than information from the media. In most cases, the margin of discussant over media congruence is substantial. The only exceptions occur in Japan and Hong Kong, where Table 5.1 showed that there was limited political discussion with other people, and the United Kingdom, where newspaper bias reaches its peak and voters can choose from a wide variety of partisan papers.

A less obvious inference from these data, but one of even greater importance for the nature of political communications in contemporary democracies, is that most voters are *not* deeply embedded in an information context that supports their own partisan preferences. In no country are a majority of voters in agreement with any of their information sources. This reflects a change from the highly stylized European model of earlier times in which societies deeply stratified along regional, class, and religious lines were thought to embed voters into homogeneous microcontexts in terms of partisanship (Lipset and Rokkan 1967a; Tingsten [1937] 1974). This model is epitomized by the 'pillarized' structure of Dutch society just a few decades ago (Lijphart 1975; Irwin and Dittrich 1984). Surprisingly, it is Greece and the United States that exhibit the highest levels of embeddedness among our country cases in the 1990s. The United Kingdom exhibits some vestiges of the traditional model, which it was so important in defining in the first place, but it does not rival either the United States or Greece in the percentage of its citizens who are embedded in a partisan intermediation context.

What seems to characterize most democracies today, especially the newer democracies, is instead a model of pluralistic voter information contexts that lack strong and homogeneous partisan signals. The pluralistic model of political communication may be more prevalent today for several reasons: First, the modern media, especially television, are

Table 5.3 Agreement between respondents' vote preferences and the perceived biases of information sources

% Agreement	United States	United Kingdom	W. Germany	Spain	Italy	Bulgaria	Chile	Greece	Hungary	Uruguay	Hong Kong	Japan
First newspaper	21	33	8	4	24	11	2	22	3	7	4	13
Television news	10	8	2	8	17	2	3	13	4	3	1	8
Spouse	43	29	20	30	15	39	7	36	27	49	7	12
First discussant	41	29	25	25	40	31	8	39	27	37	6	13

Note: Figures in each cell are percentages agreeing with the vote preference they perceive in the row information source out of all respondents.

not especially partisan compared with discussion networks and probably even the media in earlier times. Moreover, exposure to the least partisan of the media, television, is uniformly high across all the countries. Second, possibly because of the dominance of television, politics in the newer democracies is more the 'mass society' version Kornhauser (1959) described decades ago than the social-structurally based society of earlier times. Third, with more women in the workplace, more fluid social structures, and a decline in class politics, even personal discussion networks in these countries and in these times are less homogeneous politically than they once were. Without delving into the micropolitics of each of the countries, which is a different task from the one set for this chapter, we cannot pursue these hypotheses further.

Viewed from a different perspective, the level of congruence between sources and recipients of partisan messages during the political campaign may be seen as an index of a country's partisan polarization. As exposure to partisan sources that reinforce one's own partisanship increases, voters become more embedded in a homogeneous partisan information context. Aggregated to the country level, we can differentiate among our twelve cases with regard to the extent to which the flow of political information is supportive of voters' own partisan orientations. By this measure the United States and Greece, followed by the United Kingdom, Italy, and Uruguay, exhibit the most partisan embeddedness in the flow of political information. The exceptional status of the United States is particularly noteworthy in the light of the fact that these findings are based on data collected in 1992—prior to the emergence and/or increasing prominence of intensely partisan broadcast media such as Fox TV News and a plethora of radio and television 'talk shows'.[16]

At the non-partisan end of the intermediation continuum, Chile, Japan, and especially Hong Kong exhibit very little congruence in the partisanship of source and recipient of campaign messages. They have non-politicized interpersonal intermediation processes. In each case, there may be a ready explanation as to why. After a long period of especially repressive authoritarianism, Chileans were readjusting to democratic politics, and were very sensitive about polarization again between the left and the right. In the 1993 election, Japan was experiencing the temporary disintegration of the ruling Liberal Democratic Party that had dominated the country throughout the previous post-war period and continues to do so at present. Hong Kong, facing the possibility of absorption into mainland China, was witnessing the emergence of a new dominant issue in its politics that was overwhelming its previous political agenda. It is hardly surprising that the flow of biased political information in these three societies was so weakly connected to voters' electoral preferences.

A Side Glance at the Conditions of Voter–Discussant Congruence

The generally strong congruence in vote preferences between voters and their personal discussants documented above is only part of the story of interpersonal discussion of electoral politics. Beneath this pattern is a variety of characteristics of personal relationships that can modulate congruence at the individual level. Our surveys probed these characteristics in some depth in virtually all of these countries. For the primary discussant, we focus below on three of these characteristics: the nature of the relationship with the discussant, the status differential between respondents and their discussants, and the perception of their depth of political knowledge. Specifying national similarities or differences in these relationships is a critical second step towards establishing patterns in the political discussion process across modern democracies.

Respondents were asked whether their discussants were spouses, more distant relatives, co-workers, or personal friends, among other relationships. What typically characterizes these types of discussion partners is the amount of choice involved in selecting them as a discussion partner in the first place and the intimacy and longevity of the relationship. Generally speaking, one would expect that discussion partners who are more or less freely chosen and with whom we are more intimate or have a longer-term relationship would be more consonant with our vote preferences. Table 5.4 examines this expectation across eleven cases.[17]

The only consistent cross-national pattern is the substantial congruence in vote preferences between voters and personal discussants across all relationships in all countries. Only Greece, for co-workers, defies this pattern with its strongly negative association; and only the coefficients for spouses in the United Kingdom and co-workers in Hong Kong fail to attain significance. Beyond this general congruence within personal networks, though, there are no consistent patterns across all of the cases. Substantial congruence with spouses appears in most countries, but it falls off to insignificance in the United Kingdom and to only modest levels in Chile. Congruence with relatives is significant in all cases, except that the relationships for the United Kingdom, Chile, and especially Hong Kong

Table 5.4 Congruence in vote preference with primary discussant by type of relationship

	United States	United Kingdom	W. Germany	Spain	Italy	Bulgaria	Chile	Greece	Hungary	Uruguay	Hong Kong
Spouse	.40	.03	.56	.45	.62	.47	.14	.39	36	.46	.29
Relative	.42	.14	.37	.49	.44	.39	.15	.29	.42	.28	.10
Friend	.19	.57	.18	.31	.21	.56	.13	.21	.42	.22	.30
Co-worker	.17	.44	.26	.42	.18	.66	.20	-.75	.38	.24	.06

Note: Figures in each cell are tau-b coefficients between the respondent's vote preference and that perceived of the personal discussant. All relationships are significant at the .05 level except for those of spouse in the United Kingdom and of all discussants except spouse in Chile. The question about relationships was not asked in Japan.

Table 5.5 Status equality–inequality and discussant–voter congruence in vote preference

	United States	United Kingdom	W. Germany	Spain	Italy	Bulgaria	Chile	Greece	Hungary	Uruguay	Hong Kong
Spouses											
Same status	.74	.68	.70	.53	—	.52	.15	.35	—	.51	—
Unequal	.68	.74	.72	.41	—	.39	.16	.35	—	.45	—
Discussants											
Same status	.45	.61	.63	.42	—	.51	.19	.19	—	.24	—
Unequal	.42	.53	.55	.32	—	.41	.09	.35	—	.16	—

Note: Figures in each cell are tau-b coefficients between the respondent's vote preference and that perceived of the personal discussant. All relationships are significant at the .05 level, except for unequal discussant status in Chile. Status was measured by education in the United States, Spain, Bulgaria, Chile, Greece, and Uruguay and by occupation in West Germany and Britain. No comparable measures of status were available in Italy, Hungary, or Hong Kong and Japan.

are modest. Something about the politics of the United Kingdom and Chile tends to suppress voting preference congruence within nuclear and extended families to a degree that it does not in any other place. By contrast, congruence with friends and co-workers is especially strong in the United Kingdom, and considerably higher than congruence with spouses and relatives. Co-worker congruence there reflects its history of workplace mobilization, while the low levels of congruence within the family may signal gender differences in vote preference and lingering working-class Tory propensities (Butler and Stokes 1969: 104–15). Greater congruence with non-relatives than with relatives also appears in Bulgaria, Hungary, and (for friends) Hong Kong. Without more detailed exploration, though, it is difficult to know what, if anything, these countries have in common to explain this relationship.

Social status has a long history of importance in studies of politics and voting. It was seen in much of the twentieth century as one of principal bases of electoral cleavage at the mass level, especially but not uniquely in Europe (Lipset 1959a; Lipset and Rokkan 1967b; Goldthorpe 1968). On the basis of this tradition, one would expect greater association in vote preferences between voters and their primary discussants with similar status, especially in nations where politics is aligned along social status lines. Using education and occupation as measures of objective class analysis, we identified instances where spouses and discussants had the same social status as the respondent and compared those with the same and different social status.[18]

As can be seen from Table 5.5, voters and primary discussants who have the same social status are more likely to share voter preferences across almost all countries where the data will support comparisons. Greece stands out as the exception to this pattern, for reasons that are not immediately obvious. The differences are noticeable in most cases, but they are not large, and they remain positive and significant regardless of whether status is unequal or equal. For spouse, by contrast, having the same or a different status does not modulate the magnitude of the correlations in any particular way: In four countries, spouses with unequal status are more correlated in vote preference with respondents; in five countries, the correlation is higher for spouses with equal status. The reason why the differences when controlling for status are so mixed for spouses is elusive, although it may have something to do with the gendered nature of the countries' political cleavages or the difficulties of determining family status when husband and wife have different educational and occupational status.

Since the work of Lazarsfeld and his Columbia University colleagues more than a half century ago (Lazarsfeld, Berelson, and Gaudet 1948; Berelson, Lazarsfeld, and McPhee 1954; Katz and Lazarsfeld 1955), it has been hypothesized that political communications often flow in two steps—from the political world to those who follow it most closely among the mass public, then from these 'opinion leaders' to the rest of the public. It is natural that this two-step flow would come through personal discussants, with those who follow politics figuring most prominently in the transfer of information. To test this hypothesis, the CNEP surveys included a question on whether the respondent perceived the discussant as having a lot, average, or a little political knowledge.

As Table 5.6 depicts, for the countries where discussant knowledge was measured, the congruence in vote preferences between voters and their primary discussant was greatest where the discussant was perceived to be knowledgeable. The differences are quite substantial in some cases. The pattern is not repeated with any consistency when our analysis turns to spouses. Deference to a knowledgeable discussant may become confounded when marriage is involved, especially in societies that have traditional gender roles. This hypothesis is another one that merits closer microlevel examination than we can give it here.

The Role of Partisanship in Exposure to Information Source Bias

One of the hallmarks of democracy is that voters have multiple sources of political information and can choose which ones among them to follow during a political campaign. They can read the newspapers that reflect their preferences or, where one newspaper monopolizes the local market, they can choose not to read it or to read it only selectively. They can watch the television station that is most favourable to their views. They can select their discussants or, where those discussants are imposed on them by social proximity, they can pick and choose what topics to discuss, perhaps avoiding politics altogether, and how often to discuss them. They also of course can selectively perceive or even misperceive the political messages that emanate from these sources.

A primary factor that should influence voter choice of and perception of information sources should be the partisan loyalties voters carry with them into the election campaign. Specialists on voting behaviour have distinguished between the immediate selection of candidates and parties

Table 5.6 Political knowledge levels and discussant–voter congruence in vote preference

	United States	United Kingdom	W. Germany	Spain	Italy	Bulgaria	Chile	Greece	Hungary	Uruguay	Hong Kong
Spouse											
Knows a lot	.80	—	.61	.25	.61	.50	.25	-.17	—	.62	—
Average	.64	—	.77	.29	.56	.43	—	—	—	.42	—
Knows little	.68	—	.72	.48	.50	.45	.15	.34	—	.42	—
Discussant											
Knows a lot	.45	—	.62	.37	.53	.13	.27	.44	—	.22	—
Average	.43	—	.59	.29	—	—	—	—	—	—	—
Knows little	.32	—	.56	.19	.36	.09	.17	.40	—	.15	—

Note: Figures in each cell are tau-b coefficients between the respondent's vote preference and that perceived of the personal discussant. All relationships are significant at the .05 level. No comparable measures of discussant political knowledge are available for Greece, Hong Kong and Hungary.

at election time and long-standing party identifications (Key and Munger 1959; Campbell et al. 1960: 146–67; Butler and Stokes 1969: 23–44). The existence of such party identifications as conceptually separate from the vote preference in any particular election, whatever the empirical relationships between the two, has been established in a variety of countries.[19] A long tradition of voting behaviour research shows that these party identifications frame how people think about political issues and leaders (Campbell et al. 1960: 120–45; Greenstein 1965: 55–84). It is only natural to expect long-standing party identifications to structure peoples' exposure to political information as well, especially to partisan-biased political information.

Survey respondents were asked about their partisan loyalties or party identifications in all of the CNEP countries. Many of them in each country exhibited no difficulty in responding that they had been close over the long run to one of the parties contesting the election or that they were not at all close to a party. Table 5.7 shows the distribution of those with and without these long-term partisan loyalties across eleven of our country cases.[20] The percentage of the electorate who are partisans ranges widely: At the low end, it starts at about one in five of all survey respondents in Hong Kong, where the transformation of the relationship with mainland China undoubtedly was restructuring the entire political landscape. Only about a third of the electorate are partisans in the recently democratized systems of Bulgaria, Hungary, and especially Chile, where a centre-left coalition dominates electoral politics. The most partisan electorates were found in Italy, where party mobilization has been historically strong and which experienced a major realignment of its party system in the 1996 election; and in the United Kingdom, which is a long-standing home of strong parties.

In most countries, self-identified partisans are more likely than non-partisans to view their various information sources as partisan themselves, as is shown in Table 5.8. The patterns achieve more consistency for spouses and discussants than for the media, where even expected differences are modest. For discussants, again Chile and Bulgaria march against the general pattern: Non-partisans in both countries are more likely than partisans to see their discussants as biased towards a party, and in Chile, non-partisans also are more likely than partisans to perceive bias in their spouses. It is plausible that the legacy of one-party authoritarian rule, under the Communist Party in Bulgaria and especially under the military dictatorship of Augusto Pinochet in Chile, suppressed the impact of partisanship on choice or perception of information sources there.

Table 5.7 Partisans and non-partisans

	United States	United Kingdom	W. Germany	Spain	Italy	Bulgaria	Chile	Greece	Hungary	Uruguay	Hong Kong
Partisanship											
Partisan (%)	62	87	65	37	80	32	30	53	42	63	22
No party	38	13	35	63	20	68	70	47	57	37	78

Note: Cell entries are self-declared partisan or non-partisan respondents as a percentage of all survey respondents in each country. They are responses to the first of the two traditional party identification questions, which was altered to ask about 'proximity' towards a political party to fit a variety of country contexts. Because the partisanship question was worded differently in the Japanese survey, it cannot be compared with the other countries.

Table 5.8 Perceptions of information source partisan bias among partisans and non-partisans

	United States	United Kingdom	W. Germany	Spain	Italy	Bulgaria	Chile	Greece	Hungary	Uruguay	Hong Kong
Newspapers											
Partisan (%)	54	63	25	36	42	9	4	20	6	8	8
No party	49	57	26	20	30	7	5	11	2	1	4
Television											
Partisan (%)	41	27	—	20	32	4	5	13	11	4	2
No party	34	19	—	14	36	6	9	11	2	1	1
Spouses											
Partisan (%)	60	43	36	24	48	39	22	29	31	26	8
No party	55	28	21	16	6	22	34	0	15	7	6
Discussants											
Partisan (%)	70	51	52	44	67	24	28	26	30	9	8
No party	59	34	29	22	48	32	34	0	0	2	4

Note: Cell entries are the percentages of partisans or non-partisans who perceive partisan bias in each information source. Discussants are first discussants. Japan is omitted because a non-comparable party identification question was asked there. West German television is omitted because of difficulties in identifying the most-favoured stations among the many stations covered.

By contrast, partisans are *not* more likely than non-partisans to see the newspapers they read as partisan in West Germany and Chile, and the differences between partisans' and non-partisans' views of bias in newspapers is modest in several other countries. Italy and Bulgaria join Chile as countries in which non-partisans see television as more biased than do partisans. Whatever the explanation, it is clear that, while partisanship generally produces more congruence with political information sources, especially for personal discussants, there are unique country factors at work that can moderate or eliminate this relationship. The nature of these factors must be examined in further analysis, leaving unanswered at this point some tantalizing questions about why partisanship does not play an important role in structuring the flow of political information uniformly across the democratic world.

Our analysis has established that party ties often matter in people's perceptions of source bias during an election campaign across most of the democracies. The data presented in Table 5.9 refine this analysis one step further by examining how the strength of partisan loyalties affects the relationship. This analysis began by dividing self-identified partisans into three different groups based on the declared strength of their long-term party loyalties: strong, moderate, and weak. For each category, then, we have calculated the correlation between the respondent's vote preference and the perceived candidate or party favouritism in the immediate election of each information source.

The results generally show that people with the strongest party loyalties were the most likely to be exposed to a flow of political information that supported their partisanship. The pattern achieves its greatest consistency for political discussants and, albeit to a lesser degree, for spouses. In every case but Bulgaria, strong partisans were more likely than weak partisans to have discussants with congruent vote preferences. With the exceptions of only West Germany, Spain, and Hong Kong, the pattern continued, with moderate partisans having more congruent discussants than do weak partisans. With regard to spouses, the expected monotonicity is reversed for Bulgaria at each level of partisan strength and inconsistently monotonic in Chile, the United Kingdom, and the United States.

The patterns are somewhat less consistent for the media, yet still quite consistent overall. For newspapers, in all but Chile and Hong Kong, strong partisans were more likely than were weak partisans to enjoy conformity in vote preferences between themselves and their newspapers. Moreover, only in Uruguay and again Hong Kong is the correlation lower for moderate partisans in comparison with weak partisans. For television, the same

Table 5.9 Partisanship strength and congruence in voter preference and source party bias

	United States	United Kingdom	W. Germany	Spain	Italy	Bulgaria	Chile	Greece	Hungary	Uruguay	Hong Kong
Newspapers											
Strong	.19	.29	.19	.03	.33	.36	−.08	.37	.13	.20	.00
Moderate	.20	.26	.06	.10	.08	.24	.06	.34	.01	−.00	.01
Weak	−.02	.13	.03	−.05	.05	.23	−.08	−.16	−.01	.19	.35
Television											
Strong	.40	.33	—	.05	.13	.25	.21	.23	.06	.09	.07
Moderate	.24	.14	—	.03	.27	.20	.10	.09	.02	−.02	.05
Weak	.20	.08	—	−.05	.09	.25	.12	.10	.13	−.04	−.05
Spouses											
Strong	.74	.87	.86	.60	.58	.45	.34	.62	.58	.55	.06
Moderate	.65	.73	.69	.54	.57	.48	.02	.59	.38	.42	.08
Weak	.67	.57	.38	.51	.38	.57	.12	.55	.35	.38	−.00
Discussants											
Strong	.55	.72	.61	.50	.39	.53	.78	.60	.53	.30	.44
Moderate	.40	.55	.51	.39	.27	.40	.27	.50	.41	.19	.08
Weak	.29	.42	.52	.42	.21	.39	.20	.39	.38	.14	.15

Note: Figures are tau-b correlations for the relationship between respondent vote preference and the perceived vote preference of each information source, each within categories of strength of partisanship for partisans. The coefficients for spouses of weak partisans in Germany, for spouses and discussants of weak partisans in Chile, and for discussants of strong partisans in Chile are not significant at the .05 level. Japan is omitted because a non-comparable party identification question was asked there. West German television is omitted because of difficulties in identifying the most-favoured stations among the many stations covered.

pattern of consistency appeared but with somewhat more exceptions: While the stronger partisans watch television news shows that conform to their own vote preferences more than weaker partisans in all but Hungary, the comparison between moderate and weak partisans produces four exceptions to monotonicity out of the ten cases. Taking all the intermediaries into account simultaneously, the general tendency across our sample of democracies is for the strength of partisanship to affect the relationship between vote preference and the perceived bias of information sources. Yet there is enough national uniqueness to undercut any broad cross-national generalizations. Only the United Kingdom displays the expected monotonic relationship of greater congruence across all information sources in respondent and source vote preference as partisan strength increases, although Greece, the United States, and West Germany come close. They are the countries in which partisanship structures the political communications process the most. The exceptions are so sporadic in the other countries that there is no explanation for them except to cite factors unique to each country. When it comes to explaining the role of partisanship in structuring choice of information sources, in short, cross-national tendencies are so often thwarted by national peculiarities that intensive country-by-country studies are required.

Probably the most important clue to the role of partisan strength in modulating the congruity between voter preferences and information source biases is what does not appear in Table 5.9. In most countries, especially for the mass media, the correlations between voter and information source are modest, often among even the strongest partisans. This result leads ineluctably to the conclusion that citizens of most contemporary democracies are not strongly embedded in political information environments that strongly reinforce their own partisan proclivities. Their vote preferences, in other words, are not powerfully reinforced by the political information they receive. The greatest reinforcement in country after country is provided by the oldest information source—personal discussants. When it comes to the media, especially in the newer democracies, however, citizens receive only the most modest support for their own preferences. As the media have come to dominate the flow of political information in campaigns, one can imagine that many voters across the democratic world have become less firmly anchored in their partisanship, leading to a weakened role for partisanship in voting choice. There is ample indication that this has been a trend in recent years (Dalton 2006: 176–200). Based on the data presented here for the 1990s, there is every reason to expect that it will continue.

Conclusion: Cross-National Similarities and Differences in Political Communication

Analysis of CNEP survey data from a dozen democracies across the world has shed considerable light on the flow of information from the mass media and interpersonal discussants to voters during election campaigns. It has revealed cross-national similarities and differences in exposure to and the bias of the flow of political information. It also has shown how these political communications can be modulated variously by the voter's own partisanship, sometimes even overcoming the 'framing' impact of this long-standing disposition.

There is considerable consistency across our country cases, allowing for some generalizations about political communications in democracies. Voters in all countries are highly exposed to television as a source of political news, but it is viewed almost uniformly as a source of information that contains relatively little partisan bias in its reporting on candidates and parties. Instead, personal discussants typically are seen as transmitting partisan messages, and these messages are almost uniformly seen across democracies as more congruent with respondents' own preferences than are messages from either television or newspapers. This congruence, even for discussants, is not so high, however, as to suggest that voters are deeply embedded in like-minded discussion networks, much less receiving only supportive media messages. Finally, congruence with information sources generally strengthens with increases in voters' strength of partisanship, though not to the point that even strong partisans are embedded in a cocoon of like-minded partisans or partisan media.

Several countries occasionally stood out as exceptions, or outliers, to these general patterns of political communication. West Germans' level of exposure to television news fell much below that of the other countries, whereas it was Americans who perceived the highest amount of television news bias. Exposure to political discussion was especially low in Hong Kong, which is joined by Japan in the relatively infrequent amount of partisan bias perceived in discussants. Partisan congruence between discussant messages and voter preferences was noticeably low in Chile, Japan, and Hong Kong. Discussants and spouses with *different* status showed greater congruence with the voter's own partisan preferences in Greece, but nowhere else. In Greece, Spain, and West Germany, low knowledge spouses were most congruent with voter's party preferences and strength of partisanship exhibited an inverse relationship with congruence. Several nations turn up twice as outliers in these relationships, but only Chile appears to be a deviant case warranting special treatment. It is conceivable that the deep wounds from its recent authoritarian experience and the Concertación between centre and left in its elections may have disrupted the 'normal' patterns of political communication there.

Finally, there are a few characteristics of exposure and bias that varied considerably across the democracies we studied. In some cases, these variations could be explained by other factors that we could identify. For example, exposure to political messages from newspapers varied widely, with citizens from the more affluent countries more likely to depend on newspapers for campaign news. Widespread perceptions of newspaper bias were linked to countries with nationally competitive newspaper markets, where newspapers sought distinctiveness through their political postures and readers could choose among them. Political discussion was especially low in the two East Asian study sites of Hong Kong and Japan. In other cases, especially where partisan bias was considered, there appeared to be no pattern to the results that could easily be accounted for by cross-national factors. These are cases where it is most likely that unique features of the country's politics or society affected its political communication patterns.

There is a strong hint in these patterns of important differences between the media, on the one hand, and discussants, on the other hand, as sources of political information and in the role played by partisanship. The role of the media approaches uniformity across these democracies, with few exceptions. This suggests that the powerful forces of media technology and professionalism are having a common impact across the democratic world, reducing the differences among countries. As the media become even more important as sources of information in politics, and we expect that they will, the variation in country politics should diminish. By contrast, where the role of discussants is concerned, we see a heavy imprint of a country's particular pattern of partisan politics. Discussants are the primary carriers of partisan influences. How these influences are applied depends very much on their unique political histories and the partisan cleavages they have spawned. Another feature of the contemporary democratic world, we suspect, is more pluralistic discussion networks, which over time should foster greater uniformity rather than difference in country patterns.

Our analysis of newspapers, television, spouses, and other principal discussants does not exhaust the list of important political intermediaries in democratic election campaigns. Some secondary organizations, especially labour unions and churches, have historically played an important intermediation role in electoral politics. Low membership in such organizations in almost all countries, however, makes them much less important as intermediaries for their members in recent years than either the mass media or personal discussants.[21] Since the 1990s, the advent of the Internet may have added an important new intermediary to the political communication process, but our studies pre-dated its emergence for most voters.[22] The study of political communications in the twenty-first century will need to take it into account.

Finally, our analysis has focused on only a single election in each of the dozen democracies we have included. Although patterns of political communication may be more stable than are those of other political factors, it is possible that our results are limited to this single electoral contest in each country and cannot be generalized beyond it. Replication of this analysis on other election surveys conducted in the next stage of the CNEP will go a long way towards establishing the generalizability of the results of our analysis.

6

Voting and intermediation: informational biases and electoral choices in comparative perspective

Pedro C. Magalhães[1]

As Downs famously noted, voters typically lack comprehensive information about the realm of politics: such information is costly and the incentives to obtain it are low (Downs 1957). Furthermore, rather than being exposed to the same amount of limited political information from similar sources, citizens tend to acquire it from an equally limited number of different intermediaries. Finally, such information is not necessarily neutral. Instead, it may be biased in ways that end up favouring particular candidates, parties, or positions (Zaller 1992; Huckfeldt and Sprague 1995; Beck et al. 2002).

It is therefore hardly surprising that the role of informational intermediaries should be seen as potentially consequential for electoral behaviour. In fact, the notion that voters are embedded in concrete 'informational environments'—understood as relatively stable filters for political communication that structure all kinds of information they acquire (Huckfeldt et al. 1995)—was one of the main foci of some of the very earliest efforts at systematic survey-based electoral research, such as those conducted by the Columbia University's Bureau of Applied Social Research in the 1940s and early 1950s (Lazarsfeld, Berelson, and Gaudet 1944; Berelson, Lazarsfeld, and Mcphee 1954). However, Lazarsfeld's own findings about the mass media's 'minimal effects' or the overwhelming importance of psychological predispositions as explanations of political behaviour, together with the rise of alternative approaches to the study of electoral choices—generally focusing on the role of social, ideological, or partisan predispositions on the vote—have led to general scepticism about the relevance of both interpersonal and impersonal communication for the study of voting choices (Ansolabehere, Behr, and Iyengar 1993; Zuckerman 2005).

There are two main ways in which CNEP has contributed to a reassessment of the role of informational intermediaries in electoral studies. First, it has allowed research on the influence of interpersonal communication networks on the vote to move from the use of sub-national samples of the United States (e.g. Huckfeldt and Sprague 1987, 1995) to the use of nationally representative samples of the electorate in an increasing number of democratic political systems (Burbank 1997; Liu, Ikeda, and Wilson 1998; Zuckerman, Kotler-Berkowitz, and Swaine 1998; Beck 2002; Levine 2005). Second, it has enriched the study of interpersonal discussants as sources of information by focusing on the actual interplay between the impact on the vote of social interaction networks and that of a number of other information sources located between individuals and the more remote world of politics, such as the organizations to which one belongs, the mass media to which one is regularly exposed, or even the messages conveyed by parties themselves when targeting voters through direct mobilization efforts (Beck 1991; Dalton, Beck, and Huckfeldt 1998; Beck et al. 2002; Elder and Greene 2003).

The focus on informational intermediation should be seen as more than an academic fad. It responds to a number of social and political developments that, in several ways, have made it more likely that knowledge of the political information to which voters are exposed increases our ability to explain their behaviour. In older democracies, rising levels of geographical and social mobility, post-industrialization, and secularization have led to an erosion of class, religious, and other social cleavages, as well as the decline of the electorate's anchoring in party loyalties and identifications (Mackie et al. 1992; Inglehart 1997; Evans 1999; Nieuwbeerta and Ultee 1999; Dalton 2000). In newer 'third-wave' democracies, social and political developmental leapfrogging (Gunther, Diamandouros, and Puhle 1995; Diamandouros and Gunther 2001b), together with the lack of a continuous history of partisan electoral competition (Mainwaring and Sculy 1995; Kitschelt et al. 1999; van Biezen 2003), have lead to relatively similar outcomes through different (but partially convergent) paths.

These developments have a number of important consequences for the role on informational intermediation. First, the fact that partisan predispositions and the social encapsulation of voters have weakened in many countries, has contributed to the broadening and diversification of voters' informational environments (Richardson and Beck, Ch. 5). As Mughan and Gunther note regarding the mass media, 'contemporary viewers tend to be less deeply anchored than those of a generation or two ago in social and community groupings, identification with which effectively served to insulate them against the blandishments of discordant messages' (Mughan and Gunther 2000: 20). In this way, even where social-structural changes have failed to break the tendency towards political homogeneity of personal interactions, the mass media—and particularly television, today the major source of political information in the industrialized democracies (Dalton 2002: 20)—has arguably compensated for that lack of exposure to alternative viewpoints and experiences (Mutz 1998). Moreover, even the notion that interpersonal contacts tend to occur systematically among like-minded people seems to be increasingly untenable. A growing body of evidence suggests that citizens in a varied range of democratic systems do seem to be exposed to significant levels of disagreement within their political discussion networks (Ikeda and Huckfeldt 2001), a phenomenon itself related to social and geographical mobility and the decline of partisanship (Huckfeldt, Johnson, and Sprague 2004; Huckfeldt, Ikeda, and Pappi 2005). Thus, social-structural and technological changes, combined with the weakening of partisan and social-group identities, have weakened voters' informational selectivity mechanisms and increased their exposure to views that are increasingly likely to serve as something else than mere reinforcement of their predispositions. As Huckfeldt and his colleagues put it in relation to the role of discussants, the sources of information available to voters should be seen less as 'a buffer between the individual and the external political environment' and more as 'transmitters and intermediaries that connect individuals to the events and circumstances of democratic politics' (Huckfeldt, Johnson, and Sprague 2004: 122).

Second, social and partisan de-alignment may have also increased the likelihood that those individuals who end up being exposed to discordant informational biases will also be more receptive to them. We know from a great number of studies that voters are more likely to retain those messages that reinforce their predispositions than those that do not, and may even tend to project their own preferences onto the very sources of information (Klapper 1960; Petty and Cacciopo 1981). In other cases, particularly in what concerns messages conveyed by the media, those who share a particular partisan affiliation often tend to misperceive messages as systematically biased against one's own preferences, the so-called 'hostile media phenomenon' (Vallone, Ross, and Lepper 1985; Giner-Sorolla and

Chaiken 1994). And the extent to which changes in attitudes result from exposure to persuasive messages surely depends on whether such messages are consistent with individual predispositions (McPhee, Smith, and Ferguson 1963; Zaller 1992). Thus, to the extent that 'a persuasive message must be sent and received' in order to produce influence on the receiver's attitudes (Dalton, Beck, and Huckfeldt 1998: 121) and that persuasive effectiveness is contingent on the relationship between message bias and individuals' extant preferences, the fact that an increasing number of voters approach elections with weaker party predispositions or even as non-partisans is likely to render them more receptive to the favourable or unfavourable presentations of political actors or the different rationales as to why certain stands should be adopted.

This has several implications for voting behaviour in contemporary democracies. It is today relatively well established that traditional explanations of vote choices—such as those based on the social and economic characteristics of voters or their partisan or ideological predispositions—seem to have lost some of their relevance for electoral behaviour. As Dalton puts it, 'the erosion of long-term sources of partisanship suggests that factors further along the funnel of causality can play a large role in voter choice' (Dalton 2002: 193). Therefore, one obvious line of inquiry that follows from this is related to the way persuasive messages conveyed by intermediaries may affect the more proximate attitudinal explanations of the vote, such as issue positions and evaluations of candidates or the state of the economy. Furthermore, it may even be the case that intermediaries have become directly relevant for voters' choices, regardless of whether they are effectively able to change short-term attitudes. As an increasing body of literature has suggested, voters who are highly uninformed about—and uninterested in—politics are nevertheless able to use a 'gut rationality' (Popkin 1991) and resort to 'heuristics', mental and judgemental shortcuts that yield 'dependable answers even to complex problems of choice' (Sniderman, Brody, and Tetlock 1991: 19). To the extent that partisan and social-group cues are indeed becoming less informative for voters across contemporary democracies, intermediaries may become increasingly important not only (or not so much) because they send messages that compel us to adopt views and opinions that will end up affecting our voting decisions, but rather because they are seen in and of themselves as trustworthy messengers whose perceived preferences can be directly used as a crucial piece of information on the basis of which one can decide which candidate or party should get our vote.

This chapter locates itself in this line of research about the role of information on electoral behaviour. On the basis of eleven surveys conducted throughout the last decade and a half under the CNEP network, which obtained considerable amounts of data about respondents' exposure to and content of information obtained from political intermediaries on the eve of specific elections, we examine whether the informational biases to which voters are exposed during electoral campaigns end up influencing their voting choices. In this way, we build on and extend the findings of the previous chapters in this volume, especially those concerning the extent to which both interpersonal and impersonal sources of information determine the range of political viewpoints to which different citizens end up being exposed (Richardson and Beck, Ch. 5), shape their attitudes towards vis-à-vis political institutions and officeholders (Schmitt-Beck and Voltmer, Ch. 3), and seem to stabilize the partisan loyalties on a non-irrelevant part of the electorate (Belluci, Maraffi, and Segatti in this volume).

The plausibility of the notion that informational intermediaries have an impact on voting decisions will be submitted to relatively stringent tests. Their effect on the vote will be estimated while taking into account the impact of well-established long-term individual characteristics and predispositions of voters likely to have an effect on both their voting decisions and the specific biases of the information flows to which they are exposed. Besides, we make this test stricter by ascertaining whether the fundamental processes through which such influences on the vote are exerted tend to travel beyond the specific national, political, and social setting where their theorization originated, namely, the United States. For that purpose, we can count on data based on elections that took place in a sample of political systems that present sharp differences in terms of their democratic experience, socio-economic development, political institutions, geo-cultural attributes, and democratic history.

The second section of this chapter then takes a closer look at intermediation processes, and aims at determining whether and why some types of intermediaries are more influential than others. Interpersonal communication, high levels of politicization, one-sided messages, and credibility are hypothesized as constituting features of the intermediation process that maximize the likelihood that the informational biases transmitted will contribute to change attitudes and serve as a consequential reference point for decision-making. Finally, in the third section, we focus on the specific case of mass-media outlets, using alternative measures of media bias and testing whether the degree to which media landscapes are dominated by partisan outlets makes a difference regarding the extent to which exposure to the media influences voting choices.

Informational Intermediation and Voting Choices: A Preliminary Exploration

We can start with a very general and (deceptively) simple question: does intermediation matter? Or in other words, does our knowledge of the informational biases conveyed to voters by intermediaries make a relevant addition to our ability to explain and understand electoral choices across a broad variety of political systems? The CNEP surveys provide data that allow us to give at least a preliminary answer to this question. A series of surveys under the CNEP project were conducted in eleven countries following elections that took place in the 1990s: the 1992 legislative election in the United Kingdom and American presidential election; the 1993 Spanish and Japanese legislative elections, as well as the Chilean presidential election; the 1994 legislative/presidential election in Uruguay; the 1996 legislative elections in Italy and Greece, as well as the Bulgarian presidential election in the same year; and the 1998 legislative elections in Hungary and Hong Kong. In four of these cases (Spain, Chile, Uruguay, and Greece) panel studies were conducted, with information on the respondents' recollection of the vote and other relevant campaign variables asked in the second wave. In the remaining cases, a single post-electoral survey was conducted. But in all countries, respondents were asked about the intermediaries from which they received information.

One type of informational intermediation addressed in the surveys is that provided by *interpersonal discussants*. Respondents were asked to sequentially identify the persons with whom they discussed 'important topics' more often. Depending on the surveys, respondents were then asked to identify at least two and at most five of those people. Then, following several questions about the socio-demographic characterization of discussants and their frequency of specifically political discussion, respondents were asked about their perception of which party or candidate in the election, if any, was supported by each discussant.[2] The surveys also obtained data about the *voluntary organizations* to which individuals belonged, treating them as additional potential sources of consequential political information. Respondents in each country who

213

reported belonging to any organization were asked about those that were most important for them (at least *the* most important and at most the *three* most important, depending on the survey). They were then asked about which candidate or party, if any, was supported by each organization. The mass media, of course, also played a central role in surveys about sources of political information. After reporting on their frequency of exposure to *newspapers* and *television networks*—the kinds of media outlets to which exposure ended up being higher in all countries and on which we focus here—respondents were also asked (if they were exposed at all) questions about at least the most frequently read newspaper and the most frequently watched television network, and then about whether they perceived those media outlets to have supported any specific party or candidate during the campaign (and, if so, which of them). Finally, in some cases, respondents were also asked about whether they received *contacts by political parties* themselves during the campaign, either by phone, personally, or by mail, and which parties were those.[3]

On the basis of this information, following Beck et al. (2002), we coded, for each respondent and each type of intermediary, the *net bias* to which she was exposed. Net bias was first measured by subtracting the number of specific intermediaries within each type (discussants, organizations, newspapers, television networks, and party contacts) perceived as being biased in favour of the opposition parties (or candidates) to the number of intermediaries perceived as biased for the incumbent parties (or candidates). Thus, for example, for an individual whose two most frequent discussants (except spouses or partners) were perceived as supporting the incumbent, the variable 'perceived discussant bias' initially received the value 2, while for another who perceived those two as supporting the opposition, the variable was coded −2. If only one frequent discussant was signalled as supporting a specific party, the variable was coded −1 if that discussant was perceived as supporting the opposition party, and 1 if the discussant was perceived as supporting the incumbent. Finally, respondents who perceived one of those discussants as supporting the incumbent and another as supporting the opposition received the value 0 (meaning 'no net bias'), while individuals without exposure to partisan bias at all were also coded with 0. We proceeded in the same fashion for all remaining intermediaries, using the maximum information on various intermediaries we had available in each country. Finally, since the different surveys varied in terms of the number of intermediaries in each specific type of which we were able to obtain information, variables were standardized across surveys by recoding them with just three alternative values: 1, for incumbent-dominant bias; -1, for opposition-dominant bias; and 0, for no exposure to intermediaries or no net bias. In this way, the measure attempts to capture the net bias to which citizens were exposed, taking into account the fact that, for each type of intermediary, respondents may have been exposed to more than one specific source of information and its perceived partisan bias.[4]

This particular approach immediately raises a first problem that needs to be addressed from the outset before any results are produced. At this stage, we are dealing only with *perceptions of bias* rather than with any measurement of 'actual' biases. In other words, we are relying on respondents for data about the politicization of their informational environments. It has been argued that this may produce serious problems of selective misperception or purposive selection of intermediaries, causing endogeneity problems in the analysis of their effects on voting decisions (van der Eijk 2002). However, we think the problems raised by relying on respondents' perceptions of bias may tend to be overestimated. First, all surveys took extreme care in allowing respondents to select the discussants, organizations, and political parties with which they interacted in ways that detached that selection from political considerations. Thus, discussants were identified as people with whom respondents discussed 'important matters' (rather than 'politics'), while organizations were selected on the basis of being 'most important to you' *before* any political leanings were obtained. And as for party contacts, respondents were simply asked to report about the more factual matter of whether they received any contacts or not.

In addition, several studies have shown that, whenever information about perceptions of discussants' biases can be cross-checked with information obtained from discussants themselves, respondents' perceptions do tend to be rather accurate. In a study using the 1992 American post-electoral survey also used here, where such information was indeed available, Beck and his colleagues report that 'the correlations between voters' perceptions of their discussants' vote preference . . . and the discussants' own reports ranged from 0.70 to 0.78 across the five discussants' (Beck et al. 2002: 61). Other studies have reported that levels of accuracy in the perception of discussants' preferences are considerably high across cultures (Huckfeldt and Sprague 1995; Liu, Ikeda, and Wilson 1998; Ikeda and Huckfeldt 2001).

Furthermore, as other studies have shown (Pattie and Johnston 2001; Zuckerman, Kotler-Berkowitz, and Swaine 1998), there is indirect evidence allowing us, at least, to deny the existence of a strong association

Table 6.1 The association between partisanship and perceived intermediary bias (tau-b coefficients)

	Perceived discussant bias	Perceived organizational bias	Perceived newspaper bias	Perceived TV network bias	Perceived party contact bias (personal or phone)	Perceived party contact bias (mail)
Bulgaria (n = 1,216)	.28***	.23***	.23***	−.12***	.24***	.20***
Chile (n = 1,054)	.19***	.04	.06	.04	.15***	.09**
Greece (n = 966)	.27***	.27***	.30***	.15***	.24***	.24***
Hong Kong (n = 988)	.11***	.09**	.05	−.01	−.05	—
Hungary (n = 1,520)	.34***	.12***	−.01	−.05*	.04	.05*
Italy (n = 2,502)	.27***	.14***	.14***	.01	—	—
Japan (n = 1,333)	.27***	.21***	.19***	.08***	.18***	.19***
Spain (n = 1,448)	.26***	.17***	−.04	−.11***	.07**	−.01
United Kingdom (n = 2,577)	.36***	—	.29***	−.05**	—	—
United States (n = 1,318)	.30***	.23***	−.12***	−.18***	.21***	.07*
Uruguay (n = 1,005)	.23***	.13***	.08**	.03	.21***	.07*

* $p < .05$; ** $p < .01$; *** $p < .001$.

between the respondents' partisan predispositions and their perception of the partisan inclinations of intermediaries. Table 6.1 shows the bivariate relationships between respondents' party identification and the net bias perceived in each intermediary. Party identification is coded as a trichotomous variable, with value 1 if the respondent identifies herself with one of the incumbent parties (or the party of the presidential candidate), −1 if with one of the opposition parties (or the parties of the opposition presidential candidates), and 0 for no party identification.

The results show that, although a majority of coefficients are positive and statistically significant, the strongest one (.36, between partisanship and perceived discussant bias in the United Kingdom) remains moderate in strength, showing that individuals' overestimation of homophily between themselves and intermediaries, if it exists, can certainly not be seen as overwhelming. These results, however, do lend support to the notion that misperception is most likely to occur with regard to the media—and especially television—as sources of biased information. In five of our eleven cases (Bulgaria, Hungary, Spain, the United Kingdom, and the United States), the association between partisan preferences and perceived television bias is both negative and significant. This suggests that the 'hostile media phenomenon' is likely to be pervasive in several other countries besides the United States, calling attention to the need to test the impact of media biases on the vote while taking into account other more objective measures of media content. We address this particular issue later in this chapter.

Estimating the extent to which informational biases contribute to explain voting decisions is plagued by a second potential problem besides that related to measurement. In fact, the answer to any questions about the importance of informational intermediation as an explanation of the vote crucially hinges on the particular assumptions we make about the temporal and causal order of the factors that lead to that vote. If we believe that values, ideology, or party identifications constitute persistent and long-term predispositions of voters—'already "in place" before the current campaign began and... generally not changed by short-term forces based on campaign issues or candidate personality' (Miller and Shanks 1996)—then the effects of informational biases should certainly be appraised by reference to a baseline model that includes such predispositions. This was, after all, the view of the Columbia school itself, who treated extant partisan loyalties as affecting both selection, perception, and reception of information, on the one hand, and the vote itself, on the other (Berelson, Lazarsfield, and Mcphee 1954: 277–80)—a notion that has been restated in studies of mass communications and information flows (Zaller 1992). From this point of view, we should expect, for example, that people will tend to associate and discuss matters with people they perceive to be politically similar and to adhere to organizations with which they share political inclinations that, as such, were already likely to heavily influence voting decisions in the first place. This forces us to consider the distinct possibility that a major part of the overall relationship between intermediation and voting decisions may be one of mere transmission to the vote choice of effects previously exerted by political predispositions, such as partisanship.

However, it has also been suggested that some factors commonly thought of as constituting 'predispositions', such as party identification, for example, should be conceived less as a 'durable attachment' (Campbell et al. 1960: 151) than as a 'running tally of retrospective evaluations of party promises and performance' (Fiorina 1981: 84; see also Alt 1984; Niemi and Jennings 1991). Similar hypotheses have emerged from careful analyses of panel surveys, revealing impressive changes in both the intensity and direction of partisanship over time at the individual level and leading to the conceptualization of a 'valenced partisanship', 'a storehouse of accumulated party and party leader performance evaluations' (Clarke et al. 2004: 210). From this point of view, the sort of relationships we found on Table 6.1—where partisanship is systematically (though moderately) associated with perceived informational biases—can be explained in other ways besides the role of predispositions in shaping exposure to (and perception and reception of) information. Instead, by shaping the kind of information on the basis of which we form evaluations of economic, party, and party leader performance, intermediaries can be conceived as explaining partisanship itself.

The implications of working under these contrasting assumptions can be ascertained by looking at Table 6.2. Here, we treat intermediation as a general phenomenon, and thus only the countries about which we have complete information on all kinds of perceived intermediary biases under examination here are included (thus results on nine countries are presented, all but Italy and the United Kingdom). Treating the vote as a dichotomous dependent variable (1 if vote for the incumbent party

Table 6.2 The role of intermediary biases (Nagelkerke R^2)

	Impact of social and economic characteristics	Incremental impact of intermediary biases	Incremental impact of intermediary biases after controlling for party identification	N
Bulgaria	.07	.35	.28	938
Chile	.14	.26	.18	681
Greece	.03	.35	.09	570
Hong Kong[a]	.06	.08	.04	377
Hungary[b]	.08	.24	.03	923
Japan[c]	.08	.34	.11	546
Spain	.15	.24	.11	829
United States	.08	.36	.11	774
Uruguay[c]	.02	.33	.08	501

[a] Mail contacts by parties not available.

[b] List vote in first round of elections.

[c] Religiosity not available.

or candidate, 0 if vote for any of the opposition parties or candidates), columns 3 and 4 show the estimate of what the inclusion of the bloc of all intermediation variables adds in terms of explained variance (measured by Nagelkerke R^2) to a logistic regression model of voting. However, while column 3 shows the increment in explained variance brought about by the addition of perceived intermediary biases to a baseline model built exclusively around the social and economic characteristics of voters (including sex, age, education, income, and, when available, religiosity), column 4 shows estimates of the increment in R^2 brought about by the inclusion of intermediary biases to a baseline model that also includes party identification.[5] Thus, a 'funnel of causality' strategy (Miller and Shanks 1996) is used in both cases. However, while the results of column 3 show us the net effects of intermediation once the confounding effects of unmistakably prior social and economic characteristics of voters are taken into account, the results in column 4 assume that part of the relationship between informational biases and the vote may also consist of simply mediating the effects of an individual predisposition such as partisanship. The results in column 4 provide, therefore, the most stringent test of the impact of informational biases.[6]

So, does intermediation matter? And does the answer to that question depend exclusively on our assumptions about the causal order of the factors that lead to the vote? The answers to these questions seem to be, respectively, yes and no. In all our countries, regardless of the assumptions made about the causal order of party identification and intermediation, the addition of the net biases perceived by voters in their most frequent discussants, the most important organizations to which they belong, the newspapers they read, the TV networks they watch, and the contacts received by parties and candidates always increases our ability to account for variation in the dependent variable. It is true that such enhancement is, in several cases, less than earth-shattering. This happens especially in Hong Kong and Hungary, both before (in Hong Kong) and after (in both countries) the introduction of controls for the party identification of voters. It is also true that, in all cases but Bulgaria and Chile, the net impact of informational biases drops to half or less in terms of explained variance once party identification is added earlier to the model. However, in almost all cases, and even in under the most stringent test, the portion of explained variance accounted for by intermediation biases is always larger than one-tenth of the overall variance explained by the model, and always matches or even surpasses that accounted for by social and economic characteristics. In fact, in the cases of Bulgaria and Chile,

Table 6.3 Intermediaries and short-term factors (Nagelkerke R^2)

| | With controls for social and economic characteristics and partisanship | | |
	Incremental impact of evaluations of economy and/or candidates *without* control for intermediaries	Incremental impact of evaluations of economy and/or candidates *with* control for intermediaries	N
Bulgaria	.42	.23	869
Chile	.20	.11	674
Greece	.11	.08	564
Hong Kong[a]	.15	.14	335
Hungary[b,c]	.09	.06	898
Spain	.12	.07	824
United States	.32	.22	769
Uruguay[d]	.06	.04	451

[a] Mail contacts by parties not available.

[b] Present or retrospective state of the economy not available.

[c] List vote in first round of elections.

[d] Religiosity not available.

informational biases emerge as explanations of the vote that rival the importance of partisanship itself, in spite of the fact that both socio-demographic variables and party identification were added earlier to the model.

Another way of looking at the importance of informational intermediation is to examine not how much it adds to long-term socio-demographic characteristics or partisanship, but rather how it relates to short-term factors thought to play an increasingly relevant role in the vote in contemporary democracies, such as the evaluations of the economy and candidates or party leaders. In Table 6.3, column 2 shows, for each country/election, what the incremental impact of short-term factors—evaluations of the state of the economy and/or of candidates/party leaders—would appear to be if intermediary biases failed to be taken into account as causally prior variables. However, although informational biases should certainly not be treated as long-term factors in the vote in the same way that the socio-demographic characteristics of voters, it is likely that the set of intermediaries from which individuals receive information (and the political biases contained in that information) do enjoy some amount of structural consistency and endurance beyond campaign periods, something that is particularly likely in the case of voters' interpersonal discussants and the organizations to which they belong (Liu, Ikeda, and Wilson 1998; Beck et al. 2002). Thus, the impact of short-term attitudes needs to be estimated while the confounding effects of the biases sources of information available to voters—and their role in shaping short-term attitudes—are taken into account. This is what is shown in column 3 of Table 6.3.[7]

The results show that if intermediaries are not included in our models of electoral behaviour (column 2), economy and candidate/leader evaluations emerge, in many cases, as very powerful autonomous explanations of the vote. This is especially the case in the Bulgarian, American, and Chilean presidential elections, while the introduction of evaluations of candidates and the economy still represent a very significant addition to our ability to account for voting choices in Hong Kong, Spain, and Greece. However, once intermediation is taken into account, the net impact of short-term attitudes on the voter drops in every single case. That drop is especially relevant in Bulgaria, Chile, and Spain, where nearly half of what candidate and economic evaluations had apparently contributed to the model can be accounted for simply as a transmission to the vote of the effects exerted by informational biases conveyed by political discussions, organizations, media outlets, and party communications. In other words, the results suggest that the much-heralded effect of short-term factors in electoral choices in contemporary democracies consists, at least partially, in a mediation of informational biases acquired through interpersonal discussions, associational involvement, exposure to the mass media, and party contacts.

The fact that these very general results pertain to specific elections in a small set of countries should warn us against any excessive generalization. But three main findings seem nonetheless to emerge from the previous analyses. First, although there is significant cross-national variation in this respect, knowing the kind of political biases contained (or perceived as being contained) in the information to which voters are exposed does improve our ability to predict their electoral choices. This is true even when we make rather conservative estimates of the impact of intermediation, that is, when we estimate it while controlling for the effects not only of the social and economic characteristics of voters but also of those partisan predispositions likely to affect both voting choices and the selection of information sources (and, for some authors, even seen as functional equivalents of the voting choice itself). However, we have good reasons to believe that such estimates are likely to be excessively conservative, given the accumulated evidence about the dynamic and changeable elements of partisanship itself. Although this particular investigation will not be pursued here, the point is, however, clear enough: intermediation matters, and it certainly matters more than most of the dominant approaches to electoral behaviour have given it credit for.

Second, as we saw in Table 6.3, a significant part of the effects on voting choices thought to be directly exerted by issue positions and candidate images consists, in fact, in a mediation of intermediary effects, particularly in those countries and elections where short-term factors seemed to be more determinant. Thus, these results suggest that we should guard against excessive generalization regarding the expanding role of short-term factors in determining the vote and the likely electoral instability that may ensue. Instead, voters' informational environments may work as a force that works to stabilize electoral behaviour in political systems where the personalization of politics and candidate-centred campaigns might otherwise engender extreme instability (Zuckerman, Kotler-Berkowitz, and Swaine 1998).

Finally, although we lack enough cases to make any systematic test of hypotheses at the macro-level, a few systemic patterns seem to emerge. On the one hand, Bulgaria and Chile are the two countries where intermediation exerts both a larger total effect (even when we control for party identification) and where the impact of short-term factors seem to consist more on a mediation of intermediary biases. In other words, of the three presidential elections included in our sample, two of them rank among the cases where intermediary effects are largest, with the United States tied for third place. This is not particularly surprising. Although legislative elections in parliamentary systems are not immune from a strong personalization of leadership or from campaigns fought on the basis of personal appeals (Mughan 2000; Poguntke and Webb 2004), political leaders in parliamentary systems, regardless of the electoral system, are almost invariably party leaders, who have become so by commanding support on a partisan basis. Instead, voting choices in presidential elections are, as Linz put it, always based 'on an opinion about *one* individual, a personality, promises and—let's be honest—an image a candidate projects' (Linz 1994: 11). Thus, in contests for the election of individuals under majoritarian rules, such as those in presidential elections, candidates have greater incentives to adopt vote-maximizing appeals that crosscut social and partisan bonds, weakening the importance of social-group and partisan cues in voting choices in elections where the personalistic elements introduces 'a dimension of conflict that cannot be explained wholly by socio-economic, political, or ideological circumstances' (Linz 1990: 53; see also McAllister 1996). As a result, room is opened up for a greater impact of informational biases on voters' short-term attitudes where partisan or social group is less relevant.[8]

A Closer Look at Intermediaries

The very broad analysis conducted so far has a few important and relatively obvious limitations. First, since emphasis has been given to the general effects of intermediation processes, analysis has been restricted, for comparability purposes, only to the cases where we have information about all kinds of intermediaries of interest in this chapter, excluding therefore the cases of Italy and the United Kingdom. Second, and most importantly, it has not allowed us to test specific hypotheses about the likely differences among types of intermediaries in terms of their influence on the vote. Those with whom we discuss politics, the organizations to which we belong, the political parties that convey messages during electoral campaigns and the media outlets to which we are exposed are not all equally likely to reach us with biases that are clear and consistent or, at least, perceived as such. And the intrinsic differences in the transmission and reception of information among these intermediaries, as well as in their relationship with voters, are also likely to dictate differences in their ability to foster conformity and serve as reference points for voters.

Interpersonal Discussants

There are several reasons why those with whom we discuss important issues should be the foremost and most universal source of politically consequential information for voters. Unlike what is often suggested in public and political discourse, contemporary democracies display few signs of a decline of interest in politics (Inglehart 1997; van Deth and Elff 2001) and although levels of political discussion may remain at relatively low levels between elections, campaigns do seem to be able to quickly reactivate both political interest and discussion among citizens (Topf 1995). This is confirmed by the results obtained from CNEP surveys: with the exception of Japan and Hong Kong, nearly half (and in some cases quite more) of respondents in the CNEP countries report discussing politics 'often' or 'sometimes', at least when friends and family members are concerned.

This has important consequences. When compared to other potential sources of information, discussants appear as more clearly politicized in the eyes of voters: as Richardson and Beck note, 'perceptions that spouses or other discussants supported a party were more common than feelings that other information sources were politically aligned' (Ch. 5 of this volume). Moreover, in the CNEP surveys analysed here, among those who did perceive a partisan bias in discussants, only one out of eight respondents, on average, report a disagreement between the two people with whom they discuss important matters more frequently. In other words, interpersonal discussions tend to be, for voters, not only the most prevalent source of political information, but also a source of consistently biased political information.

The fact that discussion networks are politicized in a typically one-sided way is not the only reason why the information conveyed by them should be more effective in shaping one's opinions of relevant political issues or serving as a direct guide for the vote. Two additional factors enhance their potential for influence: those who convey political information and how they convey it. On the one hand, in spite of the social changes in modern industrialized democracies that have fostered socially heterogeneous discussion networks, our choice of the people with whom we discuss important issues is still exercised within an environment characterized by a relative social closure, resulting in some amount of social homogeneity between individuals and those with whom they discuss politics. As Huckfeldt and his colleagues show, social homogeneity is not necessarily a cause of political homogeneity (Huckfeldt and Sprague 1995; Huckfeldt, Johnson, and Sprague 2004), but it does reinforce the potential for influence of the information conveyed by discussants: since the acquisition of information is always costly, individuals are likely to give more credence to cognitive and behavioural cues about politics if they come from sources with which shared interests are perceived (Huckfeldt and Sprague 1995; Beck et al. 2002). On the other hand, as Lazarsfeld and his colleagues noted long ago, influence is also likely to be stronger whenever sources of information are closer to the individual in time and space and bonds of interdependence exist among discussants, allowing for repeated contacts, the reduction of selective exposure to and perception of messages, and psychological rewards for conformity. Messages transmitted in this way can be made even clearer and less ambiguous for those who receive them, while interaction, repetition, and redundancy further allow for continued persuasion on the part of intermediaries and reasoned acceptance on the part of voters (Lazarsfeld, Berelson, and Gaudet 1944).

Organizational Bias

From all these points of view, the remaining types of informational intermediaries tend to fall short of discussants' potential for influence. The voluntary organizations to which individuals belong are perhaps those that come closest. While opportunities for interpersonal communication obviously exist in associational life, organizations are also typically formed around shared interests, something that enhances the electoral relevance and individual members' acceptance of the informational cues they convey. However, while interpersonal discussants serve as a source of information for a large number of voters across the board in many countries, organizations fail to perform the same task for other countries. While the United States, Japan, Italy and, to a lesser extent, Chile and Bulgaria, stand out as having the highest levels of associational membership in our sample of cases, other countries, such as Uruguay or Greece, are clearly nations of 'non-joiners' (Belluci, Maraffi, and Segatti, Ch. 4).

Furthermore, a comparison of the former countries shows that, regardless of levels of associational membership, the specific organizations to which individuals belong also vary significantly, with important implications for their role as sources of politically relevant information. In the United States and Chile, and in a different way in Italy or Bulgaria, the types of associations in which membership is higher are precisely those that represent interests around which social and political cleavages with electoral relevance tend to be organized, and are also, unsurprisingly, those types of organizations that tend to emerge more frequently as sources of messages perceived by their members as supporting political parties or candidates. These are the cases of *religious* organizations in United States and Chile, *unions* or *professional* organizations again in the United States, Italy, and Bulgaria, and *political parties themselves* in Bulgaria (Belluci, Maraffi, and Segatti, Ch. 4). In contrast, the case of Japan shows that levels of associational membership can be high while, at the same time, be accounted for by participation in mostly non-partisan and de-politicized organizations, such as the omnipresent Japanese neighbourhood associations.

Finally, the fact that some organizations do contribute, in some countries, to disseminate politically biased information to a significant number of citizens may not be enough to ensure that actual reception and acceptance of their standpoints is likely. Such acceptance is crucially affected by individuals' actual involvement with associational life (Verba, Schlozmman, and Brady 1995) and here, again, there are huge variations.

225

Just in our sample of cases, while active involvement is the dominant norm of associational membership in the United States and Japan, the remaining countries show much higher levels of passive membership. Similarly, as Bellucci and his colleagues show (Ch. 4), the organizations which are perceived as being more politically biased—unions and professional associations—are precisely those where involvement tends to be less intense across our sample of countries. And organizations where membership fundamentally serves instrumental goals or, in some cases, (such as with regard to some unions and professional associations) is required for employment in certain occupations are also those where psychological commitment to organizational goals is also likely to be lower (Elder and Greene 2003).

Party Contacts

Even greater problems restrict the ability of parties themselves, through electoral campaigns, to exert influence on voters. First, although parties can and do indeed contact voters, this mode of communication is usually only a small part of a party's campaign efforts in contemporary democracies. Among the nine CNEP countries for which we have information available in this respect, reliance on direct contacts made personally or by phone (in contrast with the use of mail propaganda) is only proportionally higher in those countries where parties have greater overall difficulties in reaching out to voters, such as Bulgaria or Uruguay. Conversely, with the notable exceptions of Japan and, to a lesser extent, the United States, the countries where parties are more successful in establishing contacts with voters (Greece and Spain) are also those in which the reliance on non-personalized contacts—that is, mail propaganda—is proportionally much heavier.[9]

Second, and more generally, to the extent that shared interests and mutual trust may enhance the effectiveness of discussants and organizations in providing consequential cues for voters, political parties are likely to have a harder time in emerging as influential sources of information. Parties' efforts at political proselytizing—regardless of their intensity, consistency, or form—are more obviously subjected to lack of credibility and downright rejection on the part of citizens than other persuasive messages that are less obviously self-serving, particularly in an age where citizens' trust in political institutions—and political parties in particular—is manifestly declining in both established and new democracies (Norris 1999c).

Finally, it is not even clear that parties are able to consistently reach voters with clear and one-sided messages. While they are, individually treated, obvious transmitters of such kind of messages, this may not be the case from the point of view of the receivers. Changes in communication technologies, party organization, and voting behaviour have fostered a shift in party campaigning in contemporary democracies, which has moved from the use of local machines and direct interpersonal communication between candidates and voters (with the foremost purpose of mobilizing relatively stable electoral constituencies that were already predisposed towards voting in a specific party) to a new 'chasing' strategy, aimed at reaching out to larger shares of the electorate (including unaligned voters) through heavier use of more impersonal forms of communication (Butler and Ranney 1992; Farrell and Webb 2000; Norris 2000c; Rohrschneider 2002). As a result, while voters tended in the past to receive one-sided information from parties—since narrowly defined segments of the electorate tended to remain insulated from information that contained competing biases—they are today much more likely to be the recipients of multiple and conflicting messages from different parties, a phenomenon no doubt helped by the increase in the overall resources available to modern campaigning (Katz and Mair 1994). In fact, among the nine CNEP countries of which we have information about party contacts, Japan, Greece, Spain, and the United States stand out not only as those where more voters (close to 50% or more) report having received direct contacts from parties during the campaign but also as those where more voters tend to report having been contacted by *several* parties during the campaign.[10] In this way, party messages tend to be two-sided rather than one-sided among our countries, potentially diminishing their effectiveness.

The Mass Media

The mass media constitute the fourth type of intermediary under examination here, and it is also the one where the detection of an effective impact of informational biases on the vote becomes both more complex and unlikely. Some of the reasons for this are common to those advanced for political parties. In what concerns credibility, the generally low levels of public trust in the media in the advanced industrial democracies raise immediate doubts about their potential not only for persuasion but also for effective 'priming', 'framing', or 'agenda setting' (Cappella and Jamieson 1997; Miller and Krosnick 2000; Gallup International 2003).

Furthermore, although the media in industrialized democracies have not been immune from criticism about their exclusively 'mainstream' orientation or the tendency towards excessive 'editorialization' or 'tabloidization' (see, among many, Blumler and Gurevitch 1995; Langer 1998; McChesney 2000; Mughan and Gunther 2000), most studies of media contents have been hard pressed to find strong directional biases in political coverage in the main media outlets, detecting, instead, the transmission of multiple and often conflicting biases (Dalton, Beck, and Huckfeldt 1998; Picard 1998; Gunther, Montero, and Wert 2000; Semetko 2000). This should not distract us from cases where content analysis of specific media outlets have indeed revealed the existence of strong directional biases, such as the Italian television networks, particularly after Berlusconi's rise to power (Marletti and Roncarolo 2000), or the highly partisan British press (Curtice and Semetko 1994; Semetko 2000). But while these are two cases where the CNEP surveys do show an above average perception of partisan bias among respondents, citizens' awareness of political bias on the part of newspapers and (especially) television is, in the remaining countries, fairly uncommon (Richardson and Beck, Ch. 5). Thus, most citizens in many democracies, even when they are dependent from a single media outlet in order to obtain information, are regularly exposed to 'two-sided' information flows (Zaller 1992), undercutting much of the consistency and persuasive effectiveness that messages conveyed by the media might have.

An additional obstacle to the media's ability to exert a detectable influence on voting choices is the potential gap between the actual content of messages and the way they are perceived by voters. Even when consistent biases are present on the side of transmission, there seems to be, at least in some countries, a psychological tendency on the side of reception towards systematic misperception of messages originating in the media. Unlike what occurs with other intermediaries—where, at most, projection effects seem to be present—media coverage in some countries is perceived as being systematically biased against one's own side, the so-called 'hostile media effect' (Vallone, Ross, and Lepper 1985; Giner-Sorolla and Chaiken 1994). This renders media effects less likely or, at the least, much more complex and difficult to grasp. In the case of discussants, for example, the misperception of their actual biases is not necessarily an impediment for the detection of a predictable influence of those perceived biases on the vote. Here, although a gap between content and perception may tend to weaken the level of influence exerted on the vote, perception is ultimately what really matters, since the mistaken assignment of a particular partisan leaning to a discussant does not necessarily impend on what makes her fundamentally credible as an information source (Huckfeldt and Sprague 1995: 170–3). Perception of 'bias', however, may have a whole different meaning and implications in the case of the media. Where the hostile media effect is present, neutrality (and, thus, credibility) is more likely to be assigned to those outlets whose actual biases do little but reinforce previous views. Conversely, the perception of biases in a media outlet to one which is exposed may actually neutralize whatever influence the content of their information might exert or even create a negative relationship between perceived bias and electoral behaviour, as research in the United States has shown (Beck et al. 2002; Elder and Green 2003). In fact, one should only expect the media's perceived bias to have a positive effect on the vote in those cases where the existence of such biases is common and accepted knowledge, consistent with general expectations and, thus, more likely to be an accurate depiction of actual media contents.

Testing the Hypotheses

On the basis of the previous arguments, although we have good reasons to believe that, in many contemporary democracies, social and partisan de-alignment should lead to greater attention to the role of informational intermediaries as providers of consequential stimuli and cues for electoral decision-making, we should not expect all of them to be equally important in that respect. For a majority of citizens across very different political systems, those with whom they discuss important matters seem to constitute a fundamental source of politically charged, consistently biased, and potentially influential information. In contrast, we should expect organizations, the media, or political parties themselves to produce somewhat more modest and contingent effects. They tend to be less prevalent sources of objectively (or subjectively perceived) biased information, their persuasive effectiveness for voters may be encumbered by infrequent and impersonal communication, and their credibility as providers of reference points for voters is comparatively lower, particularly in the case of media outlets and political parties.

Tables 6.4 and 6.5 show tests of these hypotheses. For each country, we present the logistic regression coefficients for each intermediary bias variable we have available for each case, determining the extent to which

Table 6.4 The effects of perceived intermediary biases on voting behaviour, I (values in cells are logistic regression coefficients; values in parenthesis are first differences)

	Bulgaria	Chile	Greece	Hong Kong	Hungary
Sex	−.12	−.17	.36	−.40	−.01
Age	−.01	−.03**	.01	−.01	.01
Education	−.17**	−.43***	−.13*	.03	.04
Income	.03	.03	.05	.00	.14
Religiosity	.19**	.03	−.02	.08	−.13
Party identification	1.58*** (48.6)	1.22*** (52.7)	2.43*** (78.5)	1.87*** (70.9)	3.04*** (90.5)
Perceived discussant bias	1.69*** (68.5)	1.53*** (64.4)	.62** (25.9)	.69* (33.0)	1.41*** (54.5)
Perceived org. bias	.73** (23.5)	.85** (39.4)	.73 (29.8)	.71 (34.0)	.23 (8.7)
Perceived newspaper bias	1.14*** (38.5)	−.09 (−4.4)	.84** (34.4)	−.13 (−6.5)	−.14 (−5.3)
Perceived TV network bias	−.69* (−23.3)	.24 (11.6)	.39 (15.8)	−1.18 (−52.8)	.11 (4.2)
Perceived party contacts bias (personal or phone)	.86 (28.2)	.47 (22.5)	.57 (23.9)	.30 (14.8)	.05 (1.9)
Perceived party contacts bias (mail)	−.53 (−18.3)	.02 (1.0)	.87* (35.5)	—	−.27 (−10.2)
Constant	.66	3.13	−.54	.25	−.72
N	938	681	570	377	923
Nagelkerke R^2	.50	.48	.61	.31	.74
Highest VIF	5.7	1.9	1.9	2.0	1.3

* $p < .05$; ** $p < .01$; *** $p < .001$.

their influence emerges even when controls for both enduring socio-demographic characteristics and partisan identification are introduced in a single-equation model. Thus, again, we subject our hypotheses to the most stringent test. However, we do exclude evaluations of candidates and of the state of the economy on theoretical grounds, conceiving of them as short-term factors unlikely to influence either the traditional long-term components of the voting decision or the intermediation channels available to voters (see Beck et al. 2002). All eleven countries of which we have data available are included. For all variables besides socio-demographic characteristics—used as mere controls and of no specific interest here—we also present, in parenthesis, 'first differences' values, representing the percentage-point increase in the probability of voting for the incumbent caused by a change on each variable across its range (from its lowest to its highest value), while the remaining independent variables are kept

Table 6.5 The effects of perceived intermediary biases on voting behaviour, II (values in cells are logistic regression coefficients; values in parenthesis are first differences)

	Italy	Japan	Spain	UK	United States	Uruguay
Sex	.08	.27	.31	.32	-.02	.16
Age	-.00	.02*	-.00	.02**	.01	.00
Education	.03	-.01	-.47***	-.03	-.05	.01
Income	—	.04	-.04	.46***	.17*	-.02
Religiosity	-.26***	—	-.20*	-.05	.47**	—
Party identification	1.78*** (70.7)	1.53*** (60.3)	2.26*** (81.0)	2.55*** (85.0)	1.77*** (63.8)	2.43*** (71.6)
Perceived discussant bias	.77*** (36.7)	1.38*** (55.7)	1.62*** (66.9)	.47** (22.3)	1.24*** (51.0)	1.17*** (31.3)
Perceived org. bias	1.09*** (49.7)	.32 (14.5)	.36 (17.8)	—	.52* (22.3)	.77 (16.7)
Perceived newspaper bias	.55*** (26.8)	.46* (20.8)	.28 (13.9)	.90*** (39.7)	-.17 (-7.1)	-.08 (-1.6)
Perceived TV network bias	-.18 (-9.0)	.69* (30.8)	.15 (7.5)	-.33 (-15.7)	-.86*** (-32.4)	.65 (13.3)
Perceived party contacts bias (personal or phone)	—	.76** (33.8)	.78 (37.1)	—	.84** (35.1)	.73* (15.8)
Perceived party contacts bias (mail)	—	.19 (8.6)	.37 (18.3)	—	-.11 (-4.7)	.50 (10.0)
Constant	.51	-2.11	1.94	-2.91	-2.91	-1.09
N	1995	546	829	2493	774	501
Nagelkerke R²	.59	.61	.57	.78	.61	.62
Highest VIF	1.1	1.6	1.6	1.5	1.3	1.5

* p < .05; ** p < .01; *** p < .001.

constant at their mean values. 'First differences' values provide, therefore, a more intuitive measure of each variable's overall impact on the vote than that provided by the logistic regression coefficients.

The results show, unsurprisingly, that the most powerful predictor of the vote in incumbent parties or candidates across the board is party identification. However, the most impressive finding here is the extent to which the perceived biases in interpersonal discussion networks contribute to explain the vote. Discussant bias in favour of the incumbent has a positive impact on vote for the incumbent in all countries, and the magnitude of that impact often rivals (in Spain, United States, Japan, and, to a lesser extent, Hungary) and even surpasses (in Bulgaria and Chile) the effects of party identification itself! In these six countries, the probability of voting for the incumbent increases by at least 50 percentage points depending on whether voters' interpersonal discussion context is mainly opposition- or incumbent-biased, even for voters with similar socio-demographic characteristics and party identifications. Interpersonal discussion biases have a statistically significant impact in all countries, confirming the previously advanced hypothesis that discussants should be the most important intermediaries in terms of their net impact on the vote. It is hardly possible to overstate how generally important these results are, especially considering the strict controls to which the analysis of the impact of intermediaries is subjected here, the enormous diversity of our cases from all points of view, and the relative abandon to which the study of contextual effects on voting behaviour has been relegated to in the last decades (Zuckerman 2005).

The effect of perceived organizational biases is, among intermediary influences, the second most important in terms of combining pervasiveness, strength, and consistency among our countries. However, although the coefficient's sign is positive in all cases, it reaches statistical significance in only four out of the ten countries of which we have data available (Bulgaria, Chile, United States, and Italy). It is hardly surprising that these four cases emerge as those where organizational biases have a statistically significant impact on the vote, since they combine two important characteristics: first, they are among the five countries where levels of associational membership are higher among our sample; second, unlike the remaining case of a country of 'joiners' (Japan), associational patterns in these countries privilege types of organizations that are plugged into politically relevant social cleavages, such as labour unions, professional associations, and religious organizations, not to mention political parties themselves.

Party contacts produce much less consistent results. For the purpose of this analysis, we separate interpersonal (by phone or in person) from impersonal (by mail) party contacts, in order to test the hypothesis that the former are more likely to produce greater acceptance on the part of voters and thus a greater net impact on the vote. Generally speaking, that is precisely what tends to happen: the coefficients for perceived biases in personal or phone contacts by parties all have positive signs, are significant in three cases, and exert a comparatively strong effect in two of them—United States and Japan—while perceived biases in mail party contacts only make a positive and significant difference on the vote in Greece. Nevertheless, effects of party contacts are quite modest in comparison with what occurs with discussant bias, and it is interesting to note how the coefficients for mail contacts are even negative in three cases—the United States, Bulgaria, and Hungary—suggesting how party propaganda is closer to engendering modest hostile reactions on the part of voters than the opposite.

The Problem of Media Effects

The findings reported in the previous section, covering a very diverse range of political systems and types of elections, go a long way in ascertaining the relative importance and significance of different types of informational intermediation in contemporary democracies. However, they still leave unanswered important questions, particularly those concerning the role of the media. As we see in Tables 6.4 and 6.5, effects on the vote are positive and significant in the cases of perceived newspaper bias in Japan, Italy, Greece, and (especially) Bulgaria and the United Kingdom, but are absent in the remaining cases. Moreover, effects of perceived television network biases are simply absent in most cases. In fact, they are even negative and significant in Bulgaria and the United States (at least in 1992, prior to the advent of Fox News and the flourishing of highly partisan television talk shows): in these cases, the stronger the perceived pro-incumbent biases, the more likely were voters to choose the opposition candidates instead.

It is not entirely clear what we should conclude from these findings. We had anticipated earlier that, in spite of the trend towards partisan de-alignment in advanced democracies and its potential effects on diminishing selective exposure to and reception of media messages, informational intermediation by the media should still be less likely to make a difference on the vote than, for example, interpersonal discussants. However, findings such as those obtained for the effects of perceived bias TV networks in Bulgaria and the United States suggest important potential problems in our analysis. What accounts for these puzzling negative effects? Should the absence of significant effects of perceived television news contents in the remaining cases be safely interpreted as a result of the inherent inability on the part of media outlets to exert a net influence on voting decisions? And even if this is true, what might cause it: the fact that partisan predispositions predetermine both media exposure and the vote, or the remaining shortcomings of the media as an influential intermediary (such as two-sided information flows, impersonal communication, lack of credibility, or misperception)? And why, nevertheless, should the perception of newspaper bias emerge as relevant for the explanation of one's vote in some cases and not others?

In fact, it is likely that these results tell us less about how the media contents to which voters are exposed influence their choices than about the gap between those contents and people's perception of them. Several additional steps need to be taken to address this specific problem. Previous studies using the American component of CNEP used not only respondents' perceptions of bias in the media but also content analysis of a representative sample of newspapers and television news services in the United States in order to measure their actual bias. Dalton, Beck, and Huckfeldt (1998) show that biased newspaper editorials did have a positive—though modest—impact on the vote in American presidential elections. At the same time, Beck and his colleagues (Beck et al. 2002) found that exposure to news articles (in contrast with editorials) had no impact on the vote, while perceptions of a pro-Clinton bias in television had a negative effect on the vote for Clinton. However, by testing the effect of *both* perceptions *and* actual contents of media messages, their findings and conclusions were made more robust: while the absence of newspaper effects can be explained by the inconsistency or absence of partisan biases in newspaper coverage during the 1992 campaign, the negative effect of the perceived bias of television networks (which persists after controls for actual biases are introduced) can be now clearly related to the 'hostile media phenomenon'.

A similar analysis is attempted in this section, focusing on four country cases and using, for each of them, information on media outlets gathered from expert judgements and secondary content analysis data. There are considerable cross-national differences among these four countries with regard to the extent to which media outlets tend to provide politically one-sided messages to their readers and viewers. Bulgaria and Italy are characterized by a strongly partisan media landscape. In the former, the partisanship of the press was particularly strong well into the mid-1990s. Although privately owned newspapers have expanded in circulation since then, the two newspapers with the widest circulation in the early 1990s were controlled by the two major parties in Bulgaria: *Duma* (controlled by the BSP and the successor of *Rabotnichesko delo*, the official newspaper of the Communist Party) and *Demokratsya* (controlled by the Union of Democratic Forces). Although their circulation subsequently declined (with one of them going bankrupt) and the print media in Bulgaria have become increasingly independent from parties, at the time of our survey these two newspapers were the major elements of what was, by Western standards, a highly partisan print media landscape (IREX 2003; Schmitt-Beck and Voltmer in this volume). Although less blatant, partisanship was (and, in this case, remains) relatively strong among television networks. As Schmitt-Beck and Voltmer note in a Chapter 3, Bulgarian National Television has always been highly vulnerable to political interference on the part of the government due to its dependence on state subsidies and governmental control over existing broadcast regulatory bodies. Accordingly, private stations were the only counterbalance to governmental dominance over televised political news (Schmitt-Beck and Voltmer in this volume; also see IREX 2003).

Italy represents a comparable situation, although open partisanship of news content has tended to be more intense in television rather than in the newspapers. Following years of consensual *lottizazione* practices, through which the main political parties controlled its own channel of the public television network (RAI), Silvio Berlusconi took advantage of the absence of media regulation throughout the 1980s to create a media empire that ultimately led to his control of the three main private television channels: *Canale 5, Italia 1*, and *Rete 4*. These were blatantly used for his political purposes, which ultimately made a decisive contribution to the victory of his *Forza Italia* in the 1994 elections (Ricolfi 1994). However, between 1994 and 1996, and in spite of Berlusconi's strenuous efforts to pack RAI's governing board, he failed to completely control the news coverage made by RAI's three main channels (although that would change following his election victory in 2001). Instead, as content analyses of television coverage by Marletti and Roncarolo revealed (2000: 240), while *Forza Italia* obtained more favourable coverage in *Rai Due* (due to the disappearance of the Italian Socialist Party that previously controlled it) and in *Rai Uno* (controlled by formed factions of the Christian Democrats), *Rai Tre*'s coverage in 1996 continued to favour left-wing parties as in the past.

The level of partisanship of Italy's newspapers is somewhat lower, although still significant. The largest newspapers in Italy tend to be seen as relatively balanced and moderate in partisan and ideological terms. *Corriere della Sera* (the largest newspaper in the country) and *La Stampa* (which has consistently ranked as the third or fourth largest) are highly respected media outlets, controlled by large media and industrial groups independent from Berlusconi. They practise a general avoidance of taking stands either with the left or the right (Stille 2000) although, in the early 1990s, they tended to be seen as moderately leftist-leaning (Pucci 1996). Similarly, newspapers like the *Resto del Carlino* and *La Nazione* are generally seen as moderately leaning to the right (Pucci 1996). There are, however, several important exceptions to this pattern of relative moderation. By 1996, Berlusconi's Fininvest had already obtained control over a major national newspaper (*Il Giornale*), promptly sacking its founder (Indro Montanelli) for lack of responsiveness to the new owner's political priorities. Conversely, *La Reppublica*, created in 1976, became by the mid-1990s the main voice of the left, joined by two smaller publications—*L'Unità* and *Il Manifesto*—further to the left and with direct links with political parties.

A substantially different pattern can be observed in the United Kingdom where a blatantly partisan press has coexisted with balanced and moderate television news coverage (Semetko 2000). Although formally and institutionally independent from political parties, British newspapers are among the most partisan media in Western Europe. In the 1992 election, *The Times*, the *Daily Express*, and the *Daily Telegraph* were biased in favour of the Conservatives, joined by the *Sun* and the *Daily Mail*, whose coverage of the Labour Party was particularly negative. Conversely, the *Daily Mirror* and (an exception among non-tabloids) *The Guardian* covered the Conservatives in a more negative light, and were joined by the usually circumspect *Financial Times* in endorsing Labour—Semetko (2000: 363–5). In contrast, television news programmes in Britain have provided more balanced treatment of political issues in general and electoral campaigns in particular. Although we lack data for the 1992 elections, content analysis of coverage of the 1997 elections shows that television news broadcasts were only slightly negative towards the Conservatives among the *BBC*, *ITN*, and *SKY* (Semetko 2000: 365–7).

Finally, with regard to Spain, content analysis of television news coverage in the 1993 electoral campaign shows visible but slight biases in favour of the PSOE government in public television, offset by even more modest biases in favour of the opposition's PP by the private networks, *Tele5*, *Antena 3*, and *Canal+*. Overall, 'the Spanish television media were quite pluralistic and inconsistent in their patterns of bias' (Gunther, Montero, and Wert 2000: 61). The partisan and ideological leanings of the centre-left *El País* and the centre-right *ABC* are widely acknowledged, although content analysis of their coverage of the 1993 election campaign revealed moderate biases in favour of the PSOE and the PP, respectively. The third major national newspaper, *El Mundo*, was perhaps different in the sense that it focused explicitly on uncovering scandals involving the PSOE government, but this has not prevented observers from detecting 'generally modest political biases of news coverage by newspapers, radio, and television' in early 1990s Spain (Gunther, Montero, and Wert 2000: 75).

Given this complementary body of contextual information, we can supplement our previous analyses based on respondents' *perceptions* of bias by incorporating measures of partisan bias as determined by skilled outside observers. On the basis of these content-analysis data, we coded newspapers and television networks in the four countries as incumbent-biased, opposition-biased, or balanced/neutral.[11] We then followed the same procedure used previously for net *perceived* bias, subtracting the number of newspapers and television networks to which each individual reported being most exposed to and coded as opposition-biased to those coded as incumbent-biased. Finally, for both newspapers and TV networks, variables were then standardized with values 1 (dominant exposure to incumbent-biased outlets), −1 (dominant exposure to opposition-biased outlets), and 0 (no exposure, exposure to balanced/neutral media, or no net bias in exposure).

Table 6.6 starts by comparing, for each of the four countries and each of the main types of mass media considered, two measures of association: the extent to which voters' partisan predispositions correlate with their *perceptions* of bias in the media outlets, results that had already been presented in Table 6.1; and the extent to which such predispositions correlated with our new variables of *actual exposure* to biased outlets. For each type of outlet, we also present the correlation between perceived bias and actual bias. Some interesting findings emerge. First, it appears that, in all these countries, voters do tend to read the newspapers that objectively fit their political predispositions (as the positive and

Table 6.6 Party identification and media biases (tau-b coefficients)

	Association between party ID and exposure to incumbent-biased newspapers	Association between perceived bias and exposure bias	Association between party ID and exposure to incumbent-biased networks	Association between perceived bias and exposure bias
Bulgaria (n = 1,216)	.32***	.57***	.04	−.02
Italy (n = 2,502)	.18***	.31***	.16***	.29***
United Kingdom (n = 2,577)	.27***	.64***	−.05*	−.10***
Spain (n = 1,448)	.11***	.22***	.08**	.20***

* $p < .05$, ** $p < .01$, *** $p < .001$.

significant coefficients in column 1 suggest). This tendency is, unsurprisingly, stronger in those cases where the press is more openly partisan (Bulgaria and the United Kingdom). However, as Newton and Brynin (2001) have noted in the case of Britain, important minorities of citizens still tend to read newspapers whose biases are inconsistent with their partisan predispositions. In fact, all correlations between party identification and exposure to biased newspapers are relatively weak, even in the cases of the UK and Bulgaria. In the former, more than one-third of the voters who tended to be more exposed to one type of newspaper than another and identified with either Labour or the Liberal Democrats were, in fact, more exposed to newspapers favouring the Conservative Party. And in Bulgaria, among those who identified with parties opposing Stoyanov's UDF and read any of the major newspapers, about 11 per cent still reported reading the *Demokratsya*. The mismatch between partisan predispositions and actual television biases is even starker, as the highest tau-b value is only .16, for the Italian case. Thus, as we previously noted regarding other intermediaries, partisan predispositions and informational biases are only weakly or moderately correlated, suggesting that self-selection is not an obstacle to intermediary influence and opening up the possibility that informational biases do more than just reinforce previous predispositions. As we can see, this also applies to the case of media biases, even when 'actual' rather than 'perceived' biases are used.

However, the results also suggest that citizens' misperceptions of the biases of the media to which they are exposed is, in some cases, rampant.

For example, in Italy, in spite of the historical *lottizazione* of public television networks and Berlusconi's blatant use of his private networks for political purposes, about one of every four voters who were dominantly exposed to networks that content analysis showed to have supported the opposition perceived them as supporting the incumbent, and vice versa. As a result, the correlation between perceived biases contained in the network news to which individuals were exposed and the actual biases of those networks is a moderate .29, and it is even weaker in the remaining countries. Things are somewhat different with regard to newspapers, particularly in the cases of Bulgaria and the United Kingdom. Here, voters' perceptions of the biases contained in the newspapers they read tend to match rather well our assignments of incumbent- or opposition-biases to those newspapers on the basis of expert sources (with tau-b values around .60). In other words, the blatant partisanship of the press in these two countries leaves less room for doubt about the political leanings of each media outlet, leading voters to make correct assignments of bias. However, this is not the case in the cases of Italy and Spain with respect to newspapers, especially in the latter (.22), where the newspaper market is dominated by newspapers without clear or strong partisan positions. This suggests that the findings in the previous section regarding the effects of media biases on voting behaviour are likely to be affected by our reliance in perceptions as measures of such biases.

Table 6.7 takes us further in that respect: dealing with the cases of Bulgaria, Italy, the United Kingdom, and Spain, it replicates the analyses of voting behaviour presented in Table 6.5, but adding our 'exposure to biased outlets' variable to the previously used perceptions of bias.

The comparison of Table 6.7 with Table 6.5 is relevant in several respects. In all four countries, the explanatory power of our model increases in relation to that used in Table 6.5—very modestly in Spain and the United Kingdom, but less so in Bulgaria and Italy—with the addition of the media exposure variables to our previously used perceptions of bias. Besides, in all four cases, at least one of the two new media exposure variables emerges as statistically significant. In Spain, where the exclusive use of perceptions of media bias rendered no significant media effects whatsoever, it turns out that the greater exposure to the public television than to the private channels on the part of voters does have a modest but still statistically significant impact on the decision to vote for the incumbent party. And in the 1992 British elections, greater exposure to

Table 6.7 Intermediary influences on the vote in four countries (values in cells are logistic regression coefficients; values in parenthesis are first differences)

	Bulgaria	Italy	UK	Spain
Sex	−.13	.14	.31	.31
Age	−.01	−.01	.02**	−.01
Education	−.11	−.00	−.02	−.47***
Income	.03	—	.45***	−.07
Religiosity	.19**	−.23***	−.04	−.20*
Party identification	1.52*** (46.7)	1.77*** (66.6)	2.54*** (84.9)	2.21*** (78.3)
Perceived discussant bias	1.68*** (68.3)	.71*** (32.5)	.45** (21.4)	1.62*** (65.9)
Perceived organizational bias	.70** (22.4)	1.00*** (44.3)	—	.42 (19.7)
Perceived newspaper bias	.64 (21.6)	.40*** (18.8)	.62*** (28.4)	.18 (8.5)
Exposure to incumbent-biased newspapers	2.22*** (68.4)	.46*** (21.9)	.47** (21.9)	.50 (23.3)
Perceived television network bias	−.48 (−16.1)	−.39*** (−18.1)	−.32 (−15.2)	−.03 (−1.4)
Exposure to incumbent biased TV networks	.92*** (20.0)	.94*** (34.0)	−.18 (−8.5)	.35** (16.3)
Perceived party contacts bias (personal or by phone)	.78 (25.5)	—	—	.82 (37.2)
Perceived party contacts bias (mail)	−.60 (−20.6)	—	—	.35 (16.5)
Constant	1.20	1.08	−2.98	2.04
N	938	1995	2493	829
Nagelkerke R^2	.54	.62	.79	.58

* $p < .05$; ** $p < .01$; *** $p < .001$.

Conservative than to Labour newspapers also had a positive and significant effect on the vote, even after controls for socio-demographic characteristics, remaining intermediary biases, and partisanship are used, confirming the results of previous researches (Newton and Brynin 2001). Similarly, in Bulgaria and Italy, the effects of newspaper biases on voting behaviour are confirmed, and appear to be better captured by using the actual exposure to incumbent- or opposition-biased newspapers rather than perceptions of bias, something that is particularly (and predictably) visible in the politically saturated press environment of mid-1990s Bulgaria. Conversely, in these two cases, the only results we had previously obtained concerning effects of television network news were that the variables measuring perceptions of bias had *negative* signs. However, the variables measuring actual exposure to incumbent- or opposition-biased networks now have the predicted *positive* sign: while greater exposure to private TV networks increased the likelihood of voting for Stoyanov in Bulgaria, greater exposure to the private TV networks (as well as *Rai Uno* and *Due*) increased the likelihood of a vote for the opposition to *Ulivo* in Italy.

Furthermore, the comparison of the relative impacts of these exposure variables, measured in terms of the increase in probability of a vote for the incumbent caused by a change on each variable across its range while the remaining independent variables are kept constant at their mean values (first difference), is consistent with the notion that the potential for influence on the part of the media increases the more they tend to present voters with clear and unambiguously one-sided messages. For example, exposure to the different but generally balanced British television networks makes no difference in voting choices, while the effect resulting from differential exposure to either the public or private networks in Spain is, although significant, smaller than in the cases of Bulgaria or Italy. Conversely, in these last two cases, where levels of politicization of television networks were (especially in the latter) significantly stronger, so were the effects on the vote of exposure to different television networks. On the other hand, while differential exposure to incumbent- or opposition-biased newspapers makes predictably no difference in the Spanish case once partisan predispositions are taken into account, it makes a very strong difference in the Bulgarian and (to a lesser extent) the British and the Italian cases.

Finally, it is also interesting to note the effects of perceptions of bias once the variables measuring the actual biases of media contents are introduced in the model. The perception that the respondent's preferred newspaper supported a candidate or party retains an autonomous positive effect on the vote (significant in Italy and Britain, almost so in Bulgaria) regardless of the newspapers' actual partisan leanings. In contrast, once the actual bias of the television networks one watches is introduced in the model, all variables measuring perceptions of television bias have *negative* signs, reaching statistical significance in Italy and approaching it in both Bulgaria and the United Kingdom. This suggests important differences in the political uses of (and expectations towards) different types of media outlets. The mere perception that newspapers in sharply partisan press landscapes (Bulgaria, Italy, and the United Kingdom) support a particular party or candidate seems to work in and of itself as a significant informational cue for voters. Conversely, regardless of the way in which biased political information conveyed by television networks shapes voters' opinions and affects their voting decisions (particularly in the Italian and the Bulgarian cases), the perception of bias in television networks *undermines* their credibility as a source of information and may even produce, as in the case of Italy, negative effects on the vote.

Conclusion

Early on, we set out to submit two ideas to empirical scrutiny. The first was that, across sharply different political systems and societies, the informational environments of voters should always affect their political behaviours and choices. There are several reasons why we believed that might be the case. Voters in contemporary democracies seem to be increasingly disconnected from the social, economic, and partisan ties that previously structured their political choices, causing their electoral decisions to be made on the basis of short-term factors—evaluations of economic conditions, governmental performance, issue positions, and personal attributes of political leaders and candidates—all of them potentially shaped by the political information accessible to voters. Besides, such information is always limited, it comes from a limited number of potentially biased sources, and the exposure to particular biases is itself becoming less predetermined by voters' waning predispositions. Finally, among voters to whom politics is normally a distant realm of events and social-group or partisan cues are becoming less informative and relevant, the political stands taken by other trustworthy sources of information with whom voters established relative stable social ties can become, in and of themselves, politically consequential. The second idea advanced here was that not all informational intermediaries that connect individuals to the realm of politics are equally likely to have a decisive impact on political choices. Interactive and repeated communication with credible and consistently politicized sources of information—such as that which tends to take place with interpersonal discussants—is potentially more influential as a source of both persuasive messages and trustworthy and usable political cues. In contrast, impersonal communication, lack of perceivable shared interests, and ambiguous or multiple and contradictory messages understandably diminish the potential for influence.

Our initial assumptions were generally confirmed. Even after strict statistical controls are introduced, informational intermediaries and the political and partisan biases voters perceive in them seem to exert a significant impact on voting choices, by shaping the kind of short-term attitudes that are more proximate to the vote and, in some cases, also by serving as a direct reference for electoral decisions. Although much additional research is needed in this respect, the net impact of intermediary biases on the vote also seems to be greater in elections and countries where partisan cues and predispositions are themselves less relevant, like, for example, in presidential elections. And as predicted, among the range of relevant intermediaries, the people with whom voters discuss political issues end up being, by far, the most important and consequential sources of information in a wide range of contemporary democracies. Therefore, the recent calls for greater attention to the 'micro-social contexts' of voting, particularly those constituted by individuals' networks political discussions (Beck et al. 2002; Zuckerman 2005) receive strong support from our results, underlining the limitations of traditional approaches to voting based exclusively on social cleavages, psychological attachments, ideological placements, economic perceptions, or leadership evaluations.

We also found that the focus on individuals' informational environments should not necessarily be narrowed down exclusively to networks of interpersonal communication and interaction, powerful and important as they may be. In fact, in several elections in some countries, other intermediaries also seem to have mattered. Thus, although the organizational links between politics and voters seem to have indeed loosened in the last decades (Daalder 2002), membership in associations may still help to provide voters with relevant cues and persuasive messages that guide their voting decisions. That contribution seems to be contigent on the nature of associational life in each country. Organizational biases only make a difference in those countries where membership levels are highest, and, among these, where such associational life adheres to one of two models: either a 'post-totalitarian' model of strong party politicization of most relevant sectors of civil society (like in the Bulgarian case in the mid-1990s); or one of involvement with voluntary associations which, although formally apartisan, plug into resilient and electorally relevant social and political cleavages, such as those organized around religious identities (United States and Chile) or the occupational structure (Italy).

Similarly, we also saw that, although the detection of media effects is made difficult by gaps between the contents of messages and voters' perceptions of them, exposure to particular sources of impersonal communication also makes a decisive difference in some countries, particularly those where media landscapes are dominated by strongly partisan outlets. Furthermore, although modern campaigning is characterized by the ability of multiple parties simultaneously to reach out to a large mass of voters, party contacts emerge as the less consequential sources of political information in our set of countries. In this way, propaganda and campaign efforts seem to be mostly effective not so much in actually swinging voters in favour of a particular party, but rather in neutralizing the ability of other parties to do so. However, there remain cases where all-encompassing targets and impersonal communication are still combined with more targeted efforts using direct interpersonal contacts. The United States and Japan are the cases in point, where the adoption of 'chasing' strategies with the use of modern media and advertising technologies has not completely displaced the traditional role of 'electoral machines' and parties' direct mobilization of social networks, causing direct party contacts to have a comparatively strong impact on the vote. Finally, in all these instances of effective intermediary influence, there seems to be at least one common thread that had already accounted for the particularly strong influence on voting decisions exerted by discussion networks: the clear and one-sided politicization of the information conveyed by intermediaries, whose influence is further enhanced by the possibility of interpersonal communication (in the case of organizations and party contacts).

Several major challenges emerge for further research in this area. First, the fact that we relied mainly on respondents' perceptions in order to measure intermediary biases and determine their impact on voting decisions remains open to criticism. It is true that, to a certain extent, perception of a message's bias is a necessary condition for such message to exert a change in individual attitudes. However, the reliance on perceptions also raises potential problems, related to the possibility of projection effects or, conversely, hostility effects such as those uncovered for media messages in some countries, which may lead to over- or under-estimation of intermediary influence or even to the more fundamental problem of endogeneity. Throughout this chapter, we addressed these issues by suggesting—on the basis of data on partisan predispositions—the relative weakness of projection effects concerning party, discussant, and organizational biases, and by showing how the use of expert judgements on the biases conveyed by specific media outlets can allow us to overcome the problem of misperception. However, further comparative research would provide greater assurances in this respect if reliance on perceived biases could be complemented with the availability of more systematic data on the actual partisan biases of intermediaries, as studies dealing with the United States have already demonstrated (Beck et al. 2002).

Second, the causal mechanisms that connect the biases conveyed (or perceived as being conveyed) by the sources of information available to voters and the decisions they ultimately make are in need of further enlightenment. Causal paths are particularly in need of further investigation. Is the effect of intermediation mainly indirect, shaping the individual short-term attitudes that are more proximate to the vote, such as evaluations of the state of the economy or of party leaders or candidates? Or is it also direct, with intermediary stances serving as direct reference points for voting decisions, regardless of the short-term attitudes? In other words, does intermediation change attitudes or does it serve as a direct informational shortcut for decisions? Furthermore, as we saw in the last section, the fact that exposure to media outlets known to have particular partisan stands has an effect on the vote *regardless* of individual perceptions of their biases raises interesting possibilities. Intermediaries seem to be able to influence voting decisions in ways that dispense with voters' actual perceptions of their stands, that is, neither by changing the attitudes of voters through direct persuasion nor by serving as explicit and direct reference points for decisions. In other words, effects such as 'framing', 'priming', and 'agenda setting', well-known varieties of media effects more subtle than persuasion, are not necessarily an exclusive of the mass media as an information source, and the extent to which they may be exerted by other intermediaries requires further study.

Finally, although our use of a 'most-different-systems' design provides some assurances here about the wide cross-national importance of informational intermediation in the understanding of process and trends in electoral behaviour, wider samples of country cases are needed in order to ascertain the extent to which the strength and direction or intermediation effects are themselves affected by relevant systemic factors. Judging from the previous sections, types of elections (presidential v. parliamentary), levels of human development and cognitive mobilization, levels of partisanship in media markets, patterns of associational life, and different prevalent modes of campaigning (not to mention different party systems and varieties of party organization) are all plausible candidates for systemic variations that are likely to interact with the types of intermediaries that make a decisive net difference on voting decisions and the overall contribution they provide to the understanding of electoral choices in modern democracies.

Coding of Variables

Variables	Spain 1993 legislative election	Bulgaria 1996 presidential election (First round)	Japan 1993 legislative election	Chile 1993 presidential election	Italy 1996 legislative election (proportional vote)
Socio-demographic					
Sex	Male: 1; female: 2	Male: 1; female: 2	Male: 1; female: 2	Male: 1; female: 2	Male: 1; female: 2
Age	Respondent's age at time of survey	Respondent's age at time of survey	Respondent's age at time of survey	Respondent's age at time of survey	Respondent's age at time of survey
Education	First wave: eight-point scale from 'none' (1) to 'doctorate' (8)	Six-point scale from 'less than primary' (1) to 'five year university' (6)	Fourteen-point scale from 'grade school' (1) to 'college or university' (14)	First wave: eight-point scale from 'no studies' (1) to 'complete university studies' (8)	Seven-point scale from 'no schooling' (1) to 'university diploma' (7)
Income	First wave: six-point scale from 'Under 50,000 ptas' (1) to 'more than 350,000 ptas' (6)	Nine-point scale from 'Under 5,000 levs' (1) to 'more than 100,000 levs' (9)	Eleven-point scale from 'Under 2,000,000 Yen' (1) to '15,000,000 Yen and over' (11)	First wave: ten-point scale from 'under 50,000 pesos' (1) to 'more than 600,000 pesos' (10)	Unavailable
Religiosity/Church attendance	First wave: subjective religiosity five-point scale from 'atheist'/'other religion'/'indifferent'(1) to 'very good catholic' (5)	'How often to you go to church?' Six-point scale from 'does not go' (1) to 'everyday or almost' (6)	Unavailable	First wave: subjective religiosity five-point scale from 'no religion/other religion' (1) to 'very Catholic' (5)	'Church attendance last year?' Five-point scale from 'never' (1) to 'at least once a week' (5)
Predispositions					
Party identification	Second wave: PSOE (1); other parties (−1); no party ID (0)	UDF (1); other parties (−1); no party ID (0)	Party leaning: LDP (1); other parties (−1); no party (0)	Second wave: PDC (1); other parties (−1); no party (0)	Closeness to party: Ulivo (1); other parties (−1); no party (0)

Variables	Spain 1993 legislative election	Bulgaria 1996 presidential election (First round)	Japan 1993 legislative election	Chile 1993 presidential election	Italy 1996 legislative election (proportional vote)
Informational intermediaries					
Perceived discussant bias	Among two most frequent discussants of important topics, spouses, or partners excluded: more discussants perceived as having voted for incumbent than for opposition (1); more discussants perceived as having voted for opposition than for incumbent (−1); no discussants, or no perception of discussant vote, or as many incumbent as opposition discussants (0).				
Perceived most read newspapers' bias	Among at least one and at most two—depending on countries—of the most read newspapers during the campaign: more newspapers perceived as biased towards the incumbent than the opposition (1); more newspapers perceived as biased towards the opposition than the incumbent (−1); no newspapers, no perception of bias, or as many incumbent as opposition newspapers (0).				
Perceived most watched TV networks' bias	Among at least one and at most two—depending on countries—of the most watched TV networks during the campaign: more TV networks perceived as biased towards the incumbent than the opposition (1); more TV networks perceived as biased towards the opposition than the incumbent (−1); no TV networks, no perception of bias, or as many incumbent as opposition TV networks (0).				
Perceived organizational bias	Among at least one and at most three—depending on countries—of the organizations individuals belong: more organizations perceived supporting the incumbent than the opposition (1); more organizations perceived as supporting the opposition than the incumbent (−1); no organizations, no perception of organizations' support, or as many incumbent as opposition organizations (0).				Unavailable
Perceived personal or telephone party contacts' bias	More contacts by incumbent parties than by opposition parties (1); more contacts by opposition parties than by incumbent parties (−1); no contacts or as many contacts by incumbent as by opposition parties (0).				
Perceived mail party contacts' bias	More contacts by incumbent parties than by opposition parties (1); more contacts by opposition parties than by incumbent parties (−1); no contacts or as many contacts by incumbent as by opposition parties (0).				

State of the economy	How would you describe the present economic situation: very bad (1), bad (2), average (3), good (4), or very good (5)?	How would you describe the present economic situation: very bad (1), bad (2), average (3), good (4), or very good (5)?	Unavailable	How would you describe the present economic situation: very bad (1), bad (2), average (3), good (4), or very good (5)?	In your opinion, over the last twelve months, the economic situation in Italy has grown worse (1), remained the same (2), or improved (3)?
Candidate/leader evaluations	Difference between Gonzalez's feeling thermometer (0–10) and average of other candidates	Difference between Stoyanov's feeling thermometer (0–10) and average of other candidates	Unavailable	Difference between Frei's and Pinochet's feeling thermometer (0–10)	Not used
Vote	PSOE (1); other parties (0)	Stoyanov (1); other candidates (0)	LDP (1); other parties (0)	Frei (1); other candidates (0)	Ulivo (1); other parties (0)

249

Variables	Hong Kong 1998 legislative election	Uruguay 1993 legislative election	Hungary 1998 legislative election first round	United States 1992 presidential election	Greece 1996 legislative election
Socio-demographic					
Sex	Male: 1; female: 2	Male: 1; female: 2	Male: 1; female: 2	Male: 1; female: 2	Male: 1; female: 2
Age	Respondent's age at time of survey	Respondent's age at time of survey	Respondent's age at time of survey	Respondent's age at time of survey	Respondent's age at time of survey
Education	Twelve-point scale, from 'none' (1) to 'graduate studies' (12)	First wave: nine-point scale, from 'none' (1) to 'complete university' (9)	Seven-point scale from 'did not attend school' (1) to 'university degree' (7)	Nineteen-point scale from 'none' (1) to 'doctorate' (19)	First wave: twelve-point scale, from 'none' (1) to 'postgraduate' (12)
Income	Five-point scale of income quintiles	First wave: eight-point scale from 'less than 1,000 pesos' (1) to 'more than 20,000 pesos' (8)	Five-point scale of income quintiles	Six-point scale of annual income, from $14,999 or less (1) to 'more than $75,000' (6)	First wave: six-point scale, from 'less than 100,000 dracma' (1) to 'more than 700,000 dracma' (6)
Religiosity/Church attendance	Subjective religiosity four-point scale, from 'not religious' (1) to 'very religious' (4)	Unavailable	'Frequency of mass attendance': six-point scale from 'never' (1) to 'weekly' (6)	'Church attendance': three-point scale, from 'never' (1) to 'weekly' (3)	First wave: four-point scale, from 'never' (1) to 'every sunday' (4)
Predispositions					
Party identification	DP (1); other parties (−1); no party ID (0)	First wave: Nacional (1); other parties (−1); no party ID (0)	MSZP (1); other parties (−1); no party ID (0)	Republican (1); other (−1); no party ID (0)	First wave: PASOK (1); other parties (−1); no party ID (0)
Informational intermediaries					
Perceived most read newspapers' bias	Among at least one and at most two—depending on countries—of the most read newspapers during the campaign: more newspapers perceived as biased towards the incumbent than the opposition (1); more newspapers perceived as biased towards the opposition than the incumbent (−1); no newspapers, no perception of bias, or as many incumbent as opposition newspapers (0).				
Perceived most watched TV networks' bias	Among at least one and at most two—depending on countries—of the most watched TV networks during the campaign: more TV networks perceived as biased towards the incumbent than the opposition (1); more TV networks perceived as biased towards the opposition than the incumbent (−1); no TV networks, no perception of bias, or as many incumbent as opposition TV networks (0).				

Perceived discussant bias	Among two most frequent discussants of important topics, spouses, or partners excluded: more discussants perceived as having voted for incumbent than for opposition (1); more discussants perceived as having voted for opposition than for incumbent (−1); no discussants, no perception of discussant vote, or as many incumbent as opposition discussants (0).	Among two most important discussants, spouses or partners excluded: discussants' parties recoded on the base of respondents' voting behaviour and question about whether discussants voted 'the same way'. Then, discussant bias obtained as in other cases.
Perceived organizational bias	Among at least one and at most three—depending on countries—of the organizations individuals belong: more organizations perceived supporting the incumbent than the opposition (1); more organizations perceived as supporting the opposition than the incumbent (−1); no organizations, no perception of organizations' support, or as many incumbent as opposition organizations (0).	
Perceived personal or telephone party contacts' bias	More contacts by incumbent parties than by opposition parties (1); more contacts by opposition parties than by incumbent parties (−1); no contacts or as many contacts by incumbent as by opposition parties (0).	
Perceived mail party contacts' bias	Unavailable	More contacts by incumbent parties than by opposition parties (1); more contacts by opposition parties than by incumbent parties (−1); no contacts or as many contacts by incumbent as by opposition parties (0).

251

cont.

Variables	Hong-Kong 1998 legislative election	Uruguay 1993 legislative election	Hungary 1998 legislative election first round	United States 1992 presidential election	Greece 1996 legislative election
State of the economy	How would you describe the present economic situation: very bad (1), bad (2), average (3), good (4) or very good (5)?	How would you describe the present economic situation: very bad (1), bad (2), average (3), good (4) or very good (5)?	Unavailable	Evolution of the economy in the past two years: worse (1); same (2); better (3)	How would you describe the present economic situation: very bad (1), bad (2), average (3), good (4) or very good (5)?
Candidate/leader evaluations	Difference between Lee's feeling thermometer (0–10) and average of other party leaders	Difference between Ramírez's feeling thermometer and average of leaders of main factions with remaining parties	Difference between Horn's feeling thermometer (0–10) and average of other party leaders	Difference between Bush's feeling thermometer (0–10) and average of other candidates	Difference between Simitis's feeling thermometer (1–10) and average of other party leaders
Vote	DP (1); other parties (0)	Nacional (1); other parties (0)	MSZP (1); other parties (0)	Bush (1); other candidates (0)	PASOK (1); other parties (0)

cont.

Variables	United Kingdom 1992 legislative election
Socio-demographic	
Sex	Male: 1; female: 2
Age	Respondent's age at time of survey
Education	Six-point scale, from 'none' (1) to 'college degree' (6)
Income	Four-point scale of income quartiles, from lowest (1) to highest (4)
Religiosity/Church attendance	Six-point scale, from 'never/practically never' (1) to 'once a week or more' (6)
Predispositions	
Party identification	Conservative (1); other parties (−1), no party ID (0)
Informational intermediaries	
Perceived most read newspapers' bias	Among the two most read newspapers during the campaign: more newspapers perceived as biased towards the incumbent than the opposition (1); more newspapers perceived as biased towards the opposition than the incumbent (−1); no newspapers, no perception of bias, or as many incumbent as opposition newspapers (0).
Perceived most watched TV networks' bias	Among the most watched TV network during the campaign: perceived as biased towards the incumbent than the opposition (1); perceived as biased towards the opposition than the incumbent (−1); no exposure to TV network, no perception of bias (0).
Perceived discussant bias	Among two most frequent discussants of important topics, spouses, or partners excluded: more discussants perceived as having voted for incumbent than for opposition (1); more discussants perceived has having voted for opposition than for incumbent (−1); no discussants, no perception of discussant vote, or as many incumbent as opposition discussants (0).
Perceived organizational bias	Unavailable
Perceived personal or telephone party contacts' bias	Unavailable
Perceived mail party contacts' bias	Unavailable
Vote	Conservative (1); other parties (0)

APPENDIX 6.2

Coding of Media Exposure Variables

Variables	Bulgaria 1996	Spain 1993	Italy 1996	UK 1992
Exposure to incumbent-biased newspapers	More newspapers biased for incumbent than for opposition (1); more newspapers biased for opposition than for incumbent (−1); no exposure, as many newspapers for incumbent as for opposition, neutral newspapers (0).			
Coding of newspapers	Incumbent-biased: *Demokratsya* Opposition-biased: *Duma*	Incumbent-biased: *El País* Opposition-biased: *ABC, El Mundo*	Incumbent-biased: *La Reppublica, L'Unità, Il Manifesto; Corriere, La Stampa, Messaggero* Opposition-biased: *Il Giornale, Resto del Carlino, La Nazione*	Incumbent-biased: *The Sun, The Mail, The Times, The Express, The Telegraph* Opposition-biased: *The Mirror, The Guardian, The Financial Times*
Exposure to incumbent-biased TV networks	More networks biased for incumbent than for opposition (1); more networks biased for opposition than for incumbent (−1); no exposure, as many networks for incumbent as for opposition, neutral networks (0).			
Coding of TV networks	Incumbent-biased: private channels Opposition-biased: BNT	Incumbent-biased: TVE Opposition-biased: *Antena 3, Telecinco*	Incumbent-biased: *Rai Tre* Opposition-biased: *Rai Uno, Rai Due, Canale 5, Italia 1, and Rete 4*	Incumbent-biased: none Opposition-biased: BBC, ITN, Sky

7

Value cleavages and partisan conflict

Richard Gunther and Kuan Hsin-chi

'Bush, Dems to War Over "Values"'. As the headline of the 9 July 2004 issue of *USA Today* announced, the 2004 presidential election campaign would involve conflict between the incumbent President and his Democratic challenger over 'values'. Are such values conflicts unique to the United States, or do they appear in other democracies? Is a focus on values useful in accounting for voter choices in contemporary democratic elections? Despite greatly increased interest in values as foci of electoral conflict and competition, empirical political scientists have lacked a systematic conceptual apparatus that could be employed to analyse conflicts over 'value cleavages' within democratic electorates. And there have been very few concerted efforts by scholars in the field of comparative politics to develop analytical schema that might transcend national boundaries in systematically mapping electorally relevant value cleavages.

This chapter is a preliminary attempt to map the attitudinal underpinnings of partisan preference in seven countries on the basis of a multidimensional and cross-nationally comparable battery of questions dealing with socio-political values that have commonly had considerable relevance to partisan politics. These items were deduced from attitudinal domains inherent within major political ideologies that emerged over the past three centuries and have had considerable impact on party development, electoral behaviour and, more generally, political conflict in many countries, particularly in Western Europe. As we demonstrate, these values have exerted a profound impact on electoral behaviour in several countries even after the effects of other determinants of the vote have been 'controlled' in previous stages of a stepwise multivariate analysis. Indeed, in three of the four countries within which coherent values clusters emerged from previous stages of analysis, the explanatory power of these values is substantially greater than that of all social-cleavage variables combined. Most strikingly, we see that in the United States partisan differences over these values have become extremely polarized, and that nearly 40 per cent of the variance in the vote for George Bush versus John Kerry is 'explained' by these values, even after the effects of the respondents' religiosity and socio-demographic characteristics had been taken into consideration. We also see that the addition of our intermediation variables to the standard multivariate voting models very substantially increases their predictive power: in the case of the United States by an additional 45 per cent of the variance in the vote, raising the percentage of the vote explained to over 75 per cent.

This study is preliminary in several ways. First, it is an initial attempt to examine attitudinal structuring in a subset of only seven of the thirteen countries included within the second phase of the CNEP. The battery of values questions on which this analysis is focused was developed in 1993, after several CNEP surveys had already been conducted. Thus, comparable data for the full array of countries analysed in this book was not available. Second, this analysis is preliminary and limited in scope in so far as it is based on a battery of questionnaire items that is admittedly eurocentric. The latter characteristic is the result of the fact that this segment of the questionnaire was developed prior to the inclusion in this cross-national research project of Latin American, East European, Asian, and African countries. Accordingly, as we see, some of these attitudinal dimensions do not 'travel well'. The next stage of the CNEP III will include additional items tapping into values and attitudes that have greater relevance in these other parts of the world. Nonetheless, we believe that exploring the extent to which these attitudinal domains are relevant cross-nationally is an essential first step towards the development of a more comprehensive study of the values and attitudinal dimensions that underpin partisan preferences.

The electorates that will be analysed in this chapter are those of Spain, Greece, Chile, Uruguay, Hungary, Hong Kong, and the United States. These cases vary both geographically and with regard to their respective political trajectories over the past century, so they provide for an adequate test of the utility of a values focus on electoral behaviour. Only one of them—the United States—can be regarded as an old or long-established democracy. Two of these countries, Spain and Greece, are Southern European countries that were re-democratized in the mid-1970s. Two, Chile and Uruguay, are South American countries that were re-democratized about a decade later. Hungary was democratized following the collapse of the Soviet Bloc in 1989. Unlike the United States, Spain, Greece, Chile, and Uruguay, Hungary's late nineteenth and early twentieth century political development was devoid of any extended period of organized partisan politics, and its democratization process unfolded in the aftermath of over four decades of Communist rule. And Hong Kong is still not a democratic polity: the 1998 Legislative Assembly election analysed here is the first that the territory had experienced following its emergence from British colonial rule, and its status within the People's Republic of China makes its evolution into a fully democratic system problematic. As we argue in this study, these differing trajectories of political development have resulted in significant differences regarding the clustering of value orientations, and with respect to their impact on partisan politics.

We begin this chapter by examining the distribution of these value orientations within these seven electorates. This will be followed by an exploration of the extent to which these value cleavages are linked to individual self-placements on the left–right continuum. In this respect, we will be gaining insights into the varying meanings of 'left' and 'right' (or 'liberal'/'conservative') in different countries. We then examine the extent to which these values cluster together in different countries. Given that the very designation of the value dimensions included within this segment of the CNEP questionnaire was determined by the salience of these value cleavages in the development of political 'ideologies' in Western Europe over the past three centuries, this exercise will, from one perspective, explore the extent to which these ideological divides are reflected at the mass level in the two Western European countries included in this part of the analysis—Spain and Greece. It will also explore the extent to which this West European 'template' fits the clustering of attitudes and the development of value cleavages in a sample of non-West European democracies—in the United States, Uruguay, Chile, Hungary, and Hong Kong. After concluding that the 'ideological families' present in some of these countries differ somewhat from the configurations hypothesized in the 'West European template', we develop values scales that more accurately capture the values cleavages found in each country.

Finally, in those four countries where value clusters emerged as strong and coherent, we measure their impact on electoral behaviour. We will incorporate scales of values (based on the previous rounds of dimensional analysis) as independent variables in Logit equations, alongside other items that are commonly found to be powerful determinants of voting decisions. Among these are the 'intermediation' variables that the research undertaken by Pedro Magalhães (in this volume) found to be of great significance in predicting the vote.

In this chapter, we also set forth a speculative theoretical framework linking all of these stages of analysis, and attempting to explain why specific values cleavages emerge in some countries and affect the vote in a remarkably persistent matter, while in other countries no coherent dimensional structure emerges at all and the electoral impact of these values is nil. This explanatory framework involves three distinct political processes that may span over a century of a country's political evolution. The first process is historical, in which elites at some point in the past convert these socio-economic values into overt lines of political conflict. In the second state, which is primarily an intellectual process, the value conflict is perpetuated into political ideologies. A third process is then required before these historical and ideological developments can be linked to electoral behaviour today. This involves information-intermediation through organizational channels, the most important of which is the political party and its allied secondary associations. The formulation of an ideology may be an essential prerequisite for the crystallization of value clusters, but unless that ideology is embraced by a political party and used as a vehicle for the mobilization of sectors of the electorate over several decades, it is unlikely to have much relevance for electoral behaviour today.[1] Accordingly, the absence of post-materialist parties in the seven countries studied here—in contrast with Germany, for example (see Shull 1999)—is an additional reason why we find that those values have no significant electoral impact. Even ideologies that had once served as the basis of social movements that moved millions of persons—such as Anarchism and Anarchosyndicalism in Spain (e.g. Esenwein 1989; Corbin 1993)—may completely disappear if they are not embraced by partisan organizations that will work to perpetuate them over the following decades. Conversely, conflict over values can be greatly exacerbated and a polity can become polarized if pragmatic, catch-all parties are effectively replaced by more activist-dominated ideological political parties, as Fiorina (2005) argues has taken place in the United States since the early 1990s.

As the various chapters in this book have demonstrated, parties often have allies in this process of partisan intermediation of information flows, particularly in the form of secondary associations and the communications media. Accordingly, the final step in our analysis will involve the dissemination and perpetuation over time of these value cleavages through information channels with systematic partisan biases. In short, we argue that the partisan-biased flows of information through these channels helps to disseminate, perpetuate, and strengthen these value cleavages, and link them to specific electoral choices.

A Gap in the Electoral Behaviour Literature

The existing literature on electoral behaviour is strikingly devoid of systematic comparative analyses of the impact of values cleavages on voting. One likely reason for this gap in the literature is that the paradigms that have dominated the study of electoral politics over the past fifty years have largely ignored value cleavages among voters in democratic societies. The 'intermediation' approach developed by Lazarsfeld and his collaborators[2] focuses its analytical efforts on channels through which partisan information is conducted and disseminated throughout the public, and not with the specific content of that information or the manner in which it resonated with previously existing clusters of values or beliefs at the level of the individual voter. The Michigan paradigm (see Campbell et al. 1960) did heavily involve a psychological dimension and focused on the attitudes and beliefs of individual voters. But this approach has largely limited its attention to standing partisan loyalties, in interaction with highly transient attitudes towards individual candidates and 'issues' that emerge in the course of election campaigns. The predominant European approach (e.g. Lipset and Rokkan 1967a; Rose 1974) was rooted in a social-structural paradigm. It conceptualized electoral conflict as competition based on structural cleavages involving religious affiliation, class position and, if relevant, language, culture, and ethnicity. It subsequently grafted onto this social-cleavage base a concern with psychological or attitudinal orientations of voters, but operationalized this in the form of survey respondents' placing themselves and relevant political parties and actors on a one-dimensional left–right continuum. Finally, the 'economic-voting' paradigm introduced by Downs (1957) and further elaborated by Tufte (1978), Fiorina (1981), and many others attempts to explain electoral outcomes largely as the product of voters' reactions to short-term economic conditions. In short, none of the dominant paradigms in the electoral-behaviour literature deals explicitly with the kinds of clashes over values that have increasingly captured the attention of politicians and journalists, particularly in the United States since the 1990s.

A second reason why we suspect that value cleavages have been neglected in cross-national comparative studies is methodological. Most comparative studies of electoral behaviour focus their analytical efforts on objectively definable social-structural variables, such as socio-economic class status, membership in trade unions or religious organizations, and demographic characteristics of respondents. These objectively definable factors are relatively easy to measure with standardized and cross-nationally comparable questionnaire items. Very few deal extensively with the attitudinal underpinnings of partisan preferences. It is true that single-country studies of public opinion and voting behaviour in the Michigan tradition do include substantial numbers of attitudinal variables relating to campaign issues and evaluations of candidates, but these generate data that, by their very nature, are not cross-nationally comparable. Campaign issues are situational and transient—not only are issues largely country-specific and not usually relevant cross-nationally, but they vary greatly in salience from one election to the next. And the personal qualities of candidates are by their very nature subjective, particularistic, and non-comparable. Lacking a more stable grounding in durable socio-political values or belief systems at the mass level, these kinds of variables do not 'travel well', even from one election to the next within a single country.

Third, intellectual trends in the United States since the end of the Second World War were generally unfavourable to the study of value differences as factors underlying political behaviour. While such works as Almond and Verba's *Civic Culture* (1963), Inglehart's *Silent Revolution* (1977), and Putnam's *Making Democracy Work* (1993) have kept alive the intermittent, limited popularity of culture or values in political studies, the academic climate was largely dominated by the diffuse belief in an 'end of ideology' (Bell 1960; Maxman 1968) resulting from modernization. At a superficial level, this is grounded in the belief that the West has already reached the status of 'the good society'. At a deeper level, some social scientists believe that positivistic empiricism and behaviouralism are at least to some extent incompatible with normative concerns with the good society or the state of humankind. Concerns over the dictum of value neutrality have made many such scholars hesitant to plunge into the study of values (cf. Hechter 1993). And the resulting neglect of normative orientations in studies of electoral behaviour has not been remedied by the emergence of 'culturalist' studies as an alternative paradigm. This is due in part to the regrettable fact that culturalist and behaviouralist literatures do not engage one another. The isolation of adherents to these two schools of analysis from each other also results from the fact that the 'thick description' tradition within which most culturalist studies are set does not regard the enterprise as a cumulative science and is not oriented towards generating testable hypotheses or cross-nationally applicable findings (Geertz 1973). As a result, in those studies which make an effort to link these different (and somewhat incompatible) traditions, the impact of culture and values on behaviour lurks in the background as a value-formation process (Chong 2000) or analytical narrative (Bates et al. 1998).

Those few attitudinal variables that are regularly included in cross-national comparative studies of electoral behaviour tend to be of two types. First, as noted above, comparative studies often include very generic measures of voters' basic ideological orientations—most commonly as measured by self-placement on a left–right continuum or self-description as liberal or conservative. While variables of this kind often have considerable explanatory power in accounting for subsequent voting decisions, the precise meaning for voters of these generic distinctions is rarely examined. Moreover, the use of left–right or liberal/conservative scales presupposes a one-dimensional array of relevant attitudes, despite the fact that some of the seminal studies in the field of voting behaviour (such as Seymour Martin Lipset's *Political Man*) clearly revealed that such concepts as 'liberalism' and 'conservatism' in the United States have separate 'economic' and 'social' components. Second, a number of cross-national surveys have included comparable attitudinal measures, but these have focused almost exclusively on one single attitudinal domain—such as 'postmaterialism' (Inglehart 1979, 1997) or attitudes measuring support for democracy (Norris 1999a)—rather than attempting to map and examine the electoral impact of a broad array of socio-political attitudes.

We are not arguing that values have not been studied extensively. Max Weber's 'Protestant ethic' and Talcott Parsons' pattern variables are well-known classics that treat values within the general framework of culture. Interest in values and political conflict was greatly stimulated by the seminal works of Inglehart (1971, 1977, 1984) and his thesis that the cleavage structures underlying politics in Western nations had changed from class-based to value-based. The ensuing 'new politics' debate, however, focused almost exclusively on just one dimension of value conflict—materialism versus postmaterialism—and its impact on support for old versus new parties, particularly among younger voters. Within this tradition, the work of Oddbjørn Knutsen (1988, 1995) emerged in the mid-1990s as the most important study of the impact of values on party choice.

Over the past two decades, the World Values Surveys (WVS) have systematically collected data concerning an extraordinarily wide array of values in (as of the year 2002) eighty-one countries. But these surveys have produced data that are strikingly different from the socio-political values that we analyse in this chapter. Rather than focusing on values that have had a direct relevance for partisan conflict in a number of countries (which was the starting point for our questionnaire-item design), most of the WVS items involve highly personal orientations that are not necessarily relevant to politics: they tend overwhelmingly to involve abstract concepts such as the value of hard work and thrift, trust in other people, respect for authority, satisfaction with life, economic security, tolerance of homosexuals, love of parents, and so on (see Inglehart et al. 2004). Those few items relevant to politics involve fundamental attitudes towards democracy (such as those we analysed in Chapter 2 of this volume) and trust in government and its institutions. Somewhat more politically relevant are cross-national studies that grew out of the debate over 'Asian values'.[3] But like the other studies in the WVS project, these are concerned with the implications of values for democracy in the abstract, not for the structuring of cleavages that affect electoral behaviour. A similar example of work that studies political values without addressing the issue of the anchoring of voting preferences in value cleavages is that of Miller, White, and Heywood (1998), which evaluates socialist, nationalist, liberal, and democratic values and their implications for political change.

To our knowledge, there are very few studies that analyse the empirical relationship between value orientations and partisan preferences. Paramount among these are those undertaken by Shalom Schwartz and his collaborators (e.g. Caprara et al. 2005 on electoral behaviour in Italy; Barnea and Schwartz 1998 on Israeli electoral politics). This work, however, seeks to anchor voting choices in fundamental value dimensions relevant to the personality of individual voters, and involves such generic value dimensions as universalism, benevolence, hedonism, power, achievement, stimulation, self-direction, tradition, conformity, and security. As will soon become clear, our approach focuses on the electoral impact of socio-political values that are conceptually closer to those incorporated within contemporary political ideologies and party programmes.

Somewhat closer to our approach is the seminal work of Milton Rokeach (1973). Believing that values are important parameters of political ideologies, Rokeach examined the relationships between two value dimensions (freedom and equality) and four ideologies (communism, socialism, capitalism, and fascism) on the basis of the writings of polemicists like Lenin.

He subsequently employed his model to differentiate among activists and more passive members of these parties. 'Values and Political Partisanship' (Hardiman and Whelan 1994), growing out of the larger European Value Systems project (Ester, Halman, and de Moor 1994), is another study roughly similar to ours. These researchers concluded that, apart from socio-demographic variables, five dimensions of value orientation are particularly useful in explaining support for political parties of the left versus right. They are: left versus right self-placement; left versus right on economic issues; liberalism on issues of sexual morality; confidence in establishment institutions; and post-materialism.

The closest approximation of our approach is that of James McCann (1997), who links specific issue stands of voters to more durable value orientations, which are, in turn, rooted in two distinct dimensions which he calls 'egalitarianism' and moral 'traditionalism' within the American electorate in 1992. Also similar in some respects to our approach is the analysis of voting choice by Knutsen and Scarbrough (1995). Their model of electoral behaviour includes two different kinds of cleavage variables: structural variables, consisting of class (measured by occupation, education, and income) and religion (measured by church attendance); and value variables, relating to religious–secular, left–right materialism,[4] materialism–postmaterialism structural variables, and party choice. Using a methodological approach (discriminant analysis) different from ours, they nonetheless reach the same conclusion as we set forth at the end of this chapter—that value orientations are, in general, more important determinants of the vote than structural variables.[5] With these few exceptions, there are very few studies that systematically and cross-nationally analyse the electoral impact of socio-political values.

Nine Basic Attitudinal Orientations

The battery of questionnaire items dealing with socio-political attitudes and values in the CNEP surveys was developed with two seemingly contradictory objectives in mind. On the one hand, these items were written in an effort to go beyond the extreme generality and generic quality of the one-dimensional left–right continuum. Here, our objective was to be more specific in terms of identifying differing attitudinal domains that may underpin the left–right continuum, or may have political relevance independent of voter self-placement on the scale. On the other hand, the high specificity and idiographic nature of campaign issues needed to be replaced by more durable value orientations (i.e. those which are stable over time and likely to affect electoral behaviour over several decades, and not just in the context of a single election campaign), as well as by those more likely to be politically relevant in a number of countries. These value orientations are of an intermediate level of generality. They are not as basic as those which are often studied by social psychologists or those included in the WVS. The values explored here are *socio-political orientations* relevant to varying (indeed, competing) 'visions of a more desirable society'. They underpin the adoption of specific stands taken on the issues that emerge in the course of election campaigns.[6]

The modus operandi of this item-development effort (initially undertaken in preparation for the 1993 Spanish survey) was to create questionnaire items that would tap into the principal ideological clashes that have characterized partisan politics in Western Europe over the past century.[7] In many instances, the sets of conflicting values and the ideologies that were based on them had their origins in political events that transpired in the eighteenth and nineteenth centuries. The first of these pitted 'classical liberalism' against defenders of an *ancien régime* characterized by established state religion, authoritarian rule under a monarch, particularistic privileges of aristocratic classes, and mercantilist economic policies. In its rejection of the 'old order', classical liberalism embraced the primacy of individual liberty and equality in citizenship rights. This entailed an explicit rejection of established religion, aristocratic privileges, and authoritarian rule. Classical liberalism also had an economic dimension, striving to replace 'statist' economic policies, corporatism, and mercantilism with free market capitalism based on individual initiative. Accordingly, we wrote two questionnaire items tapping into a *Traditional Conservatism* domain, with individualism and liberalism as its antithesis. The first of these, *ReligLib* is an item in which respondents (in all countries except the United States[8]) were asked to choose between the following two alternative phrases: 'Defend our traditional religious and moral values' and 'Respect the freedom of individuals to be and believe whatever they want'. Respondents were asked to place themselves on a 10-point scale, with the two alternative phrases anchoring the extreme ends of this continuum. A second item associated with individual liberties, *OrderLib*, is one in which respondents were asked to choose between 'Maintain[ing] law and order' and 'Defend[ing] civil liberties'. We believed that these two items would help to define a *Traditional Conservative* versus liberal domain of political attitudes, although a consideration of the economic dimension of classical liberalism was reserved for the following cluster of values.

By the mid-to-late nineteenth century, liberal regimes had been established in most Western European countries, and free-market capitalism (to varying degrees) served as the framework for economic development. One unfortunate side effect of nineteenth-century capitalism was that it allowed for the emergence of extreme economic inequality and considerable suffering on the part of the newly urbanized, industrial working classes. In reaction against this liberal social and economic order, socialism emerged as an opposing political ideology.[9] In its classic formulation, socialism stressed economic equality and the replacement of private enterprise by collectivist forms of ownership of the means of production. And solidarity among the working classes was seen as a principal vehicle for bringing about this change. Three items were written to tap into this *Socialist* attitudinal domain. *EqualInd* posed to respondents a choice between 'There should be a more equal distribution of wealth', and 'There should be more incentives for individual initiative'. *PrivPub* asked respondents if they preferred to 'Privatize public enterprises' (reversing policies that had been implemented by many Socialist governments—and others—earlier in the twentieth century), or to 'Maintain existing public enterprises'. Finally, *Compete* tapped into the solidarity among workers that was to serve as the vehicle for achieving these policy objectives. This question asked respondents if they believe that they should 'Work hard and compete, so that you can get ahead at work', or 'Avoid competition with fellow workers in order to maintain good relations'. (It should be noted that 'classical liberalism' is captured by negative responses to items tapping into both the Traditional Conservatism and the Socialist ideological positions, with the latter capturing the free-market capitalism dimension of classical liberalism.)

Nowhere in Western Europe did a classically Socialist party come to power prior to the mid-twentieth century. Accordingly, a more moderate *Social Democratic* alternative began to emerge which was believed to have broader electoral appeal to the middle classes and individuals with more centrist political values.[10] This revisionist ideology took for granted the continuing existence of capitalism, but at the same time was oriented towards substantially improving the lives of previously exploited members of the working class through the implementation of various government programmes—including universal education, and social-welfare protection for the unemployed, the disabled, and other individuals who are not able to actively participate in the labour force. And these government programmes, in turn, would require the levying of increased levels of taxation, preferably through progressive taxes that redistribute wealth from the haves to the have-nots. The Social Democratic orientation was to be measured by *ServTax*, in which respondents were asked whether they preferred to 'Improve government services and social assistance' or 'Reduce taxes'. It should be noted that higher taxes and these government programmes (often characterized as 'government intervention in the economy') both directly clashed with some of the precepts of classical liberalism, as well as with traditional conservatism.

In the post-Second World War era, a new set of value orientations began to emerge. These represented a reaction against policies stressing economic development at all costs, often at the expense of environmental degradation. They also stressed individual 'self-realization', and were often hostile towards various kinds of organizations, especially political parties, that were associated with 'the establishment'. These *Postmaterialist* orientations emerged relatively late in the twentieth century, according to theories advanced by Ronald Inglehart and his collaborators, because they were credible only for those individuals raised in an environment of plenty, whose 'material needs' had been satisfied. Postmaterialist values include concern over the state of the environment, as well as an assertion of individual autonomy vis-à-vis organizations and 'power elites' associated with 'the establishment'. One item written to capture some of these concerns, *EcoGrow*, posed as alternative responses, 'Protect the environment, and try to make her cities and countryside more beautiful' versus 'Encourage economic growth without environmental restrictions on business'. And *Particip* was intended to capture the self-realization and autonomy dimension of postmaterialism. It asked respondents if they preferred to 'Increase citizen participation in government decision making' or if they believed that 'Government should quickly make decisions based on the knowledge of experts'.

Finally, in the late twentieth century, another 'values' issue was politicized by political and religious elites in some countries, particularly the United States. This involves abortion. Given its centrality in the debate over 'family values' in the United States, we decided to include an *Abortion* item in this part of the questionnaire in which respondents were asked if they believe that 'Abortion should always be illegal', or that 'Abortion should be legal' (with the exact wording of this item varying from country to country depending on the legal status of abortion). Although it was not part of the original conflict between classical liberals and defenders of the *ancien régime*, we suspected that it would be associated with the predominantly religious *Traditional Conservatism* cluster.

We took steps to prevent the hypothesized inter-item clustering from emerging as an artefact of the order in which these questions were asked, or of a response-set bias resulting from excessive consistency in the way responses were scored, by scattering similar items across this section of the questionnaire, and by reversing the direction of an anticipated left–right array for about half of the items. In order to allow for the subsequent construction of attitudinal scales, however, prior to the analysis of these data items were re-scored in such a manner as to have '1' on this continuum always reflect a 'leftist' stance, '10' represent the most conservative orientation, and values ranging between those two extremes representing intermediate positions.

In Table 7.1, we present the mean scores resulting from responses to these questionnaire items in each of the seven countries included in this part of the study. This table also presents mean scores of respondents' self-placement on the 10-point left–right continuum. In order to impose some consistency on the presentation of this large volume of data, these countries have been arrayed from left to right in accord with respondents' mean scores on the left–right continuum. Before we enter into a discussion of cross-national differences regarding these basic values, a few cautionary notes concerning the application of the left–right continuum to political studies in differing world regions are in order. It is clear that left–right is a concept familiar to West Europeans, as evidenced by the

Table 7.1 Mean scores (and standard deviations) on values items

	Spain	Hungary	Greece	Chile	Uruguay	Hong Kong	United States
ReligLib	4.3	3.7	5.5	6.3	4.9	3.5	4.4
	(3.2)	(3.1)	(3.6)	(3.6)	(3.4)	(2.6)	(3.3)
OrderLib	6.1	7.5	6.3	7.4	5.7	3.6	6.7
	(3.1)	(2.8)	(3.3)	(3.1)	(3.3)	(2.5)	(2.8)
Abortion	5.2	3.1	3.7	7.0	5.5	—	5.1
	(3.2)	(2.8)	(3.4)	(3.7)	(3.7)		(3.5)
PrivPub	4.9	3.8	5.7	4.8	3.7	5.2	5.4
	(3.0)	(3.0)	(3.5)	(3.3)	(3.1)	(2.9)	(2.3)
EqualInd	5.1	5.5	7.4	5.6	6.0	7.7	5.4
	(3.1)	(3.3)	(3.4)	(3.7)	(3.4)	(2.5)	(3.1)
Compete	4.9	7.4	7.4	6.1	5.3	7.0	7.3
	(3.1)	(2.9)	(3.0)	(3.6)	(3.4)	(2.7)	(2.4)
Particip	3.7	5.7	4.1	4.2	4.4	4.2	3.4
	(2.8)	(3.2)	(3.2)	(3.4)	(3.3)	(2.7)	(2.3)
EcoGrow	2.8	4.8	3.3	2.7	3.2	4.0	3.4
	(2.3)	(3.0)	(2.8)	(2.6)	(2.8)	(2.8)	(2.4)
ServTax	4.7	6.0	4.7	4.2	4.4	6.9	5.1
	(3.0)	(3.2)	(3.2)	(3.5)	(3.0)	(2.5)	(2.7)

fact that only 6 per cent of Spaniards and 11 per cent of Greeks were unable to place themselves on this 10-point scale. This is not the case with citizens in Eastern Europe and Hong Kong, and in several Latin American countries. Between 27 and 38 per cent of respondents in Hungary, Chile, Uruguay, and Hong Kong were incapable of responding to this questionnaire item. In Hong Kong, moreover, over 40 per cent of respondents who did provide answers to this question placed themselves at position 5 on the 10-point scale, suggesting that many of them are 'false centrists' (i.e. those who guess at a response by placing themselves at the exact middle of the scale) for whom this left–right distinction has little or no meaning. The United States ranges between the strong left–right orientation of European voters and the much weaker political relevance of that dimension elsewhere. The liberal/conservative distinction is a common element in political discourse in the United States, and fewer than one quarter of Americans surveyed in our 2004 post-election study were incapable of describing themselves in these terms. Overall, as we see below, the left–right dimension provides a useful means of ordering the presentation of data in most countries, and in every case, the placement of party systems on this continuum serves as a very useful device for making sense of otherwise complex data. The methodological utility of this scale, moreover, is consistent with a substantial body of data suggesting that voters in many countries make use of this continuum as a means of simplifying the often complex reality of partisan choice and assisting them in making electoral choices.

As can be seen from the data presented in the first row of Table 7.1, Spanish voters appear to be the most leftist or progressive among the citizens surveyed, while American respondents were the most conservative. Numerous empirical studies have shown that these ideological self-designations are strongly related to voting choice in Spain and Greece, while the liberal/conservative distinction is a highly salient characteristic of partisan competition in the United States.[11] But to what extent is the simple left–right variable relevant to electoral behaviour in other countries? And how do these left–right self-designations relate to other value dimensions? The remaining 'values' data in this and the following table provide some answers to these questions.

With regard to *ReligLib*, the item distinguishing between respect for traditional religious values, on the one hand, and individual liberties, on the other, a somewhat different rank ordering of countries appears. Respondents in Hungary, Hong Kong, and Spain have adopted the most progressive stance, while Chile appears to be by far the most conservative on traditional religious matters. Moreover, responses to these questionnaire items are skewed to one side or the other in these countries: 40 per cent of Hungarians and 33 per cent of Spaniards placed themselves at position 1 on this scale, while 37 per cent of Chileans opted for position 10. Greeks, in contrast, were very closely balanced between the two extremes: the percentages of respondents placing themselves at positions 1 and 10 in Greece were 26 and 27 per cent. The mean score for the American item cannot be directly compared with that of the other countries since its wording had been changed in preparation for the expansion of this cross-national research project into Muslim countries that were considering the adoption of *sharia* law. Nonetheless, despite the fact that the wording of this item had been substantially 'toughened', it is noteworthy that 13 per cent of respondents placed themselves in category 10, in full agreement that 'Our religious beliefs should provide the basis for the laws of our country' (with a total of 28% located within categories 7 through 10), while 37 per cent were at the extreme opposite end of this scale (category 1), believing that 'No single set of religious beliefs should be imposed on our country'. In comparative perspective, however, the relatively low standard deviation for the distribution of responses to this item in the United States does not suggest that Americans are abnormally polarized over this value.

The *OrderLib* item, in contrast, does not differentiate countries from one another very substantially, with the one notable exception being Hong Kong. Most respondents in the other countries appear to prefer the more conservative option, highly valuing the maintenance of law and order over protection of individual liberties. Hong Kong, however, is clearly different. Given the 'special status' of Hong Kong within the People's Republic of China, and the widespread fear that civil and political liberties might one day be replaced by coerced subservience to an authoritarian regime, it appears that the great majority of respondents in Hong Kong are strongly committed to the defence of civil liberties.

A similar pattern emerges from our examination of responses to the *Abortion* item. Again, most Chileans have adopted a conservative stance on this issue, with 50 per cent of respondents placing themselves in position 10 on this scale. At the other end of this distribution we find Greeks and Hungarians, 46 per cent of whom place themselves in position 1 on this scale. And at the middle of this continuum, we find Spaniards, Uruguayans, and Americans: the mean of their responses are very close to the middle of the 10-point scale, and their distributions into the two extreme positions, 1 and 10, are most closely balanced—23 per cent versus

17 per cent in Spain, 31 per cent versus 29 per cent in Uruguay, and 29 per cent versus 19 per cent in the United States. These findings raise an important question: if Americans are no more polarized in their stands on abortion than are citizens of other democratic systems, why has political conflict over this issue been so sharply divisive in the United States, while it has not been politically salient elsewhere? As we argue below, the answer to this question is closely related to information 'intermediation' and electoral mobilization by partisan elites and their allied secondary associations.

A totally different pattern emerges from our examination of attitudes towards public sector enterprises versus privatization (*PrivPub*). Here, Greeks and Americans are more conservative than other respondents (although their mean scores of 5.7 and 5.4 are not far from the exact centre of the continuum), while Uruguayans and Hungarians most strongly prefer to maintain public sector enterprises. The most noteworthy conclusion to be derived from these data, however, is that the majority of respondents in all the other countries prefer the maintenance of public sector enterprises over privatization. These popular preferences stand in contrast with the wave of privatization that has dominated public policies worldwide over the past two decades.

Modal opinions are more clearly skewed to the right, however, when we examine responses to *EqualInd*, the item asking respondents if they preferred a more equal distribution of income over maximization of individual incentive. In Spain and the United States, the mean response is very slightly to the left of centre, while in Greece, Uruguay, and Hong Kong, decidedly conservative opinions are held by most voters. Most of the citizens surveyed in these studies favour incentives that spur competition and reward hard work.

This conclusion is more directly corroborated by responses to a question (*Compete*) asking if respondents preferred solidarity with their fellow workers over working hard and competition with them. Only in Spain was the mean for all respondents significantly to the left of centre, while in Greece, Hong Kong, Hungary, and the United States, individual competition was strongly preferred by most respondents.

When we examine the notion of increased citizen *Participation* in government decision-making, the modal response jumps back to the left of centre in most countries. Only in Hungary does the majority of respondents favour decision-making by experts over increased citizen participation. The most pronounced 'participatory' orientation is embraced by respondents in the United States, followed closely by Spaniards.

By far, the most lopsided clustering of opinion involves support for protection of the environment versus unregulated economic development (*EcoGrow*). In no country does a majority favour the 'conservative', pro-business alternative. And in Spain, Greece, Uruguay, and Chile, the percentage of respondents opting for position 1 on the 10-point scale exceeds 44 per cent. It is clear from these data, as well as from the consistently low standard deviations measuring polarization of responses to this item (ranging from just 2.3 to 3.0) that a much stronger consensus opinion emerges in defence of the environment than concerning any other item in this battery of questions. Most strikingly, in sharp contrast with the policies of the Bush administration, fewer than 10 per cent of American respondents placed themselves in the four categories towards the right side of this value scale.

Finally, when we turn our attention to improved government services versus cutting taxes (*ServTax*), substantial cross-national differences emerge. Respondents in Spain, Greece, Chile, and Uruguay clearly opt for the maintenance of high-quality government services, while low taxes are preferred by a slight majority in Hungary, and by a considerable majority in Hong Kong. American respondents were slightly skewed towards the provision of government services over low taxes (again, in sharp contrast with the policies of the Bush administration).

The standard deviations across all items in each country provide a general indication of the extent to which these various political cultures are polarized. Seen from this perspective, the consistently high standard deviations in Chile for all items except those relating to environmental protection and maintenance of law and order reflects a high degree of polarization. Given the recency of the Pinochet dictatorship and the brutality of its subjugation of those it regarded as dissidents, this polarization is not surprising. Similarly, it has often been noted (see, e.g. Papayannakis 1981; Mavrogordatos 1983) that Greek political culture was greatly polarized by the civil war of the late 1940s, the harsh repression of the 'colonels' regime' of 1967–74, and the virulent anti-communism and abridgement of civil and political liberties for those on the left under the quasi-democratic governments that ruled between those two violent interludes. This polarization is reflected in these figures. Conversely, it is the *absence* of polarization among Americans that is most noteworthy. While the standard deviations for *ReligLib* and *Abortion* are significantly higher than those for the other items, seen in comparative perspective they are not abnormally high, and are substantially lower than the standard deviation scores for Chile. One might be tempted to conclude from these data that the so-called 'culture war' in the United States is, indeed a 'myth' (Fiorina 2005). As we argue below, however, a more complex multivariate analysis reveals that these value cleavages have a profoundly divisive impact on American electoral behaviour. In setting forth an explanation of this paradox, we argue that divisive conflict in a democratic political system is not merely a reflection of its citizens' fundamental attitudinal orientations, but is, instead, a product of a number of other factors, including biased flows of political information to segments of the electorate (the central focus of the CNEP) and the electoral mobilization strategies of parties and their leaders.

Ideology and the Clustering of Attitudes

While data concerning public attitudes towards these individual value-based attitudes may be interesting in themselves, our primary concern is to determine if they are systematically related to one another in accord with the four ideological orientations described above. Our first approach to addressing this issue involves an exploration of the relationship between responses to these individual items and self-placement of respondents on the left–right continuum. To what extent does the left–right scale reflect fundamental value orientations?[12]

Table 7.2 presents Pearson's r statistics measuring the correlation between each of these value orientations and respondents' self-placement

Table 7.2 Correlations (Pearson's r) between left–right self-placement and values items

	United States	Uruguay	Spain	Greece	Chile	Hungary
ReligLib	**.44*****	**.34*****	**.35*****	.14***	.11***	.10**
OrderLib	**.39*****	**.34*****	**.25*****	**.22*****	.08**	−.02
Abortion	**.47*****	.17***	**.31*****	.15***	.08**	.11**
PrivPub	**.24*****	.17***	.16***	**.23*****	.16***	.05
EqualInd	**.36*****	−.05	.08**	**.21*****	.09*	−.03
Compete	.15***	**.23*****	.18***	.06	.07*	.01
Particip	.09**	**.20*****	.04	.07*	.04	−.02
EcoGrow	**.22*****	.00	.06*	.08*	.03	.01
ServTax	**.44*****	.08*	.11***	.06	.07*	.09**
Smallest n in column	— (1,367)	(651)	— (1,296)	(810)	— (1,235)	(1,029)

* Correlation is significant at the .05 level; ** Correlation is significant at the .01 level; *** Correlation is significant at the .001 level.

272

on the left–right scale (except in Hong Kong, where the values battery was administered in a different survey which did not include left–right self-placement). We first examine these data country by country, in an attempt to determine if certain patterns hold up cross-nationally.

The country where these socio-political value orientations are most strongly and consistently associated with left–right self-designation is the United States. As can be seen from these data, all three of the traditional conservative/liberal items are strongly associated with the left–right scale, as are attitudes towards a more egalitarian distribution of income, and better public services versus tax cuts. In three additional respects, the American survey's findings are noteworthy. The first of these concerns maintaining the quality of government services versus tax cuts: in no other country is the population so divided along this aspect of the left–right division; in all other countries, the provision of high-quality government services is embraced by both the left and the right. Second, in no other country are attitudes towards the environment also polarized along this continuum; everywhere else, there is a strong consensus in favour of environmental protection on both the left and the right. The contrast between the 'politicized' polarization of attitudes towards the environment and social services (i.e. when examined in conjunction with the left–right continuum) and the lack of significant polarization of these American values when their distributions are examined separately presents us with an intriguing paradox whose explanation is to be found in the intermediation functions performed by parties and other secondary associations, the media, and personal networks. Third, while traditional conservative values, attitudes towards the environment, and the social welfare state, and preferences regarding equality versus individual initiative sharply polarize Americans, the items dealing with competition among co-workers, and a populist conception of political participation are not strongly related to the left–right continuum. We will later find that this pattern is further reflected in the clustering among these socio-political values, and will attempt to explain this significant departure from the 'West European template'.

Uruguay does not depart substantially from the standard West European pattern except with regard to one important variable. All three of the items associated with the traditionalist religious/liberal cleavage are closely linked to left–right self-designation, as are two of the three items that we suspect are related to a 'socialist' orientation. Curiously, however, the relationship between left–right and the EqualInd item (measuring the respondents preferences regarding a more equal distribution of income vs. strong incentives for individual competition) is not only statistically insignificant, but is of the wrong sign. One interpretation of the weakness of this relationship involves the fact that the distribution of incomes in Uruguay is remarkably egalitarian, and as a result, income redistribution has not been a salient or divisive political issue in Uruguayan politics for decades. With regard to the postmaterialist dimension, the item measuring preferences for increased citizen participation in government decision-making (*Particip*) is significantly related to a leftist stance, but the item involving environmental protection is not. Instead, support for environmentalist policies is so widespread that it does not distinguish those on the left from the right.

In Spain, it is clear that the three attitudes that we posited were associated with a traditionalist conservative versus classical liberal orientation are most strongly related to left–right self-designations. *ReligLib, OrderLib,* and *Abortion* produce correlations (Pearson's r) ranging from .25 to .35. Also significantly related to left–right positions are individual items that we hypothesized were associated with Socialist or Social Democratic orientations. In contrast, the two attitudes that we believe are associated with postmaterialism are not substantially linked to the left–right division in Spanish politics.

In Greece, the traditional conservative/liberal cleavage is weaker in terms of its relationship with the left–right continuum, although it is still statistically significant at a high level. Instead, attitudes that we hypothesized are most closely related to Socialist orientations (*PrivPub* and *EqualInd*) appeared to be more crucial in defining the meaning of left–right. Finally, it is interesting to note that both of the items representing the postmaterialist domain are related (albeit very weakly) to the left–right continuum at a level of statistical significance greater than .05. In no other country surveyed here do we see a similar finding.

In Chile and Hungary, it is *absence* of left–right polarization with regard to these values that is most striking. In Chile, only attitudes towards privatization of public enterprises comes close to having a moderate level of association with left–right self-placement. And while the correlation between left–right and the ReligLib item is significant at the .001 level, its overall weakness is quite striking. In Hungary, what is most striking is that left–right self-designations are not at all related to six out of the nine values included in this battery of questions. Only attitudes towards maintaining traditional religious values, abortion, and taxation versus government services are significantly associated with the distinction between left and right, and none of them is even of moderate strength. This lack of rooting of left–right self-placement in basic values, as well as the relatively high percentage of respondents who were incapable of placing themselves on the left–right continuum, suggests that the Hungarian population is not divided by these particular attitudinal orientations in any consistent or coherent manner.

Examining the relationship between the left–right continuum and these socio-political value orientations from a cross-national perspective, we see that the strongest and most consistent relationships are those involving *Traditional Conservative* versus classical liberal beliefs. With the exception of Hungarian attitudes towards maintaining law and order, all three of the value orientations that we hypothesized would fall within this cluster are significantly associated with left–right self-designations, and everywhere except Hungary and Chile these correlations are reasonably strong. The three items that were intended to tap into a *Socialist* orientation are more weakly and inconsistently related to respondents' left–right self-designations. This association is strong only among Americans and Greeks. Survey respondents in Spain, Chile, and Uruguay are divided along the lines of left versus right only with regard to one or two of these three items, and only to a moderate level of association. Quite strikingly, Hungarians are not at all divided along these lines. Similarly, the *Social Democratic* item, separating those preferring the maintenance of government services over tax cuts, is strongly related to left–right orientations only in the United States. In the other countries, this link is either weak or is absent altogether. Finally, in *no* country are *Postmaterialist* values strongly and consistently linked to left–right self-designations. Only in Uruguay and the United States does one or both of these two items produce a moderate correlation with left–right. In short, the Traditional Conservative/liberal cleavage appears to be most strongly and consistently rooted in left–right self-designations in these countries, while postmaterialism appears to be almost irrelevant to this classic ideological continuum.

Having explored the bivariate linkages between each of these values and the left–right scale, let us turn our attention to the structure of inter-item correlations among these values. Tables 7.3a through 7.3g summarize the results of two different kinds of analyses of these interrelationships. The first eight columns of data present the correlation coefficients (Pearson's r) measuring the bivariate associations among each of these items. The three or four columns to the right of each table present the factor loadings resulting from factor analyses of all of these items. These statistics are the results of an Oblimin Rotation of the Principal Components analysis of these data.[13]

As can be seen from the data presented in Table 7.3a, Spanish respondents conform most closely to the clustering among these value orientations that we hypothesized at the beginning of this chapter. The first factor produces high factor loadings and strong inter-item correlations among all three of the items that we hypothesized would constitute an attitudinal dimension reflecting ideological differences between Traditional Conservatives, on the one hand, and liberals, on the other. Also consistent with our initial hypotheses, the three items tapping into Socialist attitudes form a distinct cluster, although both the inter-item correlations and factor loadings are somewhat lower than we observed with regard to the traditionalist-religious versus liberal dimension. The two postmaterialist items are also associated with each other in the predicted manner, although very weakly (with the percentage of variance explained by that fourth factor barely above the 11.1 that would have resulted from random chance). However, the environmental-protection item (*EcoGrow*) loads almost equally strongly on the fourth factor, along with *ServTax*, and the zero-order correlation between those two items (.15) is stronger than that linking *EcoGrow* with its putative postmaterialist partner, the item tapping into preferences for direct participation in decision-making versus deference to experts (.13). This pattern emerges more clearly in Greece and several other countries, leading to a modest reconceptualization that departs from the four 'ideal types' from which these items were drawn.

In the case of Greece, as can be seen in Table 7.3b, there is again a clear clustering of attitudes along the Traditional Conservative/liberal dimension, as well as among the three items that we associate with traditional Socialist orientations. As in the case of Spain, *ServTax* and *EcoGrow* are located in the same cluster, but in this instance are joined by the second putative postmaterialist item, *Particip*. And no stand-alone postmaterialist dimension is apparent in these data. This leads us to posit that concern with the environment had taken its place alongside maintenance of the welfare state and a strengthening of citizen participation within what we call a *Modern Social Democratic* cluster. While this is not what one could have predicted on the basis of initial formulations of the social democratic alternative by the likes of Eduard Bernstein or Anthony Crosland, this linkage between maintaining government services and social assistance (the core of the 'social-welfare state') and protecting the environment is consistent with the stands taken by most centre-left or social democratic parties in recent years. More generally, this suggests

Table 7.3a Factor analysis[a] and correlations (Pearson's r) among values

	ReligLib	OrderLib	Abortion	PrivPub	EqualInd	Compete	Particip	EcoGrow	Factor 1	Factor 2	Factor 3	Factor 4
Spain												
ReligLib	—								**.801**	-.044	.056	.032
OrderLib	.42***	—							**.728**	-.020	.069	-.151
Abortion	.39***	.29***	—						**.694**	.188	.107	-.040
PrivPub	.04	.03	.11***	—					.092	**.708**	-.187	-.126
EqualInd	.07*	.04	-.01	.11***	—				-.221	**.567**	.329	-.116
Compete	.14***	.13***	.13***	.17***	.11***	—			.270	**.642**	.091	.136
Particip	.11***	.12***	.11***	.01	.07**	.03	—		.155	-.017	**.836**	.053
EcoGrow	.06*	.07**	.08**	.02	.02	.09**	.13***	—	.074	.092	**.532**	**-.494**
ServTax	.06*	.13***	.08**	.06*	.07*	.02	.00	.15***	.094	-.032	-.019	**-.896**
Percentage of variance explained (%)									21.5	13.6	12.5	11.3

* Correlation is significant at the .05 level; ** Correlation is significant at the .01 level; *** Correlation is significant at the .001 level.
[a] The factor loadings reported are those of the Pattern Matrix resulting from an Oblimin rotation of the Principal Component analysis.

Table 7.3b Factor analysis and correlations (Pearson's r) among values

	ReligLib	OrderLib	Abortion	PrivPub	EqualInd	Compete	Particip	EcoGrow	Factor 1	Factor 2	Factor 3
Greece											
ReligLib	—								.072	.058	**.766**
OrderLib	**.30*****	—							.216	-.105	**.653**
Abortion	**.25*****	.16***	—						-.133	.059	**.637**
PrivPub	.01	.09**	.07*	—					**.732**	.003	.076
EqualInd	-.02	.03	-.04	.23***	—				**.621**	.363	-.098
Compete	.15***	.16***	-.03	.22***	.05	—			**.578**	-.369	.183
Particip	.01	-.04	-.04	.04	.12**	-.03	—		.212	**.430**	-.058
EcoGrow	-.03	-.02	-.01	-.02	.07*	-.06	.12***	—	.023	**.677**	-.006
ServTax	-.03	-.01	.03	-.05	.07*	-.16***	.04	.22***	-.195	**.689**	-.006
Percentage of variance explained (%)									18.5	15.2	13.3

* Correlation is significant at .05 level; ** Correlation is significant at .01 level; *** Correlation is significant at .001 level.

278

that the stands taken by political elites and party organizations may play a crucial role in determining the clustering of attitudes into ideological packages.

As in Greece and Spain, among respondents in the United States (see Table 7.3c), the three Traditional Conservative items load on the same factor, and are strongly correlated with one another. But the other relationships do not accord well with the West European template, particularly with regard to direct citizen *participation* in political decision-making (whose relationship with other variables is either extremely weak or of the wrong sign), and the three items initially hypothesized to fall within a socialist value cluster—*PrivPub*, *Compete*, and *EqualInd*. Indeed, the latter is most strongly associated with *ServTax*, the item tapping attitudes towards taxation and the social welfare state, and the environmental protection item, *EcoGrow*. Moreover, as we saw in Table 7.2, the relationships linking *Compete* and, especially, *Particip*, on the one hand, and left–right self-designation, on the other, are rather weak. Even more strikingly, *PrivPub* loads more strongly on the first factor, and correlates more strongly with the traditional conservative and religious values than it does with those associated with the socialism cluster that so clearly emerges in several other countries. These findings make good sense: the United States has never had an electorally significant socialist party, and it had the smallest 'para-state' sector (largely limited to municipal utilities generating and/or distributing power and water) of any industrialized society. Thus, there have been very few public business enterprises to privatize. In the absence of a socialist party and the kinds of political conflicts associated with a socialist agenda, aberrant factor loadings and inter-item correlations result from this examination of putatively 'socialist' values in the United States. Indeed, the most politically salient privatization effort in the late 1990s and early 2000s has involved public support for private elementary education systems (both religious and 'charter schools'). Accordingly, in the case of the United States we shall refer to the four items falling within that cluster as constituting a *Fundamentalist Conservative* value cluster. Conversely, the two 'modern social democratic' items (*EcoGrow* and *ServTax*) are both very strongly associated with *EqualInd*, tapping into preferences for a more equal distribution of income. Since the defence of basic public services (especially social services), environmental protection, and progressive income-distributive taxation and expenditure policies have been core concerns of the Democratic Party over the past three decades (during which concerns over protection of the environment were added to the party's New Deal values), we shall refer to this attitudinal

Table 7.3c Factor analysis and correlations (Pearsons' r) among values

	ReligLib	OrderLib	Abortion	PrivPub	EqualInd	Compete	Particip	EcoGrow	Factor 1	Factor 2	Factor 3
United States											
ReligLib	—								**.807**	.122	.035
OrderLib	.32***	—							**.640**	.012	.335
Abortion	.48***	.27***	—						**.779**	.187	-.066
PrivPub	.21***	.18***	.20***	—					**.410**	.371	.291
EqualInd	.07**	.01	.11***	.12***	—				.057	**.735**	.143
Compete	.10***	.20**	.05*	.14***	.15***	—			.153	.160	**.787**
Particip	.01	-.04	.01	-.04	.11***	-.12***	—		-.002	.262	**-.574**
EcoGrow	.02	-.07**	.09***	.12***	.25***	-.07**	.16***	—	.019	**.661**	-.327
ServTax	.16***	.08***	.18***	.21***	.37***	.03	.10***	.34***	.251	**.757**	-.052
Percentage of variance explained (%)									24.2	17.2	12.5

* Correlation is significant at .05 level; ** Correlation is significant at .01 level; *** Correlation is significant at .001 level.

domain as constituting a *Modern Democrats* value cluster. Finally, the absence of a postmaterialist cluster of values in the United States is noteworthy. The populist *participation* item is not consistently linked with any other meaningful value cluster. It loads on Factor 3 with the *Compete* item, but since this linkage involves a sign reversal that makes no sense, this clustering and the weak bilateral association on which it is based ($r = -.12$) will be ignored, and these two items will be excluded from subsequent analysis.

Analyses of data from Uruguay produce item clusters that are similar to those found in Greece. As can be seen in Table 7.3d, the Traditional Conservative/liberal variables are strongly linked with one another. Similarly, pro-environmentalist orientations and support for maintaining government services are moderately linked into what we have called a Modern Social Democracy cluster of items. Again, this is distinct from the classical, early-twentieth-century formulation of social democratic revisionism, but clearly reflects contemporary stands taken by parties of the centre-left in many countries. It should be noted, however, that this Modern Social Democracy cluster combines two variables that are very weakly linked to each other (Pearson's $r = .13$). As we will see in the subsequent round of analysis, this cluster is very weakly linked to patterns of partisan preference, and will be dropped from the final multivariate analysis in this chapter. Another significant departure from our expectations involves the looseness of relationships among Socialist values, *EqualInd*, and *PrivPub* (whose bivariate correlation is only .10). This is consistent with the data presented in Table 7.2, in which the relationship between the preference for a more equal distribution of wealth and the left–right continuum was not only found to be statistically insignificant but of the wrong sign. An additional aberration is their link to the desire for increased citizen participation. Accordingly, in order to distinguish the resulting clustering of items combining two of the three 'socialist' values with the desire for increased citizen participation, we shall re-label this dimension Participatory Socialism. Finally, the 'worker solidarity' item, *Compete*, weakly loads on the same factor as the Traditional Conservative items. Accordingly, we shall refer to this factor as more generic Conservatism. But *Compete* is also moderately linked to one of the core socialist items. These aberrations provide further evidence that the West European clustering of values hypothesized earlier in this chapter may not 'travel well' to countries whose histories and cultures are quite different. Nonetheless, the clustering of these attitudes is reasonably strong and sufficiently consistent with our expectations as to enable us to carry the analysis of slightly

Table 7.3d Factor analysis and correlations (Pearson's r) among values

	ReligLib	OrderLib	Abortion	PrivPub	EqualInd	Compete	Particip	EcoGrow	Factor 1	Factor 2	Factor 3
Uruguay											
ReligLib	—								**.709**	.092	−.023
OrderLib	.39***	—							**.734**	.171	.018
Abortion	.24***	.26***	—						**.600**	−.134	.303
PrivPub	.13***	.16***	.05	—					.272	**.658**	−.094
EqualInd	−.07*	−.04	−.10*	.10**	—				−.239	**.662**	−.160
Compete	.20***	.24***	.13***	.19***	−.02	—			**.497**	.323	.275
Particip	.13***	.15***	.13***	.15***	.13***	.09**	—		.283	**.495**	.315
EcoGrow	.06	−.01	.00	.07*	−.01	.04	.05*	—	.041	.197	**.479**
ServTax	−.01	.04	.12***	−.05	.04	−.07*	.08*	.13***	.018	−.045	**.821**
Percentage of variance explained (%)									21.5	13.7	12.8

* Correlation is significant at .05 level; ** Correlation is significant at .01 level; *** Correlation is significant at .001 level.

reformulated clusters of values through all of the following stages of analysis.

The clustering of these attitudes among Chileans (see Table 7.3e) presents us with no surprise with regard to the classic Traditional Conservative/liberal cluster. Both the factor loadings and the corresponding bivariate correlations are reasonably strong, and they are consistent with our initial expectations. The other two clusters, however, represent significant departures from our West European template. Unlike the Modern Social Democracy cluster, *EcoGrow*, *ServTax*, and *Particip* are also linked with *EqualInd*. While these variables are consistently linked in a manner that makes sense politically (since Socialist parties most commonly include individuals with both what we have referred to as Socialist and Modern Social Democratic attitudes), these factor loadings are not very strong, and the bivariate correlations that underpin them are extraordinarily weak. We shall nonetheless place them in the same category as the other Modern Social Democratic value clusters. Similarly, the linking of *PrivPub* and *Compete* in Factor 3 also makes sense, and seems to reflect a commitment to individual competition within a free-market economy. We will call this cluster *Capitalism*, and since its two variables elsewhere fall within the Socialism cluster, we shall regard it as part of that political family. But the absence of a statistically significant link between these two variables and *EqualInd* clearly distinguishes this factor from anything remotely resembling West European Socialism. Overall, with the single exception of the strong Traditional Conservative/liberal cluster, the lack of structure among these values is the most striking feature of these political cultural orientations in Chile.

Given the extraordinarily low correlations between virtually all of these values items and self-placement on the left–right continuum that we observed for Hungary in Table 7.2, it is not surprising to find that the clustering of these attitudes is messy and confusing. We do find in Table 7.3f that a clear postmaterialist dimension (Factor 4) emerges from both the factor analysis and bivariate correlation between the two relevant items, although the latter is very weak. The other three factors all depart in significant ways from the West European template advanced at the outset of this investigation. Two of the three items that we initially hypothesized would form a Socialist cluster are linked, but they are associated with what was originally hypothesized would emerge as a distinct Social Democratic item in Factor 2, generally representing a centre-left orientation in politics. Factor 1 combines respect for traditional religious beliefs and opposition to abortion with preferences for the privatization of public

Table 7.3e Factor analysis and correlations (Pearson's r) among values

	ReligLib	OrderLib	Abortion	PrivPub	EqualInd	Compete	Particip	EcoGrow	Factor 1	Factor 2	Factor 3
Chile											
ReligLib	—								**.739**	-.103	.097
OrderLib	.25***	—							**.594**	-.216	.257
Abortion	.25***	.16***	—						**.688**	.002	.050
PrivPub	.11***	.12***	.07*	—					.078	.000	**.770**
EqualInd	-.09**	-.07**	.01	.03	—				-.199	**.530**	.258
Compete	.12***	.16***	.11***	.17***	.01	—			.234	-.046	**.668**
Particip	-.04	-.04	-.06*	.00	.14***	-.06*	—		-.102	**.568**	.009
EcoGrow	-.06*	-.14***	-.03	.00	.05	.00	.06*	—	-.118	**.520**	-.027
ServTax	.01	-.03	.01	-.03	.11***	-.02	.15***	.16***	.165	**.673**	-.184
Percentage of variance explained (%)									18.7	14.4	11.4

* Correlation is significant at .05 level; ** Correlation is significant at .01 level; *** Correlation is significant at .001 level.

Table 7.3f Factor analysis and correlations (Pearson's r) among values

	ReligLib	OrderLib	Abortion	PrivPub	EqualInd	Compete	Particip	EcoGrow	Factor 1	Factor 2	Factor 3	Factor 4
Hungary												
ReligLib	—								**-.701**	-.232	.104	-.218
OrderLib	.10***	—							-.091	-.216	**.739**	.006
Abortion	**.26*****	.02	—						**-.739**	-.133	-.087	.066
PrivPub	.08**	-.01	.09**	—					**-.493**	**.477**	.041	-.186
EqualInd	-.16***	-.08**	-.10***	.12***	—				.159	**.752**	.014	.088
Compete	-.02	.17***	.05	.05	.08**	—			.102	.218	**.722**	-.048
Particip	-.07*	-.04	.00	-.07*	.05	.03	—		-.041	.012	.169	**.796**
EcoGrow	-.17***	-.07*	-.06*	-.04	.07*	-.04	.14***	—	.219	.054	-.251	**.668**
ServTax	-.18***	-.08**	-.09**	.05	**.29*****	.03	.02	.06*	.171	**.663**	-.038	.042
Percentage of variance explained (%)									17.9	13.9	13.0	12.0

* Correlation is significant at .05 level; ** Correlation is significant at .01 level; *** Correlation is significant at .001 level.

enterprises (which also is associated with the variables in Factor 2). These items are rather weakly related to one another at the bivariate level. Finally, Factor 3, which links support for law and order with support for individual initiative and competition, emerges as a puzzling combination of variables that are rather weakly correlated with each other. In the aggregate, the most important conclusion concerning the dimensional configuration of attitudes in Hungary is that they are extraordinarily weak, they significantly depart from the initial ideological template, and in several respects the combination of these values makes little sense. The individual items falling within these weak clusters of variables are also not systematically related to the left–right continuum, which in many countries helps to structure political competition.

Similarly, the configuration of values in Hong Kong (Table 7.3g) also departs markedly from our West European template. *ReligLib* is moderately associated with *OrderLib*,[14] but it also forms part of a cluster (Factor 1) with *EqualInd* and *ServTax*. Stronger evidence of the lack of structuring of these attitudes in a manner comparable to that posited in our West European template can be seen in the fact that the associations between the first two and the latter two variables are of opposite signs. In contrast with the placement of these individual value orientations on the left–right continuum in most of the countries we have examined, this suggests that those who are religious and value law and order over individual liberties are also in favour of greater equality in the distribution of income and more generous government services (even if the latter entails higher taxes). While this clustering of attitudes is moderately strong and may make sense in the context of Hong Kong's society and culture, it departs substantially from our West European model. As in Chile, *PrivPub* and *Compete* form a separate cluster (Factor 3), although their bivariate correlation is extraordinarily weak (.09). Finally, a conventional postmaterialist cluster emerges (linking *Particip* with *EcoGrow*), but the bivariate association (.13) between these two variables is not very impressive. Overall, Hong Kong, whose culture and history are the least similar to all the other countries examined here, also departs most markedly from the West European model of value clusters.

Let us now submit a modified 'West European template' of value clusters to a more rigorous test by performing a confirmatory factor analysis. On the basis of our general finding that 'postmaterialism' does not emerge as a strong value cluster, while 'Modern Social Democracy' appears in most countries as a more plausible interpretation of the relationships among the two putatively postmaterialist items and attitudes towards the modern

Table 7.3g Factor analysis and correlations (Pearson's r) among values

	ReligLib	OrderLib	PrivPub	EqualInd	Compete	Particip	EcoGrow	Factor 1	Factor 2	Factor 3
Hong Kong										
ReligLib	—							**.678**	.111	-.044
OrderLib	.22***	—						**.612**	.307	.055
PrivPub	.08**	.07**	—					.274	-.057	**.634**
EqualInd	-.21***	-.13**	.00	—				**-.556**	.294	-.378
Compete	-.03	.01	.09***	.10***	—			-.112	.058	**.734**
Particip	.01	.16***	-.04	.05*	-.06*	—		-.090	**.759**	-.099
EcoGrow	-.03	.02	-.02	.05*	-.04*	.13***	—	-.067	**.633**	.071
ServTax	-.19***	-.16***	-.10***	.12***	-.01	-.03	-.01	**.569**	-.037	-.202
Percentage of variance explained (%)								19.4	15.1	13.9

* Correlation is significant at .05 level; ** Correlation is significant at .01 level; *** Correlation is significant at .001 level.

social welfare state, we reformulated the template to include three factors: Traditional Conservatism and Socialism (both as originally formulated), now joined by a Modern Social Democracy cluster composed of *ServTax*, *EcoGrow*, and *Particip*. As can be seen in Table 7.4, the RMSEA statistics generated by this confirmatory factor analysis (with lower scores indicating better 'fit', and scores approaching .1 indicating poor fit) suggest that the three-factor model works very well in Spain and Chile, and reasonably well in Uruguay, Greece, Hong Kong. This three-factor 'West European Template' did not fit well with the American value clustering, and was so inappropriate for item interrelationships in Hungary that no solution emerged from the analysis, while aberrant characteristics emerging from the preceding analysis of Hong Kong precluded its entry into this stage of the analysis.[15]

Table 7.4 Results of confirmatory factor analysis of three-factor 'West European template'[a]

	RMSEA
Spain	.049
Chile	.047
Uruguay	.061
Greece	.063
United States	.083
Hungary	Could not estimate
Results of confirmatory analysis of two-factor model[b]	
United States	.062

[a] The three-factor model consists of the Traditional Conservatism, Socialism, and Modern Social Democracy clusters.
[b] The two-factor American model includes the Fundamentalist Conservative and Modern Democrats clusters.

In the case of the United States, the reason for the inability to reach an acceptable solution through the confirmatory factor analysis is obvious: as we saw in Table 7.3c, there is no socialist cluster of values, and as we saw in Table 7.2, two key items (*Compete* and *Particip*) are only weakly associated with the left–right continuum, and are linked to each other in a separate factor that makes no sense. Let us therefore reconstruct value clusters on the bases of their respective patterns of bivariate association and knowledge of those values that have been highly salient in electoral competition between Democrats and Republicans over the past two decades. Accordingly, we replaced the three-factor West European template with a two-factor model composed of the Fundamentalist Conservative and Modern Democrats clusters (consisting of *ReligLib*, *OrderLib*, *Abortion*, and

PrivPub, in the first instance, and *EqualInd*, *EcoGrow*, and *ServTax*, as the second). As can be seen in Table 7.4, this two-factor model fits the patterns emerging from the American data much more closely.

Ideological Cleavages and Partisanship

We now turn our attention to the extent to which the value clusters that emerged from our country-by-country exploratory factor analyses are related to differing partisan preferences among voters in each of these countries. Accordingly, we shall henceforth set aside the 'West European template' (whose case-by-case applicability we have tested) and deal with the actual clustering of variables that resulted from the exploratory factor analysis for each individual country. Scales were constructed by simply adding together the scores (ranging from 1 to 10 for each value item) for those items that the preceding factor analyses determined were clustered together. Accordingly, the resulting value scales were: Traditional Conservatism in Spain, Greece, and Chile; a more generic Conservatism in Uruguay, and Fundamentalist Conservatism in the US; Socialism in Spain and Greece; a somewhat variable Modern Social Democracy in Spain, Greece, Uruguay, and Chile; Modern Democrats in the United States; Participatory Socialism in Uruguay; Capitalism in Chile; and postmaterialism in Spain, Hungary, and Hong Kong. Scales based on the other (unnamed) aggregations of variables that emerged weakly from the factor and bivariate correlation analysis in Hungary and Hong Kong were also computed and analysed.

Table 7.5 presents a general overview of the strength of the bivariate relationship between each of these value scales and vote for party or parties of the left versus right in each country. The resulting Pearson's r statistic can be regarded as a measure of the degree of polarization of the party system on that value dimension. Seen from a cross-national perspective, these data suggest that value clusters associated with religious-based conservatism (Traditional Conservatism in Spain, Uruguay's more generic Conservatism, and Fundamentalist Conservatism in the United States) deeply divide voters in those countries, while even in Greece (which has historically lacked a politically relevant religious cleavage) this association is of moderate strength. In Chile, despite the fact that earlier rounds of analysis found that the Traditional Conservative cluster is by far the most tightly constrained and polarizes citizens more strongly than in any of these countries, there is virtually no electoral impact of these values.

Table 7.5 Correlations (Pearson's r) between value scales and partisan preference

	United States	Spain	Greece	Uruguay	Chile	Hungary	Hong Kong
Tradit. Con.		**.32*****	**.21*****		.05		
Conservatism				**.41*****			
Fund. Conserv.	**.50*****						
Socialism		**.25*****	**.32*****				
Part. Socialism				**.22*****			
Capitalism					.12**		
Mod. Soc. Dem.		.09**	.10**	.08	.03		
Modern Dems.	**.44*****						
Postmaterialism		.00				−.04	.09**
Other 1						.08*	.08**
Other 2						.01	.08*
Other 3						.00	

(We attempt to explain this seemingly aberrant finding in a later section of this chapter.) From a cross-national perspective, among all the values clusters examined in this study, these religious-based value conflicts appear to have the most pervasive impact on electoral behaviour, although (as we shall argue) the behaviour of political elites can mute or prevent such value differences from becoming politically salient.

Value clusters somehow involving socialism (i.e. those focusing on equality, worker solidarity, and/or public ownership of the means of production) also strongly polarize voters in Greece and Spain, while in Uruguay this cleavage is of moderate strength. The Modern Democrats values (involving income equality, the provision of government services, and environmental protection) most deeply divide Republicans from Democrats in the United States, while the divisive impact of the Modern Social Democracy value cluster in this same political family is much weaker (or non-existent) in the other democratic systems.

Postmaterialism emerges as a statistically significant determinant of the vote for parties of the left versus right only in Hong Kong. When we examine this relationship between values and the vote on a party-by-party basis, we see that in Spain the Izquierda Unida coalition (established in an attempt to link with the Communist Party a variety of small groups with postmaterialist issue concerns) does disproportionately attract voters on one side of this value cleavage. But overall, the irrelevance of this weakly defined value cluster to electoral behaviour in these countries stands in sharp contrast with the disproportionate attention that has been given to the study of postmaterialism in comparative politics over the past few decades. It is clear that values are profoundly important politically, and that postmaterialist attitudes in most of these countries have been included within the programmatic appeals of Modern Social Democratic parties. But postmaterialism as a stand-alone value dimension has very little if any impact on partisan politics in most of the countries analysed in this study.

In short, the value clusters posited in the West European template or in country-specific variations on that model exert a considerable impact on partisan politics in the United States, Spain, Greece, and Uruguay, while in Chile the one values cluster that most strongly emerged from the preceding dimensional analysis—traditional conservatism—does not have a statistically significant impact on electoral behaviour. In Hungary and Hong Kong, the weakness and incoherence of the clustering of values noted in the previous rounds of factor analysis is parallelled by the absence of linkage with partisanship. In North and South America, and in Western Europe, however, these values appear to be of great importance as bases of electoral mobilization. As we see in the following multivariate analyses, the relationships between partisan preferences and these values clusters remain strong even after the standard social-structural variables have been introduced as control variables in previous steps of the Logit analysis. We also see that these values are closely associated with party identification, although the 'direction of causality' underpinning these relationships is unclear (and, most likely, reciprocal). We regard party identification as, in many respects, the long-term encapsulation of values which can (in long-established democracies) be passed along from generation to generation even without an accompanying intergenerational transmission of values. Party ID is therefore entered into the equation in the last step as a measure of some residual variation that the values and social structural variables had not accounted for.

Before undertaking that multivariate analysis (which aggregates vote for party or parties of the left vs. party or parties of the right as the dependent variable), let us explore the specific impact on the vote for each of the major parties in Spain, Greece, Uruguay, and the United States. Accordingly, the next step in this analysis was to divide the electorates of these countries into three groups, separating respondents into the upper (right) quartile on each value dimension, the lowest (left) quartile, with the remaining group composed of the roughly 50 per cent of respondents whose value orientations placed them closer to the middle of each of the scales. Having re-coded these scale values for each respondent in this manner, simple crosstabs by party vote were constructed, with parties arrayed from left to right.

As we can see from the data in Table 7.6a, supporters of the left-wing Izquierda Unida (IU) coalition in Spain are highly skewed towards the left with regard to each and every one of these ideological dimensions. Fully 52 per cent of IU voters fell within the top quartile of respondents on the Traditional Conservatism scale, 41 per cent were in the top quartile on the Socialism scale, 43 per cent were from the most postmaterialist quartile, and 37 per cent fell within the most leftist quartile on the Modern Social Democracy scale. At the other end of the left–right continuum, we find that supporters of the conservative Partido Popular (PP) are substantially more Traditionally Conservative than are most Spaniards, and they are also significantly less pro-socialist in their values as well. What is perhaps most striking in this table is that those who had cast ballots for the governing PSOE in the 1993 parliamentary election were almost a perfectly representative cross sample of the Spanish electorate as a whole with regard to each and every one of these value dimensions. In every instance, the percentage of PSOE voters in each quartile did not

Table 7.6a Values quartiles by vote

Spain

Vote	Left quartile	Middle	Right quartile	(N)
Traditional Conservatism (tau-b = .32)				
Izquierda Unida	52.3%	42.1%	5.6%	(107)
PSOE	22.0	54.2	23.8	(478)
Partido Popular	12.0	40.9	47.1	(325)
Full sample	23.2	49.5	27.5	(1,419)
Socialism (tau-b = .22)				
Izquierda Unida	40.6%	44.3%	15.1%	(106)
PSOE	26.1	53.3	20.6	(433)
Partido Popular	14.2	47.7	38.1	(310)
Full sample	23.4	49.3	27.7	(1,332)
Postmaterialism (tau-b = .05)				
Izquierda Unida	42.6%	39.8%	17.6%	(108)
PSOE	19.4	54.9	25.6	(468)
Partido Popular	28.8	42.4	28.8	(323)
Full sample	27.7	46.6	25.7	(1,406)
Modern Social Democracy (tau-b = .11)				
Izquierda Unida	36.9%	45.0%	18.0%	(111)
PSOE	26.3	47.1	26.7	(480)
Partido Popular	19.6	49.7	30.7	(326)
Full sample	26.3	47.6	26.1	(1,426)

deviate significantly from the percentage of Spanish survey respondents as a whole. This provides further support for the common observation (e.g. Puhle 2001) that the Socialist Party (PSOE) had by that time succeeded in converting itself into the quintessential 'catch-all' party. In contrast, IU's electorate much more clearly reflected the partisan composition of this coalition among communists and assorted postmaterialist groups. In terms of the extent to which these value dimensions divide Spanish voters, it is noteworthy that the Traditional Conservatism scale has by far the strongest association with partisan preferences. While this is consistent with the traditionally divisive impact of the religious cleavage in Spanish society earlier in the twentieth century, its strength is somewhat puzzling in so far as party leaders had scrupulously avoided taking polarizing stands on religious issues (at least prior to the 1993 election, when this survey was conducted) and parties had eschewed institutional ties to religious organizations. Strikingly low in their capacity to distinguish among partisan electorates are orientations regarding postmaterialism and Modern Social Democracy. With the exception of the markedly postmaterialist IU electorate, neither PSOE nor PP voters departed significantly from the national average regarding postmaterialist values. The Modern Social Democracy dimension does distinguish IU from PP voters, but the differences are not that great. Instead, it appears that even supporters of the centre-right Partido Popular widely endorse the principles commonly associated with the modern social welfare state and protection of the environment.

In the case of Greece (Table 7.6b), it is the Socialism dimension that most clearly differentiates supporters of parties of the left from parties of the right. This is particularly true with regard to the highly skewed distributions on the scale of supporters of the communist KKE and the conservative Nea Demokratia. Supporters of the centre-left PASOK and of the left coalition in the 1996 parliamentary election clearly tended towards the left on the scale, although by far the largest block of their supporters were located near the moderate middle of this continuum. Consistent with the findings of many other studies, the traditional conservative dimension does not so sharply divide parties of the left from those on the right, and orientations of voters along the Modern Social Democracy dimension are even more weakly associated with partisan preference. The absence of a traditional religious cleavage in Greek politics[16] appears to have softened the polarizing potential of the broader concept of traditionalist conservatism, while Greeks appear to share with Spaniards a consensual embrace of the precepts and policies of the modern social welfare state.

Table 7.6b Values quartiles by vote

Greece

Vote	Left quartile	Middle	Right quartile	(N)
Traditional Conservatism (tau-b = .19)				
KKE	34.1%	40.9%	25.0%	(44)
Left coalition	35.5	51.6	12.9	(62)
PASOK	25.7	47.5	26.8	(354)
Nea Demokratia	13.7	46.3	40.0	(255)
Full sample	24.4	46.9	28.7	(907)
Socialism (tau-b = .29)				
KKE	46.2%	46.2%	7.7%	(39)
Left coalition	33.3	46.3	20.4	(54)
PASOK	29.8	53.8	16.5	(346)
Nea Demokratia	12.5	43.0	44.5	(256)
Full sample	25.7	47.9	26.5	(877)
Modern Social Democracy (tau-b = .13)				
KKE	39.5%	41.9%	18.6%	(43)
Left coalition	33.9	52.5	13.6	(59)
PASOK	25.8	48.2	26.0	(361)
Nea Demokratia	19.3	48.0	32.7	(269)
Full sample	24.9	48.3	26.7	(926)

Table 7.6c Values quartiles by vote

Uruguay

Vote	Left quartile	Middle	Right quartile	(N)
Conservatism (tau-b = .31)				
E. Progresista	47.4%	44.8%	7.7%	(194)
Nuevo Espacio	45.2	41.9	12.9	(31)
Partido Nacional	17.6	43.4	39.0	(136)
Partido Colorado	15.0	50.3	34.8	(187)
Full sample	25.4	47.9	26.7	(921)
Participatory Socialism (tau-b = .15)				
E. Progresista	32.8%	52.9%	14.2%	(204)
Nuevo Espacio	26.7	43.3	30.0	(30)
Partido Nacional	15.7	46.4	37.9	(140)
Partido Colorado	22.8	45.1	32.1	(184)
Full sample	24.5	49.4	26.0	(939)
Modern Social Democracy (tau-b = .07)				
E. Progresista	31.9%	45.4%	22.7%	(207)
Nuevo Espacio	22.6	51.6	25.8	(31)
Partido Nacional	25.9	46.9	27.3	(143)
Partido Colorado	21.2	52.8	25.9	(193)
Full sample	25.1	50.7	24.2	(967)

In Uruguay (Table 7.6c), we see that the two traditional parties (the Partido Colorado and Partido Nacional) are clearly differentiated from their rivals on the left (Nuevo Espacio and the Espacio Progresista) by the Conservatism cleavage (tau-b = .31) and, to a much lesser extent Participatory Socialism dimension (.15). Perhaps the biggest surprise to emerge from the Uruguayan data is the complete absence of partisan differences with regard to the Modern Social Democracy dimension. Again, as in the cases of Greece and Spain, there appears to be widespread support for social services provided by the government and environmental protection policies that transcends partisan boundaries.

In sharp contrast, Table 7.6d presents the most striking results to emerge from this stage of the analysis. Voters in the United States are profoundly divided along the lines of the two value clusters that emerged from our analysis. Polarization between Republicans and Democrats along the Fundamentalist Conservative/liberal dimension is much sharper even than is found in Spain—which earlier in the century experienced a civil war between anti-clericals and supporters of traditional, conservative Catholicism. Similarly, the Modern Democrats dimension divides American voters much more deeply than does the Socialism dimension in Greece— which experienced a civil war between communists and conservatives in the late 1940s. Given the absence of comparable survey data from earlier American elections, we cannot precisely determine the extent to which these findings reflect a recent polarization of the United States' electorate along these value cleavages. If we can regard frequency of attendance at religious services as a surrogate for our predominantly religious value cluster, however, survey data reaching as far back as 1952 indicate that a profound partisan polarization of religiosity has occurred. In presidential

Table 7.6d Values quartiles by vote

United States

Vote	Left quartile	Middle	Right quartile	(N)
Fundamentalist Conservatism (tau-b = .45)				
Kerry	44.1%	45.8%	10.1%	(681)
Bush	7.9	48.8	43.2	(629)
Full sample	26.7	47.3	26.0	(1,310)
Modern Democrats (tau-b = .40)				
Kerry	38.1%	49.4%	12.5%	(678)
Bush	8.8	46.7	44.5	(625)
Full sample	24.0	48.1	27.9	(1,303)

elections prior to the 1990s, the difference in the vote for the Republican versus Democratic candidate between regular churchgoers and those who rarely or never attend religious services averaged just over 5 per cent; since 1992, however, the average difference has been consistently between 22 and 26 per cent.[17] As noted by Fiorina, moreover, this linkage 'between religion and presidential voting did not develop gradually. Rather, it emerged suddenly and dramatically in 1992'—the same year in which presidential candidate Pat Buchanan ominously proclaimed 'culture war' at the Republican National Convention. These data provide prima facie evidence (as predicted by the July *USA Today* headline with which we began this chapter) that in the November 2004 election, Republicans and Democrats did, indeed, 'War Over Values', and that the 'culture war' in the United States is no 'myth' (*pace* Fiorina[18]). We more rigorously re-examine this claim later in this chapter.

Values, Intermediation, and the Vote

This final stage in our analysis re-examines the link between socio-political values and partisan preferences within the context of multi-variate models of electoral behaviour. By treating these value orientations as independent variables, alongside others that have commonly been found to be significant determinants of the vote, we can 'control' for the causal impact of those other variables, and therefore isolate the independent impact on partisan preference of these values clusters. In addition, we shall also include in these equations the three sets of intermediation variables that have been analysed in other chapters of this book—partisan biases in the flows of information through secondary organizations, the mass communications media, and face-to-face contact with discussants. The dependent variable in all stages of this analysis will be a vote in the previous parliamentary election for a party or parties of the left versus those on the right, or, in the United States, for George Bush or John Kerry in the 2004 presidential election.

An initial glance at the zero-order relationship between these value scales and vote for party or parties of the left versus right produces striking but somewhat misleading results. The percentages of the variance in the vote (as measured by Nagelkerke R^2 statistics) 'explained' by these value scales alone (i.e. when they are entered into Logit equations as the only independent variables) is most impressive. In Greece, 21 per cent of the variance in the vote is accounted for by three value scales alone

(Traditional Conservatism, Socialism, and Modern Social Democracy); in Spain, the percentage of explained variance (with Traditional Conservatism, Socialism, Modern Social Democracy, and Postmaterialism) is 22 per cent; in Uruguay, 25 per cent is accounted for by Conservatism and Participatory Socialism;[19] and in the United States, fully 49 per cent of the variance in the vote for the Republicans versus Democrats is explained by the Fundamentalist Conservative and Modern Democrats value clusters. These zero-order relationships between values and vote can be misleading, however, in so far as they may be 'standing in' for other causal relationships. In addition, there may be considerable conceptual overlap between our measures of values and causal factors commonly associated with what we have posited as alternative paradigms of electoral behaviour. For example, to what extent might 'socialist values' be embedded within class position, or 'traditionalist conservative values' be associated with religious affiliation. In order to estimate the unique, additive impact of these subjective values orientations on the vote, as distinguished from those commonly analysed in accord with the structuralist 'social cleavages' model of voting, we introduce several standard determinants of the vote as control variables.

This analysis will proceed in a forced step-wise manner in which blocs of independent variables will be entered into the equations one at a time, with the incremental contribution to that equation's R^2 as our measure of the causal impact of that set of variables. In the first step, a number of socio-demographic variables commonly found to influence the vote (age, gender, education, and various measures of socio-economic class) will be entered in one bloc. In the second stage, we add religion to these socio-demographic control variables. Accordingly, the cumulative R^2 produced by this second equation can be regarded as a rough measure of the explanatory power of the 'social-cleavage model' of voting that has served as a dominant paradigm in European electoral studies over the past four decades. In the third step of this analysis, we will add as independent variables those values clusters that emerged from the preceding dimensional analysis of each country. This is followed by a fourth step, in which the aforementioned three sets of intermediation variables are added to the Logit equations.

In the first stage of the multivariate Logit analysis, variables indicating the age, gender, educational attainment, and socio-economic status of the respondent were introduced.[20] The numbers presented in the first row of Table 7.7 reflect the Nagelkerke R^2 that resulted from this first step in the analysis. As can be seen in that table, these socio-demographic control variables explained 11.6 per cent of the variance in the vote in Spain (pitting the conservative Partido Popular against the socialist and communist parties), 11.2 per cent in Uruguay (with the dependent variable being vote for the traditional Colorado and Nacional parties vs. the new parties of the left, Espacio Progresista and Nuevo Espacio), 1.8 per cent of the vote for Bush versus Kerry in the United States, and just .4 per cent in Greece (in electoral competition between the conservative Nea Democratia and the parties of the left and centre-left [PASOK, the communists and the left coalition]).

Table 7.7 Multivariate Logit analyses of vote for parties of the left vs. right: incremental and cumulative R^2 (percentage of variance explained)

	Spain	Greece	Uruguay	USA[a]
Socio-demographic controls	.116	.004	.112	.018
Religion	.119	.032	.061	.107
Value scales[b]	.118	.193	.153	.382
Organization partisan contact[c]	.031	.064	.107	.047
Media bias	.036	.148	.032[d]	.029
Discussant Bias	.178	.073	.094	.088
Cumulative R^2 (Pct. explained)	**.598**	**.514**	**.559**	**.671**
N	814	664	440	1,138

[a] It is important to note that African-American respondents were removed from the sample prior to running these Logit equations. This is because the impact of ethnicity (a variable that is not politically relevant in the other countries in this study—which therefore would have made these results non-comparable) was otherwise impossible to extricate from the variables measuring religiosity in the United States. African-American evangelical Protestants are the most strongly Democratic voters in the sample, while White Evangelical Protestants and 'non-traditional Christians' were the most strongly Republican. Since the only effective way to operationalize religiosity in this extremely heterogeneous population is to enter these various religious categories in a bloc as a set of dichotomous 'dummy variables' (in contrast with the ordinal ranking of degree of religiosity in those countries in which one single religion is overwhelmingly dominant), this artificially inflated the impact on the vote of 'religion' by 'smuggling' ethnicity into the equation. If African-Americans had not been eliminated, the incremental R^2 figures would have been .024% for the sociodemographic controls, .149% for religion, .329% for values, .036% for organizational membership, and .035% for radio and television bias, producing a cumulative R^2 of .573% for this equation (n = 1,287).

[b] For Spain, the value scales entered into the equation in this second step were Traditional Conservatism, Socialism, Modern Social Democracy, and Postmaterialism; for Greece, they were Traditional Conservatism, Socialism and Modern Social Democracy; for Uruguay, Conservatism, and Participatory Socialism; and for the United States, Fundamentalist Conservatism, and Modern Democrats.

[c] Includes contact from political parties and from secondary organizations to which the respondent belongs.

[d] In Uruguay, no significant or consistent biases in television or radio coverage of partisan politics were perceived by respondents. Accordingly, only bias in newspaper coverage was included in this stage of the analysis in this and all subsequent tables.

In the second step, the respondent's level of religiosity was added to the equation.[21] Religiosity exerted the strongest influence over the decision to vote for a party of the left or right in Spain (where it explained 11.9% of the variance in the vote), followed closely by the United States (10.7%). Religion exerted a much weaker influence on voting behaviour in Uruguay (where it explained 6.1% of the variance in the vote) and, especially, in Greece (which lacks a tradition of political conflict over religion). It should be noted that the cumulative R^2 produced by the end of this second step of the analysis (.235 in Spain, .173 in Uruguay, .125 in the United States, and .036 in Greece) is a rough indicator of the extent of social-cleavage anchoring of partisanship in these countries. With regard to the two Southern European cases, these results are entirely consistent with the findings of previous studies indicating that electoral behaviour in Spain by the 1993 election was moderately well anchored in that country's social structure (after having been much more deeply rooted in cleavages in previous elections), while electoral competition in Greece—a country lacking in deep economic or religious cleavages—lacks social structural 'anchors of partisanship' (see Gunther and Montero 2001*b*).

In the third step of this analysis, the aforementioned values scales were added to the socio-demographic control items as independent variables. The numbers presented in the third row of Table 7.7 indicate that these socio-political values exert a considerable influence on voting behaviour within all four electorates, even after the impact of socio-demographic and religious variables have been taken into consideration. These values clusters are by far the strongest predictors of the vote in three of the four cases, and only in Spain is their impact less (by 0.1%) than that of another variable, religion. Indeed, the extent of partisan polarization along these values cleavages in the United States is truly remarkable, explaining an additional 38.2 per cent of the variance in the vote after the full impact of the two sets of social-cleavage variables has been 'controlled'. These findings from the American case are the most striking results to emerge from our cross-national analysis of electoral behaviour. Voters in the United States in 2004 were profoundly divided along the lines of the two value clusters that emerged from our analysis. While this polarization began in the early 1990s, these data suggest that the emphasis by the Bush campaign on 'family values', abortion, and other fundamentalist conservative issues exerted a strongly polarizing influence on the American electorate.

We next turn our attention to the impact of a subset of intermediation channels on the vote. We should note at the outset that the status of 'religiosity' is one that straddles the 'social-cleavage' paradigm and the

CNEP focus on intermediation. One could argue that participation in the activities of a particular church exposes an individual to flows of politically relevant information from that secondary organization that may be biased in favour of one party or another, particularly in so far as religion has been politicized in some countries. (Indeed, in a future study, more detailed analysis of flows of partisan information within churches during the 2004 American presidential election will help to separate the electoral impacts of religion-as-structural-conduit-of-political-information, on the one hand, from religious-doctrine-as-basis-of-values, on the other.) If we had chosen to regard religious affiliation as an intermediation variable and (according to the logic of analysis followed in this section of the chapter) entered it into the equations after the values scales, its impact would have been much reduced, and that of the values scales increased by an equivalent amount. Despite the ambiguities surrounding the status of religion (i.e. as a 'cleavage' vs. 'intermediation' indicator), we have chosen to present the more 'conservative' estimate of the impact of these values. Accordingly, in terms of causal processes, we are assuming that religiosity helps to forge some of the values whose political impacts we are examining in this chapter.

In addition to presenting a conservative estimate of the impact of values by entering these variables into equations following the introduction of the aforementioned 'control variables', it should also be noted that our estimate of the impact of intermediation variables on the vote, measured only in the last step of this analysis, is also very 'conservative'. By adding these only in the last steps in this analysis, we are giving full credence to the 'selective exposure' hypothesis, according to which individuals choose their preferred information channels in accord with their previously established values or partisan inclinations (as will be explicit in a later round of this analysis). This ordering does not take into consideration the likelihood that, over the long term, values and partisan preferences may be shaped by the cumulative impact of exposure to biased information. Such long-term processes, however, cannot be explored using single-wave, cross-sectional data such as those on which most of these CNEP surveys were based.

The first set of intermediation channels to be analysed involves flows of information through secondary organizations. In the theoretical framework within which we are placing this analysis, the flow of information to voters through intermediation channels with partisan biases plays an important role in making those value orientations salient during election campaigns. In CNEP surveys, respondents are given an extensive battery of questions about the extent of their involvement in secondary associations of a wide variety. Among these are questions concerning which party (if any) was favoured in communications from that organization to the survey respondent. This perception of bias, for each of the groups to which the respondent belonged, served as the basis for creating a scale measuring organization bias in favour of the party or parties of the left versus the party or parties of the right.[22] In addition, the flow of information to voters through direct contacts with representatives of political parties (by phone, mail, or in person) were added as independent variables in this fourth step of the analysis. As can be seen from the data presented in the fourth row of Table 7.7, secondary associations exerted a significant influence on voting decisions in each of these three countries, explaining an additional 3.1 per cent of the variance in the vote in Spain, 4.7 per cent in the United States, 6.4 per cent in Greece, and 10.7 per cent in Uruguay. It should be noted that the aggregate-level impact on the vote of these secondary organizations is lowered by the fact that only 19 per cent of Greeks, 20 per cent of Uruguayans, and 25 per cent of Spaniards belong to organized groups of any kind (as compared with 47% of Americans affiliated with organizations). For those minorities who do belong, the impact of partisan biases of secondary associations is quite substantial.

The fifth row of data in Table 7.7 presents the incremental contribution to R^2 resulting from the addition to these Logit equations of blocs of variables measuring partisan biases (based on perceptions of our survey respondents) in news coverage by newspapers, television, and radio news broadcasts, and, in the cases of Spain and the United States (where the relevant variables had been included in the post-election questionnaires), radio, and television 'talk shows'.[23] When examined individually, these sources of media bias differed substantially from one country to another, and in a manner consistent with the general characteristics of each country's media system. With regard to newspapers, Greek dailies were intensely partisan: the zero-order tau-b measuring the association between the respondents' newspapers biases, on the one hand, and the respondent's vote in the previous election was .36, as can be seen in Table 7.8. In the light of the fact that 59 per cent of Greeks do not read a daily newspaper, the extent of partisan 'pillarization' of this communications medium must be regarded as extreme. Significant partisan segmentation of the newspaper market in Spain and Uruguay is also reflected in their respective correlations (tau-b) of .16 and .14. Again, the aggregate impact on the vote of this intermediation channel is reduced by the fact that 57 per cent of Spaniards and 31 per cent of Uruguayans do not read newspapers. In the United States, however, there was no statistically significant relationship between perceived partisan bias of the respondent's daily newspaper and his or her vote. This reflects the non-partisan nature of most American newspapers and their increasing reliance on national news distributed by non-partisan news services. These data are also consistent with the findings of an analysis of data from the CNEP I 1992 American presidential survey.[24]

Table 7.8 Correlations (tau-b) between intermediation bias and vote for party/parties of left vs. right

Intermediation channel	Spain	Greece	Uruguay	United States
Organizational contacts	.16	.27	.30	.32
Party contacts	.10	.40	.29	.33
Newspapers	.16	.36	.14	—
Television news	.14	.27	—	.18
TV talk shows	—	M.D.	M.D.	.25
Radio news	.17	.19	—	—
Radio talk shows	.05	M.D.	M.D.	.32
Discussant bias	.49	.35[a]	.44	.58

Note: All correlations significant at .000 level.

[a] The items measuring the partisan preferences of discussants in Greece were not as precise as those for other countries (i.e. they asked if the discussant voted for a 'different party' than the respondent, rather than identifying the specific party), so this correlation probably underestimates the strength of the relationship.

Greece also exhibited the strongest partisan polarization with regard to television news: the zero-order tau-b correlation between perceived bias in broadcasting and vote for parties of the left versus right was .27. Spain and the United States exhibited moderate levels of impact of television-news bias on electoral behaviour (.14 and .18, respectively), while survey respondents in Uruguay perceived no significant partisan bias in television's coverage of the news. The political bias of radio networks in Spain and Greece had a moderate impact on the vote, producing tau-b scores of .17 and .19, respectively, while, again, there was no perceived bias in radio coverage of the news in Uruguay. In the United States, the most intensively partisan sources of political information were 'talk shows' on television and, especially, radio, where 40 per cent of listeners perceived a pro-Republican bias (as compared with just 14% who regarded their preferred programmes as pro-Democratic). The tau-b measures of association between partisan bias and the vote were .25 and .32, respectively, for television and radio talk shows. This intense politicization stands in sharp contrast with comparable shows in Spain (the only other national survey to include questions concerning these communications media).

Spanish television talk shows were perfectly balanced in the aggregate between programmes that favoured parties of the left and right, and no programme was perceived as markedly partisan, while radio talk shows were very weakly partisan (.05).

Including these media-bias variables as the last step in a multivariate analysis of the vote for parties of the left and the right, results in a somewhat more modest picture of the impact of intermediation. Having already controlled for the respondent's values, religion, socio-demographic characteristics, and organizational affiliations, the incremental contribution of media bias that emerged from this fifth step in the analysis amounted to 2.9 per cent in the United States, 3.2 per cent in Uruguay, and 3.6 per cent in Spain. The impact of media bias in Greece, however, remained very strong—exceeding all other blocs of variables entered into the equations except values.

In the final step in the multivariate analysis presented in Table 7.7, the political preferences of discussion partners were added to the equations. As Pedro Magalhães demonstrated in the preceding chapter, these face-to-face contacts have a powerful impact on the vote. The zero-order tau-b correlations between 'discussant bias' and the vote (see Table 7.8) ranged from .44 in Uruguay to .49 in Spain to .58 in the United States, while the somewhat lower correlation of .35 in Greece is partly an artefact of a different questionnaire item wording.[25]

The Net Impact of Previously Unexplored Variables

The cumulative impact of all of the clusters of independent variables included in these efforts to explain variation in the vote for parties of the left versus right is quite substantial. The influence of socio-demographic, religious, values, and intermediation variables combined accounts for 51 per cent of the variance in the vote for parties of the left versus right in Greece, 56 per cent in Uruguay, 60 per cent in Spain, and an astounding 67 per cent of variance in the vote in the American 2004 presidential election. But let us break down these aggregate figures to determine the separate impact of different causal processes.

As noted earlier in this discussion, the cumulative R^2 resulting from the addition of the first two rows of data provides a general indication of the extent of 'social-structural anchoring' of the vote in each country. As has been noted elsewhere (Gunther and Montero 2001b), Spain's electorate was rather deeply divided along class and religious lines (although by 1993 this social-structural anchoring had weakened substantially after reaching a peak in 1982). Adding together the combined impact of the socio-demographic control variables (age, education, gender, and affluence) and religiosity, the data in Table 7.7 indicate that these social-cleavage variables explain 23.5 per cent in the variance in the vote for parties of the left versus right in the 1993 election. In that earlier study, Greece emerged with the weakest social-structural anchoring—which is not surprising given the absence of a tradition of conflict over religion and the relatively egalitarian distribution of wealth. This is reflected in our finding that all of these social-cleavage variables combined explained just 3.6 per cent of the variance in the vote. The American electorate is also quite weakly divided along class lines, while partisan polarization among religious denominations (excluding from the analysis African-American Evangelical Protestants, since that variable measured the electoral impact of ethnicity more than it did religion, *per se*) was moderate, but increasing substantially in recent years. The net result is that religion and the socio-demographic control variables explained 12.5 per cent of the variance in the vote for George Bush versus John Kerry in 2004. Uruguay was roughly equal to Spain with regard to the impact of socio-demographic factors, but the less polarizing impact of religion gave it an intermediate level of 17.3 per cent of variance explained by these social-cleavage variables.

When we turn our attention to the added explanatory power of these values and intermediation variables (i.e. subtracting out the incremental R^2 contributed by the socio-demographic control variables and religiosity), our ability to predict the vote increases dramatically. As noted above, the addition of the values clusters to these equations increases their predictive power by 11.8 per cent in Spain, 15.3 per cent in Uruguay, 19.3 per cent in Greece, and 38.2 per cent in the United States. In the latter three cases, the explanatory power of the values variables was substantially greater than that of the socio-demographic and religious variables combined. Our three sets of intermediation variables also substantially enhance our ability to predict the vote for parties of the left versus right—by an additional 16.4 per cent of the variance in the vote in the United States, 23.3 per cent in Uruguay, 24.5 per cent in Spain, and fully 28.5 per cent in Greece—even after the impact of all of the preceding values and social-structural variables had been taken into consideration.

As noted in the introduction, these intermediation variables have been almost completely neglected in the existing literatures on electoral behaviour ever since the final book published by Lazarsfeld and Merton (1954), while the values variables have, to our knowledge, never been analysed in this way before. And yet we find that the addition of these two largely unexamined sets of independent variables increases the explanatory power of the standard social-cleavage model of the vote by an additional 36.3 per cent of the variance in the vote in Spain, 38.6 per cent in Uruguay (over twice the percentage of variance explained by the standard social-cleavage variables), 47.8 per cent in Greece (over 13 times the total predictive power of the social-cleavage model!), and an astounding 54.6 per cent in the United States (over four times the explanatory power of the religious and socio-demographic variables combined).

A Theoretical Framework

How can we account for the greatly varying findings that have emerged from this examination of socio-political values and their links to electoral politics? Why have these values clusters crystallized so clearly in some countries, while our dimensional analysis clearly revealed that in other countries they do not hold together in any coherent manner? And why do these value clusters have such a significant impact on electoral behaviour in some countries and not in others? Let us address these crucial questions by setting forth a speculative interpretation of the historical origins and perpetuation of these values clusters, and their impact on electoral behaviour. We shall then examine data from a final round of multi-variate analysis that tests some of the spin-off implications of our theoretical framework.

We hypothesize that these cross-national differences are explained by four political processes. The first involves the historical origins of these value-cleavage lines in conflict among political and intellectual elites. These conflicts made certain sets of values in certain countries politically relevant, and polarized society along those lines at some point in the past. Conflict over the direction of political systems in the future evolution of society is a universal in the realm of politics, but the exact nature of these conflicts varies substantially over time and among geographical regions. In some countries, it may pit religious elites against anti-clericals (such as in several Continental European countries) while in others (such as Hong Kong or the United States prior to the 1980s), it does not. The politicization of values and their crystallization into distinct clusters among segments of the population should be expected to vary accordingly from one country to the next, although the clustering of values in countries with similar political histories should be expected to be more alike than those which had followed greatly different historical trajectories.

These differing patterns of political conflict may help to explain why some values are politicized and clustered together within a given polity at some key historical moment, but why do they persist as lines of political division (or conversely, as the basis of the internal unity of politically active groups) even after the original conflict had faded or disappeared altogether, sometimes even centuries later? The formulation of political ideologies reflecting these cleavage lines is a key variable that addresses this question. In their efforts to mobilize their supporters, political elites and their intellectual allies incorporate specific appeals into elaborate arguments rooted in clearly definable socio-political values.

Most commonly, these ideologies are formulated by proponents of sweeping social, political, or economic change rather than by defenders of the status quo. In the case of Western Europe in the eighteenth and early nineteenth centuries, when classical liberalism was being elaborated as an ideological basis for opposition to the *ancien régime* and its replacement by a more individualistic, free-market society, the old order was not defended in its time by those advancing a persuasive intellectual argument, notwithstanding a few exceptions (such as the writings of Edmund Burke). Instead, West European conservatism emerged as a coherent intellectual stance much later (in the 1860s through 1880s), in reaction against a greatly altered socio-political status quo. It was only around the turn of the twentieth century that Christian Democratic ideologies—inspired by *Rerum Novarum* and the corporatist reaction against both socialism and capitalism—were formulated and disseminated by new Catholic parties. And the neo-conservative movement only emerged in the late twentieth century, largely in reaction against the social welfare state (and, in the United States, against abortion and the alleged erosion of 'family values').

Two other value clusters—Socialism and Modern Social Democracy—were also perpetuated and disseminated on the basis of ideologies formulated in the mid-nineteenth to mid-twentieth centuries in reaction against the excesses of free-market capitalism. It is noteworthy that the one set of values included in our initial template that has failed to crystallize into a coherent cluster at the mass level, postmaterialism, lacks a concise ideological statement of any kind. Indeed, as Kitschelt (1989) and others have noted, 'Green' or 'Left-libertarian' movements/parties are extraordinarily heterogeneous and loose aggregations whose members are united by what they oppose rather than what they propose to put in its place. Thus, the articulation of a clear ideological statement appears to be a key ingredient in the crystallization of values into the clusters we have analysed in this chapter.

A third crucial variable is the embrace of that ideology by an organized political party. The consequence of this institutionalization process is the 'freezing' of these patterns of value conflict and their perpetuation over time. Indeed, once officially adopted as a party's defining principles, it is often difficult to modify a party's ideology to fit with altered social conditions even when powerful arguments are advanced about the contemporary irrelevance of the original *Weltanschauung* underpinning its programmatic commitments and about the extent to which an outmoded ideological orientation is alienating potential voters. This point is clearly illustrated by the protracted internal struggles within West European Socialist parties in the second half of the twentieth century. Despite Anthony Crosland's powerful critique in the 1950s, for example, it was not until four decades later that the Labour Party abandoned its commitment to nationalization of the means of economic production. Conversely, a second reason for the absence of a coherent or politically relevant postmaterialism cluster in the preceding waves of analysis is that it has never been embraced and articulated as a distinctive political ideology by any significant political parties in the countries examined here (with the partial exception of the IU coalition in Spain). At the same time, many of its core environmentalist themes and demands for increased citizen participation have been 'coopted' by previously established social democratic parties, and even by some centre-right parties (see Klingemann, Hofferbert, and Budge 1994).

How are ideologically rooted value packages conveyed from intellectual and political elites to ordinary citizens? It is highly unlikely, for example, that all but the tiniest minority of socialist-party voters have ever read Marx, and yet somehow key elements of Marxist views on society and economy have been embraced by Greek and Spanish voters. This is where the fourth crucial set of variables comes in—involving intermediation and the specific channels through which politically relevant information flows to voters. Parties, obviously, play a key role in formally adopting one ideology or another, or by systematically incorporating its programmatic precepts into its electoral-mobilization messages. Repeated, year after year, these appeals can be internalized by their respective sets of supporters as justifications for their voting decisions. But by the late twentieth centuries, the era of the mass-membership party had waned, and parties could no longer count on direct proselytizing at public meetings and campaign rallies. Other channels of communication must be relied on.

Allied secondary organizations constitute one important conduit for value-based partisan appeals. In many Western European countries, explicit links between parties and the church have provided channels for the flow of this biased political information, especially in the case of Catholic Action lay organizations and the like. In the United States since the 1980s, close contacts between the Republican Party and fundamentalist churches and pastors, and the incorporation of religious-based themes into public statements and electoral appeals have achieved the same result. On the left, trade unions have often served as 'transmission belts' for the flow of partisan information and for the mobilization of working-class voters. We have seen some evidence that these organizational channels remain important, but impressionistic evidence has suggested that their electoral impact has declined over the past several decades.

The mass communications media have increased in importance as the mobilization capacity of secondary associations has declined. In this chapter, we have examined the electoral impact of newspapers, television, and radio, and we found that their significance is, in some instances, quite substantial. In Greece, reading a politically biased newspaper has a considerable impact on voting choice—second only to the values clusters that have been the principal focus of this chapter—even after controls for a broad array of variables have been introduced.

Thus, our efforts to explain these cross-national differences involves four political processes. The first is historical, in which the principal actors are political and intellectual elites who convert values and beliefs into overt lines of political conflict. The second is intellectual, in which sociopolitical values are embedded within clearly articulated political ideologies. The third is organizational, involving the freezing of ideological commitments within political parties (cf. Lipset and Rokkan 1967a). And the fourth involves intermediation, specifically, the mobilization strategies and behaviour of parties and allied organizations relating to the ongoing dissemination of these politicized value orientations among segments of the population. In short, political and intellectual elites may have been the key actors that politicized values and polarized society along those lines in the past, while political parties and their supportive intermediation channels are the key actors in making historical conflicts relevant to present-day political behaviour. If elites had clashed over entirely different sets of values in the past, if these value conflicts were not embedded within political ideologies and adopted by political parties, and/or if communications media fail to convey this partisan-biased information, then we should not expect to find a similar clustering of socio-political values. Let us briefly re-examine our empirical findings with regard to several of these key political processes.

We began our examination of these issues by setting forth, in highly simplified terms, the emergence of classical-liberal perspectives as a reaction against a status quo defined by monarchical authoritarianism, aristocratic privilege, established state religion, and mercantilist or statist economic policies. When classical liberalism, in turn, had become the dominant ideology underpinning politics and economics in the mid-nineteenth century, the most significant ideology formulated in reaction against its excesses stressed economic equality, solidarity among the working classes, and collectivist approaches to ownership of the means of production, with Marxist socialism as the most politically relevant variation on these themes in most Western European countries. Contrasting somewhat with the maximalist socialist agenda, the more moderate, reformist social-democratic alternative to the excesses of free market capitalism, while not fundamentally challenging the basis of that economic order, called on government to formulate policies which would ameliorate the undesirable social consequences of that economic system. Finally, in reaction against primacy given to economic development by classical liberalism, socialism, and social democracy alike, postmaterialists emerged in the late twentieth century to emphasize values involving protection of a threatened environment, and the autonomy of individuals against established organizations. These four clusters of attitudes defined the Western European template with which we initiated our analysis.

We quickly discovered, however, that postmaterialism constituted an extremely weak attitudinal cluster in two of these countries (Spain and Hong Kong), and simply failed to emerge as a coherent stand-alone value configuration in the others. Instead, in accord with political programmes that have been articulated and implemented by modern social democratic parties, these post-materialist values are combined with the original social democratic commitment to the provision of government services and social assistance. In short, these findings do not provide substantial support for postmaterialist theory, but they do fit well with the reality of contemporary partisan politics in many countries.

Among the cases examined here, Spain most closely conforms to this pattern of value-based conflict over the course of its political history. Conflict between traditionalist conservatives and liberals was manifested in three civil wars (the Carlist Wars of 1833–40, 1846–48, and 1872–75), which strongly politicized a deep religious cleavage in Spanish society.

In the final decades of the nineteenth century, a Socialist Party (Partido Socialista Obrero Español [PSOE]) emerged to challenge the two liberal parties that dominated the Restoration Monarchy (1825–1923). The PSOE (whose statement of ideological principles included some segments written by Karl Marx himself), however, was not the only challenger on the left to challenge the status quo in the early twentieth century. It was joined by powerful Anarchist and Anarchosyndicalist movements (which were the dominant leftist forces in many parts of the country). Traditionalist conservatives, liberals, and the left (in addition to Basque and Catalan nationalist parties) engaged in increasingly rancorous conflict throughout the Second Republic (1931–36), which culminated in civil war and eventually a right-wing authoritarian dictatorship that lasted until 1975. When democracy was restored in 1977, political parties emerged representing traditionalist conservatism (Alianza Popular, which eventually moved towards the centre and was reborn as the Partido Popular [PP]), Socialism (the PSOE and, to some extent, the Partido Comunista de España), and liberalism (whose adherents were scattered among the electorates supporting the Unión de Centro Democrático, the PSOE and, by the late 1980s, the PP). And like all West European Socialist parties, the PSOE was undergoing a transformation that eventually led to the predominance of Modern Social Democracy as its ideological orientation and guiding principles in government (1982–96). The importance of this institutionalization of value cleavages is reflected in the fact that all traces of Anarchism and Anarchosyndicalism (which had been extremely powerful in the 1930s) are completely absent. By their very nature, neither Anarchism nor Anarchosyndicalism establish political parties; accordingly, there was no institution which would perpetuate and disseminate these socio-political values over the following decades. The data we have examined in this preliminary study reveal a striking conformity of the structure of Spanish mass opinion with the hypothesized patterns. And these ideological cleavages have proven to be impressively durable, persisting until well after organized conflict over a particular value had abated. Conflict over the traditionalist conservative/liberal value dimension (or, in social-structural terms, along the lines of the religious cleavage) remains the single most powerful factor differentiating parties from the left and right at the national level, despite efforts by leaders of both parties of the left and right to sidestep the explosive potential inherent in these issues. Concerning less traditionally divisive issues, however, the extent of polarization regarding protection of the environment and continuing support for the social welfare state is quite moderate, accurately reflecting the moderate and incrementalist policy stands of the two major parties prior to the 1993 election.

The political development of Greece followed an entirely different trajectory. No division over the predominant status of the Orthodox Church has emerged to affect patterns of partisanship and interparty conflict (at least not since the mutual ethnic cleansing of Greece and what is today Turkey in the early twentieth century). Accordingly, the extent to which the Greek party system is divided between supporters of traditionalist conservatism, on the one hand, and liberalism, on the other, is much less than we observed in Spain. Nonetheless, the early-twentieth-century conflicts surrounding the liberal reforms of Eleftherios Venezelos have left a lasting mark on Greek politics, as manifested in the clustering of the three variables that we hypothesized would constitute this ideological orientation. Of far greater polarizing impact are interparty divisions along the left–right continuum, as well as along the lines of the 'socialism' dimension. As has often been argued, this cleavage is a legacy of the deep divisions between a communist left and conservative governments during the civil war of the late 1940s and under the quasi-democratic regime that existed during the period between 1949 and the colonels' coup in 1967. Consistent with this interpretation, it is notewor-thy in Table 7.6b that polarization along this ideological dimension is most extreme with regard to those supporting the communist KKE and the conservative Nea Demokratia. In contrast, the Pan-Hellenic Socialist Movement (PASOK), the principal party to the left centre, is supported by an electorate that is not substantially different from the Greek population as a whole concerning this attitudinal domain. The PASOK electorate is also indistinguishable from the full sample of Greek survey respondents with regard to our 'modern social democracy' dimension—a reflection of the moderate, centre-left policies that this party has adopted over the past decade. This lack of polarization of the PASOK electorate is, in part, a result of the complete absence of a 'socialist' party in Greece prior to the mid-1970s. Accordingly, the party's founder, Andreas Papandreou, was able to create a broadly eclectic 'catch-all' party through the unification of a number of different centrist and leftist groups who had opposed the colonels' authoritarian regime: these included socialists, ex-communists, and 'technocrats', as well as individuals who had been members of the populist centre Union, led in the 1960s by Papandreou's father George (see Puhle 2001). The heterogeneous nature of this electoral clientele is reflected in the lack of polarization of the PASOK electorate along the lines of this Socialism dimension.

Uruguay's development followed a 'Western' trajectory completely atypical for Latin American countries.[26] It was characterized by early (although 'dependent') modernization, a stable democracy (at least until the late 1960s), and a strong and active civil society with the liberal and pluralistic values of European immigrants. Its ethnically and socially homogeneous population has been only moderately divided by a cleavage between capital and labour. The boom of its cattle and grain-based export economy which continued until the 1950s laid the ground for ambitious distributive policies in the first three decades of the twentieth century, giving Uruguay the world's first modern welfare state in the 1930s. The 'Uruguayan model' also included the early establishment of a highly participatory and competitive party democracy and a 'party state'. Two well-organized traditional parties, the Colorados and the Blancos (or Nacionalistas), were successful until the 1960s in maintaining high rates of participation and electoral mobilization, and in continuously reforming the political institutions. But the Uruguayan model fell into crisis when revenues from traditional export goods began to shrink after the end of the Korean War, leading to cutbacks in its distributive politics. This, in turn, increasingly undermined the legitimacy of Uruguay's particular form of democratic politics, leading ultimately to the establishment of an authoritarian regime dominated by the military and their technocrats in 1973. In 1985, however, a negotiated transition brought democracy back. The deeply rooted democratic consensus that the military was unable to erase contributed substantially to a rapid consolidation of the new democracy in the early 1990s, which, in the Latin American context, is a unique success story. Despite the electoral and institutional reforms of 1996 and the emergence of two minor, more 'modern' political parties, the country's economic recovery and its ability to adapt to the demands of a more globalized economy were impeded (until the realigning election of 2004) by the persistence of the two traditional parties, institutional conservatism, entrenched corporatist, and bureaucratic practices, and some of the peculiarities of the old Uruguayan model. The structure of value cleavages in Uruguay reflects this political trajectory: the 'modern social democracy' cluster does not divide parties, given the widespread consensus in support of the long-standing welfare state, and the main partisan battle lines pit the 'participatory socialism' of the new parties (Espacio Progresista and Nuevo Espacio) against the 'conservatism' of the two traditional parties (Nacional and Colorado).

The pronounced polarization of the American electorate is a product of deep divisions and increasing rancour among rival party elites over the past two decades. In Congress, where genteel 'folkways' once constrained the expression of conflict, interparty civility has broken down since the 1980s, accelerating after Newt Gingrich's election as Speaker of the House, the attempts to impeach President Clinton, and especially over the course of the George W. Bush administration. This elite-level polarization has acquired deep roots in the political culture as a result of sustained efforts by the Republican Party to mobilize religious fundamentalists as the party's core constituency. The issue of abortion was heavily politicized, in sharp contrast with the avoidance of this potentially divisive issue by political elites of both left and right in most other Western democracies. Interparty conflict has also focused on the social-welfare state and even environmental protection policies, which in most other Western democracies have both been consensually embraced by parties of left and right. What emerged by the end of this process is a sharply polarized political system within which partisan rancour and incivility has reached a level almost unique among contemporary established democracies. This dramatic transformation underlines the importance of political elites in determining the character of political conflict, and undermines the credibility of socio-economic reductionist arguments about how socio-economic modernization will culminate in 'the decline of ideology'.

Conversely, in the case of Chile the strategies and behaviour of present-day political elites help to explain why a cleavage between traditional religious conservatives and more secular socialists has not been reflected in patterns of electoral conflict. The exploratory factor analysis with which we began this empirical study revealed a tight clustering of values within the traditional-conservative domain, and the standard deviations presented in Table 7.1 suggested that opinions with regard to these issues were more sharply divided than in any other country explored in this chapter. Given the existence of a highly religious population and an explicitly confessional Christian Democratic party, on one side, and significant socialist and communist parties (which are typically anti-clerical), on the other, one might have anticipated a deep partisan division over this issue. Instead, opposition to Pinochet's authoritarian regime involved close collaboration between Socialists and Christian Democrats in a pro-democratic alliance with various liberal and other groups. Moreover, as Tironi and his colleagues have argued (2000), one of the key events that contributed to the unravelling of support for Pinochet's authoritarian regime was the popular mobilization surrounding a visit to Chile by the Pope. Thus, traditionally conservative religious Chileans saw no incompatibility between their religious beliefs and support for democracy, while secular or potentially anti-clerical Chileans saw that those with strong religious beliefs were their allies in the struggle for democracy. This alliance continued into the post-Pinochet democratic era, and the existence of the Concertación coalition has substantially contributed to a reduction in the divisive potential of the religious cleavage in Chilean society. Whatever religious cleavage exists in Chilean society runs through the Concertación coalition, rather than dividing it from the right-wing opposition parties,[27] preventing the predominantly religious Traditional Conservative/liberal dimension from being reflected in patterns of partisan conflict between left and right.

The other countries analysed in this chapter, Hungary and Hong Kong, followed greatly different political trajectories, and were therefore not affected by these same kinds of ideology-crystallizing forces. Accordingly, the Western European template breaks down as an adequate map of value configurations. Since the battery of questionnaire items used in this multivariate analysis was derived specifically from that template, this study did not find a coherent structure of values in these other countries. The next stage of this research project (CNEP III, within which several Asian and African countries have been incorporated), therefore, will add to this Western European core a number of additional value questions that should have greater resonance and political relevance in a wider array of countries.

Even within the constraints of the older CNEP II core questionnaire, we found in an earlier chapter of this volume that a different kind of value—involving support for democracy as the most preferable form of governance—can have considerable relevance for electoral behaviour. Indeed, the presence of a 'democracy' cleavage deeply divides the party systems of both Hong Kong and Chile. As we saw in Chapter 2, Chileans supporting the Concertación coalition and supporters of the Democratic Party in Hong Kong overwhelmingly endorse democracy as 'the best form of government for a country like ours'. In contrast, strikingly high percentages of those who voted for the pro-Pinochet opposition in Chile and the pro-Beijing DAB in Hong Kong either openly endorsed non-democratic forms of government or indicated indifference towards the type of political regime that would govern their countries.

Two conclusions can be drawn regarding the relationship between attitudes towards democracy and the value clusters we have analysed in this chapter. The first is that both can have a substantial impact on partisan preferences. The second is that the emergence of a link between fundamental support for democracy and lines of partisan conflict is entirely contingent on the stands taken by key party leaders during the transition to democracy. Where outgoing authoritarian elites collaborate with or (at least) do not oppose the process of democratization (as in the cases of Spain, Hungary, Uruguay, and the 'hierarchical' military elite in Greece), no politically significant division over support for democracy will emerge. Conversely, as Gunther, Montero, and Torcal argued in Chapter 2, where the elites of the predecessor regime oppose democratization (as in Bulgaria and Chile), or where prominent political elites make clear their preference for some non-democratic alternative (as in the case of the pro-Beijing DAB in Hong Kong), partisan competition will be rooted at least in part in conflict over democracy. It is important to note that this role of elites in converting democratic values into a politically salient line of partisan division fits perfectly with the theoretical framework advanced in this chapter.

Nonetheless, despite the similarity in causal processes, empirical analyses indicate that attitudes towards democracy and the socio-political value clusters explored in this chapter occupy separate attitudinal domains. Only in Spain was support for democracy weakly linked with three of the four values scales at an acceptable level of statistical significance. In other countries, there were no significant correlations between these orientations towards democracy and the other socio-political values.[28] In short, political disaffection and fundamental democratic orientations do not appear to be embedded in these other basic values structures.

Values, Left–Right Orientations, and Party Identification

Having elaborated our theoretical framework and described the ways in which our empirical findings can be interpreted in light of differing political trajectories over the preceding decades, let us test hypotheses linking these value clusters and party identification or left–right self-placement, which many scholars function as repositories of cumulative experiences and historical memories, and as conceptual devices that help to simplify voting choice. In Tables 7.6a–d, we presented detailed information about the relationship between these value clusters and the vote for individual parties in Spain, Greece, Uruguay, and the United States. Let us now examine the extent to which these value clusters are embedded within these broader attitudinal orientations.

In Table 7.9, we present the correlations (Pearson's r) among these value clusters, left–right self-placement, and identification with parties of the left or right. As can be seen, the Traditional and other 'conservatism' value clusters are strongly associated with left–right self-designations in Uruguay, Spain and, especially, the United States, and are moderately correlated in Greece (which has historically lacked a divisive religious cleavage). The relationships between the socialism clusters (Socialism and Participatory Socialism) and the Modern Democrats cluster in the United States, on the one hand, and left–right self-placement, on the other, are a mirror image of the preceding findings: this relationship is the strongest in the United States and Greece, while it is somewhat weaker in Uruguay and Spain (whose Socialist party in 1993 had become the quintessential

Table 7.9 Correlations (Pearson's r) among value clusters, party identification, and left–right self-designation

Spain

	Party ID	TradCon	Socialism	PostMat	Soc.Dem
Traditional Conservatism	.24***				
Socialism	.17***	.11***			
Postmaterialism	.01	.16***	.08**		
Modern Social Dem.	.02	.14***	.08**	.46***	
Left–right self-desig.	.47***	.40***	.22***	.07*	.12***

United States

	Party ID	TradCon	ModDem
Fundamentalist Conservatism	.42***		
Modern Democrats	.44***	.19**	
Left–right self-desig.	.64***	.57***	.46***

Greece

	Party ID	TradCon	Socialism	Soc.Dem
Traditional Conservatism	.12**			
Socialism	.29***	.10**		
Modern Social Dem.	.08*	−.03	−.02	
Left–right self-desig.	.59***	.25***	.33***	.15***

Uruguay

	Party ID	Conserv.	Part.Social
Conservatism	.10**		
Participatory Socialism	.06*	.17***	
Left–right self-desig.	.25***	.40***	.16***

* Significant at .05; ** Significant at .001; *** Significant at .000.

catch-all party). The Modern Social Democracy clusters in Spain and Greece (where conservative parties have not sought to dismantle the social welfare state) are weakly associated with left–right distinctions. And the postmaterialism cluster (which emerged from our dimensional analysis of these countries only for Spain) is very weakly linked to left–right orientations. It is interesting to note that party identification is more weakly associated with these clusters than is left–right self-designation—even in the United States. To a considerable degree, the lower score for party identification is a result of the relatively small portion of the electorate in some of these countries who identify with parties: the percentage of respondents stating that they identified with one of the major nationwide political parties of the left or right was 52 per cent in the United States, 44 per cent in Greece, 31 per cent in Spain, and just 20 per cent in Uruguay.

However it is measured, these value clusters are strongly related to left–right and partisan orientations. This is particularly true of left–right self-placement. When the respondent's position on the left–right scale was treated as a dependent variable in an OLS multiple regression equation, with the value scales entered into the equation as independent variables, the resulting R^2 was .43 in Spain, .42 in Uruguay, .37 in the United States, and .35 in Greece. That is, between 35 and 43 per cent of the variance in left–right self-designation is 'explained' by these values clusters.[29]

When we turn our attention back to the analysis of voting decisions, it is necessary to set aside our interest in the left–right continuum, and restrict our focus to party identification. This is for two reasons. The first is that there is an extremely high level of colinearity between left–right self-placement and identification with a political party (amounting to .64 in the United States and .59 in Greece), such that entering both as independent variables in the same equation would be methodologically problematic. Secondly, since the dependent variable in our analysis is vote for party or parties of the left versus party or parties of the right, to include left–right self-placement as an independent variable would verge on tautology.

When we enter party identification as an independent variable in a step following the inclusion of values, religion, and socio-demographic controls (see Table 7.10), we increase the percentage of the variance in the vote explained by an impressive 36.3 per cent in Greece, by more moderate levels of 19.5 and 18.7 per cent in Spain and the United States, respectively, and by a very modest 6.6 per cent in Uruguay (where only one voter out of every five claims to identify with a party). These data indicate that, even though the values dimensions explored previously in this chapter are 'embedded' within both left–right self-designations and party ID, psychological identification with a particular political party involves some additional characteristics that have an independent influence over voting decisions.

Table 7.10 Multivariate Logit analyses of vote for parties of the left vs. right: incremental and cumulative R^2 (percentage of variance explained)

	Spain	Greece	Uruguay	United States
Sociodemographic controls	.116	.004	.112	.018
Religion	.119	.032	.061	.107
Value Scales[a]	.118	.193	.153	.382
Party ID	.195	.363	.066	.187
Organizational contact	.014	.007	.080	.010
Media bias	.017	.043	.028	.012
Discussant bias	.111	.033	.073	.041
Cumulative R^2 (% explained)	**.690**	**.675**	**.573**	**.757**
N	814	664	440	1,138

[a] For Spain, the value scales entered into the equation in this second step were Traditional Conservatism, Socialism, Modern Social Democracy, and Postmaterialism; for Greece, they were Traditional Conservatism, Socialism, and Modern Social Democracy; for Uruguay, Conservatism and Participatory Socialism; and for the United States (Ohio), Traditional Conservatism and Modern Democrats.

In the last steps of this analysis, we return to an exploration of political intermediation. Earlier in this chapter (see Table 7.8), we examined the bivariate relationships between these intermediation variables and the vote. We then included these intermediation variables in multivariate equation—along with religion, the socio-demographic controls, and values scales—so that the effects of those other variables could be 'controlled'. By ordering the analysis in this manner, we explicitly attributed any 'overlapping' variance to those other variables, thereby ignoring the possibility that, over the long term, biased flows of information through those channels might help to mould socio-political values. Nonetheless, we saw that these intermediation variables still had a very strong impact on voting decisions, with incremental contributions to the percentage of the variance in the vote ranging from 16.4 per cent in the United States to 28.5 per cent in Greece. Let us adopt the same approach to measure the impact of these intermediation processes after controlling for the effects of partisan identification.

It should be noted that this ordering of variables entered into the equation implies that any overlapping variance is strictly the product of 'selective exposure'—that is, that respondents choose to read certain newspapers or watch/listen to news programmes that will support their previously established partisan preferences. Somewhat less plausibly, it is also assumed that individuals choose which organizations they will join (even labour unions and professional associations) and which individuals they will discuss politics with (even family members) on the basis of their partisan orientations. Since this approach completely ignores any influences these biased information flows might have with regard to the development of partisan attachments (the reverse order of causality), the resulting incremental R^2 figures represent the *most conservative* estimate of the impact of intermediation on the vote. Given the inability of single-wave cross-sectional data to measure the long-term impact of such re-socialization processes, this analytical strategy is reasonable if not unavoidable.

As can be seen in the data presented in the last three rows of Table 7.10, the apparent impact of these intermediation variables is reduced by the prior imposition of controls for party ID but remains quite substantial. These results suggest that the impact of intermediation channels 'overlaps' somewhat with that of party ID, but even this most conservative estimate of their impact indicates that they still exert enough influence over the voting choice as to determine the outcome of otherwise close elections. In the United States, these intermediation variables explained an additional 6.3 per cent of the variance in the vote for John Kerry versus George Bush (in an election whose margin of victory was less than 3%), while in Greece, Spain, and Uruguay they added 8.3, 14.2, and 18.1 per cent, respectively, to the predictive power of these multivariate equations. These findings are consistent with the theoretical framework set forth in this chapter.

Concluding Observations

The socio-political values that we have explored in this chapter can serve both as sources of continuity and change, depending on the value stands embraced by parties and their leaders over time. We have argued that the occurrence of elite conflicts at some critical point in a country's history is a prerequisite for the politicization of values and the coherence of their clustering together. But we further argued that in order for these value clusters to be relevant to electoral behaviour, they must be embedded within a political ideology, embraced by a political party, and disseminated by that party and its allied intermediation channels over the following decades. In short, these value orientations become closely entwined with political ideology and with partisanship, but they do so in a manner which is substantially affected by the images, programmatic appeals, and electoral mobilization strategies of political elites and their parties. In countries whose democratic historical trajectory is long and occasionally interrupted by regime changes, candidates and parties may come and go but these values-based orientations may be perpetuated by embedding within more durable partisan orientations. Conversely, even in long-established democracies, such as the United States, political parties can adopt mobilization strategies involving these values that have a direct bearing on their changing electoral fortunes—shifting their bases of support by emphasizing different values and, perhaps, increasing their respective shares of the vote accordingly. But they may do so at the expense of polarizing a country's political culture and debasing the quality of democratic accountability and discourse.

8

Conclusions: processes of intermediation, electoral politics, and political support in old and new democracies

Hans-Jürgen Puhle, José Ramón Montero, and Richard Gunther

This book is about processes of political intermediation and their impact on electoral politics and the mechanisms of political support in old and new democracies. It has undertaken systematic, cross-national analyses of three themes that are central to the study of democratic politics. One refers to the various ways and modes in which political attitudes, opinions, and values are interrelated, connected to partisan preferences, and influenced by political biases. The second addresses the different channels through which messages flow from parties and candidates to voters, and the ways in which these information flows affect voting decisions and political participation. And the third focus concerns the various forms of political support (or its absence, respectively) in a democracy, the mass-level attitudinal grounding (or even prerequisites) of democratic consolidation, and the relationship between opinions and beliefs regarding satisfaction with the performance of a particular democratic system, on the one hand, and fundamental support for democracy, on the other. While all these three themes are important for old and new democracies alike, obviously the third one is particularly important (and eventually can even become crucial) for newly established or re-established democracies.

In this concluding chapter, we try to summarize the principal findings of this book, put them into a broader perspective and explore their relative achievements and limitations. First, we address the basic questions that have structured our enquiry into the relationship between political intermediation and democracy, and the most important answers we have found. Then, the findings of the chapters of this volume are discussed in greater detail, first with regard to citizens' fundamental orientations towards democracy and the impact of the mass media, followed by references to the weight and influence of secondary associations and social networks, to the factors of biases and partisanship, and to the role of intermediation in the complex processes in which opinions, preferences and values are transformed into politicized, and eventually mobilizing, positions and decisions. Finally, we reflect on the extent to which the findings of this book, especially with regard to the utility of a renewed focus on information intermediation might enhance the explanatory potential of social science, and speculate about how new research questions and theoretical issues may have been triggered by trying to answer the older ones.

On the whole, and besides the more particular findings and impacts discussed here, the essential message of this book also implies that political intermediation and its repercussions are more complicated, and in themselves more mediated and filtered than it had been assumed; that intermediation is a set of complex multistage processes characterized by many intervening factors and constellations, embedded within a given economic, cultural, social, and political context, with distinctive historical trajectories behind it, but open to adaptation and change; that in these processes agency and contents matter very much, hence, that elites and political objectives are important. It should also be noted that although our findings allow us to make some generalizations with regard to the different degrees of the impacts of the different forms and channels of intermediation, for example, their categorical scope and meaning remains often limited, there are also many exceptions, and change over time can be crucial. This also applies to the various differences between 'old' and 'new' democracies, for example, in the degree of flexibility or malleability of the mechanisms of intermediation, or in the general impact and weight of the media: The differences exist, but they have turned out to be less clear-cut and categorical than had been assumed.

Electoral Intermediation and Democracy: Some Questions and Answers

As noted in the Introduction, the CNEP I was launched in 1990, and its first round which was based on surveys undertaken in 1990 and 1992, focused on a limited number of established democracies (Germany, Great Britain, the United States, and Japan; in 1996 Italy was added). Since its subsequent extension, in a second round during the 1990s, to a number of countries which had recently transited from authoritarian or post-totalitarian rule to democracy (Spain, Chile, Uruguay, Greece, Bulgaria, and Hungary), and the inclusion of the special case of Hong Kong, the general interest of the project has been particularly guided by a number of basic and still unanswered questions concerning the relationship between political intermediation, on the one hand, and democratic legitimacy, on the other, in old and new democracies. For a number of reasons, and considering the nature of the data available, the focus of the chapters presented in this volume had to be operationalized and narrowed down to some extent: from political to electoral intermediation (i.e. intermediation around election processes), on the one hand, and from the broad and all-encompassing syndrome of democratic legitimacy to the somewhat smaller and more manageable, but still rather complex and ambitious issue of political support and support for democracy, on the other. So this book is *not* a conventional elections study. It is rather a detailed examination of the mechanisms of electoral intermediation and their impact on political mobilization and electoral behaviour, starting out from the processes of intermediation and their relationship with the voters' perceived interests, their normative and ideological backgrounds, preferences and values clusters, on the one hand, and with political actors, elites, institutions, and some of the relevant factors influencing and framing democratic consolidation or stability, on the other. The basic categories are therefore values and partisan preferences, the flows of information, their agents and contents, and turnout.

Our focus on political intermediation has allowed us to undertake a new and detailed examination of the linkages between citizens and their political elites and institutions. In this book, we have been particularly concerned with three different types of linkages. One involves the intermediation of secondary associations (i.e. trade unions, religious groups, business organizations, civic groups, and so on) between citizens and political elites. A second involves direct face-to-face contacts within social networks (i.e. among family members and with neighbours, friends, or co-workers). And the third, which of course has become increasingly important in the last three decades, involves direct contacts between elites and masses through the communications media. As Morlino (2004) has underlined, the vitality and overall quality of democracy in these systems is very much a function of how well these communication functions are performed (also see Diamond and Morlino 2005). Democratic legitimacy requires certain preconditions, among which—besides a basic societal trust, a minimum consent on norms, rules, and procedures and the respective institutional prerequisites—the citizens' unequivocal support for democracy, in terms of opinion, values, attitudes, and behaviour, is of particular importance.

The central question was, how the outcomes of the various ways and modes of intermediation affect those aspects of democratic legitimacy that are reflected in terms of political support, and particularly in electoral mobilization and behaviour in old and new democracies. The comparison between established and more recent democracies, one of the basic characteristics of the design of the CNEP project, not only provides unique opportunities to test our hypotheses and findings in and under categorically different settings and conditions. It also contributes to the enlargement and refinement of our knowledge in an important, but so far underinvestigated sector of the study of political transformations: the particular impact and weight of the mechanisms of political intermediation in processes of transitions to and consolidation of democracy, or, in case, of the stabilization and entrenchment of what has recently been characterized as 'defective democracy' (cf. Merkel, Puhle et al. 2003; Merkel 2004; Puhle 2004). Particularly in the many cases of the latter, where we find a democratic electoral regime, but significant 'defects' in one or more of the other 'partial regimes' of consolidated or 'embedded' democracy (political liberties/public arena, effective power to govern, horizontal accountability, and civil rights/rule of law), the impact of the processes and mechanisms of intermediation can be of crucial importance.

To what extent do the successes, failures, or stagnation of the processes of democratization depend on the impact of the channels, actors, and contents of political intermediation? This question has so far not received much systematic attention by the literature on regime transformation and democratization, and the few existing answers are deceptively simplistic. This is most surprising, as almost all of the major approaches to the study of democratic consolidation, when defining the relevant factors, dimensions, or partial regimes of consolidation, have, among other things, referred to various subjects and areas where important aspects of intermediation and their impact for political support come in. We can find them, among others, in the dimensions of attitudinal and behavioural consolidation (cf. Gunther, Diamandouros, and Puhle 1995), in the arena of civil society, the extent of mobilization, the mechanisms of support, or in the impact of the long-range trajectories of development of particular countries and their characteristic constellations, for example, for the particular degree of authoritarian or bureaucratic traditions in a given society, for the composition and legal status of the various media, or for what, in our volume, Bellucci, Maraffi, and Segatti have called a country's 'associational configuration' (cf. Linz and Stepan 1996; Merkel and Puhle 1999; Puhle 2002*b*).

As argued in greater detail in the Introduction to this book, it makes sense, with questions like ours, to go back to the Columbia approach to the study of voting behaviour: it is the only one explicitly focusing on the mechanisms of intermediation as factors that may influence the voters' choice. It also recognizes that people tend to vote in groups or, better, in ecological constellations and through interactive processes, and not as isolated individuals. Hence it is, at the same time, open for the logic of the social-cleavage approach, where it might apply—though increasingly in residual dimensions and forms—and for integrating the rich evidence collected along the lines of the Michigan school. Both cleavages and values, identifications and 'feelings' are important and can have a high explanatory potential provided that they are not conceived as 'crystallized', static 'facts', but rather as the outcomes of interactions and as dynamic processes in themselves, reflecting the complex trajectories behind socio-economic and cultural contexts, 'embeddedness', and—a factor of key importance—changes over time.

Our analysis, however, has gone far beyond the traditional Columbia approach. Among other things, it has attempted to be terminologically more explicit and clearer, and to shed some light on the conceptual confusion surrounding the different components of political intermediation. It has also tried to elaborate more systematically on some of their basic indicators and on some of their most relevant stages. Moreover, we hope to have identified one of the most sought-after missing-link factors needed to explain why, in a given setting and situation, some cleavages or value orientations function as stronger anchors of partisanship than others. Here, 'politicization' makes all the difference, and has become, in various interactions and at different levels, a key element of what one day might be a multistage theory of political mobilization and voting: politicization of interests and opinions, of values, of values clusters and values cleavages (as well as residual social cleavages), of normative orientations and ideologies, of secondary associations, interactions, and affiliations of any kind. As Richard Gunther and Kuan Hsin-chi have shown in Chapter 7, politicization is to a high degree the outcome of the interactions of processes of political intermediation, and depends on many factors, contexts, contacts, and biases intervening in these processes.

In this regard, politicization of either a single issue, a set of values, or a cluster of orientations basically means relating these issues, values, or orientations to the public sphere, to electoral choice, and to political decision-making. Important here are not only the selection of politicized issues or orientations and the various filters accounting for it, but also the degree of politicization as such and the degree to which issues and orientations are politicized along partisan lines. Politicization and partisanship usually reside close to each other. One of the characteristic features of the partisan syndrome, however, is that the intermediation between individual partisanship and partisan politics through the channels of interpersonal networks, secondary associations, and the various kinds of the media potentially functions as a two-way street, even if at certain stages one or the other direction may prevail.

The evidence collected in the chapters of this volume also indicates that politicization and, finally, mobilization are products of various subsequent, at times also overlapping or intermittent, interactions of intermediation at different stages which require more detailed analysis, tests, and controls. Above all, they require a theory. A typical set of informed assumptions of such a multistage theory of political mobilization and voting (yet to be more systematically developed) may, for example, imply some of the following steps. First, a characteristic set of opinions, interests, and values of one or more individuals becomes, usually through conflict over an issue, transformed into a values cleavage. Then the values cleavage becomes politicized and subsequently built into a more comprehensive ideology which then, in turn, has to be adopted by a political party or a candidate in order to have further repercussions. The adopted ideology containing the politicized values cleavage then is fed into the various channels of intermediation (with different impacts). Whether the individual, in the end, becomes mobilized or not by the mediated message, depends on his or her selective perception in another interaction in which the filters again may be values- and ideology-based. In addition to the implied general problématique of the structural change of cleavages (and values), which also requires more theoretical grounding and broader empirical tests, these mechanisms of selectivity are a key issue of which we do not know very much and should try to learn more in the next round of investigations.

The several chapters of this volume take different paths for addressing these questions and formulating their particular answers. In Chapters 2 and 3, the authors explore the various attitudinal and behavioural dimensions of democratic support, discontent and political disaffection, their relationships with intermediation, and their significance for political behaviour and democracy. Chapter 2 focuses its attention on secondary associations (especially parties and party elites) and, to a much lesser degree face-to-face discussions, while Chapter 3 presents a detailed analysis of the various mass communications media and their impact on these democratic attitudes. The fourth, fifth and sixth chapters treat electoral mobilization mechanisms as dependent variables. They examine partisan biases and their embeddedness within primary and secondary groups in society, and the mobilizational impacts of the three most important modes of intermediation through the channels of secondary associations (Chapter 4), and of the mass media and interpersonal social networks (Chapter 5). Chapter 6 takes one step farther and links these biased information flows (as well as those directly from parties) to the vote. And Chapter 7 focuses on the relationship between partisan conflict and values cleavages and explains a large variance in the vote by taking into consideration the three channels of intermediation, some usual variables related to electoral choice, and above all socio-political values clusters.

Intermediation, Political Participation, and Attitudes Towards Democracy

In Chapter 2, Richard Gunther, José Ramón Montero, and Mariano Torcal examine the attitudinal and behavioural dimensions of the relationship between modes of intermediation and support for democracy. Rejecting the far too common indiscriminate analysis of a heterogeneous set of items tapping 'attitudes towards democracy', they begin their analysis by carefully examining the dimensionality of these orientations among the citizens of seven CNEP countries. Using a variety of research techniques (including exploratory and confirmatory factor analyses and examination of bivariate correlations among items), they find that these commonly used questionnaire items cluster into three conceptually and empirically distinct groups—political discontent, political disaffection, and democratic support. They further speculate that much of the inconsistency in the findings of numerous published studies of such attitudes may be attributed to the fact that previous scholarship failed to take into account the substantial differences among these three clusters, or (as in the classic formulation by Easton [1965]) dealt with them as constituting only two attitudinal domains.

The behavioural correlates of these three clusters of attitudes are decidedly different one from another, with decidedly different implications for various facets of democratic theory and the performance of democracy. Those who hold attitudes of political discontent express their feelings by voting against the incumbent party in elections. This is perfectly in keeping with the fundamental tenets of representative democracy, and is essential for holding incumbent governments accountable for their performance in office. Those who are disaffected from politics tend to abstain from active involvement in most forms of political activity. The exception is that (at least in the seven countries whose citizens' attitudes and behaviour are examined in this chapter) they tend to vote about as regularly as citizens who are not disaffected. The broader systemic implications of this finding pertain most directly to the quality of democracy. Self-marginalization from the flow of political information through our standard intermediation channels means that these individuals possess less (and less accurate) political information on which reasoned and informed voting choices can be based. This may significantly undermine the 'accountability' dimension of democratic performance. Of greatest theoretical concern for new democracies is the finding that those who do not possess attitudes supportive of democracy tend to support anti-system political parties (at least in those political systems where anti-system parties exist). While generally low levels of democratic support may not pose a direct threat to the prospects for survival of a new regime, support for parties which directly challenge the legitimacy of that democracy may (as argued in several studies of democratic consolidation such as Gunther, Diamandouros, and Puhle 1995; Linz and Stepan 1996) present a real possibility of regime destabilization over the long term, with the simultaneous challenge to the legitimacy of the Weimar Republic from both left and ultranationalist right being the classic example. Empirical evidence of the separability of these attitudinal domains is of considerable theoretical importance, particularly with regard to common assertions in the 'democratic transitions' literature that support for democracy and regime legitimacy is directly contingent on satisfaction with its performance. We find significant and consistent evidence that it is not.

These three clusters of orientation towards democracy relate to intermediation processes in different ways. With regard to all three, however, questions of 'direction of causality' are considerable, and cannot be answered using single-wave, cross-sectional survey data of the kind on which this project is based. It is not possible to establish either temporal or causal precedence of one variable over another. The weakest link involves political discontent, except for the strong association between dissatisfaction and partisan preference or membership in a labour union supportive of a particular political party. What we cannot determine is whether political discontent leads to a decision to vote against the incumbent party, or whether a prior partisan predisposition leads individuals to evaluate the government's performance differently (with partisans of the incumbent party more favourably evaluating its performance, and opposition supporters being more critical), and that this prior partisanship determines both the level of attitudinal discontent and the vote against the government party. The case of union membership, however, is more clear cut, and is compatible with the notion of 'encapsulation' that is so nicely analysed in Chapter 4.

The statistical association between low levels of support for democracy and vote for anti-system parties is more pervasive cross-nationally (except where anti-system parties do not exist), but here, again, questions of direction of causality cloud our interpretation of the nature of this relationship. It may be that individuals not supportive of democracy are drawn to anti-system parties in the conventional sense of voting decisions following attitudinal orientations. But where do these attitudes towards democracy come from? Since the cases examined in Chapter 2 are new democracies, it is unlikely that such orientations could have been products of formal socialization since schools under the non-democratic predecessor regime typically disseminated anti-democratic cues and formal instruction. Therefore, a 'childhood-socialization' explanation of their development is not credible. Rather than being primordial, such attitudes should be seen as malleable in response to salient political events and circumstances, cues, and mobilization strategies by political elites and their supportive party organizations. In short, if this order of causality is to be entertained, then these intermediary agents—political parties—play an extremely important role in developing fundamental attitudes towards democracy. And in accord with that interpretation, Torcal's (2002c) 'transition and consolidation effect' fits very well with the cross-national patterns that emerge from this analysis. Where the elites of the non-democratic predecessor regime resisted democratization (as in Bulgaria and Chile), there is a strong correlation between vote for the parties that they or their followers created and the holding of non- or anti-democratic attitudes. Conversely, where the predecessor elites were either irrelevant to the process of democratization (as in Uruguay and Greece) or played active, constructive roles in the transition (as in Spain and Hungary), there is no such empirical relationship.

The strongest links between these attitudes towards democracy and our intermediation channels involve the disaffection cluster. But here again, the problem of endogeneity precludes a simple, straightforward interpretation of the relationship. The disaffected tend to be less exposed to political information and intermediation via secondary associations, interpersonal networks, and the media, and they are less involved in political activities except voting (in these countries, at least). But can we conclude that some previously existing disaffection leads individuals to be less exposed to these intermediation channels and involved in their various formal and informal linkages? Does non-involvement in societal organizations and politicized interpersonal networks contribute to the development of attitudes of disaffection? Or are political disaffection and social marginalization component parts of a seamless syndrome of societal alienation?

The findings discussed in Chapter 2 demonstrate the relevance of political intermediation outside electoral politics. As in new democracies those orientations have been recently formed, they do not pre-date electoral behaviour and should be seen as open to the influence and mobilization strategies of political elites, their organizations, and other intermediary agents which can play an important role in shaping the attitudes towards democracy. Moreover, the findings on the relationship between citizens' satisfaction with the performance of a democracy and their fundamental support for a democratic regime have particularly contributed important new insights into the mechanisms of legitimacy and legitimation in processes of democratic consolidation. However, they go beyond that and challenge the conventional wisdom on what may be called the support side of democracy, in that they establish the category of 'political disaffection' (regarding the democratic regime) as an autonomous attitudinal dimension distinct from more specific 'discontent' and what Easton called 'diffuse support' for democracy.

In Chapter 3, Rüdiger Schmitt-Beck and Katrin Voltmer focus on the media as agents for shaping and disseminating political orientations. Their objectives are quite ambitious: they explore the impact of exposure to the media on several aspects of political orientations and behaviour in six countries that have undergone transitions from different types of dictatorial regimes, especially with regard to interest in politics, political knowledge, evaluation of political parties, satisfaction with democracy (a key component of the previous chapter's 'political discontent' cluster), democratic support, and political participation. Their central concern is to determine if media exposure is generally supportive of democracy in these new democracies, or if it contributes to the development of a 'media-malaise' syndrome, including feelings of distrust, disaffection, apathy, or alienation. Their most general finding is that media exposure does have a substantial multifaceted impact on the development of various kinds of attitudes and that, contrary to the media-malaise hypothesis, these influences are generally positive with regard to orientations which both ground democratic support and foster citizens' political involvement. They subject the hypothesized impact of the media to a strict empirical test that generates 'conservative' estimates of the impact of the media by introducing several control variables into their multivariate analyses. For each of their six dependent variables, they undertake two rounds of blockwise multiple regression analysis. The first includes all of the controls as independent variables, and the second adds to the equations various measures of media exposure. The difference between the explanatory power of the two equations is a measure of the incremental impact of the media. None of their findings provide support for the media-malaise hypothesis, although they do find that different types of media (e.g. the high-quality press vs. tabloids, and public television vs. private TV channels) vary significantly with regard to their impact on the development of these democratic orientations. In general, Schmitt-Beck and Voltmer conclude that the media contribute to the enhancement of feelings of competence among the citizens, to political mobilization, and to mediating between two levels of democratic consolidation in linking the institutional and attitudinal dimensions. Cynicism and disenchantment, where they exist, are at least not caused by the media. Schmitt-Beck and Voltmer have found enough evidence to suggest that media effects should be conceived of as interactive processes in which individual selection and choice continues to play a crucial role, for better (in triggering the dynamic transactional processes of the 'virtuous circle') or for worse (in leaving the uninterested behind). Hence, the media 'are not created equal', and the individual medium matters very much.

Exposure to high-quality newspapers, for example, substantially increases the political knowledge of their readers. It is also associated with high levels of political involvement, although Schmitt-Beck and Voltmer issue the usual warnings about the proverbial 'chicken-and-egg' problem with regard to this finding: it is not clear from these data if quality-newspaper readership motivates political involvement, or if those who are most interested and active in politics seek out high-quality newspapers. In contrast, tabloids have much less of this kind of impact, although it is noteworthy that tabloid readership is not conducive to negative orientations towards democratic politics. Empirical findings concerning the impact of television are also quite nuanced. It varies from one type of broadcaster to another (public broadcasting vs. private sector commercial channels), and even more substantially from one country to another. Following the news on television generally contributes to political interest and seems to encourage participation, but its impact on political knowledge varies considerably from one country to another. The common denominator (as argued by Gunther and Mughan [2000*a*, 2000*b*]) is the extent to which a particular medium presents to the reader/viewer/listener a substantial amount of policy-relevant political information, as compared with superficial coverage of politics and/or a focus on non-political 'news' events or personalized trivia. Accordingly, exposure to media with a high information content (e.g. the high- or middle-quality press, as contrasted with tabloids) has a much more positive impact than those disseminating low-quality or superficial political information (e.g. many television networks), although the latter mostly seems to have no influence at all. Overall, Schmitt-Beck and Voltmer conclude that the media are better characterized as *seedmen of democracy* rather than its *gravediggers*. In particular, the impact of media exposure appears to be strongest with regard to several dimensions of what has been referred to as 'cognitive mobilization', especially with regard to political interest and knowledge, which facilitates citizen participation in democratic politics, and enables voters to make informed choices. And these aspects of political participation, in turn, directly contribute to a democratic system's capacity for holding political elites accountable for their performance in office. Finally, Schmitt-Beck and Voltmer also conclude that 'context matters'. These media effects are much stronger in the most recently established democracies than in older democratic systems, and the varying contexts of different media systems have significant independent impact. In other words, the media effects are found to be the more influential the younger a democracy is. This is also an interesting finding which will be worth pursuing further in the next phase of the CNEP, with more countries at different stages of democratic transition and consolidation in our data set.

Intermediation, Political Values, and Electoral Mobilization

From the late nineteenth through the mid twentieth centuries, secondary associations served as the political intermediaries par excellence with regard to partisan electoral mobilization. This was particularly true with regard to mass-based parties and their religious or trade union allies. In Chapter 4, Paolo Bellucci, Marco Maraffi, and Paolo Segatti systematically examine the various facets of organizational membership as a context and mechanism for electoral mobilization in the 1990s. Setting aside political parties as organizational channels for mobilizing voters (to which we return in Chapter 6), they explore the various ways that secondary associations are relevant to this process, by politicizing their members, conveying explicit partisan cues, encouraging them to vote, and directly channelling their electoral support to specific parties. When all of these functions are performed successfully, the net effect is the 'encapsulation' (Bartolini and Mair 1990; Bartolini 2000) of portions of the electorate within communities exposed to homogeneous and reinforcing flows of political information and partisan appeals, as several scholars (e.g. Lijphart 1975; Irwin and Dietrich 1984) claim was characteristic of the Netherlands during the first half of the twentieth century. Bellucci, Maraffi, and Segatti analyse this channel for intermediation in ten old and new democracies in an effort to determine whether and to what extent secondary associations still successfully perform these functions. They find that the associational configuration and the levels of membership of a particular country are remarkably context dependent, as are the modes and mechanisms of interest intermediation.

The authors structure their analysis in accord with the expectation (which proves to be well founded) that intermediation processes will vary substantially in accord with the type of secondary association, and with the political history of each country. They argue that the extent of encapsulation of an electorate is a product of several variables, and they structure their analysis accordingly. The first of these is the share of the electorate that belongs to at least one secondary association. They find enormous cross-national variation in this regard, ranging from 85 and 72 per cent, respectively, in the United States and Japan, to a quarter or less of the population in Bulgaria, Spain, Hong Kong, Hungary, Uruguay, and Greece. A second crucial variable is the extent to which secondary associations are politicized. Here, they find considerable differences among various types of organizations: trade unions, economic organizations, and professional associations are the most politicized. They are followed, in order of partisan commitment, by religious organizations and civic non-religious groups. Another key variable (for which there are also considerable differences cross-nationally and among different types of associations) is the level of involvement of their members and their attentiveness to information channelled to them within the association. All of these, the authors find, substantially affect the extent to which secondary associations retain the ability to politically encapsulate their members.

Overall, the authors conclude that the ability of secondary associations to determine the electoral preferences of their members is limited but still politically significant, that context matters (especially with regard to cross-national differences in active membership and the extent of partisan politicization of the organization), and that, for achieving politicization, the mechanisms of political exposure, information, and persuasion are critical. Secondary organizations nowadays politicize a smaller segment of the electorate than they may have done in the golden age of the mass parties. In addition, the process of politicization by secondary associations has become more mediated, and less direct. Associational membership is no longer *per se* an indicator directly measuring organizational politicization (an assumption that underpins the use of 'nominal membership' as an independent variable in conventional election studies). The capacity of organizations to influence the electoral behaviour of their members is contingent on their ability to increase their members' subjective perception of their political surroundings by disseminating information and mobilizing their members politically. Here, the different types of secondary associations differ in their capabilities and capacities to do so—a factor that CNEP data can measure accurately for incorporation into the empirical analysis of electoral behaviour. Accordingly, the authors construct estimates of the extent of encapsulation of the electorates in these countries on the basis of the percentage of *coherent voters*—that is, those who belong to a voluntary organization, perceived political messages from it, and voted for a party or candidate supported by their association. Overall, they find that 7 per cent of all respondents in their pooled data set are coherent voters, and that there was considerable cross-national variation in the size of the encapsulated portion of the electorate, ranging from 1 per cent in Hungary and Hong Kong to 13 per cent in Japan. In general, the level of encapsulation is higher in older, established democracies than in new democratic systems (except Bulgaria). At the individual level, those who were most strongly influenced by these organizational flows of information are the unemployed, the poorly educated, males, active participants within their organizations, and union members. As the authors conclude, it is difficult to determine the extent to which political encapsulation has declined over the past century since we lack quantitative data of this kind from the so-called golden era of mass politics. But it appears that some kind of decline has taken place. Nonetheless, secondary associations remain as significant channels of political information, especially with regard to their functions as 'cues' or 'short cuts' that lower the cost of information acquisition for their members. And to widely varying degrees, cross-nationally, they continue to serve as anchors for political partisanship (see Gunther and Montero 2001).

In Chapter 5, Bradley Richardson and Paul Beck investigate the impact and significance of partisanship and partisan messages in the flow of political information from personal discussants and the media during election campaigns. They begin with the observation that very little campaign information flows to voters directly from the candidates and the parties, that most information is conveyed to voters by intermediaries, and that, as it passes through these intermediary channels, information is processed in such a manner that it rarely reaches the voters unchanged. Thus, exposure to different intermediary information sources, the kinds of information processed and communicated, and the extent to which the messages support the voter's political preferences constitute characteristic elements of a political communication process and have a substantial impact on the 'social calculus' of voting (Beck et al. 2002). The authors point out, in particular, that 'exposure' is also an act of choice, that people selectively perceive and filter the messages they receive, and that hence their own political predispositions and partisan loyalties (or at least proximity) can affect the flows of information. There are three distinct facets of these information flows that are dealt with by the authors: first, respondents are exposed to political information from personal networks—that is spouses and other personal discussants (friends, co-workers, extended family)— and from newspapers and television; second, voters perceive partisanship or partisan bias of the political messages; and third, the voters' own partisanship is related to the information they seek and receive, and these communications are filtered through 'partisan lenses'.

Richardson and Beck find a strong line of cross-national similarities among their twelve (in some cases eleven) countries from which some generalizations could be drawn. Their chapter, however, is full of methodological caveats with regard to limited inferences, and it also shows an equally strong line of exceptions and considerable variations awaiting further explanation. On the general side, their findings have verified the assumption of the dominant role of television as a source of political information throughout the world, with the relative exception of West Germany and Japan, where newspaper readership is very high. Television is especially predominant in the former communist countries due to the lack of traditions of an independent press. Much more variability was found regarding levels of exposure to newspapers, ranging from highs of 96 per cent in Japan and 84 per cent in the United States, to 40 per cent in Greece and 34 per cent in Uruguay. Their analysis demonstrates that affluence is positively correlated with newspaper reading, but that the extent to which citizens rely on newspapers or perceive them as partisan depends on other factors present in a country's particular social and political constellations. With regard to political discussion within personal networks, cross-national variability is equally high, and also difficult to explain without recurring to individual country factors. Here, the two Asian cases of our study, Hong Kong and Japan, show the least frequency, and countries with a more recent authoritarian past generally rank low.

With regard to both exposure to and perceptions of partisan bias, the authors find that, on the whole, the media were seen by respondents as much less biased than personal discussants. Television, in particular, was regarded as relatively unbiased across most nations. Even in countries where its perceived bias was higher—like Italy and the United States, or to a lesser degree the United Kingdom and Japan—it was considered to be below the partisan bias of personal discussants. Newspapers were generally seen as somewhat more biased than television (with the exception of Spain), though, on the whole, not as heavily biased as personal discussants either. Except for Greece, the press was regarded as considerably less biased in newly democratized countries than in longer-standing democracies. The notorious outliers here were West Germany and the United Kingdom, where a majority reported reading a partisan newspaper—a finding that may reflect the long traditions of a politicized press, the nationwide distribution of newspapers covering the whole partisan spectrum, competition, and other market mechanisms (such as the strength of low-quality tabloids) in these two countries.

In contrast, personal discussants were seen as the most biased sources of political information almost everywhere, with the exception of Japan and Hong Kong, where personal discussion is more limited, and the United Kingdom, where newspaper bias ranks higher. Their partisan messages were usually more congruent with, and presumably exerted a stronger influence on the respondent's own preferences than the messages from television and newspapers, the more so the stronger the voters' partisanship was. The strength of this congruence, however, was not so high as to suggest a deep embeddedness of the voters in like-minded networks of information and discussion, as would have been assumed by older cleavage-oriented studies of the 1960s (e.g. Lipset and Rokkan 1967a). There seems to be an overall trend (somewhat stronger in new democracies) towards a more pluralistic model of political communication. This appears to be due to the mechanisms of the new mass media, but also to the many underlying tendencies of social and political change, including more fluid social structures, the disappearance of traditional socio-political 'milieus', etc. (although a preliminary glance at some of our CNEP III data suggests that this trend may have been sharply reversed in the United States since 2000). Among the twelve cases compared by Richardson and Beck, the level of congruence between sources and recipients of partisan messages—which may also be seen as an index of partisan polarization—was highest in the United States (as early as in 1992!) and in Greece, followed by the United Kingdom, Italy, and Uruguay, with Chile, Japan, and Hong Kong at the lower, non-partisan end of the intermediation continuum.

Similarly, the voters' long-term partisanship or party proximity channels the flow of information and affects perceptions of partisan bias, but not uniformly and not to the extent initially anticipated. Such influences are greater the stronger one's partisanship is, and they vary by country. They are stronger in the United Kingdom, and, to a lesser degree, Greece, the United States and West Germany, and weaker in other countries. And there are many variations corresponding to the different channels of intermediation (eventually varying between spouse and other discussants). On the whole, the authors come to the conclusion that there may be a general trend towards greater uniformity concerning intermediation through the mass media, but that considerable national differences remain regarding personal discussions of politics, most likely in accord with the country's particular political history. Once again, we find that context matters in intermediation and electoral processes.

In Chapter 6 Pedro Magalhães systematically explored, in a broader and methodologically disciplined comparative approach, the effects of perceived informational biases on electoral choices in eleven (in some parts nine) of the CNEP countries taking into account all the various channels of intermediation for which data have been generated in our project. Preliminary steps in this analysis involved an extensive effort to standardize variables (unavoidably losing some countries for some questions for which data were not available), and development of a scheme for calculating 'net biases' in the flow of information through each of these intermediation channels. He then undertook a logistic analysis of voting in these countries including our intermediation items and several standard control variables (age, gender, education, and income), using two different measures of the impact of intermediation: incremental contributions to R^2 resulting from the addition of intermediation variables in a forced stepwise Logit analysis, and 'first difference' values generated using that analytical technique. In addition to estimating the explanatory power of our intermediation variables, he also submitted the findings of several chapters of this volume to a number of severe and stringent tests by adding sociodemographic control variables and party identification to these equations. The perceived biases that are taken into account are not only those of the usual four intermediaries relating to discussants/social networks, secondary associations, and the media (newspapers and television networks), but also those of party contacts (personal or by phone, and by mail). The author addresses three principal issues. First, he sets the stage by asking the categorical question of whether or not intermediation matters, and what its particular weight might be with regard to our assumptions about the temporal and causal order of factors affecting voting choice. Secondly, a closer and comparative look at the various channels and processes of intermediation helps to clarify whether and why some types of intermediaries are more influential than others. Finally, for the four countries for which information concerning the partisan biases of individual media channels was made available by content analyses and/or the judgements of country experts, he went beyond the respondents' perceptions and subjected hypotheses on the electoral impacts of such biases to a demanding, multi-method empirical test.

The findings of this chapter are particularly rich and insightful, and they tend to raise a substantial number of additional new questions. Magalhães starts out from two hypotheses. The first states that the informational environments of the voters should have an impact on their political behaviours and choices due to the shrinking structural ties and long-term orientations, to the limitations and biases of available information, and to the random selectivity of exposure. The second advances the proposition that not all informational intermediaries are equally likely to make a decisive difference on these choices: in particular, that interactive interpersonal communication should tend to be more influential and persuasive than impersonal communication through secondary organizations and the media.

Both assumptions are generally confirmed by the evidence assembled. Intermediation matters, and it matters more than it has been given credit for so far. Even under most stringent tests, the portion of explained variance of the vote accounted for by intermediation biases is larger than one-tenth of the overall variance explained, and always matches or surpasses that accounted for by social and economic characteristics. In Bulgaria and Chile, the weight of informational biases as explanations rivals partisanship itself, even after strict controls by the usual socio-economic variables (sex, age, education, income, religiosity) and party identification have been applied.

It is of particular interest that the author is also able to demonstrate that the informational intermediaries and the partisan biases voters perceive in them help to shape the short-term attitudes which are commonly included in single-country election studies, including the evaluation of the economy, issue positions, and the images of candidates or party leaders. As Magalhães states, the results suggest that the effect of such short-term factors in electoral choices in contemporary democracies consists, at least partially, in a mediation of informational biases acquired through interpersonal discussions, associational involvement, exposure to the mass media, and party contacts. This is the more important in countries and elections where short-term factors seem to be more influential. Here, the voters' informational environment (including some of its quasi-institutional aspects) may work as a partial *Ersatz*-anchor, stabilizing the electoral behaviour in political systems otherwise prone to instability. Another overall impact of the intermediation effects involves some systemic patterns. As the cases of Bulgaria, Chile, and, to a lesser degree, the United States suggest, the net impact of informational biases seems to be greater in presidential elections (with less clear-cut party cleavages), and smaller in parliamentary elections, a finding which corresponds to some of the positions advanced by Juan Linz (cf. Linz 1990; 1994).

In a closer comparison of the various kinds of intermediaries Magalhães finds that the people with whom voters frequently discuss political issues (interpersonal discussants) are by far the most important and consequential sources of information. They are perceived and acknowledged as being biased and partisan, and they have a number of structural advantages: they are stable, close to the respondent, to some degree homogeneous, and they serve as low-cost sources of information. Discussion networks are politicized in a one-sided way. These results point to the limitations of voting studies based exclusively on social cleavages, individual attitudes, ideological orientations, economic perceptions, and leadership evaluations, and back up the author's plea for paying greater attention to the 'micro-social contexts' of elections, and in particular to discussions within the individual's personal networks. Organizational and associational links also matter, though much less so, and dependent on trajectories, performance and degree of politicization, making a real difference only in cases of 'post-totalitarian' party politicization of social life (as in Bulgaria) or of associations still strongly tied to electorally relevant social and political cleavages, such as religious identities (as in the United States and Chile), or occupational structure (as in Italy). The same could apply to some of the media effects in communications systems which are dominated by strongly partisan agents.

In many cases, however, the media may lack a strong directional bias, transmit more multiple or conflicting biases, or even be systemically misperceived, and hence not have much of an impact. Magalhães demonstrates this convincingly with regard to the effects on the vote of perceived television network biases which are simply absent in most cases (and negative in Bulgaria and the United States), whereas those of perceived newspaper biases are positive and significant, particularly in Bulgaria and the United Kingdom, but also in Japan, Italy, and Greece. The findings of the additional survey on the structure of media outlets and content analysis of four country cases (Bulgaria, Italy, the United Kingdom, and Spain), besides showing a high degree of variation with regard to partisanship, and balance and moderation both in the print media and television, are consistent with the notion that the potential for influence of the media increases the more they tend to present voters with clear and one-sided messages. They also suggest important differences in the political effects and repercussions of different types of media outlets. While the perception of a partisan bias in newspapers mostly seems to be accepted as a legitimate part of information, the perception of bias in television networks usually undermines their credibility and produces negative effects (as in the case of Italy). The least consequential source of political information and influence seem to be party contacts of the various kinds, with some exceptions in countries with a longer tradition of canvassing and communicative interpersonal party contacts, like the United States or Japan. In many cases, we also find a more pluralistic pattern that corresponds to the mechanisms of the still dominant type of the catch-all party (cf. Kirchheimer 1966; Puhle 2002*a*), which disseminate to voters multiple and conflicting messages from different parties which neutralize each other. On the whole, the fact that a bias is perceived as partisan, does not reduce its impact, especially when it is enhanced by the possibility of interpersonal communication. The degree (and the mere fact) of partisan politicization, however, remains crucial. Magalhães also identifies some methodological challenges that should be taken into account for further research (and which will be taken up in the next stages of CNEP). Among them, he correctly counts the need to cope with the problems of reliance on perceived bias, of misperception and projection effects (which might better be addressed by including more systematic data on the actual biases of intermediaries), and the need to further explore causal paths. From the evidence we have, it cannot yet be told how short-term intermediation really is, whether its effects are mainly indirect or also direct, or whether they change attitudes or serve as a direct informational short-cut for decisions. It also remains unclear how the facts and various facets of exposure itself (despite the perceived bias) actually work, how we can deal with such effects 'more subtle' than persuasion (e.g. 'framing', 'priming', and agenda setting) in intermediaries other than the mass media, and which systemic, institutional, and inter-actional factors particularly condition (and have a recognizable impact on) the strength and direction of intermediation effects more in general.

Finally, Richard Gunther and Kuan Hsin-chi in Chapter 7 have sub-stantially enhanced our ability to 'explain' electoral behaviour by adding another important set of variables to our analysis of partisan conflict and electoral behaviour. They included socio-political values and values clusters in multivariate analyses of voting preferences. The impact of these values variables was subjected to severe empirical tests in which controls for standard determinants of the voter (religion, income, age, gender, and education) were introduced into previous stages of the multivariate analysis. And in subsequent steps of the analysis, party identification or left–right self-designation (depending on the country in question) were also added to the equation. Finally, our intermediation variables were included, providing the most stringent possible test of their impact on voting choice. The authors find that intermediation effects remain robust and retain much of their causal impact even after the party identification and values variables, religion, and the sociodemographic controls have been taken into account. In fact, intermediation is found to play a funda-mental role in making values relevant to the voting choice. But the most significant set of findings presented in this chapter is that these socio-political values have a very substantial impact on voting behaviour—explaining nearly 40 per cent of the variance in the vote in the 2004

American presidential election, even after the causal impacts of religiosity, age, income, gender, and education had been controlled in previous steps of the analysis.

The behavioural impact of these socio-political values had not been previously examined in cross-national empirical studies of voting. The World Values studies rigorously compare the distribution and some of the behavioural correlates in over eighty countries, but these orientations are generally quite abstract and relate to fundamental dimensions of personality rather than the kinds of orientations that are most commonly objects of partisan conflict. Most election studies, in sharp contrast, include questions dealing with campaign 'issues', but these tend to be transient, specific to individual countries and elections, and not susceptible to cross-national analysis. The socio-political values examined by Gunther and Kuan are located between these two extremes on the specificity/abstractness continuum. They were derived from the political ideologies that have fuelled partisan conflict in Western industrialized democracies over the past century. Since they had not been included in studies of electoral behaviour in both Western and non-Western democracies in the past, this study began with a systematic analysis of the dimensional structuring of these attitudes, to see if the 'West European template' of values (originally hypothesized as falling into four categories—traditional conservatism, socialism, social democracy, and 'postmaterialism') do, indeed, cluster together in the anticipated manner. With the exception of 'postmaterialism', which was subsumed within a broader 'modern social democracy' dimension, these values were found to cluster in this manner in Spain and Greece, and with some slight variations in Chile, Uruguay, and the United States. No coherent dimensional structuring was found among respondents in Hungary or Hong Kong, however. In terms of impact on electoral behaviour, these values were strongest in the United States, followed (in descending order) by Greece, Uruguay, and Spain, and they had little or no impact on voting decisions in Chile, Hungary, and Hong Kong.

Gunther and Kuan go beyond analysis of these quantitative data and develop the basic lines of a multistage theory in order to explain why some traditional values cleavages have remained strong anchors of partisan politics in some countries, and in others not. To a large extent, the answers to these questions involve intermediation. First, a given set of values has to be transformed into a values cleavage and has to be politicized through conflict over an issue at the elite or the mass level. Second, these politicized values cleavages are built into a comprehensive political ideology. Third, in order to have an impact on politics, this ideology has to be adopted and articulated by at least one political party. Embedded into party belief systems or ideologies, values cleavages can be 'frozen' and perpetuated over time, and they can eventually outlast the original issue or politicized conflict by centuries. And, fourth, in order to become relevant for voting, these values-based political statements have to be fed again into the channels of intermediation and go through the usual filters of selective exposure and choice which, as the authors demonstrate, are also to a large extent values based. So the intermediation and values variables together can explain more variance in the vote than would one or the other of them alone. Even after the effects of political and sociodemographic variables have been taken into consideration, these two sets of variables add another 26 per cent to the share of the variance in the vote explained for Spain; 28 per cent in Greece, 33 per cent in Uruguay, and an astounding 45 per cent in the United States. This is an important achievement which at the same time opens up a broad space for future conceptual and empirical work.

Looking Back, Looking Ahead

The findings of the preceding chapters have important implications for a number of fields and problems we have outlined in the Introduction. They also affect the general ways in which we have been looking at some key issues and paradigms of political science, particularly with regard to the relationship between the various modes and stages of electoral intermediation, and political intermediation more in general, on the one hand, and the scope and direction of mobilization, politicization, and support for democracy, on the other. And they can help to identify questions that remain open and to restructure our future research priorities. In addition, they have underlined the need to look more carefully into the various enabling or confining conditions, and constellations of the different medium- and long-term trajectories particular countries have followed on their way into modernity. This approach of 'different trajectories' which should not be confounded with the cage of 'path dependency', has so far inspired many useful and innovative differentiations and typologies in many fields of social science research, most notably of the studies of modern capitalism, state building, and bureaucracies, of social security systems and the welfare state, or lately even of media systems (cf. Rueschemeyer, Stephens, and Stephens 1992; Mann 1986; Hall and

Soskice 2001; Esping-Andersen 1990; Hallin and Mancini 2004), but has so far not been paid much attention in the analyses of regime transformation, democratization, or political intermediation (some exceptions being Gunther, Diamandouros, and Puhle 1995; Merkel and Puhle 1999; Puhle 2004).

One of the basic messages of this volume is that taking into account the effects of electoral and political intermediation substantially enhances the explanatory potential of the analysis of institutions and elites, interests, factions, cleavages, and social and political interactions. Bringing the intermediation and values variables into the analysis does not, however, imply an abandonment of either the Michigan or social-cleavages approaches to electoral analysis: as we pointed out in the Introduction, the incorporation of these kinds of variables into this field of study is compatible with and can enrich both of those other research traditions.

Some key findings of this current study, however, might help to focus future research, and these bear reiteration at this point. First, ideology matters. And it may matter twice, at two different levels. The existing political and ideological positions like those reflected by the values cleavages are fed into the channels of intermediation providing a further potential for politicization both in a general and a partisan sense. Parties matter, as agents of politicization and mobilization; but partisanship is also an issue of intermediation. Here another filter comes in—selectivity, or, for the moment, selective exposure (which has to be distinguished from mobilization). And selectivity, again, among other things, can be conditioned by prejudice, opinions, 'values' preferences, ideology, or the feeling of being more or less close to a certain party, be it measured in terms of party identification or in terms of the correspondence between self-placement and party placement on a left/right continuum.

Intermediation matters. This implies that it is not enough to look only into attitudes or the elements of 'social capital' in analyses of support for democracy. We must also examine interactions among the various actors in politics and civil society, at the elite and at the mass levels, as well as institutions, and their patterns of continuity or change. With regard to intermediation, elites seem to matter more than the masses, because it is they who take the lead and who define the channels and pre-structure the contents of intermediation. Elites therefore matter. They do not, however, operate on a *tabula rasa*, but in a given society. Hence the particular developmental trajectories of their respective societies, their biases, imbalances, critical junctures, and conflicts are relevant, including the aspects of the dark side of associational life, like the undemocratic tendencies in the society of Weimar Germany (cf. Collier and Collier 1991; Puhle 2002*b*).

Conflicts matter, like interests, factions, and ideologies. But political conflict is not a primordial thing. It has to be created and crafted, even transported by adequate energies, campaigns, and movements. It is always politically construed, through intermediation and subsequent processes of mobilization and politicization. Politicization matters. And the construction of political conflict is in itself political. Hence, in the end, politics matters.

The findings presented in this volume will also help to structure the leading questions for the next round of the CNEP III. Besides enlarging the focus and the empirical sample of the project to include African, Asian, and additional Latin American cases, this new round will provide additional opportunities to test some of the basic hypotheses of the present volume for verification and generalization based on a broader sample of countries, ranging from the most affluent post-industrial societies to the less-developed world. In particular, we will be able to determine the extent to which the findings summarized above are to be modified methodologically or theoretically, and whether we can generate new insights concerning the relationship between late modern and premodern mechanisms of interaction (the 'leapfrogging' syndrome, cf. Gunther, Diamandouros, and Puhle 1995). Moreover, by undertaking 'second wave' surveys in a number of CNEP I and II countries, we will be able to monitor and attempt to explain patterns of change (or continuity) over time. These may include changes at the elite level (such as increases or decreases in polarization or the 'ideologization' of politics), at the mass level (involving varying levels of partisan attachment or fundamental support for democracy), and at the institutional level (involving the nature of parties or various aspects of the intermediation process). In the end, we hope to learn more about the various ways that intermediation affects fundamental characteristics of politics in the democratic world.

Notes

Chapter 1

1. Since this work is the starting point of the CNEP project, we elaborate much more extensively on this approach later in this chapter.
2. A partial exception can be found in some segments of Seymour Martin Lipset's *Political Man*, published in 1960 (see Manza and Brooks 1999: 13–14).
3. Among the immense literature within and about the Michigan approach, particularly insightful commentaries can be found in Beck (1986); and the edited volumes by Jennings and Mann (1994) and MacKuen and Rabinowitz (2003) in honour of Warren E. Miller and Philip E. Converse, respectively.
4. On 'retrospective voting', see Key (1966) and Fiorina (1981); and on 'sociotropic' voting, see Kinder and Kiewiet (1979).
5. Cogent critiques of this approach include Bartolini (2002), Green and Shapiro (1994), and Lago (2005: ch. 5).
6. See Bartolini (2002: 84). Gunther and Kuan demonstrate why these assumptions of uni-dimensionality are unwarranted in their study of socio-political values in this volume.
7. Among many works adopting this or similar perspectives, see Popkin (1991), Sniderman, Brody, and Tetlock (1991), Zaller (1992), Lupia and McCubbins (1998), Lupia, McCubbins, and Popkin (2000), and Jones (2001).
8. The CNEP involves the active participation of a number of leading scholars. The German team, headed by Max Kaase (International University Bremen), Hans-Dieter Klingemann (Free University of Berlin), Manfred Kuechler (Hunter College), Franz-Urban Pappi (University of Mannheim), Rüdiger Schmitt-Beck (University of Duisburg), and Katrin Voltmer (University of Leeds), was the first into the field with an extremely ambitious study of the first post-war all-German election. The original American principal investigators, Paul Allen Beck (Ohio State University), Russell Dalton (University of California at Irvine), and Robert Huckfeldt (University of California at Davis), analysed the 1992 presidential election. Subsequently, Paul Beck and Richard Gunther (Ohio State Unviersity) undertook an analysis of the 2004 American presidential election. The British team from Oxford and Strathclyde universities (John Curtice, Anthony Heath, and Roger

Jowell) included CNEP core questionnaire items in the 1992 British Election Study. The Japanese team, headed by Hiroshi Akuto (University of Tokyo), Scott Flanagan (Florida State University), and Bradley Richardson (Ohio State University), studied the 1993 parliamentary election. The Spanish team, which included José Ramón Montero (Universidad Autónoma de Madrid and the Centro de Estudios Avanzados en Ciencias Sociales, Instituto Juan March), Richard Gunther (Ohio State University), and Mariano Torcal (Universitat Pompeu Fabra, Barcelona), conducted a panel survey before and after the 1993 parliamentary election. They also undertook a follow-up survey of the Spanish electorate following the 2004 parliamentary election. The Chilean team undertook surveys following the elections of 1994 and 2000 under the direction of Eugenio Tironi (Catholic University of Chile). Co-principal investigators of the Uruguayan panel study of the 1994 election were Pablo Mieres (Universidad de la República) and Richard Gunther. The 1996 Italian election study was undertaken by the Cattaneo Institute's Committee for the Study of the Political Transition. The three members of the Istituto Cattaneo's large team of research collaborators who have been most active in CNEP are Paolo Bellucci (Università di Siena), Marco Maraffi (Università di Milano), and Paolo Segatti (Università di Milano). The study of the Greek parliamentary election of 1996 was headed by Nikiforos Diamandouros (then director of Greece's National Centre for Social Research [EKKE] and currently the European Ombudsman) and Ilias Nicolacopoulos (University of Athens). The survey of the 1996 Bulgarian presidential election was headed by Georgi Karasimeonov (director of the Institute for Political and Legal Studies, Sofia) and Richard Gunther. The co-principal investigators of the 1998 Hungarian parliamentary election were Tibor Gazso (Századvég Policy Research Center) and Richard Gunther. The study of the 1998 Legislative Council elections in Hong Kong is under the direction of Kuan Hsin-Chi and Lau Siu-kai (Chinese University of Hong Kong). The 1999 Indonesian study was directed by Saiful Mujani (State Islamic Institute) and R. William Liddle (Ohio State University).

9. Having completed two stages of this project, the next stage, CNEP III, will further expand the geographical scope of the project through the addition of African, East Asian, and Latin American democracies, as well as follow-up surveys in CNEP I and CNEP II countries that will make possible an analysis of changes in intermediation patterns and other aspects of democratic politics in the course of more than a decade. By the beginning of 2006, new CNEP surveys had been conducted in Spain (2004), Greece (2004), Indonesia (2004), Uruguay (2004), South Africa (2004), the United States (2004), Taiwan (2005), Portugal (2005), Mozambique (2005), the People's Republic of China (2005), and additional surveys were planned for Italy (2006), Mexico (2006), and at least one additional African country.

10. This snowball research is based on earlier work by Huckfeldt (1986). Also see Huckfeldt and Sprague (1987, 1995) and Beck et al. (2002).

11. Among many studies, see Joslyn (1984), Iyengar (1991), Zaller (1992); Ansolabehere, Behr, and Iyengar (1993).

12. The substantial differences between cross-national comparative studies and monographic single-country studies in this regard are, we suspect, the result of the fact that campaign issues are usually quite transient (even within a single country over time), while the personal qualities of candidates are by their very nature particularistic and non-comparable.

13. There is no 'something blue' about the happy union of this path-breaking research tradition with the more recently established paradigms for the study of electoral behaviour.

Chapter 2

1. The authors would like to express their deep gratitude to Lorenzo Bursattin for his collaboration and assistance in conducting the various rounds of confirmatory factor analysis that play such a significant role in this empirical study. This chapter expands on the analysis presented in Gunther and Montero (2006).

2. e.g., Montero, Gunther, and Torcal (1997) and Gunther and Montero (2000, 2006). Also see Hibbing and Theiss-Morse (1995) and Klingemann (1999).

3. In our view, this latter claim is patently incorrect. Citizens who have recently experienced a transition from a dictatorship are able to both distinguish between authoritarian and democratic rule, and to separate their evaluations of system performance (satisfaction) from their support for the current democratic regime (legitimacy). See Morlino and Montero (1995) and Rose, Mishler, and Haerpfer (1998: ch. 5).

4. For enlightening discussions of satisfaction with the performance of democracy and/or democratic institutions, see Schmitt (1983), Fuchs, Guidorossi, and Svensson (1995), Remmer (1996), Anderson and Guillory (1997), Nye (1997), Anderson (1998a, 1998b), Norris (1999b), Newton and Norris (2000), Foweraker and Krznaric (2000), and Linde and Ekman (2003). For a critique of alleged analytical deficiencies in this indicator, see Canache, Mondak, and Seligson (2001). The October 2001 edition of the *International Political Science Review*, edited by Richard I. Hofferbert and Christopher J. Anderson, was devoted to the theme of 'The Dynamics of Democratic Satisfaction'.

5. This point is also stressed in Klingemann (1999) and Hofferbert and Klingemann (2001); also see Hibbing and Theiss-Morse (1995). For different conceptions of disaffection, see Morlino and Tarchi (1996) and Pharr and Putnam (2000), although the latter never presents an explicit definition of disaffection.

6. The Portuguese item asked respondents about the following statement: 'Democracy may have problems, but it's better than any other form of government'. Thirty-three per cent of respondents strongly agreed with this statement, and another 48% agreed; only 4% and 1%, respectively, disagreed or strongly disagreed, while 14% said they did not know how to respond. In 1985, and with an identical item format, *DemAuth* was included in the Four Nation Study of Portugal, Spain, Greece, and Italy. The percentages of those survey respondents who selected the democratic alternative ranged between 61% in Portugal (with 23% not answering this question) and 87% in Greece, with Italy and Spain falling between these two extremes with 70% of those interviewed supporting democracy (See Morlino and Montero 1995: 236).

7. Those items with agree/disagree response categories were recoded as follows: agreement was coded as 1, disagreement as 3, and 'it depends', 'neither' or 'both' as 2, with a non-response coded as missing data.

8. It should be noted that there were no significant differences between the results obtained from this Varimax rotation and an Oblimin rotation (whose results are not presented in the table). Not only were the factor loadings resulting from these two approaches very similar, but the percentage of variance explained was identical, with respect to each of the factors for all three countries.

9. These findings have been remarkably consistent over time; similar results were obtained from analysis of data collected in 1979 and 1982 post-election surveys, which included many of the items that were subsequently included in the CNEP surveys. See Maravall (1997: ch. 5); also see Torcal (2001, 2002*a*: ch. 3), which reach the same conclusions using different data-sets, variables, and statistical analyses.

10. In a confirmatory factor analysis, a specific structure of clustering among variables is hypothesized and empirically tested. This approach not only generates 'goodness-of-fit' statistics, but also allows for the calculation of correlations among the variables within each cluster and between these 'implicit factors'.

11. Factor loadings for the three items in the discontent cluster (except for the one item set initially at 1.00) ranged between .61 and .87 for Spain, .55 and .94 in Uruguay, and .51 and .80 in Greece. Factor loadings among items in the disaffection clusters ranged between .48 and .50 in Spain, .95 and .98 in Uruguay, and .98 and 1.14 in Greece.

12. The RMSEA is a goodness-of-fit statistic that is sensitive to the number of estimated parameters in the model, which is to say, its complexity. Values less than .05 indicate very good fit, and values as high as .08 reflect reasonable errors of approximation, while values above .10 indicate poor fit.

13. It should be reiterated that, unlike the *DemBest* item used in the CNEP surveys, which provided only three possible responses (agree, disagree, and 'it depends') with regard to the statement that 'Democracy is the best political

system for a country like ours', the Portuguese 2002 election study allowed respondents to strongly agree, agree, disagree or strongly disagree with the proposition that 'Democracy may have problems, but it's better than any other form of government'.

14. Within the discontent cluster, the factor loadings for the *GovPerf* and *DemSat* variables are just .15 and .10, respectively (with *EconSit* set = 1.0); and within the disaffection cluster, *DontCare* has a factor loading of just .14 (with *PolComp* set = 1.0).

15. Among the discontent items (with *PolitSit* set at 1.0), *EconSit*'s factor loading was .74, and that of *DemSat* was .50; among the disaffection items (with *PolComp* equal to 1.0), the factor loading for *NoInflu* was .88, and that of *DontCare* was .80.

16. This finding is consistent with those of Mishler and Rose (2002) and Evans and Whitefield (1995). While the former study found that in seven Central and East European democracies the impact of political perform-ance is greater than that of economic performance (and its impact is increasing), the latter study found that the combined impact of five dif-ferent variables measuring current, prospective, and retrospective assess-ments of the performance of the economy in eight post-Soviet Eastern European democracies explained less than 5% of the variance in support for democracy.

17. Unfortunately, none of our standard 'satisfaction' items was included in this survey. The closest to our item tapping satisfaction with the economic situ-ation of the country is a question (*EconCon*) measuring the respondent's confidence that the economy will improve in the coming year. The Hungar-ian questionnaire also lacked an item dealing with the respondent's level of satisfaction with the performance of democracy. As a means of fleshing out the satisfaction dimension, a measure of the respondent's confidence that his or her financial situation will improve over the coming year (*RespCon*) was included in the analysis. Despite these differences in the face content of the satisfaction items, the data presented in Table 2.3 are perfectly compatible with our earlier findings: the two economic optimism measures are highly intercorrelated.

18. The correlations among the three latent factors in the confirmatory factor analysis range from .02 to .04.

19. Adam Przeworski wrote shortly after the collapse of communism in Eastern Europe, 'As everyone agrees, the eventual survival of the new democracies will depend to a large extent on their economic performance. And since many among them emerged in the midst of an unprecedented economic crisis, economic factors work against their survival' (Przeworski 1991: 95). Some scholars have even suggested that the legitimacy of established Western democracies is increasingly dependent on their economic performance (see Fuchs and Klingemann 1995: 440).

20. In the case of Hungary, *EconCon*, and *RespCon* (reflecting confidence in the condition of the economy) were used instead.
21. It should be noted that Newton departs significantly from Putnam's argument. Putnam (1995*b*: 666) claims that 'causation flows mainly from joining to trusting', while Newton (1999*a*: 16–17) has argued that the direction of causality may flow in the opposite direction.
22. Each of the items measuring membership in various types of organizations was rescored such that a numerical value of 0 was assigned when an individual stated that he or she was not a member of the organization in question, while a value of 1 reflected membership in that organization. Scale values were computed by simply adding together all of the reformatted items. Accordingly, those not belonging to any organization received scores 0, those belonging to one organization a score of 1, those belonging to two organizations had a score of 2, etc. Since few individuals in these countries belonged to more than one or two organizations, several of these categories were very sparsely populated. Since these skewed distributions would have depressed various measures of association, these categories were recoded to reflect (depending on the distribution of respondents in each country) membership in one or more, or two or more organizations. The actual distributions of respondents among these categories with regard to political organizations (parties and trade unions) are as follows: in Spain, Greece, and Chile, 92% belonged to no organizations and 8% to one or more; in Uruguay, 95% did not belong to a political organization and 5% to one or more; in Hungary, 13% belonged to one or more political organization, while 87% did not; in Bulgaria, 23% of respondents belonged to one or more political organizations, while 77% did not; and in Portugal, 12% belonged to trade unions (and the questionnaire did not include an item tapping membership in political parties). With regard to non-political organizations: in Spain, 14% belonged to one organization, 6% to two or more, while 80% did not belong to any organization; in Greece 12% belonged to one organization, 3% to two or more, and 85% to no organization; in Uruguay, 8% belonged to one or more organizations, while 92% belonged to none; in Chile, 23% belonged to one organization, 10% to two or more organizations, and 67% belonged to none; in Hungary, 91% did not belong to any organization, while 9% belonged to one or more; in Bulgaria, 6% belonged to one or more organizations, while 94% belonged to none; and in Portugal, 1% belonged to two or more organizations, 7% belonged to one, and 92% belonged to none.
23. To undertake this analysis, a scale was created measuring the number of organizations to which respondents belonged. This is based on an extensive battery of questions in which respondents were asked whether they belong to over a dozen different types of organizations. Two of these were organizations directly involved in politics: these are membership in political parties and in trade unions. The others were organizations that ordinarily are not so

directly involved in politics: these included professional associations, fraternal organizations, youth organizations of various types, sports organizations, etc. Two different scales were constructed by adding together positive responses to questions about each type of organizational membership (with membership scored as 1 and non-membership coded as 0). The range of the scales was from 0 to as much as 5 (with the latter capturing those respondents belonging to five different organizations). Most respondents either did not belong to any organization or belong to only one. Thus, sparsely populated response categories (usually measuring membership in three or more organizations) were collapsed into fewer categories in order to normalize the distribution of responses and facilitate statistical analysis.

24. Independent variables in this multivariate analysis included age, sex, education, subjective social class identification, income, party identification, left–right self-placement, frequency of discussion of politics, membership in political organizations, and membership in non-political organizations. With our standard measure of democratic support as the dependent variable, the R^2 statistic measuring the percentage of variance explained was just .07 in Greece, .04 in Chile, and .01 in Hungary and Portugal. Only in Bulgaria did it reach .17, and the β score for the variable measuring membership in non-political organizations amounted to just .10 (significant at the .01 level). Membership in political organizations in Bulgaria was not statistically significant in this OLS analysis.

25. This conclusion is very similar to one defended by rational-culturalists, who contend that support for democratic norms relates to the effect of national parties on the development of party systems, the separation of constitutional matters from everyday political competition, and the success of left-wing parties (Evans and Whitefield 1995: 512–13; Rose and Mishler 1996: 50; Teorell 2002).

26. In order to control for the partisan contamination of perceptions of the economic and political situation of the country, we re-ran these same correlation and factor analysis procedures after controlling for partisanship. Among those who identify with a party belonging to the pro-democratic and progressive Concertación alliance, the tau-b statistics linking *DemBest* to the three dissatisfaction measures was reduced to −.02, −.06 and −.18, respectively, with only the relationship with *DemSat* being statistically significant (@ .01). The factor analysis revealed that the three discontent measures formed one attitudinal dimension (with factor loadings ranging between .610 and .650) that was much less strongly linked to the *DemBest* measure of support for democracy (whose factor loading on that dimension declined to .326).

27. On the 1999–2000 campaign, see Garretón (2000) and Torcal and Mainwaring (2003).

28. Among the many studies analysing political and parties elites in Central and Eastern Europe, see Higley, Pakulski, and Weslowski (1998) and Higley and Lengyel (1999).

29. Indeed, respondents in our 1998 CNEP Hungarian survey who were former members of the Hungarian Communist Party were actually *more* supportive of democracy than were non-members: 78% of former communists selected the democratic response to the *DemAuth* question (vs. just 63% of other respondents), and former communists were also more supportive of democracy in their responses to the *DemBest* questions, with 76% selecting the democratic alternative (vs. 71% of others) (also see Kitschelt et al. 1999: ch. 8).

30. On the transformation of the right in Southern Europe, see Pappas (2001). For Greece, the best study of the consolidation of democracy in Greece is Karakatsanis (2001); for Portugal, see Maxwell (1995) and Costa Pinto and Freire (2003); For Spain, there is an extraordinarily large number of studies of the role of elites in the transition to democracy in Spain: e.g., Gunther (1992), Linz (1993), and for a partial but extensive list of such works, see Gunther, Diamandouros, and Puhle (1995: 415–21). Also see Linz and Stepan (1996: chs. 6–9).

31. The Spanish data were derived from a 1979 post-election survey by DATA, S.A., under the direction of Richard Gunther, Giacomo Sani, and Goldie Shabad. Generous financial assistance was provided by the National Science Foundation under grant no. SOC77-16451. The opinions, findings, and conclusions expressed in this work, however, are those of the authors and do not necessarily reflect the views of the National Science Foundation. (For additional information about this survey, see Gunther, Sani, and Shabad 1986.) The very large national sample used in that survey (5,439 respondents) makes it possible to analyse the attitudes of the small percentage of Spaniards who supported the extreme-right Unión Nacional and other parties of the extreme right.

32. 1979 and 1982 data were from post-election surveys conducted by DATA, under the direction of Richard Gunther, Juan Linz, José Ramón Montero, Hans-Jürgen Puhle, Giacomo Sani, and Goldie Shabad. For further information about these surveys, see Gunther, Sani, and Shabad (1986) and Linz and Montero (1986).

33. This continuity is documented in many other surveys undertaken in Chile since the mid-1980s: see, e.g., Alaminos (1991) and the series of Latino barómetro surveys since 1995. In 2002, e.g., just 50% of Chilean respondents selected the pro-democratic response to the *DemAuth* questionnaire item.

34. These data are from the Four Nation Study, undertaken in the spring of 1985 in Portugal, Spain, Italy, and Greece under the coordination of Giacomo Sani and Julián Santamaría.

35. Indeed, we predict that if electoral turnover were to occur in Chile, bringing the post-pro-Pinochet party to power, there would be a 'sign reversal' with regard to the relationship between support for democracy and the discontent items.

Chapter 3

1. The data analysed in this chapter were collected in the context of the CNEP II project, directed by Richard Gunther, José Ramón Montero, and Hans-Jürgen Puhle. The Bulgarian and Hungarian data come from post-election surveys (Bulgarian Presidential Election 1996, N = 1,216; Hungarian Parliamentary Election 1998, N = 1,500), the other surveys are pre- and post-election panel studies (N for the first wave of the 1993 Spanish Parliamentary Election is 1,448; for the Greek 1993 Parliamentary Election N = 966; for the 1993 Chilean Presidential Election N = 1,305; and for the 1994 Parliamentary Election in Uruguay, N = 1,005).

2. For descriptions of the media systems of our country samples, see Dimitras (1997) and Zaharopoulos and Paraschos (1993) for Greece; Gunther, Montero, and Wert (2000), de Mateo (1997), and Bustamante (1989) for Spain; Wilke (1996) for Uruguay; Tironi and Sunkel (2000) and Delgado Rühl (1994) for Chile; Sükösd (2000), Lánczi and O'Neil (1996), and Gergely (1997) for Hungary; and Nikolchev (1996) and Tzankoff (2002) for Bulgaria.

3. The relatively high membership rate reported for Chile is largely due to religious organizations to which many people belong (22%). In East Germany, the membership rate is inflated by members of trade unions. Before democratization unions had been part of the official system of 'mass organizations', and in 1990 more than a third of all citizens were still members of these organizations. Although they merged with West German trade unions, they rapidly lost members in the following years.

4. For each, we based these assessments on evaluations provided by at least two experts. We are greatly indebted to the following colleagues for sharing their expertise with us: Eleni Dimitrakopoulou, Nicolas Demertzis, Manina Kakepaki, Paola Kanta, and Clio Kenterelidou (Greece); Pablo Mieres and Christoph Wagner (Uruguay); Eugenio Tironi, Markus Moke, and Hans Blomeier (Chile); Tamas Fricz, Csilla Machos, and Gabor Tóka (Hungary); Georgi Karasimeonov and Plamen Georgiev (Bulgaria).

5. It should be kept in mind that this description of the media in our sample countries refers to the particular time when the surveys of our study were conducted and may have changed since then. For example, the Bulgarian party press has declined in significance since the 1996 election, and *La Epoca* is no longer being published.

6. The equation treating 'political participation' as a dependent variable treats political interest, political knowledge, and attitudes towards parties as control

variables in the previous step of the analysis. Conversely, the equation estimating the impact of media effects on attitudes towards political parties had controlled for the impact of political participation, interest, and knowledge by entering those variables into the previous equation. Satisfaction with the performance of democracy controls for the impacts of political interest, knowledge, participation, and attitudes towards parties. And estimates of the impact of the media on Democratic Support included satisfaction with democracy along with those other four control variables.

7. Findings from the less conservative models appear in the bottom rows of the tables. To save space, the coefficients for the control variables, which are very similar to the conservative models, are not displayed in these tables.

8. Since this newspaper still expressed sympathy for the authoritarian regime of General Augusto Pinochet (at least at the time of our survey in 1994), this negative correlation is most likely the result of this particular paper's editorial stance, rather than a general inclination of the media to present politics in a negative light.

9. Other research has also found evidence of the political irrelevance of the tabloid press in established democracies, including the notorious British case (Schmitt-Beck 1998; Semetko 2000).

Chapter 4

1. It should be noted that these characteristics of individual parties can have significant impact on key aspects of party systems such as the level of electoral volatility. While mass-based cleavage parties may be constrained by their institutionalized legacies, allied secondary organizations and their mass-membership bases help to stabilize their electoral support. Catch-all and other 'organizationally thin' parties, lacking these structural bases, may be tactically more manoeuvrable during election campaigns, but they may also fall victim to major fluctuations in electoral support from one election to the next (see Gunther 2005).

2. Political theorists have long presumed that there is a strong and positive correlation between liberal democracy and associational density and diversity. Paxton's study is one of the few to test this presumption of the reciprocal effect empirically. The effect is in the predicted direction but is weak, and so illuminates a gap between political theory and political sociology that merits additional investigation.

3. It should be noted that adding these separate percentages together exceeds the 'overall membership rate' because some individuals belong to more than one organization.

4. It must also be noted that in the United States, 'membership' in a religious organization includes for many respondents only 'belonging to a church',

while in many Catholic countries this item is understood to mean membership in a lay organization associated with the Church. But also see Martin (1990), who stresses the development of Evangelical and Pentecostal cults that insist on voluntary activity of members. Also see Verba, Schlozman, and Brady (1995).

5. Being a member of a neighbourhood association is in fact considered a sort of social duty in Japan. These organizations are subsidized by the state and perform quasi-governmental functions. See Verba, Nie, and Kim (1978: ch. 6). Also see Nakane (1970) regarding the peculiar problems of forming and joining voluntary associations in Japan, given the country's social structure and culture (especially its hierarchical nature and group ties).

6. In both cases the propensity of Italians is virtually identical to that of Americans.

7. In an earlier, tentative, model the variables 'size of community' and 'religious practice' were also included in the analysis. But there was no improvement in the goodness of fit of the model and neither of the B coefficients were statistically significant. Therefore, for reason of parsimony, they were dropped from the final model.

8. See Curtis et al. (1992) and Curtis, Bear, and Grabb (2001). For an explanation of American exceptionalism, see recently Skocpol, Ganz, and Munson (2000) and Skocpol and Crowley (2001).

9. e.g., vis-à-vis 18–29 years old, all other age cohorts have a lesser propensity to join sport associations.

10. We define as 'active' those members who reported that they were 'always' or 'often' involved in associational life.

11. This conclusion was also tested and confirmed by a comprehensive model of associational level of involvement with a logistic regression. The model that fits the data best (pseudo $R^2 = .52$, with 87% of cases classified correctly) is one where, along the usual socio-demographic control variables, we include country and association effects and the interaction among them. The country variables for Spain, Bulgaria, and Hungary show no significant difference when the United States is used as the reference category; Chile, Greece, Uruguay, and Japan have a (modest) positive impact on associational activism; only Italy and Hong Kong retain a fairly strong *negative* effect on being an active participant in the association one belongs to. On the other hand, with respect to unions, all types of associations retain their *positive* effect on members' activism, very much in line with the results of bivariate analysis, with the American 'multimember' type having the strongest impact on activism, and professional associations being indistinguishable from unions.

12. These data refer to the association regarded as 'most important' by the respondent. The question format asked whether the respondent had received any political information from the organization at the time of the elections.

13. In the case of the United States, the 'most important organization' question was not asked, so we have had to reduce this analysis to only those belonging to one organization. All other joiners are placed in a separate category, which we have called 'multi-member'. Since only 25% of all members of groups in the United States belong to only one organization, this analysis of single-group members underestimates the total number of joiners, and what we see here is the effect of strongly identified union members who are most likely to seek political information.

14. In the next phase of this research project, CNEP III, we will be able to determine the extent to which religiosity in the United States was politicized over the following decade, and measure its impact on the 2004 election.

15. Sport and recreational associations are not taken into consideration in the involvement-effect analysis.

16. These analyses are based on the following numbers of cases: for unions, 980; for religious groups 525, for sports groups, 459; for civic non-religious groups, 1,607; and for professional associations, 609. Sport and recreational associations are not taken into consideration in the involvement-effect analysis. And in Hungary and Bulgaria, a lack of respondents precludes analysis perception of party support by members of religious and civic non-religious organizations.

17. Our measure of the degree of activism is similar to that of Baumgartner and Walker (1988). It is a dummy variable that distinguishes between those who describe the frequency of their participation within the group as 'often' or 'sometimes', vs. 'rarely' or 'never'.

18. See, e.g., Verba and Nie (1972), Montero (1984), Rosenstone and Hansen (1993), Corbetta and Parisi (1994a, 1994b), Verba, Schlozman, and Brady (1995), Sani and Mannheimer (2000), Legnante and Segatti (2001).

19. It should be noted, however, that Verba, Schlozman, and Brady (1995) found that *other* modes of political participation were strongly affected by civic skills acquired through activity in non-political associations.

20. Powell (1986) and Jackman (1987) also stress that turnout rates are best explained by institutional factors.

21. Among the nine countries analysed, Chile and Greece have mandatory vote requirements. Italy had this rule for a long period, but it was changed just three years prior to our 1996 survey. Spain, Chile, Bulgaria, Greece, and Uruguay have proportional-representation electoral systems, while the others have a variety of non-PR systems.

22. It should be noted that within this category in our pooled sample over 90% are highly educated (i.e. more than secondary education). Thus, its large impact could conceal an interaction effect with education.

23. See Fiorina (2005) on the United States. Also see Hill and Matsubayashi (2005).

Chapter 5

1. Beck et al. (2002), Bennett and Entman (2001: 1–29), and Zaller (1992: 6–39, 216–64).
2. Semetko et al. (1991), Norris et al. (1999), Gunther and Mughan (2000a), and Norris (2000c).
3. The countries and year (in order) of the election in each are: West Germany (1990), United Kingdom (1992), United States (1992), Japan (1993), Spain (1993), Chile (1993–4), Uruguay (1994), Bulgaria (1996), Italy (1996), Greece (1996), Hong Kong (1998), and Hungary (1998). Of them, only West Germany (due to excessive panel mortality), the United Kingdom (because there was not space in the questionnaire to ask all questions), and Japan (because some questions, thought to be irrelevant in the Japanese context, were not asked) did not provide full information on all questions.
4. The particular countries chosen for this study were the result of voluntary involvement in the CNEP project and the ability of country teams to fund a national survey in their country. They were not selected to be a representative sample of all democracies. Yet they are diverse enough along key dimensions (e.g. old vs. new democracies, western vs. non-western, former communist vs. non-communist, four different continents, parliamentary vs. presidential systems) to provide a solid foundation for making some tentative generalizations.
5. The questions were designed to identify first those with whom the survey respondents discussed 'important matters', and only then to determine whether any of this discussion focused on politics. Table 5.1 and most of the following tables contain separate figures for spouse and first-named non-spouse discussant. These figures resulted from separate questions asked about each in eight of the countries. In Germany, Japan, the United States, and the United Kingdom, however, respondents were not asked to report on political discussion with spouses per se, even though spouses virtually always turned up as one of the discussants of important matters. To measure bias separately for spouse and first discussant, therefore, we had to create a separate spouse variable and then replace spouse with a second discussant where he or she had been reported as the first discussant.
6. We use candidate or party interchangeably in our discussion because some of the elections studied were presidential, in which the same candidates appeared on the ballot countrywide, and others were parliamentary, where different candidates were on the ballots in different constituencies or voters were casting ballots for a party list. The presidential elections were in Chile, Bulgaria, the United States, and Uruguay, and the parliamentary elections were in Germany, Greece, Hungary, Hong Kong, Italy, Japan, Spain, and the United Kingdom.
7. The German survey was conducted in 1990, the first year of the reintegration of East and West Germany, and covered the first all-German

election in sixty years. Because this election was so unusual—e.g. with an East German electorate that was participating in a democratic election for the first time in almost sixty years, media that were split between the two former countries, and with hypermobilization in the East but apathy in the West—we focus only on the independent sample drawn for West Germany.

8. The literacy and economic data come from the United States Central Intelligence Agency's *The World Factbook* on the web at www.cia.gov/cia/publications/factbook. The figures are for the early 2000s. The standard for significance for the correlations reported in the chapter is .05 level. The data from this source does not contain information on education levels, and they are difficult to compare across countries, but affluence is strongly correlated with educational attainment.

9. For Table 5.1, we include only the spouse and the first-named discussant 'of important matters'.

10. Bias is not the only relevant aspect of message content, of course. Previous research shows that messages can set the agenda of candidate or party evaluations by 'priming' certain dimensions of judgement, such as particular issues or candidate characteristics (Iyengar and Kinder 1987), and by 'framing' what is applicable to that judgement (Iyengar 1991).

11. In Chile, the parties of the centre and left formed an electoral alliance (the Concertación); we used the coalition candidate as the object for our measure of bias.

12. We rely on respondent perceptions to measure bias in this study because no other information is available. While perceptions of the receiver are not an unerring basis for determining the partisan bias of the source, empirical evidence from the 1992 study in the United States suggests that the difference between bias measured at the source and bias measured through the receiver's perceptions of the source is small (Beck 2002).

13. Rubin (1981) describes how many American newspapers deserted their partisan-press moorings in the late 1800s when their owners realized that they could profit in a mass market from advertising that would reach a wide spectrum of readers. During the 1900s, the increasing importance of advertising as the main source of newspaper revenues reinforced their movement towards non-partisanship, which in turn undermined the need for newspaper competition at the local level, thus fostering the present-day local monopolies.

14. Because our country surveys differed with regard to how many discussants the primary respondent was asked to identify, we are not able to go any deeper into the discussion networks than spouse and the first non-spouse discussant and still have comparable figures across all twelve cases. Moreover, we asked only about one television source and two newspapers sources, thus limiting comparisons to the first discussant.

15. Beyond agreement, the other possibilities are that the source is non-partisan, which especially for the media is by far the more likely stance, or has a different bias than the respondent's own vote preference.

16. A preliminary analysis of CNEP III data derived from our 2004 presidential election survey has indicated that embedded polarization did, indeed, increase over the following decade. Some of these findings will be presented in Chapter 7 of this volume, and this theme will be more extensively explored in a forthcoming volume.

17. Questions about the nature of the relationships were not asked in Japan.

18. Status was treated very stringently with only spouses and discussants having almost *identical* occupation or education levels with those of the respondents coded as the same.

19. Researchers have questioned the existence of long-term party loyalties or party identifications as separate from the vote outside the United States. Richardson (1991) has shown that people in Britain, West Germany, and the Netherlands, all countries where party identification's relevance had been questioned by prominent critics, were able to answer partisanship questions over various time intervals in ways that indicate some kind of party tie exists for many voters, and demonstrated that this party tie was stable for many persons. Richardson (1988) also has found that there is a type of 'habitual voter' in Japan who lacks a self-conscious confessed tie, yet who votes regularly for the same party, perhaps as an act of conformity to social networks. Even though psychological partisanship has appeared to have weakened to some degree in European political systems (Dalton, Flanagan, and Beck 1984; Kaase 1976; Rose and McAllister 1986; Dalton and Wattenberg 2000; Thomassen 2005; Dalton 2006: 177–200) partisan loyalty still maintains a robustness and stability relative to people's attitudes to more transient objects of politics. Overall, however, some caution is warranted in treating partisan loyalties as separate from the vote in some countries, especially those with fairly new party systems.

20. Because a different question was asked in Japan about a respondent's party loyalty, it cannot be included in the analysis.

21. Respondents in our surveys were asked about their membership in secondary organizations, and it was generally so limited and their political messages so infrequent that they were not included in this chapter's analysis.

22. CNEP III surveys conducted since 2000, however, include extensive batteries of questions concerning Internet exposure and bias. Thus, future analyses will explore their impact on campaign politics and electoral choice.

Chapter 6

1. I am grateful to Richard Gunther, José Ramón Montero, Hans-Jürgen Puhle, all participants of the 2003 and 2004 CNEP meetings and all participants

at the *Fòrum de Recerca* of the Pompeu Fabra University for the valuable comments to an earlier version of this chapter, and especially to Marina Costa Lobo for the discussions that led to its very first version, in which she collaborated.

2. In eight of the eleven surveys, questions started by asking respondents about the political leanings of spouses before questions about other people with whom important topics were discussed were applied. However, in three cases, questions were asked about discussants of any kind. Thus, in order to render results strictly comparable, we excluded spouse or partner from the analysis, and concentrated strictly on the two most important discussants excluding spouses or partners in all cases. This exclusion is probably not particularly problematic: by excluding those with whom respondents have more intimate relationships, we make the test for intermediation effects more demanding.

3. The exceptions are the United Kingdom, Italy, and Hong Kong. In the UK, questions about organizations and political party contacts were not asked. In Italy, information about party contacts is absent. Finally, in Hong Kong, no question was asked about party contacts made by mail.

4. See Appendix 6.1 for details on the coding of all variables.

5. An obvious alternative measure of individual voters' predispositions would be ideology, particularly individuals' self-placement in the left–right/liberal–conservative scale. However, while it is possible to argue that 'electoral researchers have generally accepted that the concept [of party identification] could be usefully applied in most democratic systems' (Dalton 2000: 20), the same is clearly not the case with ideological values, especially as they are commonly measured in terms of a left–right continuum. While the left–right continuum seems to be a valid measure in Western industrialized democracies (Kim and Fording 1998, 2003), when we move to the non-Western world, left and right tend to basically amount to 'cues given by political parties, denoting a party space, not an ideological space, for the electorate' (Arian and Shamir 1983; see also Finlay, Simon, and Wilson 1974).

6. This particular test should be conceived as even more (and perhaps unrealistically) stringent if we believed that party identification, as it is measured in surveys, tends to capture little else but current voting intentions (Butler and Stokes 1969; Budge, Crewe, and Farlie 1976). However, the well-documented secular decline of party identification in Western democracies in the last decades, the generic factors found to influence such decline on the basis of survey data—socio-economic modernization and cognitive mobilization (Dalton 2000)—and the fact that the impact of party identification seems to vary across countries at all levels of development and in different geo-cultural areas according to predictable institutional variables (Norris 2004) is scarcely compatible with the notion that party identification, as captured by survey data, should be seen as nothing else but a mere proxy for current voting preferences.

7. Japan is excluded from this analysis for lack of questions on both evaluations of economy and candidates in the survey.

8. It is also interesting to note that, among the six countries in which legislative elections were analysed, Spain and Japan are those in which added explanatory power of intermediation variables is highest when party identification is controlled for. These were also the two countries in the group of legislative elections which enjoyed the highest levels of socio-economic development throughout the 1990s. This should remind us of the fact that one of the foremost explanations for the declining relevance of social-group and partisan cues in voting behaviour—and thus for a more relevant role of informational intermediation—relates it to citizens' increasing levels of cognitive mobilization (Dalton 1996; Inglehart 1997).

9. In the United States, although 45% of voters report having been contacted by parties in any way, 20% report having been contacted directly by phone or personally, while 38% report having received mail propaganda. The disproportion in terms of mail contacts is much higher in Greece and Spain. In the former, 53% of voters were contacted, 43% of them by mail, while the same values for the latter are, respectively, 51% and 49%.

10. In Greece, Spain, or the United States, at least half of those voters who were contacted by parties reported contacts by *both* the opposition *and* the incumbent parties or candidates. The main exception here is Japan, where parties' ability to reach out to voters is both exceptionally high and greatly one-sided (in this case, unsurprisingly in favour of LDP candidates).

11. Thus (as can be seen in Appendix 6.2), in Bulgaria, *Demokratsya* and the private TV networks were coded as biased for the incumbent (UDF), while *Duma* and *BTN* were coded as biased for the opposition (BCP). In Italy, *La Reppublica, L'Unità, Il Manifesto, Corriere della Sera, La Stampa,* and *Messaggero* (newspapers) and *Rai Tre* (network) were coded as biased for the incumbent (Ulivo), while *Il Giornale, Resto del Carlino,* and *La Nazione* (newspapers) and *Canale 5, Italia 1, Rete 4, Rai Uno,* and *Rai Due* (networks) were coded as opposition-biased. In the UK, *The Sun, The Mail, The Times, The Express,* and *The Telegraph* were coded as incumbent-biased (Conservative) while *The Mirror, The Guardian,* and the *Financial Times* (newspapers), as well as *BBC, ITN,* and *SKY* were coded as opposition-biased (Labour). Finally, in Spain, *El País* and *TVE* were coded as biased for PSOE (the incumbent), while *ABC, El Mundo,* and the private networks were coded as biased for the opposition. Remaining outlets coded as neutral.

Chapter 7

1. The classic statement on the importance of 'institutionalization' of conflict is Barnes (1966). Knutsen and Scarbrough (1995: 494) make a similar point in their discussion of value-based 'cleavage politics'.

2. See Lazarsfeld, Berelson, and Gaudet (1948), Berelson, Lazarsfeld, and McPhee (1954), and Katz and Lazarsfeld (1955).

3. See Diamond and Plattner (1998), Nathan (1997), Shi (2003), and the East Asian Democratization and Value Change Project—subsequently named the Asian Barometer (http://eastasiabarometer.org).

4. Left–right materialism was a scale composed of items dealing with state vs. private ownership, strong vs. weak role for government in economic planning, support vs. opposition regarding redistributing wealth, and support vs. resistance on expanding social welfare.

5. Knutsen and Scarbrough have made significant contribution to the study of the relationship between values and vote choice. However, their work is limited in several aspects. First, their scope of investigation was confined to eight West European countries. Secondly, their research strategy was a secondary analysis of existing survey data drawn from different sources, with the consequence that non-comparable question items were used for comparison. This chapter tries to overcome these limitations by relying on a more comprehensive sample of different kinds of countries and producing cross-nationally comparable data based on a common battery of value items. Moreover, we prefer using multivariate regression analyses to ensure better control for potential factors of explanation.

6. This accords with the definition set forth by Milton Rokeach (1973: 5, 7, 18) who argues that a 'value is an enduring belief that a specific mode of conduct or end-state of existence is personally or socially preferable to an appositive or converse mode of conduct or end-state of existence'. To Rokeach, a value is a belief of the third kind—a prescriptive or prescriptive belief 'wherein some means or ends of action is judged to be desirable or undesirable'. Values can be distinguished from attitudes in several ways. An attitude refers to an organization of several beliefs around a specific object or a situation, whereas a value is a single but general belief, transcending specific objects or situations. A value is a standard to judge good or bad, right or wrong, and so on, but an attitude is not a standard. Finally, Rokeach argues that 'values occupy a more central position than attitudes . . . and they are therefore determinants of attitudes as well as of behaviour'.

7. The literature on these classic ideas and ideologies is huge. Pertinent examples include Conway (1995), Taylor (1960), Suvanto (1997), and Graves (1984).

8. In preparation for the inclusion into the CNEP of a number of Muslim countries contemplating the adoption of *Sharia* law, the *ReligLib* item was changed, posing a choice between 'Our religious beliefs should provide the basis for the laws of our country' and 'No single set of religious beliefs should be imposed on our country'. This is the version of the question that was included in the 2004 American presidential election survey.

9. A convenient reference is provided by Laidler (1968). Also see Lerner (1994) and Wuthnow (1989).

10. Interesting work in this regard includes Steger (1997), Howell (1980), Padgett and Patterson (1994), and Callaghan (2000).
11. See, e.g., Sani (1974), Gunther, Sani, and Shabad (1986), Sani and Montero (1986) and Westholm (1997).
12. Unfortunately, the absence of the left–right item from the Hong Kong survey which included the values battery precludes this stage of analysis of those data.
13. For our purposes, the Oblimin rotation seems to be a preferable method for both theoretical and empirical reasons. Theoretically, it is difficult to assume that these ideological dimensions are concepts independent from each other. Empirically, the Varimax components matrices for each individual country do reveal that several items load high or moderately on more than one dimension. The assumption of orthogonality cannot be sustained. Therefore it is more appropriate to use oblique rotations.
14. Abortion was not included among the items in the Hong Kong survey's 'values battery'.
15. Hong Kong was not included in this confirmatory factor analysis both because two strong sets of correlations (involving *EqualInd* and *ServTax*) were of the wrong sign, and because the absence of one variable (*Abortion*) would have precluded comparison with the RMSEA statistics for the other countries (which are based on χ^2 statistics).
16. See Gunther and Montero (2001: 101–5, 121–4).
17. Sources: For 1952–2000 presidential elections, Fiorina (2005: 69); for 2004, CNEP post-election survey.
18. This conclusion stands in sharp contrast with the title, the bold statements on the dust jacket, and the argument of the first five chapters of Morris Fiorina's 2005 book, although our findings are most consistent with the data presented in the final three chapters of Fiorina's book. This apparent inconsistency is the result of the fact that Fiorina addresses this question from two different perspectives. His assertion that there is no deep cultural cleavage in American society is based on an examination of marginals and simple comparisons between the distribution of opinion between red and blue states (at the aggregate level), between the old and the young, or between men and women. Seen from this perspective, there is no marked polarization of the American public; and this same conclusion can be drawn from the data we presented in Table 7.1 and the accompanying narrative in the text. These seemingly incompatible findings raise a fundamental question: what defines the 'real' politics in a country—the distribution of public opinion at the mass level, or the manifestation of opinion in electoral behaviour. We regard public opinion as 'raw material' which is then moulded into political behaviour through the electoral mobilization efforts of elites, the media, and partisan secondary associations. It is the mobilization of segments of the electorate into sharply opposing camps that has the most direct and powerful impact on the nature of politics in a democratic system. Political elites and parties structure the political agenda,

frame political discourse, engage in electoral competition with each other, and formulate policies, and the way they choose to perform these functions may be substantially out of step with modal public preferences. Sharply divisive conflict at the elite level, with each party's respective electorate mirroring that polarization, may be an unfortunate departure from the moderate preferences of the model voter, but it is not a 'myth'. While our interpretation clashes with the bold language used by Fiorina in many parts of his influential book, he, himself, acknowledges this undesirable reality, and attributes 'the hijacking of American democracy' to the takeover of once pragmatic catch-all parties by ideological purists and extremists. In short, he attributes the polarization of the American electorate to changes in the intermediation roles played by parties and their allied secondary associations and communications media.

19. Modern Social Democracy was excluded because an initial round of analysis found that its inclusion in the equation actually reduced the percentage of variance explained.

20. In Spain and Greece, which most closely conformed to the CNEP II core questionnaire format, the measures of socio-economic position that were used were the interviewer's assessment of the quality of the respondent's housing and neighbourhood. Extensive analyses of these two variables found that they were better measures of the respondent's degree of affluence than any other variables, especially self-report of income (which produced unacceptably high levels of non-responses, and which produce much confusion and uncertainty among respondents in economies within which workers typically have several jobs or receive considerable supplementary income that goes well beyond the stated base salary). In the United States and Uruguay, the respondent's self-report of income was used.

21. In Spain, the respondent's self-description as a 'very good Catholic', 'practicing Catholic', 'not-very-practicing Catholic', 'non-practicing Catholic', 'indifferent', 'atheist' or 'believer in another religion' was used as the indicator of religiosity. In Greece, frequency of church attendance was used; in Uruguay, the indicator was based on the respondent's self-description as 'Catholic', 'Christian', 'believer', 'deist', 'agnostic', 'atheist', 'no religion' or 'other'. In the United States, two types of measures of religiosity (based on the National Election Study standard format) were used: one of these measured frequency of church attendance; the other was based on the respondent's self-identification with a specific denomination, which was subsequently recoded into dichotomous 'dummy variables' representing White Evangelical Protestant, White mainline Protestant, Catholic, Jewish, and 'nontraditional' religious groups. In the case of the United States, it is important to note that African-American respondents were not included in this analysis, since affiliation with Black Evangelical Protestant denominations was more a measure of ethnicity (a social cleavage which is not present in the other countries in this study, whose inclusion would undermine the comparability of these empirical findings)

than of religiosity. Indeed, Black Evangelical Protestants are the strongest supporters of the Democratic Party, while White Evangelical Protestants and 'nontraditional' Christians are the most solidly Republican in their partisan preferences.

22. For each of those secondary associations that the respondent belonged to, a score of −1 was allocated if the respondent perceived the organization as favouring the party or parties of the left, +1 was assigned if the group favoured the party or parties of the right, and 0 was assigned if the organization did not favour a party. These scores were added together, resulting in composite scores that (in the case of the United States) ranged from −3 to +3. However, since very few respondents belonged to more than one organization with a partisan bias in most countries, scores were collapsed to a range of −1 to +1 for all countries. It should be noted that individuals belonging to no organizations, those belonging to groups with no partisan biases, and those who belonged to groups whose partisan biases cancelled each other out, a score of 0 was produced.

23. With regard to radio and television broadcasts, these 'bias' scales were calculated in such a manner as to compensate for the tendency of individuals to deny that news sources favouring their own personal preferences are biased. The first step in the construction of these scales was to calculate the net perceived bias of the news outlet as a percentage of its total viewer/listener/readership. Media outlets that were perceived as strongly favouring parties or candidates of the left were assigned negative net scores; those favouring parties or candidates of the right were scored positively; and scores of 0 reflect perfect balance in news coverage. For example, the ABC evening news with Peter Jennings was perceived to be unbiased by the overwhelming majority of its viewers, with the remainder claiming that it was biased split almost evenly between those thinking that it favoured Democrats and those perceiving a pro-Republican bias, giving it a score of −.9 (very slightly pro-Democratic). CNN's Headline News was perceived as slightly pro-Republican, and was given a score of +1.7. NBC evening news with Tom Brokaw and CBS evening news with Dan Rather were somewhat pro-Democratic (−6.6 and −8.9, respectively). Fox News Live, however, was seen as strongly pro-Republican, and received a net bias score of +18.3. Once these bias scores were calculated, the variable indicating which news broadcast was viewed was recoded so that *all* viewers of that programme were assigned that score (whether or not they, themselves, perceived bias). And persons who did not watch (or listen to) any such programme were given scores of 0, reflecting the fact that they were not exposed to biased information from that source. With regard to newspapers, bias scores were based on content analysis by country experts for Spain, Greece, and Uruguay. Since the overwhelming majority of the American newspaper market is dominated by small city-specific newspapers, however, it was not possible to separately

code each newspaper. Accordingly, the simple variable reflecting respondents' perceptions of partisan bias was used instead.

24. Dalton, Beck, and Huckfeldt concluded on the bases of extensive content analysis of newspaper coverage of the 1992 campaign that 'the American press does not present clear and singular messages about presidential elections but, rather, multiple messages about the candidates and the campaign' (1998: 111). They did find, however, that editorial endorsements of candidates did have an impact on electoral behaviour.

25. With regard to the United States, Uruguay and Spain, the party supported by each individual discussion partner is reported, while in Greece the respondent was only asked if the discussant supported a 'different party' or 'the same party'. Since it is not possible to determine—for a PASOK voter, e.g.—if the 'different party' was Nea Demokratia (a party of the right) or the KKE or Left Coalition (both on the same side of the left–right divide as PASOK), the impact of this discussant bias on vote for party or parties of the left vs. right cannot be so precisely determined as in the case of the other three countries.

26. We would like to thank Hans-Jürgen Puhle for providing us with the analysis of Uruguay's trajectory of political development, on which this discussion is based.

27. Indeed, when supporters of the Concertación parties are examined separately it is noteworthy that the mean scores on this Traditional Conservative scale more clearly divide Socialists from Christian Democrats (by .6 points on a 10-point scale) than they do the aggregate of Concertación supporters from the right-wing opposition (.1 point).

28. Correlations between our core measures of fundamental support for democracy (agree/disagree, 'Democracy is the best form of government for a country like ours' [DemBest]; and preferences for democratic vs. authoritarian regimes) were significant at the .001 level only in Spain with regard to Traditional Conservatism (Pearson's $r = .11$), Social Democracy (.14), and Postmaterialism (.12). Only one of these value scales (Modern Social Democracy) in Greece was correlated with DemBest at a level of statistical significance of .01 (Pearson's $r = -.09$). None of the other values scales in Spain, Greece, Uruguay, Chile, and the United States was correlated with support for democracy at a level of significance of .05 or better. Due to the incoherence of the values clusters that emerged from our analyses in Hungary and Hong Kong, these correlations were not calculated.

29. The percentages of the variance in party ID were somewhat lower, ranging from .25 in the United States to .11 in Uruguay, where only a small minority of respondents claimed to identify with a political party.

References

Aarts, K. (1995). 'Intermediate Organizations and Interest Representation', in H.-D. Klingemann and D. Fuchs (eds.).

_____ and Semetko, H. (2003). 'The Divided Electorate: Media Use and Political Involvement', *Journal of Politics*, 65: 759–84.

Alaminos, A. (1991). *Chile: transición política y sociedad*. Madrid: Centro de Investigaciones Sociológicas/Siglo XXI.

Alexander, G. (2002). *The Sources of Democratic Consolidation*. Ithaca, NY: Cornell University Press.

Allen, W. S. (1965). *The Nazi Seizure of Power*. Chicago, IL: Quadrangle Books.

Almond, G. A. (1990). *A Discipline Divided. Schools and Sects in Political Science*. Thousand Oaks, CA: Sage.

_____ (1993). 'Foreword: The Return to Political Culture', in L. Diamond (ed.), *Political Culture and Democracy in Developing Countries*. Boulder, CO and London: Lynne Rienner.

_____ and Powell, G. B. (1978). *Comparative Politics: System, Process, and Policy*. Boston, MA: Little, Brown & Company.

_____ and Verba, S. (1963). *The Civic Culture: Political Attitudes and Democracy in Five Nations*. Princeton, NJ: Princeton University Press.

Alt, J. (1984). 'Dealignment and the Dynamics of Partisanship in Britain', in R. Dalton et al. (eds.), *Electoral Change in Advanced Industrial Democracies: Realignment or Dealignment?* Princeton, NJ: Princeton University Press.

Altheide, D. L. and Snow, R. P. (1988). 'Toward a Theory of Mediation', in J. A. Anderson (ed.), *Communication Yearbook 11*. Newbury Park, CA: Sage.

Anderson, C. A. (1998a). 'Parties, Party Systems and Satisfaction with Democratic Performance in the New Europe', in R. Hofferbert (ed.), *Parties and Democracy: Party Structure and Party Performance in Old and New Democracies*. Oxford: Blackwell.

_____ (1998b). 'Political Satisfaction in Old and New Democracies', Institute for European Studies Working Paper 98.4. Ithaca, NY: Cornell University.

Anderson, C. J. and Guillory, C. A. (1997). 'Political Institutions and Satisfaction with Democracy: A Cross-National Analysis of Consensus and Majoritarian Systems', *American Political Science Review*, 91: 66–81.

—— and Tverdova, Y. V. (2001). 'Winners, Losers and Attitudes About Government in Contemporary Democracies', *International Political Science Review*, 22: 321–38.

Anduiza Perea, E. (1999). *Individuos o sistemas? Las razones de la abstención en Europa Occidental*. Madrid: CIS.

Ansolabehere, S., Behr, R., and Iyengar, S. (1993). *The Media Game: American Politics in the Television Age*. New York: Macmillan.

Arian, A. and Shamir, M. (1983). 'The Primarily Political Function of the Left–Right Continuum', *Comparative Politics*, 15: 139–58.

Ball-Rokeach, S. J. and DeFleur, M. L. (1976). 'A Dependency Model of Mass-Media Effects', *Communication Research*, 3: 3–21.

Barnea, M. F. and Schwartz, S. H. (1998). 'Values and Voting', *Political Psychology*, 19: 17–40.

Barnes, S. (1966). 'Ideology and the Organization of Conflict', *Journal of Politics*, 28: 513–30.

Bartels, L. M. (1993). 'Messages Received: The Political Impact of Media Exposure', *American Political Science Review*, 87: 267–85.

—— (2002). 'Beyond the Running Tally: Partisan Bias in Political Perceptions', *Political Behavior*, 24: 117–50.

Bartolini, S. (2000). *The Political Mobilization of the European Left, 1860–1980: The Class Cleavage*. Cambridge: Cambridge University Press.

—— (2002). 'Electoral and Party Competition: Analytical Dimensions and Empirical Problems', in Gunther, Montero, and Linz (eds.) (2002).

—— and Mair, P. (1990). *Identity, Competition and Electoral Availability: The Stabilization of European Electorates, 1885–1985*. Cambridge: Cambridge University Press.

Basperoni, G. (ed.) (1997). *ITANES 1990–1996. Italian National Election Studies. Results of the Nationwide Voter Sample Surveys Conducted by the Istituto Cattaneo in 1990, 1992, 1994 and 1996*. Bologna, Italy: Istituto Carlo Cattaneo.

Bates, R. H. et al. (1998). *Analytic Narratives*. Princeton, NJ: Princeton University Press.

Baumgartner, F. R. and Walker, J. L. (1988). 'Survey Research and Membership in Voluntary Associations', *American Journal of Political Science*, 32: 908–28.

Beck, P. A. (1986). 'Choice, Context, and Consequence: Beaten and Unbeaten Paths Toward a Science of Electoral Behavior', in H. F. Weisberg (ed.), *Political Science: The Science of Politics*. New York: Agathon Press.

—— (1991). 'Voters' Intermediation Environments in the 1988 Presidential Contest', *Public Opinion Quarterly*, 55: 371–94.

—— (2002). 'Encouraging Political Defection: The Role of Personal Discussion Networks in Partisan Desertions to the Opposition Party and Perot Voters in 1992', *Political Behavior*, 24: 309–37.

—— Dalton, R. J., Greene, S., and Huckfeldt, R. (2002). 'The Social Calculus of Voting: Interpersonal, Media, and Organizational Influences on Presidential Choices', *American Political Science Review*, 96: 57–73.

References

Bell, D. (1960). *The End of Ideology: On the Exhaustion of Political Ideas in the Fifties*. Glencoe, IL: Free Press.

Bennett, W. L. (1998). 'The Media and Democratic Development: The Social Basis of Political Communication', in P. H. O'Neil (ed.), *Communicating Democracy. The Media and Political Transitions*. Boulder, CO: Lynne Rienner.

____ and Entman, R. M. (eds.) (2001). *Mediated Politics: Communication in the Future of Democracy*. New York: Cambridge University Press.

Berelson, B. R., Lazarsfeld, P. F., and McPhee, W. N. (1954). *Voting: A Study of Opinion Formation in a Presidential Campaign*. Chicago, IL: University of Chicago Press.

Berman, S. (1997a). 'Civil Society and Political Institutionalization', *American Behavioral Scientist*, 40: 562–74.

____ (1997b). 'Civil Society and the Collapse of the Weimar Republic', *World Politics*, 49: 401–29.

Blumler, J. G. and Gurevitch, M. (1995). *The Crisis of Public Communication*. London: Routledge.

Braga de Macedo, J. B. (1983). 'Newspapers and Democracy in Portugal: The Role of Market Structure', in K. Maxwell (ed.), *The Press and the Rebirth of Iberian Democracy*. Westport, CT: Greenwood Press.

Bratton, M. (2005). *Public Opinion, Democracy, and Market Reform in Africa*. Cambridge: Cambridge University Press.

____ and Mattes, R. (2001a). 'Support for Democracy in Africa: Intrinsic or Instrumental', *British Journal of Political Science*, 31: 447–74.

____ ____ (2001b). 'How People View Democracy: Africans' Surprising Universalism', *Journal of Democracy*, 12: 107–21.

Bruck, P. A. (1993). 'Current Media Economic and Policy Problems in Central Europe', *Journal of Media Economics*, 6: 3–13.

____ and Stocker, G. (1996). *Die ganz normale Vielfältigkeit des Lesens. Zur Rezeption von Boulevardzeitungen*. Münster, Germany: Lit.

Budge, I., Crewe, I., and Farlie, D. J. (eds.) (1976). *Party Identification and Beyond: Representations of Voting and Party Competition*. London: John Wiley & Sons.

Burbank, M. J. (1997). 'Explaining Contextual Effects on Vote Choice', *Political Behavior*, 19: 113–32.

Bustamante, E. (1989). 'TV and Public Service in Spain: A Difficult Encounter', *Media, Culture and Society*, 11: 67–87.

Butler, D. and Ranney, A. (eds.) (1992). *Electioneering*. New York: Oxford University Press.

____ and Stokes, D. E. (1969). *Political Change in Britain*. London: Macmillan.

Caciagli, M. and Corbetta, P. (eds.) (2002). *Le ragioni dell'elettore. Perché ha vinto il centro-destra nelle elezioni italiane del 2001*. Bologna: IL Mulino.

Callaghan, J. (2000). *The Retreat of Social Democracy*. Manchester, UK: Manchester University Press.

Campbell, A., Converse, P., Miller, W., and Stokes, D. (1960). *The American Voter*. New York: John Wiley & Sons.

Canache, D., Mondak, J. J., and Seligson, M. A. (2001). 'Meaning and Measurement in Cross-National Research on Satisfaction with Democracy', *Public Opinion Quarterly*, 65: 506–28.

Cappella, J. N. and Jamieson, K. H. (1997). *The Spiral of Cynicism: The Press and the Public Good*. New York: Oxford University Press.

Caprara, G. V., Schwartz, S., Capanna, C., Vecchione, M., and Barbaranelli, C. (2005). 'Personality and Politics: Values, Traits and Political Choice', Unpublished manuscript.

Carrow, M. M., Churchill, R. P., and Cordes, J. J. (1998). *Democracy, Social Values, and Public Policy*. Westport, CT: Praeger.

Chaffee, S. H. and Schleuder, J. (1986). 'Measurement and Effects of Attention to Media News', *Human Communication Research*, 13: 76–107.

Chaves, M. and Gorski, P. S. (2001). 'Religious Pluralism and Religious Participation', *Annual Review of Sociology*, 27: 261–81.

Chong, D. (2000). *Rational Lives: Norms and Values in Politics and Society*. Chicago, IL: University of Chicago Press.

Clarke, H. et al. (2004). *Political Choice in Britain*. Oxford: Oxford University Press.

Collier, R. B. and Collier, D. (1991). *Shaping the Political Arena: Critical Junctures, the Labor Movement, and Regime Dynamics in Latin America*. Princeton, NJ: Princeton University Press.

Converse, P. E. (1969). 'Of Time and Partisan Stability', *Comparative Political Studies*, 2: 139–71.

—— (1990). 'Popular Representation and the Distribution of Information', in J. A. Ferejohn and J. H. Kuklinski (eds.), *Information and Democratic Processes*. Urbana, IL and Chicago, IL: University of Illinois Press.

Conway, D. (1995). *Classical Liberalism: The Unvanquished Ideal*. New York: St. Martin's Press.

Corbetta, P. and Parisi, A. (1994*a*). 'Il calo della partecipazione elettorale: Disaffezione delle istituzioni o crisi dei riferimenti partici', *Polis*, 8: 29–65.

—— —— (1994*b*). 'Smobilitazione partitica e astensionismo elettorale', *Polis*, 8: 423–43.

Corbin, J. R. (1993). *The Anarchist Passion: Class Conflict in Southern Spain, 1810–1965*. Aldershot, UK: Avebury.

Costa, P. A. and Freire, A. (eds.) (2003). *Elites, sociedade e mudança política*. Oeiras, Portugal: Celta Editora.

Cox, G. W., Rosenbluth, F. M., and Theis, M. F. (1998). 'Mobilization, Social Networks, and Turnout: Evidence from Japan', *World Politics*, 50: 447–74.

Craig, S. C. (1993). *The Malevolent Leaders: Popular Discontent in America*. Boulder, CO: Westview Press.

Curtice, J. and Semetko, H. (1994). 'Does It Matter What the Papers Say?' in A. Heath, R. Jowell, and J. Curtice (eds.), *Labour's Last Chance?* Aldershot, UK: Dartmouth.

Curtis, J. E., Douglas, E. B., and Grabb, E. G. (2001). 'Nations of Joiners: Explaining Voluntary Association Membership in Democratic Societies', *American Sociological Review*, 66: 783–805.

Daalder, H. (2002). 'Parties: Denied, Dismissed, or Redundant? A Critique', in Gunther, Montero, and Linz (eds.) (2002).

Dalton, R. J. (1984). 'Cognitive Mobilization and Partisan Dealignment in Advanced Industrial Democracies', *Journal of Politics*, 46: 264–84.

—— (1996). *Citizen Politics: Public Opinion and Political Parties in Advanced Industrial Democracies*, 2nd edn. Chatham, UK: Chatham House.

—— (2000). 'The Decline of Party Identification', in R. J. Dalton and M. Wattenberg (eds.) (2000).

—— (2002). 'Political Cleavages, Issues, and Electoral Change', in LeDuc, Niemi, and Norris (2002).

—— (2004). *Democratic Challenges, Democratic Choices: The Erosion of Political Support in Advanced Industrial Democracies*. Oxford: Oxford University Press.

—— (2006). *Citizen Politics: Public Opinion and Political Parties in Advanced Industrial Democracies*. Washington, DC: CQ Press.

—— and Wattenberg, M. P. (1993). 'The Not so Simple Act of Voting', in A. Finifter (ed.), *The State of the Discipline*. Washington, DC: American Political Science Association.

—— —— (eds.) (2000). *Parties Without Partisans: Political Change in Advanced Industrial Democracies*. Oxford: Oxford University Press.

—— Beck, P. A., and Huckfeldt, R. (1998). 'Partisan Cues and the Media: Information Flows in the 1992 Presidential Election', *American Political Science Review*, 92: 111–26.

—— Flanagan, S. C., and Beck, P. A. (1984). *Electoral Change in Advanced Industrial Democracies: Realignment or Dealignment?* Princeton, NJ: Princeton University Press.

de Mateo, R. (1997). 'Spain', in Ostergaard (1997).

Delgado Rühl, A. (1994). 'Massenmedien in Chile', in J. Wilke (ed.), *Massenmedien in Lateinamerika*, vol. 2. Frankfurt am Main, Germany: Vervuert.

Delli, C., Michael, X., and Keeter, S. (1996). *What Americans Know about Politics and Why It Matters*. New Haven, CT and London: Yale University Press.

Deutsch, K. W. (1961). 'Social Mobilization and Political Development', *American Political Science Review*, 55: 493–514.

Diamandouros, P. N. and Gunther, R. (1995). 'Preface', in Gunther, Diamandouros, and Puhle (1995).

—— —— (2001a). P. N. Diamandouros and R. Gunther (eds.), *Parties, Politics, and Democracy in the New Southern Europe*. Baltimore, MD: Johns Hopkins University Press.

—— —— (2001b). 'Introduction', in Diamandouros and Gunther (2001a).

Diamond, L. (1993). 'Introduction: Political Culture and Democracy', in L. Diamond (ed.), *Political Culture and Democracy in Developing Countries*. Boulder, CO and London: Lynne Rienner.

—— (1999). *Developing Democracy: Toward Consolidation*. Baltimore, MD: Johns Hopkins University Press.

—— and Morlino, L. (2005). *Assessing the Quality of Democracy*. Baltimore, MD: Johns Hopkins University Press.

—— and Plattner, M. F. (eds.) (1998). *Democracy in East Asia*. Baltimore, MD: Johns Hopkins University Press.

Dimitras, P. E. (1997). 'Greece', in Ostergaard (1997).

DiPalma, G. (1970). *Apathy and Participation: Mass Politics in Western Societies*. New York: Free Press.

Downs, A. (1957). *An Economic Theory of Democracy*. New York: Harper.

Easton, D. (1965). *A Systems Analysis of Political Life*. Chicago, IL: University of Chicago Press.

—— (1975). 'A Reassessment of the Concept of Political Support', *British Journal of Political Science*, 21: 285–313.

Edwards, B., Foley, M. W., and Diani, M. (eds.) (2001). *Beyond Tocqueville: Civil Society and the Social Capital Debate in Comparative Perspective*. Hanover, MA: University Press of New England.

Elder, L. and Greene, G. (2003). 'Political Information, Gender, and the Voter: The Differential Impact of Organizations, Personal Discussion, and the Media on Electoral Decisions of Women and Men', *The Social Science Journal*, 40: 385–99.

Elster, J. (ed.) (1996). *The Round Table Talks and the Breakdown of Communism*. Chicago, IL and London: University of Chicago Press.

Encarnación, O. G. (2000). 'Beyond Transitions: The Politics of Democratic Consolidation', *Comparative Politics*, 32: 479–98.

Enyedi, Z. (2003). 'Cleavage Formation in Hungary: The Role of Agency', Paper presented at the 2003 ECPR Joint Sessions, Workshop 19, Edinburgh.

Esenwein, G. R. (1989). *Anarchist Ideology and the Working-class Movement in Spain, 1868–1898*. Berkeley, CA: University of California Press.

Espindola, R. (2002). 'Electoral Campaigning and the Consolidation of Democracy in Latin America—the Southern Cone', Paper presented to the workshop on Political Communication, the Mass Media and the Consolidation of New Democracies, ECPR Joint Sessions of Workshops, 22–27 March 2002, Torino, Italy.

Esping-Andersen, G. (1900). *The Three Worlds of Welfare Capitalism*. Cambridge: Polity Press.

Ester, P., Halman, L., and de Moor, R. (eds.) (1994). *The Individualizing Society: Value Change in Europe and North America*. Tilburg, Netherlands: Tilburg University Press.

Evans, G. (1999). *The End of Class Politics?* Oxford: Oxford University Press.

_____ and Whitefield, S. (1995). 'The Politics and Economics of Democratic Commitment: Support for Democracy in Transition Societies', *British Journal of Political Science*, 25: 485–514.

Farah, B. G., Barnes, S. H., and Heunks, F. (1979). 'Political Dissatisfaction', in S. H. Barnes, M. Kaase et al. (eds.), *Political Action: Mass Participation in Five Western Democracies*. Beverly Hills, CA: Sage.

Farrell, D. M. and Paul, W. (2000). 'Political Parties as Campaign Organizations', in R. J. Dalton and M. Wattenberg (eds.), *Parties Without Partisans: Political Change in Advanced Industrial Democracies*. Oxford: Oxford University Press.

Finlay, D. J., Simon, D. W., and Wilson, L. A. (1974). 'The Concept of Left and Right in Cross-National Research', *Comparative Political Studies*, 7: 209–21.

Fiorina, M. A. (1981). *Retrospective Voting in American National Elections*. New Haven, CT: Yale University Press.

_____ (1999). 'Extreme Voices: A Dark Side of Civic Engagement', in T. Skocpol and M. P. Fiorina (eds.), *Civic Engagement in American Democracy*. Washington, DC: Brookings.

_____ (2005). *Culture War? The Myth of a Polarized America*. New York: Pearson and Longman.

Foweraker, J. and Krznaric, R. (2000). 'Measuring Liberal Democratic Performance: An Empirical and Conceptual Critique', *Political Studies*, 48: 759–87.

Fox, E. (1988). 'Media Policies in Latin America: An Overview', in E. Fox (ed.), *Media and Politics in Latin America. The Struggle for Democracy*. London: Sage.

Franklin, M. (1996). 'Electoral Participation', in L. Le Duc, R. Niemi, and P. Norris (eds.), *Comparing Democracies*. London: Sage.

_____ Mackie, T., Valen, H. et al. (1992). *Electoral Change: Responses to Evolving Social and Attitudinal Structures in Western Countries*. Cambridge: Cambridge University Press.

Früh, W. (1991). *Medienwirkungen: Das dynamisch-transaktionale Modell. Theorie und empirische Einführung*. Opladen, Germany: Westdeutscher Verlag.

Fuchs, D. and Klingemann, H.-D. (1995). 'Citizens and the State: A Relationship Transformed', in H.-D. Klingemann and D. Fuchs (eds.) (1995).

_____ and Roller, E. (1998). 'Cultural Conditions of Transition to Liberal Democracy in Central and Eastern Europe', in S. H. Barnes and J. Simón (eds.), *The Postcommunist Citizen*. Budapest: Erasmus Foundation.

_____ Guidorossi, G., and Svensson, P. (1995). 'Support for the Democratic System', in H.-D. Klingemann and D. Fuchs (eds.) (1995).

Fung, A. (2003). 'Associations and Democracy: Between Theories, Hopes, and Realities', *Annual Review of Sociology*, 29: 515–39.

Gabriel, O. W. and van Deth, J. W. (1995). 'Political Interest', in J. W. van Deth and E. Scarbrough (eds.), *The Impact of Values*. Oxford: Oxford University Press.

Garretón, M. A. (2000). 'Chile's Elections: Change and Continuity', *Journal of Democracy*, 11: 78–84.

Geertz, C. (1973). *The Interpretation of Cultures*. New York: Basic Books.

Génique, G. (1921). *L'élection de l'Asemblée à la legislature de 1849: Essai d'une rèpartition geographique des parties en France*. Paris: Rieder.

Gerber, A. S. and Green, D. P. (2000). 'The Effects of Personal Canvassing, Telephone Calls, and Direct Mail on Voter Turnout: A Field Experiment', *American Political Science Review*, 94: 653–63.

Gergely, I. (1997). *Understanding the Media in Hungary*. Düsseldorf, Germany: The European Institute for the Media.

Giner-Sorolla, R. and Chaiken, S. (1994). 'The Causes of Hostile Media Judgments', *Journal of Experimental Social Psychology*, 30: 165–80.

Glock, C. Y. (1979). 'Organizational Innovation for Social Science Research and Training', in R. K. Merton, J. S. Coleman, and P. H. Rossi (eds.), *Qualitative and Quantitative Social Research: Papers in Honor of Paul F. Lazarsfeld*. New York: Free Press.

Goguel, F. (1851). *Géographie des elections françaises: de 1870 à 1951*. Paris: Armand Colllin.

Goldthorpe, J. H. (1968). *The Affluent Worker: Political Attitudes and Behaviour*. Cambridge: Cambridge University Press.

Gosnell, H. F. (1927). *Getting Out the Vote: An Experiment in the Stimulation of the Vote*. Chicago, IL: University of Chicago Press.

Granovetter, M. J. (1973). 'The Strength of Weak Ties', *The American Journal of Sociology*, 78: 1360–80.

Green, D. P. and Shapiro, I. (1994). *Pathologies of Rational Choice Theory: A Critique of Applications in Political Science*. New Haven, CT: Yale University Press.

Greenstein, F. I. (1965). *Children and Politics*. New Haven, CT: Yale University Press.

Graves, M. A. R. (1984). *Revolution, Reaction and the Triumph of Conservatism: English History, 1558–1700*. Auckland, NZ: Longman Paul.

Gulyas, A. (1998). 'Tabloid Newspapers in Post-Communist Hungary', *Javnost and The Public*, 5: 65–77.

Gunther, R. (1992). 'Spain: The Very Model of the Modern Elite Settlement', in Higley and Gunther (1992).

—— (2004). *Attitudes Toward Democracy in Seven Countries: Dimensional Structure and Behavioral Correlates*. Studies in Public Policy #385. Glasgow: Centre for the Study of Public Policy, University of Strathclyde.

—— (2005). 'Parties and Electoral Behavior in Southern Europe', *Comparative Politics*, 37: 253–74.

—— and Diamond, L. (2003). 'Species of Political Parties', *Party Politics*, 9: 167–200.

—— and Montero, J. R. (2000). *Legitimacy, Satisfaction and Disaffection in New Democracies*. Studies in Public Policy 0140-8240. Glasgow: Centre for the Study of Public Policy, University of Strathclyde.

—— —— (2001a). 'Die Multidimensionalität der Einstellungen zur Demokratie: Das Beispiel Spanien', in M. Gräser, C. Lammert, and S. Schreyer (eds.), *Staat, Nation, Demokratie. Traditionen und Perspektiven moderner Gesellschaften. Festschrift für Hans-Jürgen Puhle*. Göttingen, Germany: Vandenhoeck & Ruprecht.

_____ _____ (2001*b*). 'The Anchors of Partisanship', in Diamandouros and Gunther (2001*a*).

_____ _____ (2006). 'The Multidimensionality of Attitudinal support for New Democracies: Conceptual Redefinition and Empirical Refinement', in M. Torcal and J. R. Montero (eds.), *Political Disaffection in Contemporary Democracies: Social Capital, Institutions, and Politics*. London: Routledge.

_____ _____ and Wert, J. I. (2000). 'The Media and Politics in Spain: From Dictatorship to Democracy', in Gunther and Mughan (2000*a*).

_____ _____ and Linz, J. J. (eds.) (2002). *Political Parties: Old Concepts and New Challenges*. Oxford: Oxford University Press.

_____ and Mughan, A. (eds.) (2000*a*). *Democracy and the Media: A Comparative Perspective*. Cambridge: Cambridge University Press.

_____ _____ (2000*b*). 'The Political Impact of the Media: A Reassessment', in Gunther and Mughan (2000*a*).

_____ Sani, G., and Shabad, G. (1986). *Spain After Franco: The Making of a Competitive Party System*. Berkeley, CA: University of California Press.

_____ Diamandouros, P. N., and Puhle, H.-J. (eds.) (1995). *The Politics of Democratic Consolidation: Southern Europe in Comparative Perspective*. Baltimore, MD: Johns Hopkins University Press.

_____ Puhle, H.-J., and Diamandouros, P. N. (1995). 'Introduction', in Gunther, Diamandouros, and Puhle (1995).

Hall, P. and Soskice, D. (eds.) (2001). *Varieties of Capitalism*. Oxford: Oxford University Press.

Hallin, D. C. and Mancini, P. (2004). *Comparing Media Systems: Three Models of Media and Politics*. Cambridge: Cambridge University Press.

Hamilton, R. F. (1967). *Affluence and the French Worker in the Fourth Republic*. Princeton, NJ: Princeton University Press.

_____ (1972). *Class and Politics in the United States*. New York: John Wiley & Sons.

_____ (1982). *Who Voted for Hitler?* Princeton: Princeton University Press.

Hardiman, N. and Whelan, C. T. (1994). 'Values and Political Partisanship', in C. T. Whelan (ed.), *Values and Social Change in Ireland*. Dublin: Gill & Macmillan.

Hechter, M. (1993). 'Values Research in the Social and Behavioral Sciences', in M. Hechter, L. Nadel, and R. E. Michod (eds.), *The Origin of Values*. New York: Aldine de Gruyter.

Hibbing, J. R. and Theiss-Morse, E. (1995). *Congress as a Public Enemy: Public Attitudes Toward American Political Institutions*. New York: Cambridge University Press.

Higley, J. and Gunther, R. (eds.) (1992). *Elites and Democratic Consolidation in Latin America and Southern Europe*. Cambridge and New York: Cambridge University Press.

_____ and Lengyel, G. (eds.) (1999). *Elites after State Socialism*. Boulder, CO: Rowman & Littlefield.

_____ Pakulski, J., and Weslowski, W. (eds.) (1998). *Postcommunist Elites and Democracy in Eastern Europe*. London: Macmillan.

Hill, K. Q. and Matsubayashi, T. (2005). 'Civic Engagement and Mass-Elite Agenda Agreement in American Communities', *American Political Science Review*, 99: 215–24.

Hofferbert, R. I. and Klingemann, H.-D. (1999). 'Remembering the Bad Old Days: Human Rights, Economic Conditions, and Democratic Performance in Transitional Regimes', *European Journal of Political Research*, 36: 155–74.

_____ _____ (2001). 'Democracy and its Discontents in Post-Wall Germany', *International Political Science Review*, 22: 363–78.

Holbrook, T. M. (1996). *Do Campaigns Matter?* Thousand Oaks, CA: Sage.

Holmberg, S. (1999). 'Down and Down We Go: Political Trust in Sweden', in P. Norris (ed.), *Critical Citizens. Global Support for Democratic Governance*. Oxford: Oxford University Press.

Holtz-Bacha, C. (1990.) 'Videomalaise Revisited: Media Exposure and Political Alienation in West Germany', *European Journal of Communication*, 5: 78–85.

Hovland, C. I., Janis, I. L., and Kelley, H. H. (1953). *Communication and Persuasion*. New Haven, CT: Yale University Press.

Howell, D. (1980). *British Social Democracy: A Study in Development and Decay*, 2nd edn. London: Croom Helm.

Huckfeldt, R. (1986). *Politics in Context: Assimilation and Conflict in Urban Neighborhoods*. New York: Agathon Press.

_____ and Sprague, J. (1987). 'Networks in Context: The Social Flow of Political Information', *American Political Science Review*, 81: 1197–216.

_____ _____ (1995). *Citizens, Politics, and Social Communication*. Cambridge: Cambridge University Press.

_____ Dalton, R., and Levine, J. (1995). 'Political Environments, Cohesive Social Groups, and the Communication of Public Opinion', *American Journal of Political Science*, 39: 1025–54.

_____ Johnson, P. E., and Sprague, J. (2004). *Political Disagreement: The Survival of Diverse Opinions within Communication Networks*. Cambridge: Cambridge University Press.

_____ Ikeda, K., and Pappi, F. U. (2005). 'Patterns of Disagreement in Democratic Politics: Comparing Germany, Japan, and the United States', *American Journal of Political Science*, 49: 497–514.

Huneeus, C. and Maldonado, L. (2003). 'Demócratas y nostálgicos del antiguo régimen: Los apoyos a la democracia en Chile', *Revista Española de Investigaciones Sociológicas*, 203: 9–49.

Huntington, S. P. (1991). *The Third Wave. Democratization in the Late Twentieth Century*. Norman, OK and London: University of Oklahoma Press.

Ignazi, P. (1993). 'Il voto del MSI: durevole ma inquieto', in M. Caciagli and A. Spreafico (eds.), *Vent'anni di elezioni in Italia, 1968–1987*. Padova, Italy: Liviana Editrice.

Ikeda, K. and Huckfeldt, R. (2001). 'Political Communication and Disagreement Among Citizens in Japan and the United States', *Political Behavior*, 23: 23–51.

Inglehart, R. (1971). 'The Silent Revolution in Europe: Intergenerational Change in Post-Industrial Societies', *American Political Science Review*, 65: 991–1017.

—— (1977). *The Silent Revolution: Changing Values and Political Styles*. Princeton, NJ: Princeton University Press.

—— (1979). 'Value Priorities and Socioeconomic Change', in S. Barnes et al. (eds.), *Political Action: Mass Participation in Five Western Democracies*. Beverly Hills, CA: Sage.

—— (1984). 'The Changing Structure of Political Cleavages in Western Society', in R. J. Dalton, S. C. Flanagan, and P. A. Beck (eds.), *Electoral Change in Advanced Industrial Democracies: Realignment or Dealignment?* Princeton, NJ: Princeton University Press.

—— (1988). 'The Renaissance of Political Culture', *American Political Science Review*, 82: 1203–30.

—— (1990). *Culture Shift in Advanced Industrial Society*. Princeton, NJ: Princeton University Press.

—— (1997). *Modernization and Postmodernization: Cultural, Economic, and Political Change in 43 Societies*. Princeton, NJ: Princeton University Press.

—— (ed.) (2003). *Human Values and Social Change: Findings from the Values Surveys*. Leiden, Netherlands: Brill.

—— and Klingemann, H.-D. (1976). 'Party Identification, Ideological Preference and the Left–Right Dimension among Western Mass Publics', in I. Budge, I. Crewe, and D. Farlie (eds.), *Party Identification and Beyond. Representations of Voting and Party Competition*. London: John Wiley & Sons.

—— Basañez, M., and Moreno, A. (eds.) (2004). *Human Beliefs and Values: A Cross-Cultural Sourcebook Based on the 1999–2002 Values Surveys*. Mexico, DF: Siglo Veintiuno Editores.

Inkeles, A. (1951). *Public Opinion in Soviet Russia. A Study in Mass Persuasion*. Cambridge, MA: Harvard University Press.

International Research and Exchanges Board (IREX). 2003. *Media Sustainability Index 2003. The Development of Sustainable Media in Europe and Eurasia*. Washington, DC: IREX.

Irwin, G. and Dittrich, K. (1984). 'And the Walls Came Tumbling Down: Party Dealignment in The Netherlands', in Dalton, Flanagan, and Beck (1984).

Iyengar, S. (1991). *Is Anyone Responsible? How Television Frames Political Issues*. Chicago, IL: University of Chicago Press.

—— and Kinder, D. (1987). *News That Matters: Television and American Opinion*. Chicago, IL: University of Chicago Press.

Jackman, R. W. (1987). 'Political Institutions and Voter Turnout in the Industrial Democracies', *American Political Science Review*, 81: 405–24.

Jakubowicz, K. (1995). 'Media as Agents of Change', in D. L. Paletz, K. Jakubowicz, and P. Novosel (eds.), *Glasnost and After. Media and Change in Central and Eastern Europe*. Cresskill, NJ: Hampton Press.

—— (1996). 'Media Legislation as a Mirror of Democracy', *Transition*, 18: 17–21.

Janowitz, M. (1975). 'Professional Models in Journalism: The Gatekeeper and the Advocate', *Journalism Quarterly*, 52: 618–26.

Jennings, M. K. and Mann, T. E. (eds.) (1994). *Elections at Home and Abroad: Essays in Honor of Warren E. Miller*. Ann Arbor, MI: University of Michigan Press.

—— and Niemi, R. G. (1974). *The Political Character of Adolescence*. Princeton, NJ: Princeton University Press.

Johnson, O. V. (1998). 'The Media and Democracy in Eastern Europe', in P. H. O'Neil (ed.), *Communicating Democracy. The Media and Political Transitions*. Boulder, CO: Lynne Rienner.

Jones, M. P. (2001). *Politics and the Architecture of Choice: Bounded Rationality and Governance*. Chicago, IL: University of Chicago Press.

Joslyn, R. (1984). *Mass Media and Elections*. New York: Random House.

Kaase, M. (1976). 'Party Identification and Voting Behavior in the West German Election of 1969', in I. Budge, I. Crewe, and D. Fairlie (eds.), *Party Identification and Beyond*. New York: John Wiley & Sons.

—— (1983). 'Sinn oder Unsinn des Konzepts "Politische Kultur" für die Vergleichende Politikforschung, oder auch: Der Versuch, einen Pudding an die Wand zu nageln', in M. Kaase and H.-D. Klingemann (eds.), *Wahlen und politisches System*. Opladen, Germany: Westdeutscher Verlag.

—— (1988). 'Political Alienation and Protest', in M. Dogan (ed.), *Comparing Pluralist Democracies: Strains on Legitimacy*. Boulder, CO and London: Westview Press.

—— (1994). 'Political Culture and Political Consolidation in Central and Eastern Europe', in F. D. Weil and M. Gautier (eds.), *Political Culture and Political Structure. Theoretical and Empirical Studies*, Research on Democracy and Society, vol. 2. Greenwich, CT: JAI Press.

Karakatsanis, N. M. (2001). *The Politics of Elite Transformation: The Consolidation of Greek Democracy in Theoretical Perspective*. Westport, CT and London: Praeger.

Karasimeonov, G. (ed.) (1990). *The 1990 Election to the Bulgarian Grand National Assembly and the 1991 Election to the Bulgarian National Assembly: Analyses, Documents and Data*. Berlin: Edition Sigma.

Katz, E. and Lazarsfeld, P. W. (1955). *Personal Influence: The Part Played by People in the Flow of Mass Communications*. New York: Free Press.

Katz, R. S. and Mair, P. (1994). *How Parties Organize: Change and Adaptation in Party Organizations in Western Democracies*. London: Sage.

—— —— (1995). 'Changing Models of Party Organisation and Party Democracy: The Emergence of the Cartel Party', *Party Politics*, 1: 5–28.

Kelley, D. and Donway, R. (1990). 'Liberalism and Free Speech', in J. Lichtenberg (ed.), *Democracy and the Mass Media*. Cambridge: Cambridge University Press.

379

Kepplinger, H. M. (1998). 'The Transformation of Politics Through the Development of the Mass Media', in H. W. Giessen (ed.), *Long-Term Consequences on Social Structures through Mass Media Impact*. Berlin: Vistas Verlag.

Key, V. O. (1966). *The Responsible Electorate: Rationality in Presidential Voting, 1936–1960*. Cambridge, MA: Harvard University Press.

Key, V. O., Jr and Munger, F. (1959). 'Social Determinism and the Electoral Decision: The Case of Indiana', in E. Burdick and A. J. Brodbeck (eds.), *American Voting Behavior*. Glencoe, IL: Free Press.

Kiewiet, D. R. (1983). *Macroeconomics and Micropolitics. The Electoral Effects of Economic Issues*. Chicago, IL and London: University of Chicago Press.

Kim, H.-M. and Fording, R. C. (1998) 'Voter Ideology in Western Democracies, 1946–1989', *European Journal of Political Research*, 18: 221–39.

_____ _____ (2003). 'Voter Ideology in Western Democracies: An Update', *European Journal of Political Research*, 42: 95–105.

Kinder, D. R. and Kiewiet, D. R. (1979). 'Sociotropic Politics: The American Case', *British Journal of Political Science*, 11: 129–61.

Kirchheimer, O. (1966). 'The Transformation of the Western European Party Systems', in J. LaPalombara and M. Weiner (eds.), *Political Parties and Political Development*. Princeton, NJ: Princeton University Press.

Kitschelt, H. (1989). *The Logics of Party Formation: Ecological Politics in Belgium and West Germany*. Ithaca, NY: Cornell University Press.

_____ (1994). *The Transformation of European Social Democracy*. Cambridge: Cambridge University Press.

_____ Mansfeldova, Z., Markowski, R., and Tóka, G. (1999). *Post-Communist Party Systems: Competition, Representation, and Inter-Party Cooperation*. Cambridge: Cambridge University Press.

Klapper, J. T. (1960). *The Effects of Mass Communication*. New York: Free Press.

Kleinnijenhuis, J. (1991). 'Newspaper Complexity and the Knowledge Gap', *European Journal of Communication*, 6: 499–522.

Klingemann, H.-D. (1999). 'Mapping Political Support', in Norris (ed.) (1999a).

_____ and Fuchs, D. (eds.) (1995). *Citizens and the State*. Oxford: Oxford University Press.

_____ Hofferbert, R. I., and Budge, I. (1994). *Parties, Policies and Democracy*. Boulder, CO: Westview.

_____ _____ _____ (1999). 'Mapping Political Support in the 1990s: A Global Analysis', in Norris (ed.) (1999a).

Knutsen, O. (1988). 'The Impact of Structural and Ideological Party Cleavages in West European Democracies: A Comparative Empirical Analysis', *British Journal of Political Science*, 18: 323–52.

_____ (1995). 'Party Choice', in J. W. van Deth and E. Scarbrough (eds.), *The Impact of Values*. Oxford: Oxford University Press.

_____ and Scarbrough, E. (1995). 'Cleavage Politics', in van Deth and Scarbrough (1995).

Kornberg, A. and Clarke, H. D. (1992). *Citizens and Community: Political Support in a Representative Democracy*. Cambridge and New York: Cambridge University Press.

Kornhauser, W. (1959). *The Politics of Mass Society*. New York: Free Press.

Krauss, E. S. (2000*a*). *Broadcasting Policies in Japan: NHK and Television News*. Ithaca, NY: Cornell University Press.

—— (2000*b*). 'Japan: News and Politics in a Media-Saturated Democracy', in Gunther and Mughan (2000*a*).

Kuan, H.-C. and Lau, S. K. (2002). 'Between Liberal Autocracy and Democracy: Democratic Legitimacy in Hong Kong', *Democratization*, 9: 58–76.

Lago, I. (2005). *El voto estratégico en las elecciones generales en España (1979–2000). Efectos y mecanísmos causales en la explicación del comportamiento electoral*. Madrid: Centro de Investigaciones Sociológicas/Siglo XXI.

Laidler, H. W. (1968). *The History of Socialism: A Comparative Survey of Socialism, Communism, Trade Unionism, Cooperation, Utopianism, and Other Systems of Reform and Reconstruction*. New York: Crowell.

Lánczi, A. and O'Neil, P. H. (1996). 'Pluralization and Politics of Media Change in Hungary', *Journal of Communist Studies and Transitional Politics*, 12: 82–101.

Langer, J. (1998). *Tabloid Television: Popular Journalism and the Other News*. London: Routledge.

Lazarsfeld, P. F. and Merton, R. K. (1954). 'Friendship as Social Process: A Substantive and Methodological Analysis', in M. Berger, T. Abel, and C. H. Page (eds.), *Freedom and Control in Modern Society*. New York: D. Van Nostrand Company.

—— Berelson, B. R., and Gaudet, H. (1944). *The People's Choice*. New York: Duell, Sloan and Pearce. (Also commonly cited as 1948 published by Columbia University Press.)

Legnante, G. and Segatti, P. (2001). 'L'astensionista intermittente, ovvero quando dicidere di votare o meno e lieve come una piuma', *Polis*, 2: 181–202.

Lenski, G. (1963). *The Religious Factor*. New York: Anchor and Doubleday.

Lerner, W. (1994). *A History of Socialism and Communism in Modern Times: Theorists, Activists and Humanists*, 2nd edn. Engelwood Cliffs, NJ: Prentice-Hall.

Levine, J. (2005). 'Choosing Alone? The Social Network Basis of Modern Political Choice', in A. S. Zuckerman (ed.), *The Social Logic of Politics: Personal Networks as Contexts for Political Behavior*. Philadelphia, PA: Temple University Press.

Lijphart, A. (1975). *The Politics of Accommodation: Pluralism and Democracy in the Netherlands*. Berkeley, CA: University of California Press.

Linde, J. and Ekman, J. (2003). 'Satisfaction with Democracy: A Note on a Frequently Used Indicator in Comparative Politics', *European Journal of Political Research*, 42: 391–408.

Linz, J. J. (1990). 'The Perils of Presidentialism', *Journal of Democracy*, 1: 51–69.

—— (1993). 'Innovative Leadership in the Transition to Democracy and a New Democracy: The Case of Spain', in G. Sheffer (ed.), *Innovative Leaders in International Politics*. Albany, GA: State University of New York Press.

____ (1994). 'Presidential or Parliamentary Democracy: Does It Make a Difference?', in J. J. Linz and A. Valenzuela (eds.), *The Failure of Presidential Democracy: Comparative Perspectives*. Baltimore, MD: Johns Hopkins University Press.

____ and Montero, J. R. (eds.) (1986). *Crisis y cambio: electores y partidos en la España de los años ochenta*. Madrid: Centro de Estudios Constitucionales.

____ and Stepan, A. (1978). *The Breakdown of Democratic Regimes*. Baltimore, MD: Johns Hopkins University Press.

____ ____ (1996). *Problems of Democratic Transition and Consolidation: Southern Europe, South America, and Post-Communist Europe*. Baltimore, MD and London: Johns Hopkins University Press.

____ Gómez-Reino, M., Orizo, F. A., and Vila, D. (1981). *Informe sociológico sobre el cambio político en España, 1975/1981*. Madrid: Euramérica.

____ Stepan, A., and Gunther, R. (1995). 'Democratic Transition and Consolidation in Southern Europe, with Reflections on Latin America and Eastern Europe', in Gunther, Diamandouros, and Puhle (1995).

Lipset, S. M. (1959*a*). *Political Man*. New York: Doubleday.

____ (1959*b*). 'Some Social Requisites of Democracy: Economic Development and Political Legitimacy', *American Political Science Review*, 53: 69–105.

____ (1981). *Political Man: The Social Bases of Politics*, expanded and updated edition. Baltimore, MD: Johns Hopkins University Press.

____ (1990). *Continental Divide: The Values and Institutions of Canada and the United States*. New York: Routledge.

____ (1994). 'The Social Requisites of Democracy Revisited', *American Sociological Review*, 59: 1–22.

____ and Rokkan, S. (1967*a*). *Party Systems and Voter Alignments*. New York: Free Press.

____ ____ (1967*b*). 'Cleavage Structures, Party Systems, and Voter Alignments: An Introduction', in Lipset and Rokkan (1967*a*).

Liu, J. H., Ikeda, K., and Wilson, M. S. (1998). 'Interpersonal Environmental Effects on Political Preferences: The "Middle Path" for Conceptualizing Social Structure in New Zealand and Japan', *Political Behavior*, 20: 183–212.

Loewenberg, G. (1971). 'The Influence of Parliamentary Behavior on Regime Stability', *Comparative Politics*, 3: 170–95.

Lupia, A. and McCubbins, M. (1998). *The Democratic Dilemma: Can Citizens Learn What They Need to Know?* New York: Cambridge University Press.

____ ____ and Popkin, S. L. (eds.) (2000). *Elements of Reason: Cognition, Choice, and the Bounds of Rationality*. Cambridge: Cambridge University Press.

McAllister, I. (1996). 'Leaders', in L. LeDuc, R. G. Niemi, and P. Norris (eds.), *Comparing Democracies: Elections and Voting in Global Perspective*. Thousand Oaks, CA: Sage.

McCann, J. A. (1997). 'Electoral Choices and Core Value Change: The 1992 Presidential Campaign', *American Journal of Political Science*, 41: 564–83.

McChesney, R. W. (2000). *Rich Media, Poor Democracy: Communication Politics in Dubious Times*. Champaign, IL: University of Illinois Press.

McDonough, P., Barnes, S., and López Pina, A. (1984). 'Authority and Association: Spanish Democracy in Comparative Perspective', *Journal of Politics*, 46: 653–88.

—— —— —— Shin, D. C., and Moisés, J. Á. (1998). *The Cultural Dynamics of Democratization in Spain*. Ithaca, NY: Cornell University Press.

Mackie, T. et al. (1992). 'Electoral Change and Social Change', in M. Franklin, T. Mackie, H. Valen et al. (eds.), *Electoral Change: Responses to Evolving Social and Attitudinal Structures in Western Countries*. New York: Cambridge University Press.

MacKuen, M. B. and Rabinowitz, G. (eds.) (2003). *Electoral Democracy*. Ann Arbor, MI: University of Michigan Press.

McPhee, W. N., Smith, R. B., and Ferguson, J. (1963). 'A Theory of Informal Social Influence', in W. N. McPhee (ed.), *Formal Theories of Mass Behavior*. New York: Free Press.

Mair, P. (1996). *Party System Change: Approaches and Interpretations*. Oxford: Clarendon Press.

Mainwaring, S. (1998). 'Party Systems in the Third Wave of Democratization', *The Journal of Democracy*, 9: 67–81.

—— and Sculy, T. R. (1995). *Building Democratic Institutions: Party Systems in Latin America*. Stanford, CA: Stanford University Press.

Mann, M. (1986). *The Sources of Social Power*, 2 vols. Cambridge: Cambridge University Press.

Manza, J. and Brooks, C. (1999). *Social Cleavages and Political Change: Voter Alignments and U.S. Party Coalitions*. Oxford: Oxford University Press.

Maravall, J. M. (1997). *Regimes, Politics and Markets: Democratization and Economic Change in Southern and Eastern Europe*. Oxford: Oxford University Press.

Markowski, R. (2003). 'Cleavage Formation and Development: Conceptualizing and Measuring Cleavages in New Democracies', Paper presented at the 2003 ECPR Joint Sessions, Workshop 19, Edinburgh.

Marletti, C. and Roncarolo, F. (2000). 'Media Influence in the Italian Transition from a Consensual to a Majoritarian Democracy', in Gunther and Mughan (2000a).

Marsden, P. V. and Friedkin, N. E. (1993). 'Network Studies of Social Influence', *Sociological Methods and Research*, 22: 127–51.

Mavrogordatos, G. (1983). *The Rise of the Green Sun: The Greek Election of 1981*. London: King's College, Centre for Contemporary Greek Studies.

Maxman, C. I. (1968). *The End of Ideology Debate*. New York: Clarion Book.

Maxwell, K. (1995). *The Making of Portuguese Democracy*. Cambridge: Cambridge University Press.

Merkel, W. (1998). 'The Consolidation of Post-Autocratic Democracies: A Multilevel Model', *Democratization*, 5: 33–67.

____ (2004). 'Embedded and Defective Democracies', in A. Croissant and W. Merkel (eds.), *Consolidated or Defective Democracy? Problems of Regime Change*, special issue of *Democratization*, 11: 33–58.

____ and Puhle, H. J. (1999). *Von der Diktatur zur Demokratie: Transformationen, Erfolgsbedingungen, Entwicklungspfade*. Opladen, Germany: Westdeutscher Verlag.

____ ____ et al. (2003). *Defekte Demokratie. Band 1: Theorie*. Opladen, Germany: Leske und Budrich.

Merriam, C. E. (1926). 'Progress in Political Research', *American Political Science Review*, 20: 1–13.

____ ([1925] 1970). *New Aspects of Politics 3rd edn*. Chicago, IL: University of Chicago Press.

____ and Gosnell, H. F. (1924). *Non-Voting: Causes and Methods of Control*. Chicago, IL: University of Chicago Press.

Merrill, J. C. and Fisher, H. A. (1980). *The World's Greatest Dailies*. New York: Hastings House.

Merton, R. K., Coleman, J. S., and Rossi, P. H. (1979). *Qualitative and Quantitative Social Research. Papers in Honor of Paul F. Lazarsfeld*. New York: Free Press.

Milbrath, L. and Goel, M. L. (1977). *Political Participation*, 2nd edn. Chicago, IL: Rand McNally.

Milev, R. (eds.) (1996). *TV auf dem Balkan. Zur Entwicklung des Fernsehens in Südosteuropa*. Hamburg, Germany: Verlag Hans-Bredow-Institut.

Miller, A. H., Goldenberg, E. N., and Erbring, L. (1979). 'Type-Set Politics: Impact of Newspapers on Public Confidence', *American Political Science Review*, 1: 67–84.

Miller, J. M. and Krosnick, J. A. (2000). 'News Media Impact on the Ingredients of Presidential Evaluations: Politically Knowledgeable Citizens Are Guided by a Trusted Source', *American Journal of Political Science*, 44: 301–15.

Miller, W. E. and Shanks, M. J. (1996). *The New American Voter*. Cambridge, MA: Harvard University Press.

Miller, W. L. (1991). *Media and Voters: The Audience, Content and Influence of the Press and Television at the 1987 General Elections*. Oxford: Clarendon Press.

____ and Niemi, R. G. (2002). 'Voting: Choice, Conditioning, and Constraint', in LeDuc, Niemi, and Norris (2002).

____ White, S., and Heywood, P. (1998). *Values and Political Change in Postcommunist Europe*. New York: St. Martin's.

Mishler, W. and Rose, R. (1999). 'Five Years After the Fall: Trajectories of Support for Democracy in Post-communist Europe', in Norris (1999a).

____ (2001). 'What Are the Origins of Political Trust? Testing Institutional and Cultural Theories in Post-Communist Societies', *Comparative Political Studies*, 34: 30–62.

____ ____ (2002). 'Learning and Re-learning Regime Support: The Dynamics of Post-Communist Regimes, *European Journal of Political Research*, 41: 5–36.

Montero, J. R. (1984). 'Niveles, fluctuaciones y tendencias del abstencionismo electoral in España y Europa', *Revista Española de Investigaciones Sociológicas*, 22: 103–47.

—— (1993). 'Revisiting Democratic Success: Legitimacy and the Meanings of Democracy in Spain', in R. Gunther (ed.), *Politics, Society, and Democracy: The Case of Spain*. Boulder, CO: Westview Press.

—— Gunther, R., and Torcal, M. (1997). 'Democracy in Spain: Legitimacy, Discontent and Disaffection', *Studies in Comparative International Development*, 32: 124–60.

Morlino, L. (1995). 'Political Parties and Democratic Consolidation in Southern Europe', in Gunther, Diamandouros, and Puhle (1995).

—— (1998). *Democracy Between Consolidation and Crisis: Parties, Groups and Citizens in Southern Europe*. Oxford: Oxford University Press.

—— (2004). 'What is a "Good" Democracy?', in A. Croissant and W. Merkel (eds.), *Consolidated or Defective Democracy? Problems of Regime Change*, special issue of *Democratization*, 11: 10–32.

—— and Montero, J. R. (1995). 'Legitimacy and Democracy in Southern Europe', in Gunther, Diamandouros, and Puhle (1995).

—— and Tarchi, M. (1996). 'The Dissatisfied Society: The Roots of Political Change in Italy', *European Journal of Political Research*, 30: 41–63.

Mughan, A. (2000). *Media and the Presidentialization of Parliamentary Elections*. Houndmills, UK: Palgrave.

—— and Gunther, R. (2000). 'The Media in Democratic and Nondemocratic Regimes: A Multilevel Perspective', in Gunther and Mughan (2000*a*).

Muller, E. N. and Jukam, T. O. (1977). 'On the Meaning of Political Support', *American Political Science Review*, 71: 1561–95.

Mutz, D. C. (1998). *Impersonal Influence: How Perceptions of Mass Collectives Affect Political Attitudes*. Cambridge: Cambridge University Press.

Nakane, C. (1970). *Japanese Society*. London: Weidenfeld and Nicolson.

Nathan, A. J. (1997). 'The Place of Values in Cross-Cultural Studies: The Example of Democracy and China', in A. J. Nathan (ed.), *China's Transition*. New York: Columbia University Press.

Neuman, R. W. (1986). *The Paradox of Mass Politics. Knowledge and Opinion in the American Electorate*. Cambridge, MA and London: Harvard University Press.

Neumann, S. (1956). 'Toward a Comparative Study of Political Parties', in S. Neumann (ed.), *Modern Political Parties. Approaches to Comparative Politics*. Chicago, IL: University of Chicago Press.

Newton, K. (1999*a*). 'Social Capital and Democracy in Modern Europe', in J. van Deth, M. Maraffi, K. Newton, and P. F. Whiteley (eds.), *Social Capital and European Democracy*. London: Routledge.

—— (1999*b*). 'Social and Political Trust in Established Democracies', in P. Norris (ed.), *Critical Citizens: Global Support for Democratic Governance*. Oxford and New York: Oxford University Press.

____ (1999c). 'Mass Media Effects: Mobilization or Media Malaise?', *British Journal of Political Science*, 29: 577–99.

____ and Brynin, M. (2001). 'The National Press and Party Voting in the UK', *Political Studies*, 49: 265–85.

____ and Norris, P. (2000). 'Confidence in Public Institutions: Faith, Culture, or Performance?', in Pharr and Putnam (2000).

Nie, N., Powell, G. B., and Prewitt, K. (1969). 'Social Structure and Political Participation: Developmental Relationships', Parts I and II. *American Political Science Review*, 63.

Nie, N. H., Verba, S., and Petrocik, J. R. (1979). *The Changing American Voter.* Cambridge MA: Harvard University Press.

Niemi, R. G. and Weisberg, H. F. (2001). 'What Determines the Vote?', in R. G. Niemi and H. F. Weisberg (eds.), *Controversies in Voting Behavior.* Washington, DC: Congressional Quarterly.

Nieuwbeerta, P. and Ultee, W. (1999). 'Class Voting in Western Industrialized Countries, 1945–1990', *European Journal of Political Research*, 35: 123–60.

Nikolchev, I. (1996). 'Polarization and Diversification in the Bulgarian Press', *Journal of Communist Studies and Transitional Politics*, 12: 124–44.

Norris, P. (ed.) (1999a). *Critical Citizens: Global Support for Democratic Governance.* Oxford: Oxford University Press.

____ (1999b). 'Introduction: The Growth of Critical Citizens', in Norris (1999a).

____ (1999c). 'Institutional Explanations for Political Support', in Norris (1999a).

____ (1999d). 'Conclusions: The Growth of Critical Citizens and its Consequences', in Norris (1999a).

____ (2000a). 'The Impact of Television on Civic Malaise', in S. Pharr and R. D. Putnam (eds.), *Disaffected Democracies: What's Troubling the Trilateral Countries?* Princeton, NJ: Princeton University Press.

____ (2000b). *Political Communication in Post-Industrial Democracies.* Cambridge: Cambridge University Press.

____ (2000c). *A Virtuous Circle: Political Communications in Postindustrial Societies.* Cambridge: Cambridge University Press.

____ (2002). *Democratic Phoenix. Reinventing Political Activism.* Cambridge: Cambridge University Press.

____ (2004). *Electoral Engineering: Voting Rules and Electoral Behavior.* Cambridge: Cambridge University Press.

____ and Inglehart, R. (2004). *Sacred and Secular: Religion and Politics Worldwide.* Cambridge: Cambridge University Press.

____ Curtice, J., Sanders, D., Scammell, M., and Semetko, H. A. (1999). *On Message: Communicating the Campaign.* London: Sage.

Nye, J. S. (1997). 'Introduction: The Decline of Confidence in Government', in J. S. Nye, Jr, P. D. Zelikow, and D. C. King (eds.), *Why People Don't Trust Government.* Cambridge, MA: Harvard University Press.

Offe, C. (1997). 'Cultural Aspects of Consolidation: A Note on the Peculiarities of Postcommunist Transformations', *East European Constitutional Review*, Fall 1997: 64–8.

O'Neil, P. H. (ed.) (1997). *Post-Communism and the Media in Eastern-Europe*. London: Frank Cass.

Ostergaard, B. S. (ed.) (1997). *The Media in Western Europe. The Euromedia Handbook*, 2nd edn. London: Sage.

Padgett, S. and Paterson, W. (1994). *A History of Social Democracy in Postwar Europe*. Cambridge: Cambridge University Press.

Page, B. I. (1996). 'The Mass Media as Political Actors', *PS—Political Science and Politics*, 29: 20–4.

Papathanassopoulos, S. (2000). 'Election Campaigning in the Television Age: The Case of Contemporary Greece', *Political Communication*, 17: 47–60.

Papayannakis, M. (1981). 'The Crisis in the Greek Left', in H. Penniman (ed.), *Greece at the Polls: The National Elections of 1974 and 1977*. Washington, DC: American Enterprise Institute.

Pappas, T. S. (2001) 'In Search of the Center: Conservative Parties, Electoral Competition, and Political Legitimacy in Southern Europe's New Democracies', in Diamandouros and Gunther (2001*a*).

Pasquino, G. (2001). 'The New Campaign Politics in Southern Europe', in Diamandouros and Gunther (2001*a*).

Patterson, T. E. (1993). *Out of Order*. New York: Knopf.

—— (1998). 'Time and News: The Media's Limitations as an Instrument of Democracy', *International Political Science Review*, 19: 55–67.

Pattie, C. and Johnston, R. (2001). 'Talk as a Political Context: Conversation and Electoral Change in British Elections, 1992–1997', *Electoral Studies*, 29: 17–40.

Paxton, P. (2002). 'Social Capital and Democracy: An Interdependent Relationship', *American Sociological Review*, 67: 254–77.

Petty, R. E. and Caccioppo, J. T. (1981). *Attitudes and Persuasion: Classic and Contemporary Approaches*. Dubuque, IA: William C. Brown.

Pfetsch, B. (1996). 'Convergence through Privatization? Changing Media Environments and Televised Politics in Germany', *European Journal of Communication*, 11: 427–51.

Pharr, S. J. and Putnam, R. D. (eds.) (2000). *Disaffected Democracies: What's Troubling the Trilateral Countries?* Princeton, NJ: Princeton University Press.

Picard, R. G. (1998). 'Media Concentration, Economics, and Regulation', in D. Graber, D. McQuail, and P. Norris (eds.), *The Politics of News, the News of Politics*. Washington, DC: CQ Press.

Poguntke, T. and Webb, P. (2004). 'The Presidentialization of Democracy in Democratic Societies: A Framework for Analysis', in T. Poguntke and P. Webb (eds.), *The Presidentialization of Politics: A Comparative Study of Modern Democracies*. Oxford: Oxford University Press.

Popescu, M. and Tóka, G. (2002). 'Campaign Effects and Media Monopoly: The 1994 and 1998 Parliamentary Elections in Hungary', in D. M. Farrell and R. Schmitt-Beck (eds.), *Do Political Campaigns Matter? Campaign Effects in Elections and Referendums*. London: Routledge.

Popkin, S. L. (1991). *The Reasoning Voter: Communication and Persuasion in Presidential Campaigns*. Chicago, IL: University of Chicago Press.

Powell, G. B. (1986). 'American Voter Turnout in Comparative Perspective', *American Political Science Review*, 80: 17–43.

Price, V. and Zaller, J. (1993). 'Who Gets the News? Alternative Measures of News Reception and their Implications for Research', *Public Opinion Quarterly*, 57: 133–64.

Przeworski, A. (1991). *Democracy and the Market: Political and Economic Reforms in Eastern Europe and Latin America*. Cambridge: Cambridge University Press.

—— and Sprague, J. (1986). *Paper Stones: A History of Electoral Socialism*. Chicago, IL: University of Chicago Press.

Przeworski, A. et al. (1995). *Sustainable Democracy*. Cambridge: Cambridge University Press.

Pucci, E. (ed.) (1996). *L'industria della comunicazione in Italia*. Milano: Guerini e Asociati.

Puhle, H.-J. (2001). 'Mobilizers and Late Modernizers: Socialist Parties in the New Southern Europe', in Diamandouros and Gunther (2001*a*).

—— (2002*a*). 'Still the Age of Catch-allism? *Volksparteien* and *Parteienstaat* in Crisis and Reequilibration', in R. Gunther, J. R. Montero, and J. J. Linz (eds.), (2002).

—— (2002*b*). 'Trajectories of Western Modernization Around the Atlantic: One World or Many?', in H. Pietschmann (ed.), *Atlantic History: History of the Atlantic System 1580–1830*. Göttingen, Germany: Vandenhoeck & Ruprecht.

—— (2004). 'Problemas de consolidación democrática y democracias defectuosas', in W. L. Bernecker (ed.), *Transición democrática y anomia social en perspectiva comparada*. México, DF: El Colegio de México.

Putnam, R. D. (1993). *Making Democracy Work: Civic Traditions in Modern Italy*. Princeton, NJ: Princeton University Press.

—— (1995*a*). 'Bowling Alone: America's Declining Social Capital', *Journal of Democracy*, 6: 65–78.

—— (1995*b*). 'Tuning In, Tuning Out: The Strange Disappearance of Social Capital in America', *P.S.: Political Science and Politics*, 28: 664–83.

—— (2000). *Bowling Alone: The Collapse and Revival of American Community*. New York: Simon & Schuster.

—— (2002). *Democracies in Flux: Social Capital in Contemporary Society*. Oxford and New York: Oxford University Press.

—— and Feldstein, L. (2003). Better Together: Restoring the American Community. New York: Simon and Schuster.

Radcliff, B. and Davis, P. (2000). 'Labor Organization and Electoral Participation in Industrial Democracies', *American Journal of Political Science*, 44: 132–41.

Ranney, A. (1983). *Channels of Power: The Impact of Television on American Politics*. New York: Basic Books.

Reisinger, W. N. (1995). 'The Renaissance of a Rubric: Political Culture as Concept and Theory', *International Journal of Public Opinion Research*, 7: 328–52.

Remmer, K. L. (1996). 'The Sustainability of Political Democracy: Lessons from South America', *Comparative Political Studies*, 29: 611–34.

Richardson, B. (1988). 'Japan's Habitual Voters: Partisanship on the Emotional Periphery', *Comparative Political Studies*, 19: 675–93.

—— (1991). 'European Party Loyalties Revisited', *American Political Science Review*, 85: 751–75.

Ricolfi, L. (1994). 'Elezioni e mass media: quanti voti ha spostato la Tv', *Il Mulino*, 13: 1031–46.

Riker, W. (1982). *Against Populism: A Confrontation Between the Theory of Democracy and the Theory of Social Choice*. San Francisco, CA: Freeman.

—— (1990). 'Political Choice and Rational Choice', in J. Alt and K. Schepsle (eds.), *Perspectives on Positive Political Economy*. Cambridge: Cambridge University Press.

—— and Ordeshook, P. C. (1968). 'A Theory of the Calculus of Voting', *American Political Science Review*, 62: 25–42.

—— —— (1973). *Introduction to Positive Political Theory*. Englewood Cliffs, NJ: Prentice-Hall.

Roberts, D. F. and Maccoby, N. (1985). 'Effects of Mass Communication', in G. Lindzey and E. Aronson (eds.), *The Handbook of Social Psychology*, 3rd edn. New York: Random House.

Robinson, J. P. and Levy, M. R. (1986). *The Main Source. Learning from Television News*. Beverly Hills, CA: Sage.

Robinson, M. J. (1976). 'Public Affairs Television and the Growth of Political Malaise: The Case of "The Selling of the Pentagon"', *American Political Science Review*, 70: 409–32.

Rohrschneider, R. (2002). 'Mobilizing Versus Chasing: How Do Parties Target Voters in Election Campaigns?', *Electoral Studies*, 21: 367–82.

Rokeach, M. (1973). *The Nature of Human Values*. New York: Free Press.

Rokkan, S. (1970). 'The Voter, the Reader and the Party Press', in S. Rokkan (ed.), *Citizens, Elections, Parties. Approaches to the Comparative Study of Processes of Development*. New York and Oslo: David McKay and Universitetsforlaget.

—— (1999). 'State Formation, Nation Building, and Mass Politics in Europe', in P. Flora (ed.), *The Theory of Stein Rokkan*. Oxford: Oxford University Press.

Rose, R. (ed.) (1974). Electoral Behavior: A Comparative Handbook. New York: Free Press.

—— and McAllister, I. (1986). *Voters Begin to Choose*. London: Sage.

—— and Mishler, W. (1996). 'Testing the Churchill Hypothesis: Popular Support for Democracy and its Alternatives', *Journal of Public Policy*, 16: 29–58.

_____ _____ and Haerpfer, C. (1998). *Democracy and its Alternatives. Understanding Post-communist Societies*. Baltimore, MD: Johns Hopkins University Press.

Rosenstone, S. J. and Hansen, J. M. (1993). *Mobilization, Participation, and Democracy in America*. New York: Macmillan.

Rospir, J. I. (1996). 'Political Communication and Electoral Campaigns in the Young Spanish Democracy', in D. L. Swanson and P. Mancini (eds.), *Politics, Media, and Modern Democracy. An International Study of Innovations in Electoral Campaigning and Their Consequences*. Westport, CT: Praeger.

Rubin, R. L. (1981). *Press, Party and Presidency*. New York: Norton.

Rueschemeyer, D., Stephens, E. H., Stephens, J. D. (1992). *Capitalist Development and Democracy*. Chicago, IL: University of Chicago Press.

Sani, G. (1974). 'A Test of the Least-Distance Model of Voting Choice', *Comparative Political Studies*, 7: 193–208.

_____ and Mannheimer, R. (2000). *La conquista degli astenuti*. Bologna, Italy: Il Mulino.

_____ and Montero, J. R. (1986). 'El espectro político: izquierda, derecha y centro', in J. J. Linz and J. R. Montero (eds.), *Crisis y cambio: electores y partidos en la España de los años ochenta*. Madrid: Centro de Estudios Constitucionales.

Sartori, G. (1998). *Homo videns: La sociedad teledirigida*. Madrid: Taurus.

Scammell, M. and Semetko, H. (2000). 'Democracy and the Media', in M. Scammell and H. Semetko (eds.), *The Media, Journalism and Democracy*. Aldershot, UK: Ashgate, pp. xx–xlix.

Schmitt, H. (1983). 'Party Government in Public Opinion: A European Cross-National Comparison', *European Journal of Political Research*, 11: 353–75.

_____ and Holmberg, S. (1995). 'Political Parties in Decline', in H.-D. Klingemman and D. Fuchs (eds.), (1995).

Schmitt-Beck, R. (1998). 'Of Readers, Viewers, and Cat-Dogs', in J. W. van Deth (ed.), *Comparative Politics: The Problem of Equivalence*. London and New York: Routledge.

Schönbach, K. (1983). *Das unterschätzte Medium. Politische Wirkungen von Presse und Fernsehen im Vergleich*. München, Germany: Saur.

Schumpeter, J. A. (1962). *Capitalism, Socialism and Democracy*, 3rd edn. New York: Harper & Row.

Schwartz, S. (1994). 'Beyond Individualism/Collectivism', in U. Kim et al. (eds.), *Individualism and Collectivism*. Thousand Oaks, CA: Sage.

_____ (1997). 'Values and Culture', in D. Munro et al. (eds.), *Motivation and Culture*. New York: Routledge.

Semetko, H. A. (2000). 'Great Britain: The End of the News at Ten and the Changing News Environment', in Gunther and Mughan (2000a).

_____ Blumler, J. G., Gurevitch, M., and Weaver, D. H. 1991. *The Formation of Campaign Agendas: A Comparative Analysis of Party and Media Roles in Recent American and British Elections*. Hillsdale, NJ: Lawrence Erlbaum.

Seymour-Ure, C. (1974). *The Political Impact of Mass Media*. London: Constable.

Shi, T. (2003). 'Does it Matter or Not? That is the Question: Cultural Impacts on the Political Process', Paper presented to the East Asia Barometer Conference held on December 8–9, 2003, Taipei.

Shull, T. (1999). *Redefining Red and Green: Ideology and Strategy in European Political Ecology*. Albany, NY: State University of New York Press.

Siegfried, A. ([1913] 1964). *Tableau politique de la France de l'Ouest*. Paris: Armand Colin.

Simon, H. A. (1982a). *Models of Bounded Rationality*. Cambridge: MIT Press.

—— (1982b). 'Rationality and Political Behavior', *Political Psychology*, 16: 45–61.

Skidmore, T. E. (ed.) (1993). *Television, Politics and the Transition to Democracy in Latin America*. Baltimore, MD: Johns Hopkins University Press.

Skocpol, T. and Crowley, J. E. (2001). 'The Rush to Organize: Explaining Associational Formation in the United States: 1860s–1920s', *American Journal of Political Science*, 45: 813–29.

—— Ganz, M., and Munson, Z. (2000). 'A Nation of Organizers: The Institutional Origins of Civic Voluntarism in the United States', *American Political Science Review*, 93: 527–46.

Slomczynski, K. and Shabad, G. (1999). 'Partisan Preferences and Democratic Commitments in Poland', Paper presented at the Annual Meeting of the American Political Science Association, Atlanta, Georgia, September 1999.

Sniderman, P. M., Brody, R., and Tetlock, P. E. (1991). *Reasoning and Choice: Explorations in Political Psychology*. Cambridge: Cambridge University Press.

Splichal, S. (1992). 'Media Privatization and Democratization in Central-Eastern Europe', *Gazette*, 49: 3–22.

—— (1994). *Media Beyond Socialism. Theory and Practice in East-Central Europe*. Boulder, CO: Westview.

Steger, M. B. (1997). *The Quest for Evolutionary Socialism: Eduard Bernstein and Social Democracy*. New York: Cambridge University Press.

Stille, A. (2000). 'The Italian Press', *Correspondence: An International Review of Culture and Society*, 6: 18–19.

Stolle, D. and Rochon, T. R. (1998). 'Are All Associations Alike?', *American Behavioral Scientist*, 42: 47–65.

Sükösd, M. (2000). 'Democratic Transformation and the Mass Media in Central and Eastern Europe: From Stalinism to Democratic Consolidation in Hungary', in Gunther and Mughan (2000a).

Suvanto, P. (1997). *Conservatism from the French Revolution to the 1990s*. New York: St. Martin's Press.

Swanson, D. L. and Mancini, P. (eds.) (1996). *Politics, Media, and Modern Democracy*. Westport, CT: Praeger.

Tarchi, M. (1997). *Dal MSI ad AN. Organizzazione e strategie*. Bologna, Italy: Il Mulino.

Taylor, O. H. (1960). *Classical Liberalism, Marxism and the Twentieth Century* [Lectures delivered at the Thomas Jefferson Center for Studies in

Political Economy, University of Virginia]. Cambridge, MA: Harvard University Press.

Teorell, J. (2002). 'Popular Support for Democracy in Russia: A Cross-temporal Comparison', Paper presented at the conference, 'Consolidation in New Democracies', Uppsala University, June 8–9.

Thomassen, J. (ed.) (2005). *The European Voter*. Oxford: Oxford University Press.

Tingsten, H. ([1937] 1974). *Political Behavior: Studies in Election Statistics*. Ann Arbor, MI: University of Michigan Press.

Tironi, E. and Agüero, F. (1999). 'Sobrevivirá el actual paisaje político Chileno?', *Estudios Politicos*, 74: 151–69.

____ and Sunkel, G. (2000). 'The Modernization of Communications: The Media in the Transition to Democracy in Chile', in Gunther and Mughan (2000a).

Tóka, G. (1995). 'Political Support in East-Central Europe', in H.-D. Klingemann and D. Fuchs (eds.), (1995).

Tökes, R. L. (1997). 'Party Politics and Political Participation in Postcommunist Hungary', in K. Dawisha and B. Parrott (eds.), *The Consolidation of Democracy in East-Central Europe*. Cambridge and New York: Cambridge University Press.

Topf, R. (1995). 'Beyond Electoral Participation', in H.-D. Klingemann and D. Fuchs (eds.), (1995).

Torcal, M. (1995). 'Actitudes políticas y participación política en España: Pautas de cambio y continuidad', Ph.D. dissertation, Universidad Autonóma de Madrid.

____ (2001). 'La desafección en las nuevas democracias del sur de Europa y Latinoamérica', *Instituciones y Desarrollo*, 8–9: 229–80.

____ (2002a). 'Disaffected Democrats: The Origin and Consequences of the Dimensions of Political Support in New Latin American and Southern European Democracies', Unpublished manuscript.

____ (2002b). 'Institutional Disaffection and Democratic History in New Democracies', *Central European Political Science Review*, 10: 40–77.

____ (2002c). 'Political Disaffection in New Democracies: Spain in Comparative Perspective', Ph.D. dissertation, Ohio State University.

____ and Mainwaring, S. (2003). 'The Political Recrafting of Social Bases of Party Competition: Chile, 1973–1995', *British Journal of Political Science*, 33: 55–84.

____ Gunther, R., and Montero, J. R. (2002). 'Antiparty Sentiments in Southern Europe', in Gunther, Montero, and Linz (eds.) (2002).

Tufte, E. R. (1978). *Political Control of the Economy*. Princeton, NJ: Princeton University Press.

Tzankoff, M. (2002). *Der Transformationsprozess in Bulgarien und die Entwicklung der postsozialistischen Medienlandschaft*. Hamburg, Germany: Lit Verlag.

Vallone, R. P., Ross, L., and Lepper, M. R. (1985). 'The Hostile Media Phenomenon: Biased Perception and Perceptions of Media Bias in Coverage of the "Beirut Massacre"', *Journal of Personality and Social Psychology*, 49: 577–85.

van Biezen, I. (2003). *Political Parties in New Democracies: Party Organizations in Southern and East-Central Europe*. Houndmills, UK: Macmillan.

van der Eijk, C. (2002). 'Design Issues in Electoral Research: Taking Care of Core Business', *Electoral Studies*, 21: 189–206.

van Deth, J. W. (1990). 'Interest in Politics', in M. Kent Jennings and J. W. van Deth et al. (eds.), *Continuities in Political Action*. Berlin and New York: de Gruyter.

—— and Elff, M. (2001). 'Politicisation and Political Interest in Europe: A Multi-Level Approach', MZES Working Paper p0014.

—— and Scarbrough, E. (1995). *The Impact of Values*. Oxford: Oxford University Press.

—— Maraffi, M., Newton, K., and Whitely, P. (1999). *Social Capital and European Democracy*. London: Routledge.

Vassilev, R. (2000). 'Problems of Democratic Transition and Consolidation in Post-Communist Bulgaria', Ph.D. dissertation, Ohio State University.

Verba, S. and Nie, N. (1972). *Participation in America: Democracy and Political Equality*. New York: Harper & Row.

—— Nie, N., and Kim, J.-O. (1978). *Participation and Political Equality. A Seven-Nation Comparison*. Chicago, IL: University of Chicago Press.

—— Schlozman, K., and Brady, H. E. (1995). *Voice and Equality: Civic Voluntarism in American Politics*. Cambridge, MA: Harvard University Press.

Voltmer, K. (2000). 'Constructing Political Reality in Russia. Izvestiya—Between Old and New Journalistic Practices', *European Journal of Communication*, 15: 469–500.

Waisbord, S. R. (1995). 'The Mass Media and Consolidation of Democracy in South America', *Research in Political Sociology*, 7: 207–27.

Warren, M. E. (2001). *Democracy and Association*. Princeton, NJ: Princeton University Press.

Weatherford, M. S. (1987). 'How Does Government Performance Influence Political Support?', *Political Behavior*, 9: 5–28.

Weaver, D. H. (ed.) (1998). *The Global Journalist. News People Around the World*. Cresskill, NJ: Hampton.

—— and Buddenbaum, J. M. (1980). 'Newspapers and Television. A Review of Research on Uses and Effects', in G. C. Wilhoit and H. de Bock (eds.), *Mass Communication Review Yearbook*, vol. 1. Beverly Hills, CA: Sage.

Weisberg, H. F. (1986). 'Model Choice in Political Science: The Case of Voting Behaviour Research, 1946–1975', in H. F. Weisberg (ed.), *Political Science: The Science of Politics*. New York: Agathon Press.

Wessels, B. and Klingemann, H.-D. (1998). 'Transformation and the Prerequisites of Democratic Opposition in Central and Eastern Europe', in Barnes and Simon (1998).

Westholm, A. (1997). 'Distance versus Direction: The Illusory Defeat of the Proximity Theory of Electoral Choice', *American Political Science Review*, 91: 865–83.

393

Wilke, J. (1996). 'Massenmedien in Uruguay', in J. Wilke (ed.), *Massenmedien in Lateinamerika*, vol. 3. Frankfurt am Main, Germany: Vervuert.

Wolling, J. (1999). *Politikverdrossenheit durch Massenmedien? Der Einfluss der Medien auf die Einstellungen der Buerger zur Politik*. Opladen, Germany and Wiesbaden, Germany: Westdeutscher Verlag.

Wuthnow, R. (1989). *Communities of Discourse: Ideology and Social Structure in the Reformation, the Enlightenment, and European Socialism*. Cambridge, MA: Harvard University Press.

Zaharopoulos, T. and Paraschos, M. (1993). *Mass Media in Greece: Power, Politics, and Privatization*. Westport, CT: Praeger.

Zaller, J. R. (1992). *The Nature and Origins of Mass Opinion*. Cambridge: Cambridge University Press.

____ (1998). 'The Rule of Product Substitution in Presidential Campaign News', *Annals of the American Academy of Political and Social Science*, 560: 111–28.

Zuckerman, A. S. (2005). 'Returning to the Social Logic of Politics', in A. S. Zuckerman (ed.), *The Social Logic of Politics: Personal Networks as Contexts for Political Behavior*. Philadelphia, PA: Temple University Press.

____ Kotler-Berkowitz, L. A., and Swaine, L. A. (1998). 'Anchoring Political Preferences: The Structural Bases of Stable Electoral Decisions and Political Attitudes in Britain', *European Journal of Political Research*, 33: 285–321.

Zukin, C. (1977). 'A Reconsideration of the Effects of Information on Partisan Stability', *Public Opinion Quarterly*, 41: 244–54.

Index

The letter f indicates a figure, n a note and t a table

AN *see* Alleanza Nazionale
Abortion questionnaire: values 266, 267t, 269–70, 271, 272t, 274, 277t, 278t, 288
Affluence and the French Worker (Hamilton) vii
African Americans 298 n
age: and political behaviour 103–4, 247t, 250t
Alleanza Nazionale (AN) (Italy) 61
America *see* United States
American National Election Studies 163
American Voter, The (Campbell et al.) xi, 9
Anarchism: Spain 310
Anarchosyndicalism: Spain 310
anti-system parties 72
Asia *see* Hong Kong; Japan
associations *see* secondary organizations
'attack journalism' 79
attitudes: political systems 20–21, 30–31
attitudinal orientations 263–72

BSP *see* Bulgarian Socialist (formerly Communist) Party
Berelson, Bernard v, 5–6, 7
Berlusconi, Silvio 194, 235, 239
bias *see* partisan bias
Blancos *see* Partido Nacional (Blanco) (Uruguay)
Britain *see* United Kingdom
broadcasting 98
   Eastern Europe 86–7
   see also mass media
Bulgaria 2, 95
   attitudes to democracy in 34, 35t, 36, 40, 41, 42, 43, 44t, 53, 54–5, 143
   electorate encapsulation in 173t, 174, 175f, 176t, 178t
   and face-to-face contacts 49

intermediary biases in 218, 219–20, 221, 222, 230t, 232, 233, 234
and mass media 86, 93, 94t, 101t, 115, 116–17, 118, 122, 134, 254t, 238, 239
   newspapers 99, 102, 111, 112, 113, 114, 125, 126, 235, 239, 241, 242, 254t
   television 112, 126, 235, 239
and organizational membership 47t, 48, 50, 225
partisan bias in 189t, 190, 193t, 200, 201tt, 202, 216t
party contacts in 226
and political information 186t, 187
political participation in 63, 64, 65t, 66, 67
political systems in 30
presidential election (1996) 247–9
and voluntary associations 144, 145t, 146, 148t, 149t, 150t, 151f, 153t, 154t, 155, 160, 161t, 162
voter-discussant congruence in 196tt, 197, 199t
and voting influences 239, 240, 241
Bulgarian Socialist (formerly Communist) Party (BSP) 54, 99, 353 n29
Bureau of Applied Social Research: Columbia University 2–6

CNEP *see* Comparative National Elections Project
Caetano, Marcelo 57
campaign issues: and voting behaviours 260
capitalism 265, 283
Catholics: and voting vii, 7
   see also Christian Democrats; religiosity: influence on voters
Chicago University *see* University of Chicago

Chile 3, 313–14
  attitudes to democracy in 34, 35t, 36, 39,
    43–5, 53, 54–6, 58t, 59–60, 142
  and economic development 271, 284t
  and electoral participation 168t
  electorate encapsulation in 173t, 175f,
    176t, 178t
  and face-face contacts 49
  intermediary biases in 218, 219–20, 221,
    222, 230t, 232
  law and order in 275, 284t
  left-right self-placements in 272t, 274
  and mass media 93, 94t, 101t, 115f, 117,
    132
    newspapers 99, 102, 110, 111, 112, 126
    television 98, 102, 110, 112, 113, 114,
    126
  and organizational membership 47t, 225
  partisan bias in 190, 193, 194, 200, 201tt,
    202, 216t
  partisan preferences in 290t, 291
  and political culture 106f, 107, 109, 132,
    271
  political information 187
  political participation in 63, 64, 65t, 66,
    67, 68, 69
  political systems in 30
  and presidential election (1993) 247–9t
  and religious values 268–9, 284t, 313–14
  and tax cutting 271, 284t
  Traditional Conservatism in 289, 290t
  and values 256–7, 267t, 283, 284t, 288
  and voluntary associations 144t, 145t,
    147, 148t, 149t, 150t, 151f, 153t,
    154t, 155, 156, 157t, 159, 161t,
    162
  voter-discussant congruence in 195,
    196tt, 197, 199t, 205–6
Christian Democrats 7, 306, 313
church attendance see religiosity: influence
    on voters
civic associations
  and electoral participation 175, 177,
    179–80
  and political information 165t, 166
civic engagement: effects on
    democracy 181–2
civil liberties
  Chile 271
  Greece 271
  Hong Kong 269
class: and voting vii–viii
  see also social status: and voting
    behaviours

Class and Politics in the United States
    (Hamilton) vii
classical liberalism 263, 306, 309
cleavages: and voting behaviours 7–9,
    16–17, 55–6, 142, 177, 209, 305–6
  see also values cleavages
co-workers: and voting behaviours 196tt,
    197
Colorados see Partido Colorado (Uruguay)
Columbia University v
  Bureau of Applied Social Research 2–6,
    208, 217, 325
  Sociology Department vi, xi, xiv
commercialization: mass media 87, 88
Communism
  Bulgaria see Bulgarian Socialist (formerly
    Communist) Party (BSP)
  Hungary see Socialist (former Communist)
    Party of Hungary
  and mass media 85–6
Comparative National Elections Project
    (CNEP) xii–xiii, xiv–xv, 2, 15–22,
    26–8, 34, 256, 314, 322–3, 345
  and mass media 97, 234
  and partisan bias 188–5, 205–6
  and political information 185–8, 209,
    211, 213, 223–4
  and values 263, 300–1
  and voluntary organizations 142
  and voter-discussant congruence 198
comparative studies: voting behaviours 261
Compete questionnaire: values 265, 267t,
    270, 272t, 277t, 278t, 279, 281, 288
Concertación coalition: Chile 314, 352 n26
Conservatism: values 264, 265, 275, 279,
    283, 288, 306
'critical citizens' 138
cross-national difference: selectoral
    behaviour 305–15
Cross-National Election Project see
    Comparative National Elections
    Project (CNEP)
culturalism: and voting behaviours 260–1
'culture wars' 21
  United States 271–2, 296

decision-making see Particip questionnaire
'defective democracy' 324
democracies 181
  third-wave 75, 180
democracy
  attitudes to 30, 31–62, 327–32
  support for 30, 92, 109, 127, 314
democratic consolidation 27, 30

democratic legitimacy 324
Democrats: United States 279, 281, 296, 297
dictatorships 57, 59 *see also* Communism
disaffection: and democracy 330
  see also political disaffection
discussants *see* personal discussants
Downs, Ed 12

East Germany *see* Germany
Eastern Europe *see also* Bulgaria; Greece; Hungary
  mass media 85–6, 103
  political participation 91
  political systems 95
Easton, D. 31
EcoGrow questionnaire: values 266, 267t, 271, 272t, 276, 277t, 278t, 279, 283, 284t, 287t
economic approach: voting behaviours 12–15, 259
economic performance: democracies 32
Economic Theory of Democracy (Downs) xi
economic voting paradigm 259
economic well-being: and citizens' attitudes 105
economies: influence on voters 249t
education
  influence on voters 247t, 250t
  and political behaviours 104
elections 234, 247–53tt, 319 *see also* voting behaviours
electoral behaviours: literature of 259–63
  see also voting behaviours
electoral intermediation: and democracy 322–7
electoral participation: turnout rates 166–71
electorates: encapsulation 171–80, 333, 334–5
elites *see* political elites
Elmira Project v, 5–6
environment *see EcoGrow* questionnaire
EqualInd questionnaire: values 265, 267t, 270, 272t, 274, 277t, 278t, 279, 281, 287t
Espacio Progresista (Uruguay) 294t, 295, 312
ethnicity 298 n
Europe *see* Bulgaria; Germany; Greece; Hungary; Italy; Spain; United Kingdom
European Value Systems project 263
extremists 182

face-face contacts: and voting behaviours 5, 48–9
  see also personal discussants
families *see* spouses
Fiorina, Morris xi–xii, 364 n18
Florida State University xii–xiii
Four Nation Study (Comparative National Elections Project) 34, 364 n34
Fraga, Manuel 57
friends: and voting behaviours 195, 196tt, 197
  see also personal discussants
Fundamentalist Conservatism: voting preferences 295, 297

gender: and political behaviour 104
General Election 1992 (United Kingdom) 239–40
Germany
  and influence of television 205
  and mass media 93, 94t
  and Nazi era vii–viii
  and partisan bias 189t, 190, 191, 193t, 201tt, 202, 203, 204
  and political information 185, 186t, 187, 188
  and voter-discussant congruence 196tt, 199t, 205
Gerth, Hans vi
Greece 3, 311
  and abortion 269, 278t
  and attitudes to democracy 34, 35t, 36, 38t, 39, 40, 41, 42, 43, 44t, 51t, 54
  and competition 270
  and economic development 271
  and electoral participation 168t
  and electorate encapsulation 173t, 175f, 176t, 178t, 179
  and face-to-face contacts 49t
  and income equality 270
  intermediary biases in 218, 220t, 221, 230t, 233
  law and order in 275, 278t
  and left-right self-placements 272t, 274, 316, 317, 318, 318t
  and legislative election (1996) 250–3tt
  and mass media 93, 94t, 101t, 115f, 117, 129, 301, 302t
    newspapers 102, 110, 125, 126, 308
    television 103, 112, 113, 114, 126
  and organizational membership 47t, 225
  partisan bias in 189t, 192, 193t, 194, 201tt, 203, 204, 216t, 290, 291
  party contacts in 226, 227

Greece (*cont.*)
  and party system 143
  political broadcasting in 87
  and political culture 106f, 107, 109, 271
  and political information 186t, 187
  political participation in 63, 64, 65t, 66,
    67, 68, 91
  political systems in 30, 95
  and privatization 270
  and religious values 268, 269, 278t, 298t,
    299
  and secondary organizations 301, 302t
  and social structure 304
  and tax cutting 271, 278t
  and values 256, 267t, 278t, 288
  and voluntary associations 144, 144t,
    145t, 146, 148, 149t, 150t, 151f,
    152, 153t, 154t, 155, 157t, 158,
    161t
  and voter-discussant congruence 195,
    196tt, 199t, 205
  and voting preferences 293, 294t, 296,
    298
'Green' parties 306

'home team' hypothesis: citizens'
  attitudes 104
Hong Kong 3
  and civil liberties 269
  and competition 270, 286, 287t
  and democracy 142, 314–15
  and economic development 271, 286,
    287t
  and income equality 270, 286, 287t
  intermediary biases in 218, 219, 220t,
    221, 230t
  left-right self-placements in 273
  and legislative election (1998) 250–3t
  partisan bias in 189t, 191, 192, 193t, 194,
    200, 201tt, 216t
  partisan preferences in 290t, 291
  political discussion in 205, 206
  and political information 186t, 187
  religious values in 268, 286, 287t
  and tax cutting 271, 286, 287t
  and values 257, 267t, 269, 286, 287t
  and voluntary associations 144, 145t,
    148, 149t, 150t, 151f, 152, 153t,
    154t, 155, 156, 157t, 158, 160,
    161t
  and voter-discussant congruence 195,
    196tt, 197, 199t
'hostile media phenomenon' 210–11,
  228–9, 234, 244

Hungarian Communist Party 56–7
  see also Socialist (former Communist)
    Party of Hungary
Hungary 2, 95
  and attitudes to democracy 34, 35t, 40,
    40t, 42–3, 44t, 52, 54, 143
  and competition 270, 285t
  and decision-making 270, 285t
  and economic development 271, 285t
  and electorate encapsulation 172, 173t,
    174, 175f, 176t, 178t, 179
  and face-face contacts 49t
  and income equality 270, 285t
  intermediary biases in 218, 220t, 230t,
    232
  and law and order 275, 285t
  and left-right self-placements 272t, 274–5
  legislative election (1998) 250–3t
  and mass media 86, 93, 94t, 101t, 115,
    116–17, 118, 122, 133
    newspapers 102, 110, 111, 126
    television 112, 113–14, 126
  and organizational membership 47t
  partisan bias in 189t, 190, 193t, 201tt,
    203, 216t
  partisan preferences in 290t, 291
  and political culture
    impact of mass media on 106f, 107,
      108
  and political information 186t, 187
  political participation in 63t, 64, 65t, 66,
    67, 68
  political systems in 30
  and privatization 270, 285t
  and religious values 268, 269, 285t
  and tax cutting 271, 285t
  values cleavages in 257
  and values 267t, 285t, 288
  voluntary associations 144t, 145t, 148,
    148t, 149t, 150t, 151f, 153t, 154t,
    155, 156, 157t, 158, 159, 160, 161t,
    162
  and voter-discussant congruence 196tt,
    197, 199t

ideological cleavages 289–96, 306
ideologies
  and attitude clustering 272–89
  importance of 344
  and political parties 307
  see also political ideologies
income distribution: influence on
  voters 247t, 250t
information *see* political information

informational intermediation: and voting choices 213–23, 239–42
intermediaries: political information 183, 208–46
intermediation *see* political intermediation
'interpersonal influence': Nazi Germany viii
interpersonal personal discussants: and political information 213, 214, 223–6
Italy 3
  attitudes to democracy in 34, 58t, 142
  and electoral participation 168t
  electorate encapsulation in 173t, 175f, 176t, 178t
  intermediary biases in 231t, 232, 233
  and legislative election (1996) 247–9t
  and mass media 235–6, 238, 239, 241, 254t
  and organizational membership 225
  partisan bias in 189t, 193t, 194, 201tt, 203, 216t
  political information 186t, 187
  and voluntary associations 144t, 145t, 146, 148t, 149t, 150t, 151f, 152, 153t, 154t, 155, 156, 157t, 160, 161t
  and voter-discussant congruence 196tt, 199t
  and voting influences 239, 240, 241
Izquierda Unida (Spain) 292t

Japan
  and electoral participation 167
  electorate encapsulation in 172, 173t, 174, 175f, 176t, 177, 178t
  intermediary biases in 218, 231t, 232, 233
  legislative election (1993) 247–9t
  and mass media 93, 94t, 244
  and organizational membership 225, 226
  partisan bias in 189t, 190, 191, 192, 193t, 194, 216t
  party contacts in 226, 227
  and party system 142
  and political discussion 206
  and voluntary associations 144t, 145t, 146, 147, 148t, 149t, 150t, 151f, 153t, 154t, 155, 158, 159, 161t, 162
journalism: Eastern Europe 86
  see also 'attack journalism'; newspapers; tabloid press
journalists: role of 83

KKE (Greece) 293, 294t
Karamanlis, Constantine 57

Labour Party (United Kingdom) 139, 307
labour unions: and electoral participation 167, 175, 177, 225, 354 n3
Latin America *see also* Chile; Uruguay
  and mass media 87–88
  and political participation 91
  political systems in 95
Lavín, Joaquín 56, 60
law and order *see* OrderLib questionnaire
Lazarsfeld, Paul F.: *see also* Colombia University Bureau of Applied Social Research v, vi, viii, xi, xii, xiii, xiv, 1, 4, 5, 7, 10, 16, 198, 208–9, 224, 259
'Left-libertarian' parties *see* 'Green' parties
left-right self-placements: and values 272–89, 315–19
Lipset, Seymour Martin vi, 7, 8
Lynd, Robert S. vi

MSI *see* Movimento Sociale Italiano (MSI)
McPhee, William N. v, 5–6, 7
malaise hypotheses 81–2
Marcuse, Herbert vi
Marxism 7, 307 *see also* Socialism
mass media 183–4, 330–2
  classification of 96–9, 125–6
  influence on democracies 75–6, 110–24
  and political bias 216t, 233–42, 244
  and political cultures 79–84, 103–18, 127
  and political information 206, 214, 227–9, 233–42
  and public opinion vi
  Nazi Germany viii
  role of intermediary biases in 232
  significance of 119–22
  and third-wave democracies 84–9
  and voting behaviours xiv, 19–20, 67, 210, 308
  see also newspapers; television
mass society theory: and voting vii–viii
media *see* mass media
media dependency: new democracies 92–6
media exposure 96–103, 129–34tt
media malaise 80–1, 331
Merton, Robert K. vi
Meyer, Gerhart E.O. v
'Michigan model': party identification' xi, xii, 259, 260
Michigan school of electoral behavioural research 9–12, 16, 136, 325
Mills, C. Wright vi

mobilization: and electoral
participation 140, 167, 168, 169, 172,
179, 326, 333–43
mobilization theory 80–1, 82
Modern Democracy: partisan
preferences 290
Modern Democrats 289
Modern Social Democracy 290, 291, 292,
293, 306, 310, 316
Modern Social Democratic clusters:
values 276, 281, 283, 286, 288–9
Movimento Sociale Italiano (MSI) (later
Alleanza Nazionale) (AN) 60–1
Muslims: and ReligLib questionnaire
363 n8

Nacionalistas see Partido Nacional (Blanco)
(Uruguay)
Nazis: Weimar Germany vii, viii
Nea Demokratia (Greece) 293, 294t
Neumann, Franz v
'new politics' debate: and voting
behaviours 261
news media: content and context 83–4
newspapers 97–9, 122, 125–6, 331
Bulgaria 235, 254t
as information sources 183–4, 185, 186,
188, 189t, 190–1, 192, 193t, 336
Italy 241, 254t
and partisan bias 194, 198, 201 t5.8, 202,
203t, 206, 216t, 340
and political cultures 127
and political information 228, 234, 235,
237–8, 239, 331–2
Spain 254t
United Kingdom 254t
and voting behaviours 5, 6, 93, 248t,
250t, 301, 302t, 308
see also mass media; tabloid press
Nuevo Espacio (Uruguay) 295, 312

Oblimin Rotation of the Principal
Components analysis 276, 349 n8,
364 n13
'opinion leaders': voting behaviours 6
OrderLib questionnaire: values 264, 267t,
269–70, 272t, 274, 275, 277t, 278t,
287t, 288
organizational bias: and political
information 225–6, 243
organizations see secondary organizations

PASOK (Pan-Hellenic Socialist Movement)
(Greece) 293, 294t, 311

PSOE (Partido Socialista Obrero Español)
(Spain) 292–3, 310
panel surveys: voting behaviours 5
Papandreou, Andreas 311
Particip questionnaire: values 266, 267t,
270, 272t, 274, 276, 277t, 278t, 279,
281, 283, 284t, 287t, 288
Participatory Socialism 281, 289, 294t, 295
Partido Colorado (Uruguay) 294t, 295, 312
Partido Nacional (Blanco) (Uruguay) 294t,
295, 312
Partido Popular (Spain) 292t, 293, 310
Partido Socialista Obrero Español see PSOE
partisan bias 341–2
political communication 188–95,
198–204, 209–10, 214–15, 218, 229,
233–42, 326, 335–7, 340–1
party candidates: influence on voters 249t
party contacts: influence on voters 226–7,
248t
party identification
influence on voters 11–12, 247t, 250t
'Michigan model' xi
party leaders: influence of 222
party systems 142–3
Party Systems and Voter Alignments (Lipset
and Rokkan) 8
People's choice, The (Lazarsfeld et al.) 5
personal discussants: influence on
voters 195–8, 205, 206, 248t, 250t,
336
personal factors: voting xi, xii
Pinochet, Augusto 55, 56, 60, 313
pluralism: and democratic
decision-making 137
policy cultures 78
political communication: partisan bias
in 188–95
political conflicts: importance of 345
political contacts: voluntary
associations 156–60
Political Control of the Economy, The
(Tufte) 13
political cultures 77–8
political disaffection 90, 330
behavioural consequences of 62–8
political discontent 32–3, 46–7, 92
behavioural consequences of 50–3, 73
Italy 60–1
political discussion see face-face-contacts;
personal discussants
political elites
and democracy 329–30
importance of 344–5

United States 313
and voting behaviours 71, 72, 182
political evolution: and values
        cleavages 258
political ideologies: and values
        cleavages 258, 289–96
political information 183–207
    and bias 208–46
    exposure to 163–6, 338–40
political information source bias: and
        partisanship 198–204
political interest 90
political intermediation 1–2, 213, 219, 222,
        245–6, 259, 322, 344–5
political participation
    and democracy 327–32
    and secondary associations 135–82
    variables in 247–54, 337–38
political knowledge 90, 127
political orientations 105
political participation 90–1, 127
political parties 127, 138–40
    anti-system 329
    and democracy 91–2
    and political information 214
    and voting behaviours 298–305
political reporting: mass media 96
politicization: and voting behaviours 325–6
Portugal
    and democracy 34, 35t, 36, 40t, 40–1, 42,
        43, 44t, 52, 54, 57
    and organizational membership 47t
    political participation in 63, 65t, 66, 67t,
        68
    political systems in 30
Postmaterialism 266, 286, 290–1, 309, 316
'predispositions': voting decisions 217–8
presidential elections
    Chile 247–9t
    United States 234, 250–3t, 319
press see newspapers
primary socialization: influence on
        voting vi
PrivPub questionnaire: values 265, 267t,
        270, 272t, 274, 277t, 278t, 279, 281,
        287t, 288
process cultures 78, 105–8
professional associations 165t, 166, 176,
        225
propaganda: and mass media 85–8
Protestants: and voting vii
Przeworski, A. 32
psychological orientations: and voting
        behaviours 9–10

questionnaires
    values 264, 265–72
    voting behaviours 19–20

radio see mass media
'rational actor' approach: government
        performance xi–xii
regime transitions: and voting
        behaviours 70–1
religion: and voting behaviours vii, 295–6,
        298t, 299, 300, 303–4
religiosity: influence on voters 247t, 250,
        308
religious associations
    and political information 165t, 166, 225
    and voting behaviours 177, 179–80
ReligLib questionnaire: values 363 n8, 264,
        267t, 268–9, 271, 272t, 274, 277t,
        278t, 286t, 288
Republican Party (United States) 295, 296,
        313
right-wing parties: Spain 58–9
right-wing regimes: and mass media 87–8
    see also dictatorships
Riker, William 13
Rochester model: study of voting 13
Rokeach, Milton 262–3, 363 n6
Rokkan, S. 7, 8, 136
Roman Catholics see Catholics

satisfaction: voters 350 n17, 355 n6
secondary organizations 137–8, 139, 182
    and democracy 182
    and electoral participation 167, 206–7,
        333–5
    influence on voters 248t, 250t
    membership of 139
    and voting behaviours xiv, 17–18, 46–8,
        49, 68, 70, 135–82, 300–1, 302t, 308
secondary socialization: influence on
        voting vi, 69–70
ServTax questionnaire: values 266, 267t,
        270, 271, 272t, 276, 277t, 278t, 279,
        283, 284t, 287t
sex: and political behaviour 247t, 250t
'social calculus': voting 183
social capital hypothesis 46–50
social class see class
social cleavages: and voting behaviours 7–9,
        16–17, 136
social contexts: voting behaviours xiii
Social Democracy 265–6, 275, 276, 279, 281
social networks research: voting
        behaviours xiii–xiv, 16–17

social-or personal-influence model:
    influence on voting vi, 135–6
social status: and voting behaviours 196
    t5.5, 197
    see also class
social-structural paradigm: voting
    behaviours 259
Socialism 293, 294t, 306, 307
    Greece 311
    left-right self-placements 316
    Participatory 281, 289, 294t, 295
    partisan preferences 290
    Spain 292
    United States 279
    values 265, 275, 289
    see also Marxism; Bulgarian Socialist
        (formerly Communist) Party
Socialist (former Communist) Party of
    Hungary 54, 57
socialization: influence on voting vi
socio-political values 21–2
    and voting behaviours 298t, 300, 342
Southern Europe
    and mass media 87
    political participation 91
    see also Italy; Greece; Portugal; Spain
Spain 3, 309–11
    and abortion 270, 277t
    and competition 270
    and decision-making 270
    and democracy 34, 35t, 36, 38t, 39, 40,
        41, 42, 43, 44t, 51t, 54, 58–9
    and economic development 271, 277t,
        280t
    and electoral participation 168t
    electorate encapsulate in 173t, 175f,
        176t, 178t, 179
    and environment 276, 280t
    and face-face contacts 49
    and income equality 270, 280t
    intermediary biases in 218, 220t, 221,
        231t, 232
    law and order in 275, 280t
    and left-right self-placements 272t, 274,
        316, 317, 318t
    and legislative election (1993) 247–9t
    and mass media 93, 94t, 101t, 115f, 117,
        130, 238, 239, 254t, 301, 302–3, 318t
        newspapers 102, 110, 126, 237, 254t
        television 112, 126, 237
    and organizational membership 47t, 48,
        318t
    partisan bias in 190, 193t, 201tt, 202,
        203, 204, 216t

partisan preferences in 290, 291, 318t
party contacts in 226, 227
and political broadcasting 87
and political culture: impact of mass
    media on 106f, 107, 108, 109
and political information 186t, 187
political participation in 63t, 65t, 66, 67,
    68
political systems in 30
and religious values 268, 269, 298t, 299,
    303–4, 318t
and secondary organizations 301, 302t
and tax cutting 271, 276
and Traditional Conservatism 290
and values 256, 267t, 276, 277t, 288
and voluntary associations 144, 145t,
    148, 148t, 149t, 150t, 151f, 153t,
    154t, 155, 156, 157t, 158, 159, 161t
and voter-discussant congruence 196tt,
    199t, 205
and voting influences 239, 240t, 241
and voting preferences 292–3, 296–7, 298
spouses: and voting behaviours 195, 196tt,
    197, 199t
Storch de Garcia, Juan J.L. vi
Suárez, Adolpho 57
surveys: voters *see* Comparative National
    Elections Project (CNEP)
system cultures 78, 106

tabloid press 86, 97–8, 102, 111, 122, 126t,
    228, 332
    see also mass media
taxation 266 *see also* ServTax questionnaire
television
    Bulgaria 98, 102, 110, 112, 113, 114, 126,
        235, 239, 240
    Chile 98, 102, 110, 112, 113, 114, 126
    classification of 126
    Greece 103, 112, 113, 114, 126
    Hungary 112, 113–14, 126
    influence of 112–14, 248t, 250t, 302–3,
        332
    as information source 183–4, 185, 187,
        188, 189t, 190, 192, 193t, 194, 336
    Italy 235–6, 241
    and partisan bias 198, 202, 203t, 204,
        205, 210, 201 t5.8
    and political bias 216t, 340
    and political cultures 127
    and political information 228, 233, 234,
        235–6, 237, 238, 239, 241
    significance of 122
    Spain 112, 126, 237

United Kingdom 236
United States 236
Uruguay 110, 112, 113, 126
use of 97, 98, 100
and voting behaviours 18–20, 93
see also broadcasting; mass media
third-wave democracies 75, 180, 209
see also Bulgaria; Chile; Greece; Hungary;
Portugal; Spain; Uruguay
trade unions *see* labour unions
Traditional Conservatism 264, 265, 275,
279, 283, 288 n, 289–90
and left-right self-placements 316
and partisan preferences 292–3
and voting preferences 289–90, 294t
transition and consolidation effect: voting
behaviours 54, 57–8
Truman, Harry S. viii
turnout rates: electoral participation
166–71

unions *see* labour unions
United Kingdom
intermediary biases in 231t, 233
legislative election (1992) 253t
mass media 93
newspapers 235, 236, 241, 239, 254t
television 236
media bias 238, 239, 244
media exposure variables (1992) 254t
partisan bias in 189t, 190, 192, 193t, 194,
201tt, 202, 203, 204, 216t
political information 186t, 188

voter-discussant congruence 195, 196tt,
197, 199t
voting influences 239, 240, 241
United States 296, 312–13
and abortion 269–70, 280t
and competition 270, 280t
and decision-making 270, 280t
electorate encapsulation in 174, 175f,
176t, 178t
and environment 272t, 273
and income equality 270
intermediary biases in 218, 220t, 221,
222, 231t, 232, 233, 234
law and order in 275
and left-right self-placements 272t, 273,
316, 317, 318
mass media 93, 94t, 301, 302t, 318t
newspapers 359 n13
and organizational membership 225, 226,
318t

partisan bias in 189t, 190, 191, 192, 193t,
194, 201tt, 202, 203, 204, 216t
partisan preferences in 290t, 291
party contacts in 226, 227, 318t
and political information 163–4, 186t,
187, 188
and presidential election (2004) 250–3tt
and privatization 270, 280t
and religious values 268, 280t, 295–6,
308, 318t
secondary organizations 301, 302t
and Socialism 279
and tax cutting 271, 273, 280t
and television 302–3
and values 256, 267t, 288
and voluntary associations 144, 145t,
146, 147, 149t, 150, 150t, 151f, 153t,
154t, 155, 156, 157t, 158, 159, 160,
161t
and voter-discussant congruence 196tt,
199t
and voting behaviours xi, 142
and voting preferences 295–6, 297, 298
University of Chicago v
University of Michigan xi
Uruguay 3, 312
and abortion 269, 270, 282t
attitudes to democracy in 34, 35t, 36, 39,
40, 41, 42, 43, 44t, 51t, 54
and economic development 271, 282t
and electoral participation 168t, 273t,
274, 282t
electorate encapsulation in 173t, 175f,
176t, 178t
and environment 273, 282t
and face-face contacts 49t
and income equality 270, 273–4, 282t
intermediary biases in 218, 220t, 231t
law and order in 275, 282t
and left-right self-placements 272t,
273–4, 316, 317, 318t
and legislative election (1993) 250–3tt
and mass media 93, 94t, 101t, 106f, 108,
109, 115f, 117, 131, 301, 302t, 318t
newspapers 99–100, 102, 110–11, 126
television 110, 112, 113, 126
and organizational membership 47t, 225
partisan bias in 190, 193t, 194, 201tt,
203, 216t
partisan preferences in 290t, 291
party contacts in 226
and political information 186t, 187
political participation in 63t, 65t, 66, 67,
68, 91

Uruguay (*cont.*)
political systems in 30
and privatization 270, 282t
and religious values 273, 282t, 298t, 299
secondary organizations 301, 302t
and tax cutting 271, 282t
values cleavages in 256–7
and values 267t, 268, 282t, 288
and voluntary associations 144t, 145t,
146, 147, 148, 149t, 150t, 151f, 152,
154t, 156, 157t, 158, 160, 161t, 162
and voter-discussant congruence 196tt,
199t
and voting behaviours 304
and voting preferences 294t, 295, 297,
298

value orientations: party support 263
values: and voting vi, 21, 296–320
values cleavages 2, 259–63, 326, 342–3, 344
Venezelos, Eleftherios 311
video malaise 80, 82–3, 84
voluntary associations
and political information 163–6
and membership 143–71, 148, 151f, 152
and participation 153t, 154t, 155
and partisan support 160–3
as percentage of population 145t, 146,
147

and political contacts 157t, 158, 159
and political information 213–14, 225–6
types of 148t
voters
and choice 14–15, 211, 213–23
and personal discussants 195–8, 205,
206
and political information 183, 184–207,
209–11, 242–6
see also electorates
*Voting: A Study of Opinion Formation in a
Presidential Election* (Berelson et al.) v,
vi–vii, 5
voting behaviours xii
intermediary influences on 239–42
study of 4–15, 28, 325
see also intermediaries: political
information
voting preferences 291–305

Weimar Germany: Nazis vii, viii
West Germany *see* Germany
Western Europe *see* Germany; Italy;
Portugal; Spain; United Kingdom
Western European template: values
clusters 286, 288–9, 342
World Values Surveys (WVS) 262, 342

Zhivkov, Todor 54